The Theory and Application of
Forest Economics

—— Colin Price ——
The Theory and Application of Forest Economics

Basil Blackwell

First published 1989

Basil Blackwell Ltd
108 Cowley Road, Oxford, OX4 1JF, UK

British Library Cataloguing in Publication Data

Price, Colin
  The theory and application of forest economics.
  1. Forestry. Economic aspects
  I. Title
  338.1'749

  ISBN 0–631–15365–9
  ISBN 0–631–15366–7 Pbk

Library of Congress Cataloging in Publication Data

Price, Colin.
  The theory and application of forest economics/Colin Price. p. cm.
  Bibliography: p.
  ISBN 0–631–15365–9
  ISBN 0–631–15366–7 (pbk.)
  1. Forests and forestry–Economic aspects. 2. Forest management.
  I. Title.
  SD393.P67 1989
  333.75–dc 19

Typeset by Joshua Associates Ltd., Oxford
Printed in Great Britain by T. J. Press (Padstow) Ltd, Padstow, Cornwall

Contents

Preface

The study of forest economics faces two equal and opposite dangers. It can become obsessed with the minutiae of particular operations in particular forests: or it can become enraptured with the elegance of algebraic generalities.

Neither the minutiae nor the generalities are objectionable in themselves. The danger lies in failure to relate theories to what happens in the forest. In the course of detailed studies, the basic principles may be forgotten: in the throes of higher mathematics, the importance of discovering something that has a use in the forest can be mislaid.

The widening availability of computers has given new powers to both extremes. In field studies, the ability to build and analyse massive data–bases becomes an excuse to gather more data: for the mathematician, simulations of bewildering complexity become possible. In the meantime, real decisions have to be made by foresters, and both the quantity of the data and the complexity of the models tend to place economics beyond where they wish to reach.

Acknowledging these dangers, this book has been, in a sense, written for people with their feet on the ground and their heads in the clouds. It starts from the assumption that economics should offer some help to forest managers: but it acknowledges that good practical decisions are ultimately based on sound theory. It is aimed particularly at students of forestry and of natural resource management, at both undergraduate and postgraduate level, but it is hoped that it will prove helpful to those who are already managers of forests, to those who are involved more generally in land management, and to those with some economics background who are simply interested in forests as an important resource. Forestry has become a topical and controversial subject world-wide: I shall be well pleased if the book helps to introduce a reflective note into what is very often an emotional debate.

The content of the book

In writing the book I have tried to steer a zigzag course between practice and theory by asking myself three questions: what decisions do we need to make? what understanding can we gain of the matters affected by the decisions? how can we translate that understanding into operational criteria for making decisions well? And, while the fundamental aim of the book is to convey general principles, I have tried to use plenty of specific examples. These examples cover a broad spread of geographical and economic conditions. Inevitably, however, my own background in the economics of plantation forestry in Britain has influenced the emphasis, and there is also much reference to conditions in countries associated with the British Commonwealth.

I have concentrated on widely known tree species, and for the sake of uniformity all physical measurements are in metric units. But for monetary units a wide range of currencies has been used, and in some examples no units are used at all. Readers are welcome to translate the units, or to scale them up or down by an order of magnitude, if that makes them more meaningful.

Some examples are based on actual data: others have been invented to demonstrate a point efficiently, though within realistic orders of magnitude. The aim is always to put over principles, not to give a handbook of actual costs and revenues, which vary so much through time and space that no general text can helpfully summarize them: the recent literature of individual countries should be perused for such information.

The subject matter naturally reflects my own interests and specialisms, and the balance will not please everyone. For example, it could be argued that machinery costing and cost–benefit analysis are matters already treated in general economics texts. I have emphasized them, firstly because not all forestry students or managers have access to such books; secondly because these works are not all written in readily comprehended language; thirdly, because I believe that, on certain points with particular importance for forestry, these texts give a wrong impression. I am thinking particularly about the rate of interest, which, as will be shown, is the central feature of forestry economics.

In devoting much space to selected issues, I have inevitably done less than justice to other aspects of a very broad subject. In particular, marketing, accounting and the economics of the forest industries are touched on only peripherally, as they bear on decisions in the forest. This is by no means to suggest that these are unimportant topics.

Nor have I given a detailed account of modern quantitative techniques. The mathematical programming aspects of these are well covered in Dykstra (1984) and Buongiorno and Gilless (1987), while Johansson and

Löfgren (1985) apply mathematical economics to forestry. There is, perhaps, a misplaced feeling that these sophisticated techniques are an alternative to traditional forestry economics. Nothing could be further from the truth: the same ideas underlie programming, algebraic and pencil-in-hand approaches, but I believe it is easier to grasp them, one at a time, in the context of particular straightforward worked examples.

In keeping with the forest-level focus, relatively little space is devoted to the wider political economy of forest development. This subject is discussed at length by Westoby (1987). Nor have I given extensive treatment to the state of world markets for forest products: IIASA's monumental work on this subject (Kallio et al., 1987) is something one could barely hope to summarize, let alone compete with.

It will be plain also that this is a book about normative economics – about what forest managers should do – rather than a guide to the observation and analysis of what they actually do in practice. One hopes, of course, that managers will actually do what they should do!

Although I have covered conventionally much of the traditional ground of forest economics, some controversial topics are also included. Many important matters remain unresolved, and it would be misleading to present forest economics simply as an agreed body of knowledge. There may be places where the arguments, and the mathematics, become hard to follow. It is worth persisting, however, because these are complexities of the real world.

The structure of the book

The book is in four parts. The first deals with the fundamental concepts needed to run a profit-orientated enterprise, with examples focused on the harvesting of timber. The second covers the managerial economics of silvicultural operations. The third is concerned with the basis on which forest decisions can be made in pursuit of social well-being. The last part considers the political economy of forestry, dealing with matters of regional and national significance.

It might seem that the latter two parts are superfluous to the requirements of practical managers. However, the need to understand the social context of forest decisions is becoming progressively clearer. Foresters may wish to have at their disposal economic techniques for making decisions that tend to the social good. But even if they do not, they would be well advised to know something of those techniques. In the developing world, finance for a plantation project may depend on an adequate cost–benefit analysis being prepared: in the developed world the public debates about forestry often centre on evaluation of social benefit and cost. Foresters ought to interest themselves in these broader matters anyway, but if interest does not *entice* them to, expediency may *force* them to.

I would like to think that the four parts and their constituent chapters follow a logical sequence of thought. There is no need, however, to set off from this point with the grim resolution of reaching the back cover via all intermediate chapters. Although economics as a subject is endlessly cross-linked, many of the chapters can be regarded as free-standing by those with some background economics.

Using the book

To avoid treading well-worn ground, I have assumed a very basic knowledge of economic concepts such as supply, demand and elasticity, but nothing beyond what is covered in the opening chapters of an introductory general economics text. An understanding of algebra and simple mathematical notation, such as summation signs and subscripts, is needed to interpret the equations. Knowledge of elementary calculus will assist fuller understanding in some places, but it is not essential.

Some users may wish to read the book only selectively, or in a different sequence. Part I could be used alone for general land economics courses, though the forestry emphasis may prove irksome. Anyone with a reasonable understanding of managerial economics and investment appraisal could glance through chapter 2 then move directly to the silvicultural economics of Part II, or to the cost–benefit analysis of Part III. For those without this grounding, chapters 2, 3, 7, 11 and 12 should give an adequate basis. Part IV, prefaced by chapters 7 and 29, and supplemented by chapters 20, 25, 26 and 28, gives an introduction to the significance of forestry in the rural and national economy.

There are certain prerequisites before selective reading within each Part will be intelligible. Chapter 3 should be read before chapters 5 or 6. Chapters 8, 9, 10 and 11 will not make sense without knowledge of discounting, which is supplied in chapter 7. The silvicultural topics in Part II can be addressed in any order, but it is advisable to read chapter 13 first. Chapter 17, which is perhaps the hardest in the book, should not be read until the meaning of chapter 12 is well-understood. In Part III chapters 22, 23 and 24 provide a foundation. Chapter 29 should be read before chapters 30 or 31. Chapter 32 draws on most of the preceding ones. Otherwise the topics can be taken in any order.

Readers who are only interested in profit-maximization can, I suppose, aim to stop reading at chapter 21, though chapters 22, 34 and 35 may give food for thought.

I have provided no suggestions for discussion topics and no self-assessment calculation questions. New examples and matters for debate should arise naturally from application of the principles discussed to local circumstances. In particular, it is highly instructive to rework the examples in the text using, for example, a different discount rate, or higher or lower costs and revenues. Anyone with access to a computer spreadsheet facility should attempt to reproduce the tables, and to observe the effect of changing each of the variables.

Acknowledgements

The author of a textbook builds very largely on what has gone before, and hence takes credit which is mostly due to others. I have not written a review of the extensive literature, which records the conclusions of earlier workers: references are given mostly to attribute ideas, to back up assertions and to supply elaborations, but there are many authors whose works I have not quoted, from Martin Faustmann onwards, who have diffusely contributed to forming this book.

I am indebted not only to this long tradition, but in a general sense to patient teachers, stimulating colleagues and enquiring students. More specifically, this book owes much to the many people who have brought to my notice problems and conditions of which I should otherwise be ignorant, and those who supplied examples, suggested modifications and identified errors in the text. The limits of space do not allow me to detail their contributions and affiliations: I simply name them here in alphabetical order, hoping that not too many have slipped my mind.

Peter Blandon, F.A. Choudhry, Jens Christensen, Don Connolly, Frank Convery, Roger Cooper, Derek Earl, Peter Greig, David Grundy, Pat Hardcastle, Rodney Helliwell, Jenny Johnson, Dilip Kumar, Roy Lorrain-Smith, Jim MacGregor, Aaron Mgeni, Ernie Misomali, C. T. S. Nair, Peter Parks, Eleanor Price, Huda Sharawi, Wink Sutton, Vincent Theobald, Terry Thomas, S. N. Trivedi, Martin Whitby.

The forestry students in the University College of North Wales, Bangor during the year 1987–88 did a great deal to detect, without malice, the prolific errors of earlier drafts, a service for which I am thankful. Any errors remaining are, of course, my own responsibility, but it would be much appreciated if readers who identify such errors would bring them to my notice.

The publishers of the following journals have kindly allowed me to reproduce, in modified form, material which I originally published in those journals: *Scottish Forestry* (in chapters 8 and 9); *Quarterly Journal of Forestry* (in chapter 15); *Forest Ecology and Management* (in chapter 30); *Environmental Management* (in chapter 31).

Thanks are due to the following for permissions to reproduce photo-graphs: Forestry Commission, Edinburgh (plates I, III, V and X); Gary Kerr (plate II); Terry Thomas (plates IV and VII); USDA Forest Service, Forest Products Laboratory (plate VI); Edwin Shanks (plate VIII); International Centre for Conservation Education (plate IX).

I am indebted to Peter Whatley for his patient copy-editing, and Carol Busia and John Davey for steering the book through publication.

Finally, I would like to say sorry and thank you to my family, who to all intents and purposes have been one under strength for the past year.

List of Abbreviations and Symbols

BCR	benefit–cost ratio
CBA	cost–benefit analysis
c.i.f.	cost, insurance, freight
C_t	costs incurred at time t
f.o.b.	free on board
GNP	gross national product
IRR	internal rate of return
MER	marginal export revenue
MEV	mean expected value
MIC	marginal import cost
NPV	net present value
PV	present value
PVC	present value of costs
PVR	present value of revenues
q	rate of return on investment
r	the rate of discount (or interest)
R_t	revenue accruing at time t
R^2	the proportion of variance of a dependent variable accounted for by variation in an independent variable
s	the proportion of extra income which is saved
SDV	summed discounted volume
SPIF	shadow price of investment funds
SPRF	shadow price of running funds
t	a point in time
T	the end of a time period, especially a rotation
UIR	urgency index ratio
VAT	value added tax
ρ	the continuous discount rate $(= \log_e(1 + r))$
∞	infinity: in this book used to indicate a perpetual series

Part I The Basics of Profit-maximizing

1 Objectives of Management and Courses of Action

Forest management is about making and implementing decisions. Every active day forest managers confront the questions: what to do? to what extent to do it? how? when? which, among alternative courses of action, to do first or at all?

Faced with such decisions, foresters can muddle along, trying to grow fine strong trees, or to prevent incursion of graziers, or simply to continue the tradition of management handed down by forebears, predecessors or teachers. Yet in a fast-changing and competitive world muddling along does not meet the requirements of the forest's role; maintaining a tradition involves actions no longer appropriate to circumstances. Foresters must seek new answers, and to do so they require some criterion of rational action.

Economics, on the other hand, is partly a behavioural science, providing an explanation of why people act as they do. It perceives actions as being directed towards objectives: the scurrying human condition of getting and spending results not from random impulses, but from purposeful response to the stimulus of prices. Producers are maximizing net returns: consumers are maximizing satisfaction within their budget.

If economics was no more than this, it could be regarded as an interesting hobby for those with a particular turn of mind. To claim the respect – and the vilification – which it has achieved in the modern world, it needs a normative element: not only to explain what producers and consumers *are* doing, but to determine what they *should* be doing, and to deliver to these economic agents rational criteria for choosing among courses of action.

Rationality, reasonableness and objectives

Rational decision-making means choosing courses of action that tend to achieve objectives. Note that 'rational' does not mean the same as 'reasonable'. People may have quite unreasonable objectives – such as becoming world dictator, or eliminating every wild plant ('weed') growing within a kilometre of their homes. Nonetheless, they are acting rationally – in accord with these objectives – if in the first instance they assassinate anyone who disagrees with them, or in the second spray the surrounding land with deadly herbicide.

In order that foresters' actions are both rational and reasonable, they must ascertain firstly that their objectives command widespread acceptance – at least within the enterprise – and secondly that what they do tends to promote achievement of those objectives. These are the criteria that justify foresters' activities: planting trees, growing them tall and strong, and felling them at maturity is irrelevant unless these actions promote desired objectives.

The position of objectives is pre-eminent in modern management science. Whereas in the past foresters might have operated under implicit objectives, nowadays explicit objectives are normally defined, like those below:

Increase timber production within the nation.
Achieve self-sufficiency in temperate timbers.
Protect and enhance nature conservation values.
Provide recreation facilities.
Encourage integrated rural development.
Maximize site productivity.
Sustain timber supplies to the company's processing industries.
Provide the community with as much of its wood requirement as possible.

The commonest type of objective is a *specific objective*, which defines the sphere of organizational operations. Most forestry organizations have an objective referring to production of timber, but that gives land managers insufficient guidance. It is also necessary to state in what direction, and to what extent, production of timber is desirable. Many environmental protection groups – the Sierra Club in the United States, the Ramblers' Association in Britain, the Chipko Movement in India – have objectives, more or less explicit, which favour *reduced* commercial timber production.

The most common specific objective is to maximize timber production. However, quite frequently, and particularly at local level, a *target* for timber production may be fixed, or perhaps a percentage self-sufficiency. The distinction between maximizing achievement of a specific objective and attaining a target may be crucial in formal decision-making.

Multiple objectives

The objectives of forestry organizations are individually good and worthy, such that no-one could reasonably oppose them. It is, for example, difficult to find serious-minded people who argue that nature conservation is undesirable. However, once an organization specifies more than one objective, a potential problem arises: it is good to have as much wood production as possible; it is good to have as much nature conservation as possible; but beyond a certain point production of more wood reduces nature conservation value, for example by disturbing fragile habitats during harvesting. The fine-sounding forest policies of many nations and organizations are riddled with such potential conflicts, and rarely contain useful clues as to how managers should resolve them. Furthermore, pursuit of most objectives is limited by the monetary or physical resources available. Given these problems, the objectives normally provided to foresters do little but underline what is fairly obvious, and hardly help at all in tackling problems in day-to-day decision-making.

One solution to this problem lies through recasting some specific objectives as targets which it is mandatory to achieve, or constraints which must not be infringed. A straightforward example of a target might be production of enough timber for a local processing industry. If the timber production objective was set like this, the nature conservation objective could be maximizing species diversity, within the requirement to achieve the target. Alternatively, environmental constraints may be set, as in the requirement of Swiss forestry that, to prevent erosion, felling should be in small groups. Within this constraint, a specific objective of maximizing timber production is pursued. The sustained yield tradition of European and North American forestry effectively sets targets for yield in every year.

Unfortunately, many objectives are not susceptible to sensible treatment as targets or constraints. For example, a target of 50% self-sufficiency may be desirable for a timber-importing country like Britain; or a constraint might be imposed that a new processing industry should not receive external funding after five years. However, it would be even more desirable that 60% self-sufficiency should be achieved, or that the industry should become independent within three years. Converting specific objectives to constraints and targets cannot reflect the desirability of going *beyond* the target, or keeping *well within* the constraint.

The difficulty becomes more acute when an organization includes forestry as one among several enterprises, as mixed-economy governments or multinational corporations may. Maximization of timber production cannot be directly compared with maximization of industrial output or flow of irrigation water. The question raised then is not 'which forestry objective takes precedence?', but 'do forestry objectives take precedence over the objectives of other enterprises?'

Profit-maximization

Chapter 23 considers ways of combining objectives into decision criteria. There is, however, an alternative. An objective may be defined to which many enterprises – many courses of action within one enterprise – contribute. The traditional economic objective of producers is maximization of profit (surplus of total revenues over total costs). In behavioural terms, this objective provides a well-tested explanatory hypothesis. It is sometimes argued that behaviour is better explained in terms of profit-satisficing rather than profit-maximizing: businesses aim at a reasonable profit level. But suppose two options both meet this target and one offers a higher profit: which is preferred? If that offering the higher profit is chosen, then profits are still being maximized.

In normative terms too profit-maximizing has appeal. For individual investors or businesspeople, profits represent command over resources for consumption or further investment. For the nation, profit represents net contribution to national wealth, and a basis for taxation. It is difficult to see why, *all else being equal*, a small profit should be preferred to a large one, or a small loss to a small profit.

Inevitably, all else is not equal: non-monetary objectives may be adversely affected by decision-making which blindly accepts profit as the measure of all good. This matter is taken up in Part III. In Parts I and II, however, it is accepted provisionally that profit-maximizing, within certain imposed and self-imposed constraints, is a useful guide to the allocation of resources *to* and *within* forestry, one which allows forestry to adapt to the needs of the world within which it is set.

The remaining chapters of part I examine: the elements of profitability – revenue, cost, taxes and subsidy; the trade-off between cash flows, especially in harvesting; the influence of time on values, on cost of machinery and roads, and on criteria of profitable investment, including investments made in conditions of risk. These are the building-blocks of forest economics.

2 The Sources of Revenue

Revenue is the positive side of profit. This chapter reviews the forms which forest revenue may take, the factors affecting it, its variation with size and location of trees, and the revenue concepts needed for rational decision-making. The difficult matter of *predicting* revenue in the long term is left to chapter 35.

The form of forest revenue

When a country is undeveloped, when population is small, and before a market economy has formalized, forests provide their benefits directly to consumers. But during development, intermediaries adopt the task of converting natural resources into consumption goods, and revenue in various forms accrues to owners of resources and providers of services.

In early development, little is known about the forest: even its geographical extent may be uncertain. Owners of large forest tracts – typically the state – can most easily obtain revenue by selling the *concession* to exploit a defined area of land, for a defined period. When species composition, density of stocking or timber quality are unknown, and when there are few qualified personnel to oversee measurement and removal of produce, this gives the most efficient use of human resources. It may also be the best method when the product offered has low value, such as salvage from a young crop killed by insects, or the right to clear logging residues for firewood. Prospective buyers are likely to survey the area themselves, relieving pressure on the state's limited resources.

If there are several potential buyers, a reasonable price may be obtained by competitive bidding. If not, corruption and collusion between business and government officials (Palo, 1987) may lead to underpricing. Further advantages and disadvantages of concessions are discussed in MacGregor (1972).

When individual valuable products such as veneer logs are scattered irregularly, as in tropical moist forests, revenues may be increased by a *royalty* system, in which a fixed sum is payable for each exploited tree, possibly with differential fees for different species and size classes. While this requires oversight of harvesting, the necessary skills are easily learnt.

Payment by volume or weight leaving the forest demands more sophisticated measurement of all or a sample of trees. The labour, skill and integrity needed increase if a different price per cubic metre is fixed for each size class.

The above are payments for *standing* value or *stumpage* of timber: forest owners' services are confined to providing access to the resource, including use of forest roads or the right to build them.

Forest owners may however go further: trees may be felled – and perhaps undergo primary processing (debranching, topping and cross-cutting) – before sale *at stump*; they may be extracted cross-country to a transport network and sold *at roadside*; they may be transported to the processing industry and sold *delivered*. In these three cases either *tree lengths* or *sorted logs* may be the unit of sale. When there is integrated ownership of forest resource and forest industries, the organization may undertake various degrees of manufacture and distribution – but this goes beyond the forester's normal concerns.

As the unit of sale shifts from area of forest to finished product, so increasingly sophisticated skills, organization and equipment are required: the latter methods arrive only as the forestry sector develops.

Forest revenue thus falls under two headings: payments for harvesting and processing operations; and a fee for the resource itself, which for a natural forest represents payment to land-owners – usually the state – and for the managed forest represents return to growers (see figure 2.1).

Demand for forest products

The ultimate source of revenue is demand from consumers for final products, as expressed in willingness to pay the market price for each product. Demand for wood products is affected by:

(a) population (quantity bought at a particular price increases, usually proportionally, with population);
(b) income per head (quantity of some goods, such as firewood, increases only slowly or may even decline with increasing national income, while other products, such as paper, form an increasing proportion of expenditure (income elasticity of demand for wood products varies widely around 1 (see Kallio et al., 1987));
(c) availability of substitute products (like fossil fuels) which reduce

demand, or complementary products (like computer printers) which increase it;

(d) state of wood processing technology (without a domestic pulp or particle-board industry, there may be no industrial demand for small roundwood);

(e) tastes for timber products (since timber is often not sold directly to consumers, but undergoes further processing, formation of tastes occurs less through consumer advertising, more through supply of information to manufacturers on strength and working properties of particular species, and through general advocacy of wood as a material);

(f) state of business activity (if the economy is recovering from economic recession, the construction industry, a major consumer of sawn timber, is active: by contrast, during descent into recession, the construction industry is more depressed than the overall economy).

Wood fulfils many purposes, some vital, some trivial, and even at high prices some is consumed. At lower prices increasing consumption per head leads to *diminishing marginal utility*, that is, the value of an extra unit of consumption declines, as units fulfil progressively less important uses. This underlies the negative slope of demand.

In a closed economy – one which, through geographical isolation or policy does not trade in world markets – these demand factors, together with the supply of products, determine the equilibrium price. For products like firewood which are costly to transport in relation to value, international trade is also unimportant: the relevant supply area is within 10–200 kilometres of the point of use. For most countries and higher-quality timber, however, price is determined at least partly by world markets, not just domestic conditions.

Derived demand

In a competitive economy, the value of a tree standing in the forest is derived from the price of final products by deducting payments (including profit margin or mark-up) for each stage of converting the tree to a consumable product: this may include retailing and wholesaling, as well as harvesting and processing. In conversion, much of the raw material may become a waste or low-value product: thus typically 1 tonne of roundwood becomes only 0.5 tonne of sawn timber, the remnant being offcuts and sawdust. On the other hand some forms of particle-board manufacture convert the entire biomass to useful products.

This process of successive deduction can be taken further back, to the forest concession, for which the maximum offered price takes account of costs of survey, building roads, and forest reinstatement (if this is a condition of the concession).

The residual value of the natural resource is usually only a small fraction of the ultimate sale value of consumer goods: even of delivered price, a third may be taken by transport and a further third by felling and extraction to roadside. Owners of managed forests may resent the greater part of final product price accruing to processes which are completed in a few weeks, leaving a meagre share to cover the 5–200 years taken to grow the trees. Nonetheless, other natural resources as well as skill and effort are dedicated to conversion, and inevitably financial rewards reflect this.

The small fraction of consumers' price accruing to forest owners makes the forest economy susceptible to fluctuations in final product price. If the price of standing timber constitutes 20% of sawnwood price, a 10% drop in world sawnwood price (which could occur overnight through shifting international exchange rates) would halve residual return to growers (see figure 2.1).

Again, disgruntled forest owners may argue that it is unfair that they bear the brunt of the price fall (though they contentedly take the benefits of disproportionate price rises!) And indeed, processing and harvesting industries may briefly absorb some of the reduction themselves, operating at reduced profit or even an accounting loss rather than allowing machinery and workers to stand idle. On the other hand it is not in foresters' ultimate interest that these intermediaries should go bankrupt. If the offered price is too low, owners of managed forests at least have the option of leaving trees to grow on until times and prices improve.

The price–size relationship

The value of a log depends on end use and processing cost. If it is well marketed, each log is allocated to the end use offering the best price. Generally, the larger the log, the wider the range of possible end uses: a veneer-quality log could be chipped for pulp, but small roundwood cannot yield veneer, and, because of high percentage conversion losses, cannot economically be turned into even small-dimension sawnwood. Composite products such as blockboard and glulam structures allow small-dimension timber to replace some uses of large sawn pieces; but this means additional cost in materials and processing, which must be deducted from final product price in deriving a return to the grower. For 'quality' products, like writing paper, made from small-dimension timber, up to 96% of the high price to consumers may be absorbed by processing cost.

Large trees are increasingly scarce, as natural forests are progressively 'creamed', and as short-rotation managed crops become more dominant in

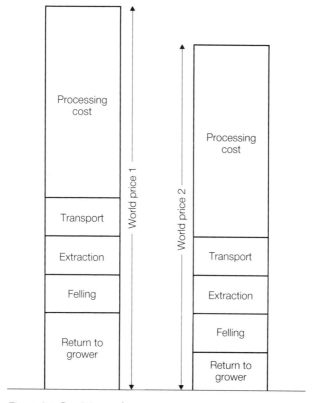

Figure 2.1 Breakdown of costs

timber supply. Hence products like veneer, for which *only* large trees are suitable, come into shorter supply, and their price reflects a scarcity value.

In general, then, a large tree or log commands a higher delivered price per cubic metre than a small one. It is also less costly per cubic metre to harvest: felling several small trees requires a repeated sequence of operations needed only once for a large one; debranching a large tree is substantially faster than an equivalent volume of small ones; attaching extraction wires, chains or ropes may take no longer for a large log than a small one; given a mechanized system, loading lorries with one large log is more efficient than with many small logs of the same total volume. Economies of handling large logs continue in processing, and the larger the log, the higher the percentage conversion to final products.

All these factors combine to produce a relationship between price per cubic metre and tree size which typically has the form shown in figure 2.2.

Plate i Variation in log diameter: the largest logs may be worth several times more per cubic metre than the smallest
(Photo: Forestry Commission)

This *price–size* relationship has great significance in harvesting and silvicultural decisions. Key features are:

(a) the intercept on the volume axis, denoting the *marginal tree size* which may just be harvested without loss;
(b) the decreasing gradient of the curve as volume increases, which reflects the facts that increasing size eventually secures no more advantageous markets, and that economies of dealing with larger sizes are gradually exhausted.

There are exceptions. The curve may rise in steps if there are several markets with well-distinguished minimum size requirements: even so

(a) economies in harvesting larger trees lead to the steps sloping upwards;
(b) variation of tree size within a stand tends to smooth the relationship between *mean* residual price and *mean* tree volume.
(c) the *proportion* of a tree convertible to high value products, with lesser probability of defect, increases gradually with growth.

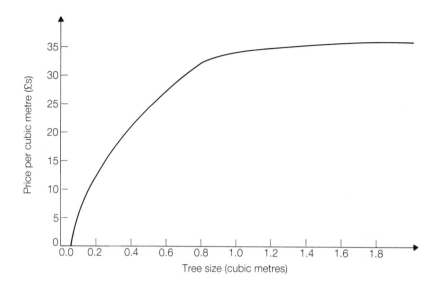

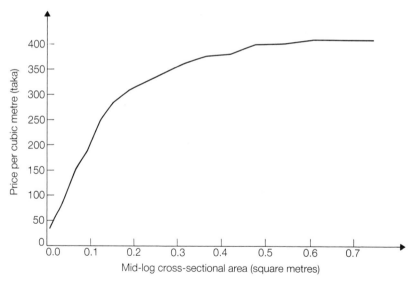

Figure 2.2 Price–size relationships
    (a) conifers in Britain (Mitlin, 1987)
    (b) teak in Bangladesh (Rahman, 1981)

Very large trees may command a huge premium for particular uses, especially veneer, or become valueless if they are so sparsely scattered that they do not justify purchase of the special equipment needed to harvest them. Small trees may have high value in special decorative markets. Highly automated, large-throughput processing industries may narrow the differential between small uniform and large heterogeneous logs. These variations must be allowed for in interpreting any generalizations about the price–size relationship.

Spatial price variation

Since haulage distance to processing industries, standard of transport infrastructure and ease of harvesting vary, the price–size relationship differs between forests, even when the same markets are supplied. In remote forests with difficult terrain, marginal tree size is much larger than in forests near processing industries and with easy harvesting conditions. In the least accessible forests, no tree may be worth exploiting, irrespective of size. It may therefore seem surprising that international trade in timber exists – even for low-value small roundwood. Such trade arises because over long distances more economical forms of transportation – trains and particularly ships – can replace lorries, which are flexible and cheaply loaded, but costly per tonne per kilometre (figure 2.3). Thus timber near a port 8000 km across an ocean may be transported to a dockside processing industry more cheaply than homegrown timber 200 km away along bad roads.

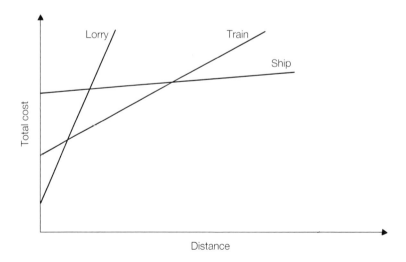

Figure 2.3 Transport costs by various modes

Processing industries may offer a premium delivered price to offset transport costs from remote timber resources. This is not charity, but discriminatory pricing in the cause of profit-maximization. Many processing firms have major fixed costs, and once these have been incurred the profit made on additional units processed is large, justifying, if necessary, a high price for the raw material. Nonetheless, paying a high price to all suppliers erodes profitability. The firm prefers a price structure attracting sufficient raw material to fill processing capacity, while paying each forest owner only what is needed to compete successfully with other potential purchasers.

Other forest products

Non-wood revenues from the forest (rental of grazings, recreation fees, water charges) have the same residual nature as timber revenues. It is true that recreational products – hunting, shooting or fishing permits, rental of accommodation, charges for entry, use of car parks or forest drives – are sold direct to consumers. But the fact remains that transport has to take place before the forest has value. For practical reasons, consumers are transported to product rather than *vice versa*, but the effect is the same: the residual value of a forest is less when remote from consumers. A low-value product – a scenically unattractive forest – is visited only if it is near residential or holiday centres, while the revenue generated by facilities in an attractive forest still depends on its accessibility. This variation in net recreation value of a forest according to its distance from population can be used to value unpriced recreation (see chapter 25).

In developed countries, recreation may provide significant revenues. In 1986–7, the British Forestry Commission derived about 3% of its income from renting forest accommodation, with a further 1% from shooting and fishing. Locally, the contribution may be even more marked. On one camp site occupying 10 hectares, recreation facilities produce a gross revenue per hectare about 100 times that of timber production! But caravan sites and forest drives do not arise spontaneously: like trees themselves, forests generate recreation revenues only after costs have been incurred. These costs too must be deducted in determining the value attributable to the natural resource.

Particularly but not exclusively in developing countries, non-wood materials such as leaves for forage or exudates and distillates (gums, resins, turpentines, etc.) are locally important – despite their collective title of 'minor forest products'. In Sudan, the exudate gum arabic may yield 99% of the revenue from growing *Acacia senegal*, the remainder being attributable to firewood (Sharawi, 1987). The economic importance of such products is enhanced by their availability early in the rotation.

Revenues in decision-making

Three revenue concepts are important in managerial decision-making. Total revenue ([price per unit of output] × [number of units]) is relevant to decisions on whether a defined course of action is worthwhile or not. In comparing two or more courses of action (how much fertilizer to apply) two other concepts are more useful: *marginal revenue* and *incremental revenue*. Although both are concerned with changing intensity of economic activity, their meanings are clearly distinguished in this book.

Marginal revenue, the addition to total revenue gained by selling one more unit of output, is the customary concept in business economics. In a perfectly competitive economy, in which no single producer has enough market share to influence price significantly, marginal revenue equals product price, and is constant over the enterprise's feasible range of output. Although timber enters world trade and therefore, apparently, faces maximum competition, competitive assumptions may not fully hold.

(a) Many forest enterprises are large: the state forest service may own most of the forest land in a country, and control production even from the land it does not own; some forest industries own major forest estates in several countries, and are dominant enough to influence market prices locally, while internationally products like chemical pulp in which there are great scale economies are oligopolistic.

(b) Since low-priced forest products like firewood cannot be transported economically over long distances, they can only be supplied to a given market by a few forests.

Taken together, these factors produce spatial monopoly, in which the market *in a given locality* is dominated by one seller.

Under these conditions, additional revenue to the dominant enterprise from selling one more unit is less than the market price, because putting more wood on the market reduces the price for all other units (unless the seller can dictate not only the quantity on the market, but price differentials between buyers). Table 2.1 shows a notional linear decline in the market-clearing price for headloads of fuelwood sold weekly from an isolated forest. Marginal revenue is always below the prevailing price, reaching zero well before potential sales are exhausted.

Readers with calculus may represent demand algebraically, and confirm that the first differential of total revenue (= marginal revenue) reaches zero at a sale volume of 200 headloads.

Inevitably, the full picture is more complex: restricting output to maintain high prices invites consumers near the market boundary to seek cheaper supplies from the next forest ownership. Thus a zone of limited competition

Table 2.1 Demand and marginal revenue

Headloads	Price (¢)	Total revenue	Marginal revenue
0	40	0	—
1	39.9	39.9	39.9
100	30	3000	—
101	29.9	3019.9	19.9
200	20	4000	—
201	19.9	3999.9	−0.1
399	0.1	39.9	—
400	0	0	−39.9

exists at the market edge, and a monopolist might use discriminatory pricing within the market area, charging the lowest price to those nearest the market boundary.

This book generally proceeds on the assumption that forest managers are selling into a market capable of absorbing extra output at a given price, but marginal revenue can always be substituted for price in the examples given.

Incremental revenue is a less familiar concept. In this book it denotes the additional revenue gained by either:

(a) applying one more unit of a specified input to a forest operation, or

(b) replacing one course of action by another, more lucrative one.

In the first case, incremental revenue may be varied continuously, as with increasing fertilizer application or extension of a plantation: in the second case the increment of revenue may be 'lumpy', as in replacement of one species by a more productive one.

Incremental and marginal revenue concepts can sometimes be used interchangeably: they give the same answer in decision-making, and the concept used is a matter of convenience. Marginal revenue is familiar and directly related to what the consumer sees as the key variable – output. On the other hand, foresters' decisions often focus on varying the *input*, albeit with the aim of increasing productivity, and optimal forestry regimes are usually prescribed in terms of recommended input rather than target output.

More importantly, foresters can increase the value of revenue in four ways:

(a) increasing *quantity* of output;

(b) increasing *quality* of output;

(c) improving *marketing* of given output

(d) changing *timing* of output.

Elementary economics texts habitually concentrate on (a), being easiest to show graphically. Much of silviculture is devoted to (b), for example, selective thinning to remove coarsely branched trees.

Marketing has been facetiously and very misleadingly defined as the art of selling something one has too much of to people who don't want it at a price they can't afford, and foresters often, quite improperly, neglect it as being too remote from their concerns or beneath their pride. However, good marketing assures the allocation of the available timber to its most suitable overall set of end uses, and as such not only promotes consumer satisfaction, but also may be the most cost-effective means of increasing revenue.

Retiming timber sales is an important option. Its revenue implications are most obvious when timber prices are changing rapidly over time, but, as chapter 7 shows, timing affects the value of revenues pervasively.

The term 'marginal revenue' makes no sense when additional revenue is derived by means other than increasing the quantity of output. By contrast, incremental revenue, which relates to additional revenues howsoever derived, applies to any course of action that improves some combination of quantity, quality, marketing and timing.

Finally, although total revenue has been separated from marginal and incremental concepts for descriptive purposes, total revenue at one level of decision-making may become incremental revenue at another. For field foresters, incremental revenue might be seen as the pay-off from fertilizing more heavily, or logging a compartment at greater intensity: total revenue is what is made from a hectare managed according to the chosen regime. For regional planners, however, trying to determine optimal supply schedules to a processing mill, incremental revenue comes from felling an additional hectare: total revenue relates to the entire supply contract.

What matters is not so much correctly applying names of concepts as getting the questions right: what (total) revenue do I obtain when I adopt this course of action? what changes (how much more – or less – revenue do I obtain) if I adopt this course of action rather than that one?

3 Cost Concepts and Decision-making

Forest economists, hybrid as they are of social and biological scientists, are congenitally prone to classifying things, a tendency nowhere more apparent than in approaches adopted to operational costs. This chapter examines the usefulness of these classifications in relation to decision-making.

One possible classification is into traditional factor-of-production categories: land, labour, capital, enterprise and raw materials. This has the virtue of appearing to be both exhaustive and mutually exclusive: every factor can be placed under one of these headings, and at first sight the categories seem distinct. There are two drawbacks, however.

1 Classification of factors of production has always been debatable: some economists argue that raw materials are simply intermediate products, got by applying labour, capital and enterprise to land; others view capital as a collection of raw materials to which continuously productive form has been given; yet others claim enterprise is just a specialized form of labour, subject to the pains of labour, subject to its rewards.

All factors of production can ultimately be resolved into:

(a) land and all that lies thereon, or more generally, natural resources including the seas and all that floats thereon, swims therein or lies thereunder;
(b) labour, in the sense of applied human effort and time;
(c) technology, including useful human skills and knowledge.

Even technology itself is ultimately the fruit of labour, and labour arose by a long evolutionary process from the land.

2 Apart from the classification being open to dispute, its whole purpose may be questioned. In profit-maximization, does it matter whether a cost represents labour or raw materials? Land and capital were once regarded as fixed costs, which could be varied only in the long term, whereas labour and raw materials could be obtained or disposed of at will. This distinction

is no longer valid in industrialized countries, where skilled labour may require years of training and where legislation defines stringently the circumstances in which it may be dismissed.

The physical location of costs

Another classification distinguishes direct cost, oncost and overheads. Direct costs are identifiably incurred at the point of physical production: they include wages paid to forest workers, outlay on chemicals for crop protection, and fuel cost.

Oncosts, normally accounted at local level, are mostly associated with employing labour (though sometimes taxation and insurance of machinery comes under this heading too). Examples are allowances for holiday pay and sick pay and for times when bad weather or machinery failure prevents working; contributions made by employers to pension schemes or national welfare funds; supervision of work. These costs are not obvious at the point of physical operation. Nonetheless, they must be paid if a contented and efficient work-force is to be retained. It is normal to sum these costs, calculate them as a proportion of direct costs, and to add this percentage to the direct labour cost of operations.

Overheads are enterprise costs which cannot easily be assigned to any particular operation, or to the needs of any particular forest. Examples are the costs of undertaking research, maintaining information services, forming organization policy and exerting political influence. Administrative and clerical services at every level from headquarters to local office are also included. Like oncost, overheads are normally added as a percentage on direct costs. Like oncost, they may easily be of similar order of magnitude to direct costs.

It is important to identify an appropriate level of overheads. A state forest service undertakes many functions related to the general well-being of forestry, including private, corporate and commercial sectors as well as state-owned forests. It would be improper to aggregate all these overheads and charge them to the state-owned forests only. It is therefore helpful if overheads can be divided into those pertaining to the *state enterprise*, those associated with *oversight of the non-state sector*, and those which, like research, benefit the whole forest economy. Realistic allocation of overheads like managerial input within the enterprise requires identification of the activities to which that input contributes (MacGregor and Balman, 1973; Openshaw, 1980).

Direct cost seems a clearly defined concept. The importance of correctly identifying and allocating overheads cannot be disputed if costings are to be realistic. The oncost concept, lying between direct and overhead categories, is harder to justify. For example, why should weekly wage be regarded as a direct cost, while weekly payments per employee to a pension fund are classified as oncosts? Why should supervision of a harvesting operation be an oncost when clerical work to sell the produce of the operation is a local overhead?

Oncost has a certain practical convenience, provided the items included are clearly demarcated, but the items could be reclassified either as direct labour cost or as overheads at the appropriate level.

Variability of cost

Given that decision-makers are concerned with changes resulting from a course of action, or from undertaking one course of action rather than another, cost may usefully be classified according to its variability. As with revenue, we can distinguish *total* cost (the cost of carrying out the complete operation on a hectare or stand); *marginal* cost (the cost of producing one more unit of a particular product); *incremental* cost (the cost of applying one more unit of a factor of production, or intensifying an operation, or switching from one operation to another). A diagrammatic representation of variability is given in figure 3.1.

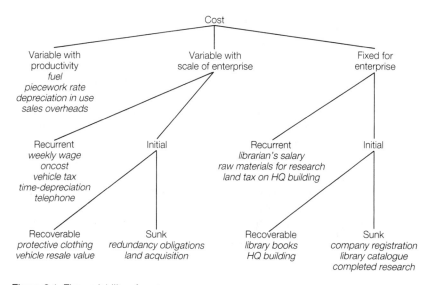

Figure 3.1 The variability of costs

This bears explanation. For costs variable with productivity, total cost rises with output, but need not rise in proportion to output or to rate of working. Greater output rate may cause more accidents and consequently sick time, so cost could rise faster than output. For costs which vary with scale of the enterprise (as judged, for example, by number of employees or capital value of the enterprise) cost per unit output declines with increasing productivity: for example, holiday pay is divided over an increasing quantity of output as labour productivity increases, while lorry licensing and insurance costs are spread over more loads carried as utilization increases. Recurrent costs are almost instantly and automatically variable with change in scale of enterprise, but the distinction between recurrent and initial costs is often only a matter of time-scale: for example, wages are paid weekly, vehicle licences monthly or yearly, whereas vehicle purchase recurs only every few years. Whether initial cost is recoverable or sunk depends on whether the item can be resold in the event of the enterprise shrinking. Since many items instantly lose sale value merely by becoming second-hand, part of initial cost, for example of acquiring vehicles, automatically becomes sunk. Some initial costs are entirely sunk, being useful only to the enterprise on that site, such as a forest road system.

Fixed costs for the enterprise tend to concentrate at headquarters. They are fixed in that they do not *necessarily* increase with scale of enterprise. These costs decline per unit size of the enterprise as well as per unit of output (Sutton, 1969). For example, the cost of negotiating an advantageous premium price for quality timber is spread over all output, while research on silviculture becomes more cost-effective if its results apply to a greater forest area. Naturally a large forest enterprise undertakes more research than a small one. But the scale of its operations in no way obliges it to do more research. If it does more, it is precisely *because* its research is more cost-effective: the total cost produces a better total pay-off because of the larger output to which it applies.

The examples in figure 3.1 have been chosen to illustrate a point: that the variability of cost need not be determined by either the factor of production involved or the location where cost is incurred. There is a *tendency* for expenditure on headquarters overheads and durable capital such as buildings to be less variable than on-site costs and raw materials expenditure. But, as far as decision-making is concerned, their important characteristic *is* variability, not physical form or location. Payment to workers illustrates the point well. With piecework (payment per unit of output) unit labour cost is constant: with plain time (payment per hour) unit labour cost varies with work rate.

Scale economies and diseconomies

Both capitalist and Marxist economists give considerable attention to scale economies, that is, cost advantages from working on a large scale. These include:

1 Labour specialization, which allows individual workers both to use their natural competence, and to acquire high skills in particular tasks. Thus there are specialist silvicultural workers, fellers, tractor drivers, all more productive – and so cheaper per unit output – than they would be working at the whole range of forestry tasks.

2 Indivisibilities, like a bridge across to a forest which costs the same, irrespective of forest size.

3 Technical economies, such as use of larger, more efficient machines.

4 Production streamlining, as might occur when a sawmill is set up to produce a long run of one product specification.

5 Discount prices for bulk purchases, for example of vehicles or fertilizer.

6 Lower allocations for contingencies, since in a large enterprise there is less chance of everything going wrong simultaneously.

Scale economies are discussed further in a forestry context in Cubbage (1983). They are also important in the pulp industry, but less so in sawmilling (Sutton, 1973). This has implications for the pattern of forests supplying them.

Cost savings usually diminish with successive increments in size. And, even if scale economies are not exhausted entirely, they may eventually be offset by diseconomies of scale. In particular, large enterprises may suffer failure of communications and top-heavy management, together with loss of incentives, sense of purpose and identification with objectives of the enterprise.

Not all activities reach their optimal scale at the same size. Thus it may be efficient for one enterprise to own and manage many large forests, in each of which harvesting is undertaken by several small contract companies.

Ways of looking at cost

1 So far, the discussion has concerned only *financial cost* – monetary outlay on factors of production. This form of cost interests accountants, but for decision-makers there are other relevant concepts.

2 *Opportunity cost* is the revenue (or benefit) forgone when a factor of production is withdrawn or withheld from an alternative course of action. The most obvious example is the opportunity cost of land for plantations, the forgone revenue in this case usually being its value to agriculture.

It should be emphasized that true opportunity cost is the *net* revenue or *profit* forgone. Thus a hectare of land taken for forestry might otherwise have yielded 50 poundsworth of food annually. But if this would have required £20 of labour, £10 of machinery and £10 of raw materials, then its opportunity cost is only £50 – (£20 + £10 + £10) = £10 per year. Alternatively, the opportunity cost could be loss of agricultural revenue if a hectare of land was taken for forestry, and its previous inputs of labour, machinery and raw materials were employed more intensively on the remaining farm area. Such intensification may actually increase farm revenue, so that opportunity cost is apparently negative (but in this case it would be possible to leave the land idle as an alternative to using it for forestry, opportunity cost hence being zero).

The relevant alternative form of production is not necessarily the *best* alternative, but the alternative in which the factor of production would actually be employed – the *expected* agricultural net revenue, rather than the net revenue achievable if the most profitable farm technology were adopted.

Opportunity cost may affect enterprises external to forestry, particularly when forestry is expanding. However, more immediately relevant to forest managers is the opportunity cost of factors already employed by the enterprise, and which, for legal, social or practical reasons, must remain so in the medium term. For example, workers have zero opportunity cost when bad weather makes normal forest production impossible. If alternative indoor work can be found, such as maintenance of machinery or manufacture of simple products, the revenue forgone by doing these jobs is zero.

At the other extreme, during seasonal peaks of labour demand (near the end of the planting season) the opportunity cost of labour probably exceeds its financial cost. The short time-scale may preclude hiring additional workers, so additional jobs can only be done by withdrawing workers from urgent work within the enterprise.

3 *Disbenefits* are effects which consumers would have preferred not to experience, the classic example being pollution. These are costs even though no monetary transaction is involved. A major development in modern economics has been in evaluating these detrimental effects and incorporating them in decisions (chapters 24–26).

Note that these are *alternative* and *mutually exclusive* ways of looking at cost, only one of which should be used to cost a given factor at a given time. It might be appropriate to add the opportunity cost of an under-occupied labour force to the financial cost of chemicals in estimating the total cost of a weeding operation, but it would be double-counting to add the financial cost of workers to their opportunity cost.

4 A fourth way of looking at cost does however incorporate elements of 1–3. *Shadow* cost is the net loss of social benefit incurred by applying a factor of production to a particular course of action. It is used extensively in Part III.

The difference between these views of cost is illustrated by the costing of labour already employed by the enterprise.

Financial cost: wage-bill plus labour oncost.

Opportunity cost: reduction in revenue consequent upon withdrawal of a unit of labour from whatever activity it would otherwise have been engaged in.

Disbenefit: whatever value the labour force places on the leisure time given up in order to work, plus the dissatisfaction caused by work conditions which include adverse weather, a difficult work environment and an above-average accident rate.

Shadow price: the value of the wage to employer, less its value to the employee, plus the forgone value of whatever product workers might otherwise have produced, plus an estimate of how much more or less pleasant is their new occupation, compared with their former one.

Costing an operation

Confronted with so many concepts and classifications, which should forest managers choose? Again the question is, what changes as a result of using a factor of production? The answer depends on the objective of the organization. If it is to maximize profits (within constraints of law and custom) then the relevant cost is the financial cost of purchasing or hiring additional factors of production, *if additional units are readily available*.

For raw materials and hire services, and in costing long-range decisions about the scale of enterprise, such availability is normal. If, however, additional units cannot reasonably be purchased within the given time period (as is normal in the short term for land, skilled labour and large machines) then the relevant cost is the opportunity cost of the required factors moved from their alternative activity within the forest enterprise. Given the question 'what changes?', managers must predict what revenue would actually be contributed by the factors, if they were not transferred. This particular exercise is not concerned with whether this alternative activity was the best alternative, although that may be the subject of a separate decision. The actual alternative may not be the best one because the world is far-from-optimal. Restrictive labour practices or mistaken management decisions at a higher level or sheer inertia may have excluded the best alternative. If individual managers cannot instate the best alternative, they should accept that the actual alternative provides the relevant opportunity cost in an imperfect world.

If the ultimate objective of forest management is not profit, but the welfare of society as a whole, then disbenefit and shadow cost become relevant, as discussed in Part III.

Work study

Defining a cost per input unit is only part of costing. The cost of an operation depends also on the number of input units required. This is not a matter of economics, but of work study.

Work study has several objectives relevant to economics:

(a) improving health and safety at work, which at a cynical minimum reduces sick pay and lawsuits for damages against the enterprise;
(b) defining a piecework rate that gives workers a realistic incentive to increase productivity, thus spreading oncost and overheads sufficiently to reduce the cost of a given operation.

But of central interest to decision-making is measurement of output rates of workers and machines. Without this information, rational economic decisions about operations cannot be taken. For labour, the aim is usually to determine a standard time: that is, the time in which a trained and motivated worker of average ability would be expected to complete a specified job in specified circumstances. On top of the 'direct' time taken to complete a single work cycle (such as felling a tree), an 'overhead' time must be added for repairs and maintenance of working tools, together with a percentage relaxation allowance which varies with arduousness of the job. Thus the standard time is:

$$\{(\text{[direct time]} + \text{[indirect time]}) \times [1 + \text{relaxation \%}]\} \times \text{[rating]}$$

where [rating] is the subjectively assessed speed of work compared with a notional average

Tables of standard times published by forestry organizations are essential sources of information in costing.

Output of machines is normally measured the other way round, as the units of output achieved in a given working time, normally an hour. Since the costing of machinery involves concepts which have not yet been treated, this vital aspect of modern forestry economics is described in chapters 8 and 9.

4 Taxes and Subsidies for the Forest Owner

The glum epigram, that nothing is certain but death and taxes, is only true in that these doleful phenomena will overtake all of us *sooner or later, in one form or another*. And, just as none of us has a sure distant foreknowledge of the manner of our deaths, so in a long-term enterprise like forestry the particular *form* and *severity* of taxation at the end of a protracted growing period is far from certain. Indeed, this uncertainty requires special economic appraisal, outlined in chapter 12.

The stoicism of the epigram is not universally shared. While some regard taxation as a phenomenon instituted by governments with the express purpose of annoying the population or sapping its ability to mount effective opposition, others question the need for taxation at a particular level or upon particular groups within the population. One function of private forestry associations is to lobby governments for more favourable tax treatment for forestry.

Taxation, of course, has positive purposes: to transfer purchasing power from individuals, making resources available for public use; to redistribute income; to penalize undesirable economic activity. These functions will be encountered in Parts III and IV.

However, in forest decision-making the important point is not to debate *why* taxation exists but to take account of the fact that it *does* exist. Taxes are costs, falling upon forest enterprises in diverse ways. In countries where forests are natural or self-regenerated, taxes may be the *only* significant cost of forest ownership. Taxes affect the profitability of forestry, absolutely and relative to other land uses and investments. They may also change the kind of silviculture which is most profitable. It is therefore vital that forest managers understand taxation and its likely impact on cash flow.

Because tax structures vary from country to country, and year to year, it serves little purpose to detail any one country's tax structure, and it would be quite pointless to list the even-more-transient *rates* of tax. Instead, this chapter examines various feasible types of tax and ways of treating them in decision-making. National forestry journals should be consulted for more local and topical information.

Taxes on products

Product taxes can be levied at a flat rate – so many £s, $s or Rs per unit of product – or at a given proportion of untaxed price. Both methods present difficulties: with the flat rate tax, in defining the unit of product; with the proportional tax, in determining actual price, given that bulk discounts and special offers cause this to vary from day to day and consumer to consumer.

Value added tax (VAT) in the European Economic Community exemplifies proportional tax. VAT is levied on the value added to a product by each enterprise. Thus an enterprise which buys small roundwood for Fr10 000, cuts it to length and points it with chainsaw services costed at Fr1000 and preserves it with creosote costing Fr2000 before selling fencing stakes nominally priced at Fr20 000, has added value of Fr20 000 – (10 000 + 1000 + 2000) = Fr7000, and it pays tax on this net sum. It is the value added by labour and enterprise. In practice, the tax is levied on the sale price, Fr20 000, of the product, and the enterprise claims a tax rebate on the Fr13 000 spent on inputs. Tax on that Fr13 000 was already paid by the enterprises supplying small roundwood, chainsaws and creosote. Actual payments would be as shown in table 4.1, with a 15% tax.

Table 4.1 Incidence of value added tax

Item	Raw cost	Tax	Gross cost
Small roundwood	10 000	1 500	11 500
Chainsaw	1 000	150	1 150
Creosote	2 000	300	2 300
Total inputs			14 950
Fencing stakes	20 000	3 000	23 000
Rebate on inputs	−13 000	−1 950	
Value added	7 000		
Net tax	7 000 × 15% = 1 050		

Forestry purchases many inputs such as chemicals, fuel and machinery, which have already been taxed under this system, and so are eligible for rebate. Its products are inputs to other industries. In the above example, the farmer purchasing fencing stakes would claim a rebate of Fr3000.

Sellers of final products cannot simply decide a desired selling price and add VAT: in a competitive market they accept the prevailing tax-inclusive sale price. Tax liability is 15% of *that value which, after tax is added, gives this sale price*.

$$T = 15/100 \times U; \quad \therefore\ U = 100/15 \times T$$
$$P = U + T = 100/15 \times T + T = 115 \times T/15$$
$$\therefore\ T = 15/115 \times P \approx 13.0\% \text{ of } P$$

where T, U, P are tax, untaxed price and post-tax price.

$$\text{Fr23 000} \times 13.0\% \approx \text{Fr3000}$$

Some products may be exempt from such taxes, particularly the essentials of life. Under UK rules firewood, like other domestic fuels, is exempt, as is timber used in house-building. Rebate on inputs can still be claimed.

The rebate system may appear unnecessarily convoluted, but it enables the tax to be levied flexibly and accurately. For example, when adding value by harvesting timber it is impossible to know what proportion of value added will eventually become tax-exempt housing timber. Only at final product stage is this determined. The house-builder, paying no VAT on house sale, but claiming rebate on the timber, ensures that the appropriate portions of timber sales, and tractor and chainsaw services, are eventually untaxed.

Some products, for example petroleum, are subject to additional *excise* taxes, often levied at a flat rate on sale or as tariffs on import to a country.

The main effect of product taxes is a mark-up on the price to final consumers. As such, they somewhat reduce the producers' price at which a particular quantity of a product can be sold. The reduced residual price of stumpage gives due allowance for product taxation: decision-makers should use prices before tax is added in calculating revenues. Similarly, where a rebate system operates, the pre-tax cost of inputs should be used in calculating operational costs. Profit to the enterprise is ultimately based on these prices.

Tax systems with no rebate would entail multiple taxation of the end product. For example, the steel embodied in a chainsaw would be taxed on purchase of steel, of chainsaw, of felled timber and of finished wooden goods. However, in systems which tax the value of product, rather than value *added* at each stage, tax is usually paid only by the final consumer; intermediate or producers' goods are unlikely to be taxed.

Taxes on factors of production

Non-rebatable taxes on products which become intermediate goods in creating other goods and services are effectively taxes on *production* of factor inputs. There may be a separate tax on *use* of inputs, like an annual tax on road vehicles. Tax on the vehicle as a *product* is paid once, whether the vehicle is used or not: the tax on the vehicle as a *factor of production* is paid periodically, but only if the vehicle is used during that period. Similarly, a payroll tax may be levied on each employee, regardless of the work done.

Land taxes are generally charged per hectare, the rate of tax depending on the particular land use. Forest land may be exempted from land tax, or treated favourably compared with urban or industrial uses. Land taxes are often collected to meet local rather than national expenditure needs.

Factor taxes increase the cost of inputs. They provide an incentive to economize on the amount of factors employed, but to use more intensively those factors that *are* employed (intensification rather than extension of land use under a per-hectare tax, longer working weeks and greater rates of worker productivity with a payroll tax, fuller utilization of a smaller number of lorries with a vehicle tax).

Differential taxes on different land uses may induce a shift from one land use to another. However, the taxes are usually less than the extra revenue gained by shifting to a more lucrative land use, especially when forestry and agricultural land undergo urban or industrial development.

Income taxation

Taxes fall on income derived from working in the forest, as in any other enterprise. They may also be levied on income derived from forest ownership, that is, the profits of the enterprise. The tax may be a fixed proportion of income, regressive (taking a smaller proportion of larger incomes) or, most usually, progressive (taking a larger proportion of larger incomes). 'Unearned income' – profit derived from investment and land-ownership rather than remuneration for labour – may be subject to higher tax rates. Every nation also has specific tax exemptions. Income taxation may fall on the profits of public companies, often at different rates from those applying to individuals.

Because of the long-term and often fluctuating nature of forest income, special provisions may be made for its taxation, tax being levied on one of the following:

1 *Actual net receipts from sales, treated in isolation*

Such a yield tax is effectively an income tax, but the rate may differ from ordinary income taxation, and be fixed independently of the non-forest income of the owner.

2 *Actual net income from forestry, aggregated with ordinary income*

In a forest of approximately normal age-class structure, net income is steady from year to year. However, where plantations have only recently been formed, a long period of net loss is likely to precede the era of annual profit. Yield or income tax laws may allow individuals to offset these losses against income from other sources. If, for example, the marginal rate of tax (the proportion of tax paid on an extra unit of income) is 50%, the owner's income from other sources is £50 000 and an area of land is afforested at a cost of £10 000, this £10 000 may be deductible from the £50 000, making the taxable income £40 000. The owner's tax liability is not 50% of £50 000 but 50% of £40 000, a saving of £5000. This provision is equivalent to a 50% grant towards planting costs. Maintenance expenditures in the plantation's early life may also be eligible.

Some items, such as purchase of land for afforestation, may be regarded as capital acquisitions rather than part of profit and loss, so are excluded. Investments in infrastructure or buildings may be allowed as tax offsets only by spreading them over time – say at 5% of their value for 20 years.

Once the forest attains net profitability, the normal rules of income taxation apply, unless special provisions are made.

3 *Average income from forestry*

Over a stand's life, periods of net cost and net revenue alternate, net cost dominating at first, but net revenue gaining ascendancy later in the rotation. On the basis of the site's productivity and prevailing prices, an average net annual income over the crop's life can be projected, and made the object of a constant annual tax (a productivity tax). In practice, this is disadvantageous, since heavy taxes are paid early in the rotation, when the stand, far from yielding cash flow to pay the tax, is incurring costs.

4 *A very nominal estimate of annual net income from forestry*

This avoids taxes early in the rotation being too onerous.

5 *A mixture of bases*

Provision may be made for alternation between actual net income (advantageous during periods of net loss), and average annual net income (which reduces annual burden during periods of profit, since the total profit is averaged over a larger number of years (the whole rotation) than the number of years in which tax is actually being paid).

Until 1988 the United Kingdom system combined (2), (4) and (5) such that forest owners could claim tax relief during the period of net cost, while making a token annual payment for each hectare of revenue-generating forest, regardless of income actually derived from it (Hart, 1986). Stands in the forest could be designated individually for either form of tax, so that relief was claimed even when the forest as a whole was generating large profits.

Taxation of profit, while reducing profitability, cannot under ordinary provisions make a profitable course of action *un*profitable, nor does it affect the *relative* profitabilities of alternative courses of action – within *and* outside the forest enterprise. On the other hand special provisions may increase the profitability of forestry compared with other investments: indeed, this is often their express purpose. They may also alter the relative profitability of options *within* forestry.

Taxation of forest capital

A mature forest represents a substantial store of wealth. Even a young stand without merchantable timber is still valued for its expected future production, and has a market value reflecting this potential.

One peculiarity of forestry as an economic activity is that the productive machinery (capital) is also the product: the tree is both the means of creating present increment, and the accumulated increment of past time periods. Similarly land is both a factor of production, and a store of wealth. The implicit ambiguities raise problems in applying capital taxes to forestry, and special provisions are frequently made.

Capital taxes fall under three headings:

(a) taxes levied periodically on *possession* of capital (property tax, wealth tax),
(b) taxes on *increase in value* of capital, and
(c) taxes on every *transfer of ownership* of capital.

Taxes on possession hit forestry particularly hard, if they are levied on 'wealth' that in fact represents an accumulation of past income (increment) that has yet to be realized. They encourage reduction of forest capital, with results discussed in chapters 13 and 16. On the other hand, exempting trees from wealth tax would be over-lenient. To avoid wealth tax either favouring forestry unduly, or penalizing it for its special characteristics, it should be levied on a capital value related to productive potential of forest land, rather than on current standing value of the crop. Whether such a productivity tax is a wealth tax, an income tax or a factor tax depends on the basis of the assessment. As it does not vary with silvicultural activities, it should have no effect upon them.

It is not normal to tax increase in capital value until the capital is transferred. Capital may be transferred by sale, exchange or gift. A *capital gain* arises if sale price of a managed forest is greater than the price at which it was acquired. Part of the increase could be due to crop increment (particularly if the forest was acquired as a young plantation), part to improved silviculture, and part to increasing physical capital, such as roads.

Inflation affects the cash value even of a forest whose distribution of tree volumes is unchanged since acquisition. Although that represents no increase in the *real* value of the forest, it may be treated as a capital gain for tax purposes, or allowance for inflation may be made.

The special nature of forest capital again needs special treatment. For example, the value of the standing crop may be treated simply as a backlog of uncashed income, to be taxed only at felling; capital value then depends only on land and infrastructure. This is an important exemption where forest income is taxed nominally. Given this provision, large capital gains only occur when forest land is converted to a different land use such as housing development or mineral exploitation. In countries where land use is stringently controlled, land with clearance for development may be scarce and highly priced, and its capital value may be many times what it was in the previous use. Capital gains realized through such increases may be subject to particularly heavy tax rates.

On the other hand, capital gains may be taxed advantageously, compared with income, giving an incentive for forest ownership as a means of tax reduction.

Capital loss normally occurs during major felling, even if the site is replanted. It may be possible to offset such capital losses against capital gains – for example, if the owner has sold other woodlands which have *increased* in value. Suppose a woodland estate was bought for £100 000, the crop felled and sold for £80 000 and the land resold for £30 000: it would be unfortunate if (for example) timber income was taxed at 50% and no relief was available on the reduction in capital value of the woodland.

Tax on capital transfer by gift may be levied on the donor or on the recipient. Tax levied on the donor is fixed, regardless of the number of the beneficiaries: the aggregate tax *on recipients*, however, may be reduced under progressive tax rates by dividing capital among many beneficiaries who have little previously accumulated inheritance. Taxation of the donor may be made under different arrangements, depending on whether transfer happens during lifetime, at death, or within a specified period before death.

A distinction may be made between transfers of personal wealth (jewelry, cars, yachts, etc.) and those of productive capital (business premises, fleet of delivery vehicles, forest land), usually favouring the latter. Special provision for forestry might be made, given that the chief value of young crops lies, not in their immediate merchantable value, but in their potential to produce *future* merchantable value. Thus payment of tax may be deferred until timber is felled. Coupled with this provision may be a further concession, that tax outstanding on standing timber is cancelled in the event of a second transfer: if, for example, two deaths occur in rapid succession.

Taxes on capital transfer cannot be evaded by encashing the forest asset and transferring cash instead: indeed, because reliefs for productive assets may thereby be lost, this stratagem may result in heavier taxation of the transfer.

Subsidies

Apart from direct revenue by sale of goods and services, a forest enterprise may derive revenue in subsidies from central or local government or from private charitable bodies. Subsidies may even exist in the financial accounts of state forest enterprises. For example, a subsidy from central funds may be given to reflect the social and environmental values of the enterprise.

Some subsidies are related to production or maintenance of goods or services which it is desired to encourage, for example, supplies of pure water. Others are intended to offset the cost of operations, particularly ones such as amenity planting that will yield a revenue, if at all, only in the long term. Differential grants may aim to promote a particular form of forestry, such as planting of native species.

Treatment of taxes and subsidies in decision-making

Professional foresters tend to treat taxes routinely under headings like enterprise overheads, or as a mitigation of profit. Such treatment does not allow sensitive accounting of the incidence of tax; it may lead to more tax than necessary being paid, or to possibilities for advantageous manipulation of the forest not being exploited. For example, treatment of a fixed tax as an overhead, on the grounds that it cannot be attributed to any particular forest operation, increases the cost *ascribed* to each operation, even though the operations do not, in fact, increase tax payments.

Yet again, the pertinent question is 'what changes as a result of adopting a particular course of action?' The relevant changes lie not just within the forestry sector, but in all the forest owner's financial affairs. Given that forestry may attract special tax treatment, the question is not 'how much net tax liability will this operation incur?', but 'how much less (or more) net tax liability will this operation incur, compared with alternative financial changes outside forestry which the owner might otherwise make, or even compared with postponing the operation till after a favourable tax change?'

To judge these matters properly needs knowledge not only of the whole tax system but also of the owner's financial portfolio. Foresters may feel that such subjects lie beyond both their competence and their interest. Nonetheless, they should be aware of them, understand why the owner's tax advisors recommend a particular course of action, and be capable of making decisions using post-tax costs and revenues. The fiscal arrangements for private forestry may be a major reason for the existence of a forest enterprise, and managers of that enterprise cannot afford to ignore them.

Subsidies are usually given specifically for a particular course of action or for employing specific factors of production. Subsidies at the time of the operation should be treated as a mitigation of cost: those given when the course of action comes to fruition are enhancements of revenue.

Taxes, subsidies and state forest services

Taxation of the state forest enterprise, or granting of subsidies from one public body to another, may appear pointless, since it merely transfers funds from one government pocket to another. That is an over-simplification.

Where taxes are a monetary equivalent of some undesirable effect such as pollution which the market fails to price, they reflect a real disbenefit to society and should plainly be treated as costs. Similarly subsidies generally reflect a benefit lying outside the interest, remit, objectives or competence to evaluate of a given organization: if that benefit is not explicitly valued, the subsidy must be.

The case is less clear when taxes function to raise revenue, as with VAT. This tax both provides a benefit to government and indicates the value, via willingness to pay, of the forestry goods produced. The post-tax price represents the benefit from production. If this (defensible) view is adopted, however, factors of production and intermediate goods must also be costed at post-tax prices, since in an equilibrium economy these represent opportunity costs, in terms of willingness to pay for alternative products.

The approach of cost–benefit analysis to non-equilibrium economies and to transfers to government is discussed in chapters 22–32.

Whether taxes like VAT are uniformly ignored or uniformly included does not affect the profit-maximizing level of production identified by the criteria in chapter 6. However, they do affect absolute profit. Excluding tax payments from public forestry accounts gives a false impression of profitability relative to private forestry and investment generally.

The profits of public forestry are not themselves normally subject to tax. Instead, some or all of the profits are remitted to central funds, and central finance may be made available by parliamentary vote, *diktat* or custom when the forest service requires cash input. The effect on forestry of such treatment of profits is discussed in chapters 18 and 30.

5 Decision-making for a Point in Time

One way of profit-maximizing is to evaluate costs and revenues for every possible combination of forest activities, and to adopt the combination giving the greatest surplus of revenue over cost. However, this approach becomes unworkably time-consuming once more than five or six activities are considered in all combinations. Much of managerial economics is concerned with practical short-cuts in decision-making. Modern computer-based decision-making techniques usually embody a structured, efficient and exhaustive approach to examining the alternatives.

This chapter examines the important elements of decision-making situations, and introduces procedures for use when only cost or only revenue is variable.

Classifying courses of action

It is helpful first to identify the circumstances in which each decision is made.

1 An *isolated* course of action can be implemented without affecting any other contemplated course of action. An example would be selling the right to collect firewood in a logged area. None of the forest's factors of production is required, and no existing market is affected.

2 *Compatible* courses of action can logically be undertaken simultaneously, but decision-makers may need to select a sub-set from among them. For example, there is nothing intrinsically infeasible about thinning every stand in the forest older than 20 years, but for practical reasons some stands are thinned in a given year, others only in due course, and others not at all.

3 *Interactive* courses of action are compatible, but the results of one course of action depend on what other courses of action are implemented at the same time. For example, a crop may be fertilized with nitrogen, or phosphorus, or potassium, or with any combination of elements. The decision to apply each element cannot be regarded separately since

(a) it may be more efficient to fertilize with one pass of a combined fertilizer rather than separately for each element;

(b) the effect of the elements may be synergic rather than additive: that is, the enhanced growth resulting from application of phosphorus alone may not be the same as the enhancement caused by *mixing the same amount of phosphorus* with a given application of nitrogen.

4 *Incompatible* courses of action are mutually exclusive: one cannot implement more than one from a group of incompatible alternatives. For example, a given hectare cannot be planted with both pure pine and pure eucalypt. (A third incompatible course of action is planting a mixed crop.) From a decision-making viewpoint, incompatible courses of action may be mutually exclusive in practice though not in logic. For example, only one of two potential bridge sites for a logging road is needed to cross a river.

Availability of factors of production and markets

In long-range planning, land may be the only significant constraint on production: if more labour, machinery or infrastructure is needed, it can be acquired; if markets for products are lacking, new industries can be encouraged. Availability of factors and markets can also be assumed when forest operations occur regularly, as in a normal forest, so that the work-force can deal with one after another, without delaying any beyond its optimal time.

In practice this steady progression does not always happen. A large acquisition may take some years to plant using the labour available: some areas will be planted immediately, others delayed a short time, yet others a long time. In the short term, moreover, many unforeseen contingencies or changes of circumstance may result in available resources becoming insufficient to implement the desired programme.

Obvious causes are natural disasters such as fire, hurricanes or insect attack, following which salvage removals might require years of work by the available labour and machinery. An excess of desirable work over available resources may also result from management changes: an unmanaged woodland consisting of overmature crops, unthinned stands and unplanted waste may be bought by a commercial enterprise. Change in economic conditions, such as a new market for small timber, may suddenly reduce optimal rotations.

Extra labour cannot be trained immediately to meet the increased work-load, machinery or contractors may not be instantly available for hire, nor, in the case of salvage felling, may markets exist to absorb increased production. Besides, the period of adjustment to new circumstances might be short in relation to the active life of a worker, machine or sawmill, so that major increase in available resources might not be economically justifiable even if physically feasible.

The same problem faces managers when the resources committed to a given programme unexpectedly change. Machinery failure or worker illness is frequent. More dramatic, widespread and prolonged is the effect of a major processing industry closing, which may hinder the felling programme for years. Finally, a change of objectives may result in some resources being diverted to operations outside the timber production working circle.

Thus there are many circumstances, pervasive rather than rare, in which resources and markets are insufficient to undertake every profitable forest operation immediately, or even at all. This is a major reason why logically compatible courses of action are not, in fact, undertaken simultaneously, and a choice has to be made about which operations should receive priority, in order to maximize the profitability of the whole enterprise. Chapter 19 treats the problem in detail.

Time scale

Decisions in forestry normally involve a time dimension. Obviously establishment and tending of plantations is undertaken for long-term revenue. But equally, intervention in natural forests influences the future growth of the remaining crop. Even 'cut-and-run' exploitation decisions, which leave the devastated forest as someone else's economic problem, need some prior investment in infrastructure and machinery.

Nonetheless, for certain categories of decision, particularly when exploitable natural forest is not in immediately short supply, the economically significant consequences of the decision occur within so short a span that time can be ignored. Given the additional complexities of considering time – detailed in chapter 7 – there is advantage in omitting time from an initial survey of decision-making.

Decision criteria for isolated and compatible courses of action

An isolated course of action should be adopted if total revenue exceeds total cost: since it interacts with no other course of action, if it makes a profit in isolation it must increase profits of the whole enterprise.

However, lack of physical interaction does not imply that a course of action is *economically* isolated. Suppose that a physically isolated area of a species suitable for ornamental use has undergone pre-commercial thinning. The decision is whether to leave the thinnings in the forest or to extract and sell them. The incremental revenue to the enterprise from selling them is *the change made to its entire receipts.* Even if thinnings from the isolated block are themselves sold in local markets at the prevailing price, the consequence may be that thinnings in other areas are sold at a lower price, or not at all. The overall addition to enterprise revenue is thus less than the direct value of sales from the isolated area (see the marginal revenue example in chapter 2). Total receipts actually decline if demand for the enterprise's product is price-inelastic. Alternatively, the product from other stands may have to be transported further to find a market at the prevailing price, and this increased cost should be deducted when determining if the course of action is profitable.

If factors of production can be varied – if, for example, labourers will work longer hours at a pre-set overtime rate and lorries can be hired for delivery – the additional cost of extracting the thinnings is directly financial. If, however, work time and rate are constrained, and if only the enterprise's own transport fleet is available, output from the isolated block can be achieved only by diverting labour and machinery from productive work elsewhere. The relevant cost is then an opportunity cost.

Choice of action when revenue is constant

In some cases revenue is fixed, for example when the manager is choosing

(a) the best among incompatible methods for undertaking a given operation, or
(b) the best combination of compatible activities to meet a given required output.

In either case, profit-maximization implies cost-minimization.

The definition of cost here follows the principles discussed in chapter 3. For example, in choosing among mechanical, chemical and hand weeding of plantations, the cost of chemicals is their financial cost. However, unless casual labour is available, labour cost during the weeding season may be an opportunity cost. Since weeding normally takes place outside the planting season, this could be a slack period in young plantations, with consequent low opportunity cost. During times of depressed markets, harvesting gangs may be available for weeding without affecting timber sales. On the other hand, in forests with heavy commercial recreation, the holiday season may coincide with the period of maximum weed growth, with high opportunity cost in forgone recreational revenues. Hand weeding might therefore be the rational choice in one forest, and chemical weeding in another, although similar working conditions existed and cash prices of factors of production were identical.

When prices vary between sites, optimal technique differs even more. In developing countries the low price of labour is likely to make hand weeding the minimum-cost method. An example of the effect of low labour cost on choice of technique appears at the end of chapter 8. Cost–benefit analysis (see chapter 28) may further emphasize the advantages of labour-intensive methods.

Choice of scale of working (whether to harvest a given volume from one large or several small coupes) entails balancing operational (as opposed to enterprise) economies and diseconomies of scale. The following economies may reduce cost per hectare in one large coupe compared with several small ones.

Labour specialization:	separate work-gangs are trained in felling and trimming, in extraction and in primary conversion at roadside, rather than the full spectrum of work being done by individuals at many scattered locations.
Indivisibilities:	minimum expenditure on ancillary site facilities such as shelters and first aid posts, and on supervision.
Technical economies:	reduction of total coupe perimeter with reduced damage to adjoining crop, and reduced expenditure on fencing browsers out of regeneration areas.
Streamlining:	in particular, better matching of operational phases – a forwarder may extract the produce of ten fellers, so concentration of felling avoids unproductive inter-site movement.
Contingencies:	a reduced set of spares on site if all chainsaws are of one type.

A consideration counting against a single large coupe is lack of flexibility. If, for example, the site is at high elevation, bad weather may preclude working; or the wash-out of a road or unsafe condition of a bridge giving access to the area may cause suspension of all harvesting. By contrast, with several working sites, workers and machines can be shifted as necessary to where working conditions are acceptable.

Detailed balancing of these factors may require more work study data or assessment of climatic and biotic factors than are readily available, but a compromise is likely to lead to two or more moderately sized and well-separated felling sites within a forest, with extraction machinery if necessary rotating between them. However, environmental constraints may favour a smaller coupe size than the cost-minimizing one.

The system of least average cost

The optimal size of production unit depends on the relative importance of fixed costs or scale economies on one hand and scale diseconomies or transport costs on the other. Nurseries supplying commercial forests have substantial costs, irrespective of level of production. In the following example, such costs amount to £50 000 annually. Marginal production cost per thousand seedlings is £40, and transport costs are £0.02 per thousand per kilometre (straight-line distance). Suppose the forest land to be supplied covers 10% of land surface, and that planting requires 2500 plants per hectare with a mean rotation of 50 years. Figure 5.1 shows the relationship between cost per thousand seedlings and the straight-line distance between adjacent nurseries.

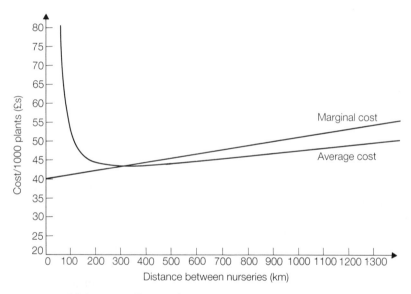

Figure 5.1 Minimum seedling supply costs

Marginal cost of supplying a thousand seedlings rises steadily as the nurseries become further apart and maximum transport cost increases. However, average cost declines initially as the fixed £50 000 is divided among more output units. Once marginal cost rises above average cost, it pulls average cost upwards again, producing the classic U-shaped curve of economics texts. In this case, a distance of about 350 km between nurseries gives lowest average costs.

If nurseries vary in cost-structure, decisions become more complex. With rising marginal supply cost in each of several production units, total cost is minimized when the marginal supply cost to any supply area boundary is the same from the production unit either side of the boundary. Thus costlier production units have a smaller supply area, or may be unable to supply economically at all.

Similar exercises can be carried out for other supply and delivery centres, though the decision is complicated by uneven distribution of forests or markets, and the anisotropy of the transport system. These problems can be overcome using computer models (e.g. Sessions and Paredes, 1987).

Selecting a set of actions with an input constraint

When one factor of production is available in fixed quantity, financial outlay on it is independent of the actions undertaken. Use of the factor in activity A makes it unavailable for activity B, or activity C: obviously an opportunity cost is involved. But is the opportunity cost equal to net revenue forgone in B, or in C? The profit-maximizing set of activities cannot be defined until their opportunity cost is determined, nor can opportunity cost be defined while it is unknown which of A, B, or C is the best option, and which the next best alternative!

The problem is resolved by changing perspective. Since cost of the constrained factor is constant, profits are maximized by maximizing the summed revenues from all chosen activities, net of variable cost of other factors.

Suppose that a forest estate owns a small sawmill, and undertakes some processing of estate produce. Three products are possible, all drawing on an ample supply of small roundwood. The most efficient product of sawing capacity, indicated by the last column of table 5.1, is post and rail fencing, despite its heavy demand on saw time. If the market for this product is limited, the next most profitable is mining timber. Note that the ratios calculated are for value added, not product price, to saw time. *What changes as a result of the sawing operation?* Instead of selling at the unconverted price of £10/m³, the timber fetches a higher price, £40, an incremental revenue of £30. By the ratio product price to saw time units, mining timber

Table 5.1 Efficiency of conversion

Product	Price/m³ of raw timber	Units of saw time	Value added per unit saw time
Unconverted timber	10	—	—
Dimensioned mining timber	22	2	6
Quartered fencing posts	25	3	5
Sawn post and rail fencing	40	4	7.5

would have appeared a more efficient use of saw capacity, but that would have ignored the value of unconverted timber itself. Two cubic metres of timber and four units of saw time can create either $2 \times £22 = £44$ from mining timber, or $1 \times £40 + 1 \times £10 = £50$ from a mix of sawn fencing and unconverted timber.

With only one constraint (saw time) the best strategy is to convert only one product. Applying a second (market) constraint, the number of products rose to two. Generally, the number of activities in an optimal strategy is not greater than the number of constraints on resources and markets.

Selecting a set of actions: linear programming

Suppose that a logging company, with a fixed time in which to exploit a concession, is limited by the capacity of both its survey team and its logging gangs. Two distinct forest types exist within the concession: type X is relatively uniform forest on steep slopes, easily surveyed and marked but with difficult conditions for logging; type Y is highly diverse forest on flat ground, time-consuming for surveyors to identify commercial trees in, but easily logged. Both types contain many valuable trees. If the surveying constraint only is considered, exploitation will be more rapid in type X, whereas the logging constraint favours work in type Y.

When two or more constraints exist, the optimal set of actions can be efficiently determined by *linear programming*. Conceptually, linear programming requires nothing more difficult than iterative calculation of ratios, as in the conversion example. Technically, however, it is a highly developed subject. Figure 5.2 presents a graphical solution of the logging problem.

Given the constraints, the more of type X that is logged, the less can be logged of type Y, the areas showing an inverse linear relationship. The line AC shows the combinations feasible within the surveying constraint, DB those feasible within the logging constraint. The area DECO is called the *feasible space* and the line DEC the *efficiency frontier*. Lines FG, F'G' and F"G" are combinations of X and Y that yield equal revenue: their gradient depends on the relative richness in commercial species of X and Y, the ratio OG:OF being the ratio of revenue per hectare in X and Y; these lines are parallel.

The profit-maximizing combination of X and Y is the point on the efficiency frontier which touches the furthest equal-revenue line from the origin, in this case point E. Points D, E and C are called *basic solutions*: optimal combinations are always basic solutions.

The constraints could also be products (a certain required minimum production), the problem being to minimize cost rather than maximize revenue. For example, forest types X and Y might be envisaged as miombo

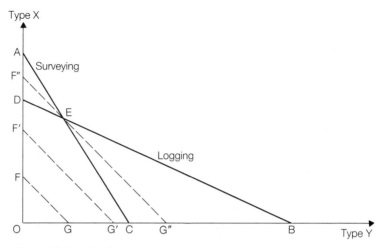

Figure 5.2 Graphical solution of linear programming problem

woodland and reforested agricultural land, or two types of coppice-with-standards. Small and large dimension material can be obtained from both types, but in different proportions. AC might represent the minimum requirement of large material, and DB that of small material. The feasible space lies *outward* of AEB, and the objective is to achieve the *lowest* of the equal-cost lines, FG. E is again the optimal combination.

Greater numbers of constraints require more sophisticated algebraic techniques.

Linear programming packages on computers normally produce, in addition to the optimal solution, a set of 'shadow prices' which represent the gain in attainment of the objective (maximum profit in this case) resulting from another unit of constrained resource becoming available. When constraints are not absolutely immovable, this helps in deciding whether it is worth taking action to alleviate the constraint.

Constrained choice among incompatible and interactive courses of action requires definition of what changes, not only between the datum of doing nothing and undertaking an activity, but between undertaking activity X1 and undertaking *intensified* activity X2. Both incremental revenues and incremental demands on constraints must be calculated in appraising the incremental activity X1→X2. Should variable costs, as of fuel or raw materials, be involved, they should be deducted from revenue. Thus the most general criterion of desirability, under a constraint, is choose in descending order of

$$\frac{[\text{incremental revenue}] - [\text{incremental variable cost}]}{[\text{incremental constrained factor of production}]}$$

The technical procedure for selecting activities under constraints is outlined in chapter 19, where it is presented with more illuminating examples.

6 Profit-maximizing Decisions

In long-term planning, or when constrained factors of production have a clearly defined opportunity cost, or when workers and machines are readily available for hire, and where large markets exist for all produce, conditions of decision-making approach those outlined in economics texts: the profit-maximizing level of activity is determined by both variable costs and variable revenues.

The planned harvest of a natural forest is used in this chapter to demonstrate both the criteria required, and the order in which a complex set of decisions should be tackled. Imagine a large expanse of forest into which there is one potentially easy road-line at the bottom of a valley (see figure 6.1). The first chronological step in implementing a logging project might be constructing a harbour for shipping logs, followed by construction of the road: *decisions*, however, should generally be taken in reverse order, the working assumption being that the prerequisite physical works *have been* undertaken. The first decision therefore concerns:

How far from the road should logging proceed?

Extraction of timber over rugged terrain is slow, so that technically loggable timber may be too expensive to move to roadside – especially using the machinery costing method proposed in chapter 9. The economic extraction limit depends on marginal cost and marginal revenue per cubic metre of timber extracted.

Marginal revenue per cubic metre on board ship is R; cost of transport along the road (*haulage*) is T per cubic metre for each of K kilometres, including a debit for increased road maintenance; that of skidder extraction is E for each of D kilometres from stump to road; felling costs are F, and chokering/loading/unloading costs L per cubic metre.

Summed costs per cubic metre $= T \times K + E \times D + F + L$

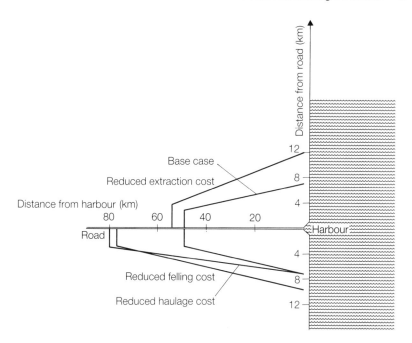

Figure 6.1 Extraction limits in natural forest

Values over several transport and extraction distances are plotted in figure 6.2, for R = $40, T = 25¢, E = $2.80 and $F + L$ = $18.

Take a distance 20 km from harbour and a point D_1 km into the forest from the road. Here marginal revenue exceeds marginal cost of delivering one more cubic metre to the port. Total profit increases by logging at this and any other distance as far as D_2. At D_3 marginal cost exceeds marginal revenue: every cubic metre logged between here and D_2 constitutes a loss. D_2 is the breakeven point.

Profits are maximized where marginal revenue equals marginal cost, the familiar criterion from the economic theory of the firm. The horizontal axis, however, is *not* quantity of output, as in economics texts, but distance. If the crop stands at a uniform volume per hectare the distance axis could be replaced by one representing volume of output, since the two would be linearly related. The first aim, however, is to determine not the optimal volume of output, but the economic limit of exploitation. This figure is more operationally useful: to find it, volume per hectare need not be known.

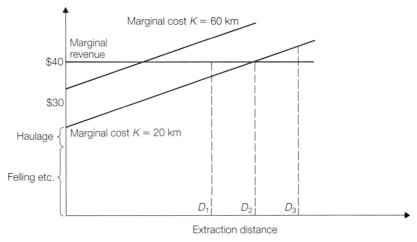

Figure 6.2 Marginal cost and revenue of extraction

How far from harbour to build the road?

If the road does not yet exist volume per hectare is crucial to the decision whether to build it. Let timber stand at 40 m³/ha in each of ten revenue classes: \$0–\$4, \$4–\$8 and so on up to \$40. (This revenue variation includes a harvesting cost penalty for smaller sizes). At any haul distance, it is now possible to determine

(a) extraction limit for each class;

(b) net value of timber brought to a 1 km length of *existing* road,

(c) global profit by exploiting all economic timber both sides of the road, given a \$30 000/km cost of building the road.

In reality the forest might be less uniform, but table 6.1 gives an initial guideline. It shows that limiting price class rises and extraction limit declines with increasing distance. (This sheds light on the general pattern of natural forest exploitation, in which the remotest areas are exploited only for the highest value categories.) With increasing distance from harbour, net value per kilometre declines rapidly at first: not only does transport erode more of the revenue at harbour, but also a smaller extent of forest, and fewer price categories are economically exploitable. As fewer trees are affected, net value declines more slowly. Beyond about 48 km, net value does not pay the cost of extending the road: global profit is maximized by exploiting only this far inland.

Table 6.1 Limits of extraction

Distance to harbour	Lowest exploitable price class	Extraction limit for $36–40 class	Net value/km	Global profit
0	$20–24	7.14		
10	$20–24	6.25	224 721	2 368 248
20	$24–28	5.36	149 152	3 882 311
30	$24–28	4.46	92 455	4 747 267
40	$28–32	3.57	52 444	5 140 024
45	$28–32	3.13	37 545	5 206 206
50	$32–36	2.68	25 960	5 207 892
75	$36–40	0.45	737	4 684 163
80	—	0	0	4 535 212

If a road had already been built, it would be worth skidding timber to it as far as 80 km from the harbour. Once the road is constructed, its cost does not change as a result of using it. However misguided the decision to build the road may have been, no regrets can redeem its cost. It is a sunk cost, since it is unlikely that the roadstone has significant resale value.

The important general principle is that *past costs have no influence on present decisions* (except, perhaps, that we may learn from their awful example to avoid making *future* expenditures without adequate economic analysis). There are two opposite and equally misplaced intuitive responses to past costs.

(a) 'The cost of this road has been so great that extraction of timber to it cannot possibly show an overall profit, so should be abandoned.'

(b) 'The cost of this road has been so great that we must make full use of it.'

To repeat, the past cost of the road changes not one whit if it is abandoned, used discreetly, or hammered to destruction. This past cost, therefore, is irrelevant to present decisions.

Is the project profitable?

Table 6.1 shows the maximum predicted global profit from the logging operation. The last question is whether this profit covers the cost of developing a harbour if none exists. If so, the sequence of decisions is implemented, this time in chronological order.

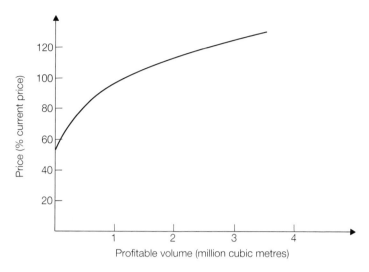

Figure 6.3 'Supply curve'

It is of interest to know how changes in costs and revenues affect the operation. As figure 6.1 shows, lower felling costs push back the extraction limit for a given size class by the same interval, lower extraction costs by a *decreasing* interval, and lower haul costs by an *increasing* interval with increasing haul distance from harbour. All increase the distance to which it is worth building a road, the number of size classes economically extractable at any location, and overall profit.

Higher prices dramatically increase profit, as they affect all the limits of exploitation (see table 6.2). A 30% price rise increases profit by 426% and economically exploitable volume by 202%. Plotting volume against price gives a picture (figure 6.3) akin to a supply curve.

Such curves give a rather misleading impression of timber abundance, suggesting that enormous additional timber supplies can be drawn forth with very modest price increases. However, the finitude of the forest, as well as the cost of exploitation, limits the long-run supply of timber from an area.

If terrain allows, it might be preferable to build several parallel roads inland. This would both make new areas of timber economically accessible, and reduce expensive cross-country skidding. The questions of optimal road density and pattern are taken up in chapter 10.

Whether to extract at all with fixed costs

Cable extraction has a more complex cost structure than skidding. Part of extraction cost by this method is a *fixed cost* of setting up the cables. Costs of

Table 6.2 'Supply curve' from natural forest

Price rise	Haul limit	Extraction limit at 40 km	Maximum profit	Profitable volume
0	48	3.57	5 208 000	1 160 000
10%	63	4.93	10 131 000	1 800 000
20%	77	6.29	17 379 000	2 580 000
30%	92	7.64	27 392 000	3 500 000

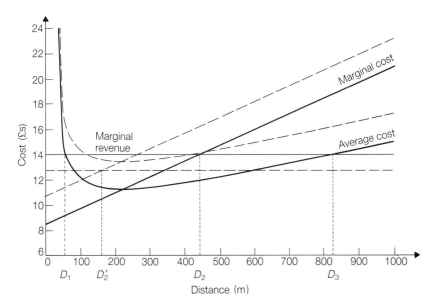

Figure 6.4 Extraction limits with fixed costs

extracting to the economic limit show the form in figure 6.4. With any extraction limit between D_1 and D_3 a profit is made: nearer than D_1, insufficient timber is extracted to cover the cost of set-up. Beyond D_3, the summed losses made by logging past the breakeven point D_2 more-than-consume the maximum profit earned by logging as far as that point.

Conventionally, marginal costs of cable extraction are rather insensitive to distance, since travel along the cable is normally rapid: thus technical rather than economic factors define the extraction limit. (However, it is argued in chapter 9 that the movement phase of cable extraction is normally undercosted.)

There are further complications.

(a) The cost of set-up is partly fixed, partly dependent on the distance over which cables and pulleys must be dragged and intermediate cable supports set up. Thus marginal cost is partly a cost of extracting an extra cubic metre and partly the extra set-up cost incurred in extending the cable system to reach that cubic metre. This is particularly relevant if commercial volume per hectare is low near the extraction limit, extra costs being spread over a small volume of extra output.

(b) The dashed lines in figure 6.4 show the marginal cost/revenue relationship for smaller trees. This size would not itself be worth extracting at all, since total cost always exceeds total revenue. However, given that the cableway has already been set up to extract larger trees, *nothing changes in respect of set-up cost* if smaller trees are extracted too, albeit to a shorter economic limiting distance D'_2. The profit margin on these smaller trees could indeed suffice to turn overall loss into overall profit.

Thus for cable systems there is a considerable hierarchy of costs which are fixed down to certain levels of decision-making. The following decisions need to be made.

(a) Should a log of given quality be extracted along a cable system which already reaches it?

(b) Should the cable be extended from a given set-up position on the road?

(c) Should the system be set up to extract to an existing road?

(d) Would profits from another cable system set-up justify extending the road?

(e) Would profits from all cable logging justify building a harbour?

Table 6.3 shows which costs and revenues are variable and which fixed in relation to each of the above decisions. Fixed costs are irrelevant to decision-making *at that particular level*.

Variation of revenue per cubic metre with tree size and quality, and variation of economically extractable volume per hectare with stand volume, tree value, length of cableway and distance from harbour also makes calculating the total revenue from cable extraction a tedious operation. A computer program is likely to help in tackling the calculations systematically.

The cable example demonstrates well the complex structure of cost, the need to identify the relevant cost for each aspect of the decision, and the

Table 6.3 Decisions in cable extraction

Decision	Move timber	Extend cable	Set up winch	Build road	Build harbour
(a)	Variable	Fixed	Fixed	Fixed	Fixed
(b)	Variable	Variable	Fixed	Fixed	Fixed
(c)	Variable	Variable	Variable	Fixed	Fixed
(d)	Variable	Variable	Variable	Variable	Fixed
(e)	Variable	Variable	Variable	Variable	Variable

right order to take decisions. The general rules are: optimize first the small things, then the large things; ask at each stage 'what changes occur in costs and revenues as a result of extending this operation, or of undertaking it at all?'

Despite the apparent intricacy of this problem, there are only two different types of decision: how far to take an operation, given that it is being done, and whether to undertake that operation at all. The first type of decision requires identification of marginal (or incremental) costs and revenues: the second requires calculation of total costs and revenues.

Maximizing and minimizing profit

Formally, one further criterion must be met to assure a profit-maximizing decision. Consider a diamond-shaped piece of low-quality land with a long axis of 2 km and a short axis of 1 km (its sides are therefore 1.24 km) – see figure 6.5. The owner wishes to lease some land to forestry, yielding an

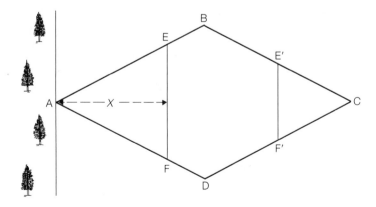

Figure 6.5 Map of proposed area for fencing

annual rent of £25/ha, rather than leave it unproductive. The forest must be contiguous with the existing area of forest west of A. The presence of a herd of deer in winter requires a deer-proof fence with annual maintenance cost of £500/km, following the sides of the area until it crosses the diamond parallel to its short axis. The length of fence AEF is 3.24X, its annual cost £1620X and its area 50X^2 ha, worth £1250X^2 in rent. Fence ABE′F′D is 2 + 1.24X long, costs £1000 + 620X and encloses an area 200X - 50X^2-100 ha, worth £5000X - 1250X^2 - 2500.

Every metre further east that EF is erected costs an extra £1.62 and encloses about 2.5X poundsworth of additional forest. Every metre further east E′F′ is erected costs an extra £0.62 and encloses about (5 - 2.5X) poundsworth of additional forest. Incremental revenue and cost from extending the forest a metre east are plotted in figure 6.6. There are two positions at which incremental cost equals incremental revenue. At 0.65 km east, profit has clearly reached a *minimum* of about £-525. Eastward from here, incremental revenue exceeds incremental cost, gradually compensating for previous losses. The breakeven point occurs at 1.24 km east, and profit is maximized (£337 per year) at 1.75 km east. Beyond this, incremental cost exceeds incremental revenue.

It is a general result that incremental [or marginal] revenue equals incremental [marginal] cost at both maximum and minimum profit. Those familiar with calculus will not find this strange, given that at the point of equality the rate of change of total profit is zero.

It is evidently crucial to distinguish maxima from minima, and figure 6.6 illustrates the criteria. At 1.75 km east, incremental cost is *rising relative to incremental revenue*: this is the test of a profit-maximizing point: at 0.65 km

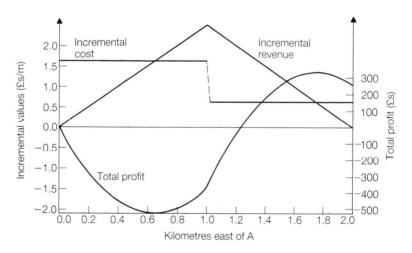

Figure 6.6 Profit minimizing and maximizing points

east, incremental cost is *falling relative to incremental revenue*, and this diagnoses a profit-minimizing point. Three or more intersections, and several maxima, may exist, in which case further calculations of total profit are needed to determine the overall maximum.

Summary

This chapter and the previous one have introduced several concepts and criteria whereby profit may be maximized, given adequate data and an ability to recognize the circumstances in which each applies.

For incompatible or interactive courses of action, incremental cost and revenue between courses of action should be calculated.

When factor constraints operate, for an isolated course of action the cost of the constrained factors is an opportunity cost.

Choice among compatible courses of action under a constraint requires selection in descending order of the ratio incremental-net-revenue: incremental-constraint.

Past costs should have no influence on present decisions.

When cost and revenue are both variable, three criteria are needed to ensure profit maximization:

(a) total revenue > total cost
(b) incremental [marginal] revenue = incremental [marginal] cost
(c) incremental [marginal] cost is rising relative to incremental [marginal] revenue.

For those familiar with calculus notation, these rules may be restated as

(a) $R > C$
(b) $dR/dQ = dC/dQ$
(c) $d^2C/dQ^2 > d^2R/dQ^2$

In taking a sequence of decisions, optimization should start at the detailed level, and work towards the major decision of whether the optimal *design* of activity is worth doing at all.

7 The Treatment of Time

Any intervention in an ecosystem triggers a sequence of ecological events. Sometimes the system is so buffered that it accommodates the change almost instantly: sometimes it is so delicately balanced that disaster can result from apparently trivial acts. Often it is foresters' deliberate purpose to intervene so as to enhance the ecosystem's future capacity to produce the goods and services required by the objectives of the enterprise.

As the scale of human activity increases, so the *in*consequential ecological intervention becomes a rarer event. Increasingly, foresters take actions where explicit consideration of the time dimension is imperative – at minimum, because intervention with disastrous long-term consequences reduces the public standing of organizations for which they work.

With the introduction of intertemporal effects comes the need to compare revenues and costs accruing at different times. Are losses of site productivity, consequent on exploitation of natural forest, more important than immediate revenue gained? Does the enhanced value of knot-free timber justify the early costs of pruning?

The point is that a £ today does not have the same value as a £ next year. Nor is a cubic metre of timber available now equivalent to one 10 years hence, any more than a cubic metre standing in the forest is equivalent to one delivered to the factory gate. Products and factors of production have *place utility*, *time utility* and *form utility*: they are valued for *where* and *when*, as well as *what* they are. Thus a Christmas tree in June has no market value, while surplus labour in the hot or dry season is valueless for the planting programme.

However, this chapter is not concerned with seasonality, but with the general progression of time – costs during one planting season compared with those of the next; Christmas trees this year and Christmas trees 10 years hence. A resource is usually presumed more valuable, the earlier it is available. Resources can be used to create capital goods, such as roads and plantations, or can be sold to generate funds for creation of capital. Since capital continuously produces other goods, the sooner it is available, the more it can yield to an enterprise. For example, a road in a plantation is more valuable if constructed after 25 years, when it can be used to extract thinnings, than after 50 years, when its use is confined to harvesting final fellings. It is on this positive productivity of capital and investment funds that our initial comparisons between time periods are based.

Since popular notions equate investment with putting money in a bank, let it be clear what economists mean by the term. Investment means incurring costs in order to increase future revenues (or save future costs). This is normally done by creating physical capital – building factories, offices, houses, planting forests, constructing roads and dams. Much investment takes place in *human capital* (education and training) and in *technological capital* (research and development). Investment can also be seen as postponement of consumption: seeds of an agricultural crop being sown rather than eaten; a maturing plantation being left to grow for five more years; small roundwood being used to fence a plantation against browsers rather than sold or burned as fuel. In each case there is an immediate opportunity cost in forgone consumption, in order that future consumption may increase.

Interest payment

Banks lend money so that individuals and organizations may exploit the ability of capital to produce a flow of products. But funds, like other resources, are limited, and to direct them to the most productive uses a price must be charged for borrowing. In capitalist economies the price, charged annually (or at lesser intervals), is *interest*. In strict Islamic and Marxist economies the idea of interest is abhorrent for respectively religious and political reasons. In Islam, interest is regarded as exploitation of fellow-humans, whereas in Marxism it represents an unearned (and therefore undeserved) return to the owners of wealth. Nonetheless, even within such economies, criteria are adopted which tend to penalize investments whose productivity is small or long-delayed (see chapter 11). Pragmatic considerations may even allow explicit interest charges.

Payment of interest (or any charge for use of investment funds) makes a $ worth more now than after one year. This is true whether money is borrowed (since a $ repaid now means less interest to pay over the next year) or deposited (since a $ now means more interest earned over the next year). If the interest rate is 10%, then $1 now is equivalent in value to $1 × (100% + 10%) = $1.10 in one year.

In forestry, periods of investment are normally such that repayment cannot be made after one year. Effectively the £1100 due on an initial loan of £1000 is re-invested for a further year, after which the repayment due would be £1100 × (100% + 10%) = £1210; £1331 would be owing after three years and so on. This is *compound interest*, the general formula for repayment due being

$$\pounds L \times (100\% + R\%)^t \text{ or } \pounds L \times (1 + r)^t \qquad (7.1)$$

where L = amount of loan
 R = percentage interest rate
 r = interest rate as a decimal
 t = duration of the loan before repayment.

Decimal format is invariably used in calculations.

Except with low interest rates, compound interest mounts rapidly and dominates economic appraisal of forestry under any but the shortest rotations, as table 7.1 shows.

Table 7.1 Repayment due on a loan of £1000

Time lapse	INTEREST RATE				
	1%	3%	5%	10%	15%
5	1 051	1 159	1 276	1 611	2 011
10	1 105	1 344	1 629	2 594	4 046
20	1 220	1 806	2 653	6 728	16 367
30	1 348	2 427	4 322	17 449	66 212
50	1 645	4 384	11 467	117 391	1 083 657
75	2 109	9 179	38 833	1 271 895	35 672 868
100	2 705	19 219	131 501	13 780 612	1 174 313 400

It is tempting (particularly for foresters) to dismiss compound interest as a mere financial abstraction. This misses the point entirely. If £1000 loaned to forestry could have been used instead to create another capital asset capable of paying £100 interest in the first year, the total of loanable funds and hence the capital assets in the second year increase by 10%; if these assets also repay 10% annually, the earning power of initial funds expands compound-wise at 10%. This is the opportunity cost of funds allocated to forestry, and if forestry yields less revenue than its opportunity cost to the economy it is no more a valuable social investment than a sound commercial venture.

The position stated is over-simplified: chapter 29 re-examines compound interest in the national context. Nonetheless, for business enterprises, it validly represents the investment decision.

Discounting

Compound interest shows the future sum of money equivalent to a sum (typically a debt) at present. Often in forestry, however, time is seen from a different perspective: a revenue is expected from a crop 50 years hence – what is the equivalent value of that sum now? This question is not easy to answer intuitively. Many foresters do not expect to be alive when the crops they plant mature; others expect to have been promoted or transferred. Anyway, it is difficult to know whether the prospect of $1 million beyond such a divide of time is really as important as it sounds.

Compound interest, however, gives a ready means of establishing the present equivalent of a future sum. What sum of money at present will become worth $1000 in 10 years, the interest rate being 10%? One can write:

$$\$X \times (1 + 0.10)^{10} = \$1000$$

$$\therefore \$X = \frac{\$1000}{1.10^{10}} = \$385.54$$

The equivalent now of some future cost or revenue or profit is called its *present value* (PV). Generalizing the above formula, the PV of a sum, $\$Y$, in t years time, when the decimal interest rate is r, can be given as

$$\frac{\$Y}{(1 + r)^t} \tag{7.2a}$$

An alternative formula found in economics texts is

$$\$Y \times e^{(-\rho \times t)} \tag{7.2b}$$

where e = the base of natural logarithms
$\rho = \log_e(1 + r)$

This form gives numerically identical results, and enables certain additional manipulations to be performed.

The process of dividing a future value by $(1 + r)^t$ to obtain a present equivalent is known as *discounting*. The rate r used in this sense is called the *discount rate*, and $1/(1 + r)^t$ the *discount factor*. As with compound interest, the effect of discounting on the economics of forestry is dramatic, as shown in table 7.2.

Mathematically, discounting simply reverses compounding. Compounding means multiplying by $(1 + r)$ once for every year forward through time: discounting means dividing by $(1 + r)$ once for every year backwards through time. Time does not go backwards, which gives discounting an aura

Table 7.2 Value of Rs1000 discounted at several rates for various times

	DISCOUNT RATE				
Time lapse	1%	3%	5%	10%	15%
5	951.5	862.6	783.5	620.9	497.2
10	905.3	744.1	613.9	385.5	247.2
20	819.5	553.7	376.9	148.6	61.10
30	741.9	412.0	231.4	57.31	15.10
50	608.0	228.1	87.20	8.519	0.9228
75	474.1	108.9	25.75	0.7862	0.02803
100	369.7	52.03	7.605	0.07257	0.0008516

of unreality. Investments yield profits, interest accrues to money deposited in banks: discounted values are less readily envisaged (though they are observable in futures markets and prices of government bonds).

However, *Homo sapiens* is not a species beholden only to the moment's impulses, but a visionary, a forecaster, a planner, who designs present actions with a view of the future. Part of that process is to assess the importance of future events in relation to present ones.

Discounting does not entirely depend, either, on the observed productivity of investments or the payment of interest. It is widely observed that individuals choose to consume products (chocolates, fuelwood) now, rather than storing them for future consumption. Some premium (for example, the 30-, 60- or 100-fold yield of seed-corn, or a positive rate of interest or profit on invested funds) is required to persuade them to postpone consumption.

Investors in capitalist economies seem indifferent between £1 now and (say) the £1.10 obtainable by investing for a year: were it not so, they would invest more, or less, until it *was* so. Hence the time preference rate (the discount placed on consumption one year hence) is often equated with the available rate of return on investment. But time preference is characteristic of human psychology in all cultures, religions and ideologies. Humans apparently give less significance to events, benefits, pleasures, pains, costs, revenues, profits, the further into the future they are expected to occur. (Chapter 29 offers an alternative explanation of human behaviour, but the one outlined is generally accepted by economists.) Thus the objections of strict Islam and Marxism to compound interest need not apply to discounting based on time preference, which exists independently of financial institutions.

Compounding and discounting

Thus there are two ways to compare cash flows accruing at different times: the method selected is a matter of convenience, as discussed in chapter 11. Correctly applied, they never yield different choices among courses of action. One approach is to compound each cost and revenue forward to some point in time, at or beyond the last cash flow. The alternative is to discount each cash flow backwards to some point in time at or before the first cash flow; in practice this is normally the present time, or the time when a course of action is initiated, referred to as time zero (or t_0).

A third possibility exists of taking some time during the investment period as the reference point, compounding forward to that time cash flows occurring before it, and discounting back those occurring afterwards.

In all cases the golden rule is to obtain the equivalent value of each cost or revenue at the chosen point in time, and *only then* to sum the figures, as in table 7.3. The necessity for compounding or discounting arises because pounds occurring at different times are *not* equal in value. It is thus clearly incorrect to sum all costs and revenues and then to compound or discount the aggregate to the reference point: such an operation is meaningless. Note also that $r = 5\% = 0.05$. This is not the same as $r = 5$, as a computation will quickly confirm:

$$8000/(1 + 5)^{22} = 8000/(1.316 \times 10^{17}) = 6.078 \times 10^{-14}$$

The effect of discounting is not as drastic as that!

The wide availability of calculators with power functions has made calculation of discount factors very easy. Previously, they were found by using logarithmic tables, or by referring to discount tables compiled for various values of r and t. Longhand calculations are extremely tedious.

Table 7.3 Two approaches to comparing revenues at different times

Felling	Year	Projected revenue	Revenue discounted to $t = 0$	Revenue compounded to $t = 22$
First thin	10	500	$500 \div 1.05^{10} = 307$	$500 \times 1.05^{12} = 898$
Second thin	14	1000	$1000 \div 1.05^{14} = 505$	$1000 \times 1.05^8 = 1\,477$
Clearfelling	22	8000	$8000 \div 1.05^{22} = 2735$	$8\,000$
Total			3547	10 375

Some useful discounting formulas

One attraction of discounting is its ability to yield compact formulas which allow rapid calculation of the summed present value of a regular cash flow occurring at intervals over many years, or extending to the indefinite future. For example, the PV of $£Y$ after one year, $£Y$ after two years, after three years and every subsequent year is

$$£Y/r \tag{7.3a}$$

If the cash flow is continuous at the rate $£Y$ per year, PV is

$$£Y/\rho \tag{7.3b}$$

where ρ is $\log_e(1 + r)$

For $£Y$ at 1, 2, 3 ... T years, PV is

$$\frac{£Y}{r} \times \left(1 - \frac{1}{(1 + r)^T}\right) \tag{7.4a}$$

and for a continuous cash flow at $£Y$ per year from 0 to T years, PV is

$$\frac{£Y}{\rho} \times \left(1 - \frac{1}{(1 + r)^T}\right) \quad \text{or} \quad \frac{£Y}{\rho} \times (1 - e^{-\rho T}) \tag{7.4b}$$

The PV of a cash flow lasting T years, then repeated in perpetuity is

$$PV_\infty = PV_T \times \frac{(1 + r)^T}{(1 + r)^T - 1} \quad \text{or} \quad PV_{T}/\left(1 - \frac{1}{(1 + r)^T}\right) \tag{7.5}$$

where subscripts ∞ and T refer to duration of cash flow.

The PV of a repeated cash flow for some specified future period is called its *capitalized* value.

Forestry economics textbooks used to abound in formulas designed for every individual management decision. Students were clearly expected to memorize these, and regurgitate them in examinations. This was always a pointless use of book-space and memory: a formula can be derived to meet every case by manipulating those given above. Indeed, readers with algebraic facility may derive the above formulas from (7.2a). With understanding, foresters may make their own formulas: without it, they will surely mis-remember or mis-apply other people's.

Inflation

Discounting is nothing to do with inflation. Discounting may reflect the productivity of investments, or it may reflect time preference, but it does not reflect decline through time in the purchasing power of money over goods.

Inflation is such a preoccupation of businesses, governments and world financial institutions that it is hard to believe that it presents no problem in comparing future cash flows. It has been stated that a £ now does not have the same value as a £ in a year, and, as far as purchasing power is concerned, this has been a common experience for humanity in the twentieth century.

But return on investment means something different: not monetary yield, but physical production. Even in a world without inflation, physical investments would yield physical products, and dividends would be paid to investors. Discounting means something different again: not that the purchasing power of a £ in a year is less than that of a £ presently, but that the possession of a given physical resource, or consumption of a given physical product a year hence, is valued less than that physical resource or product if available presently.

Take a plantation which is expected at year 40 to yield 400 m³ of a particular quality of timber, presently priced at £10/m³ standing. There are two ways to treat inflation.

1 *The monetary method*

The inflation rate is 10%. Since it is unknown whether it will rise or fall, this rate is projected for 40 years, and applied to all products. The price per cubic metre at felling will be

$$£10 \times 1.10^{40} = £452.59$$

The predicted *money* revenue is £452.59 × 400 = £181 037/ha.

Suppose the (monetary) bank interest rate is 15.5%. One who borrows £1000 expects to repay £1155 after a year, irrespective of changes in the purchasing power of the £.

PV, discounting at 15.5%, is

$$£181\ 037/1.155^{40} = £568.$$

2 *The 'real' or purchasing power method*

Part of the monetary interest rate is due to the falling value of money. Investments yield high money returns partly because the price of given physical output rises year after year. Banks must pay higher rates of interest to lenders, to compensate them for the fall in purchasing power of the £ during the period of deposit, as well as to persuade them to postpone consumption of real products. Suppose that £100 now buys 100 units of some desired product, say cans of beans, each costing £1. Because of inflation, at the end of one year each can costs £1.10. £100 deposited at 15.5% secures £115.50 in one year. The number of cans purchasable with the latter sum = £115.50/£1.10 = 105 cans. In terms of purchasing power (the number of cans purchasable) there has been a *real rate of return* of 5% on the investment. One who is indifferent between 100 cans of beans now and 105 cans of beans in a year has a *real rate of time preference or discount* of 5%.

Since the real rate of interest is concerned with purchasing power, not money, the future revenue from a forest crop is taken as its equivalent value in other commodities. At the current price of £10/m³, 1 m³ of timber can be exchanged for 10 cans of beans; there is no information suggesting that this 'exchange rate' will differ in 40 years.

In units of purchasing power over beans, then, the forest yields a return of 4000 cans per hectare in 40 years. Discounted at the real rate of 5%, this has an equivalent value of

$$4000/(1.05)^{40} = 568 \text{ cans}$$

Since the value of one can is £1, the monetary equivalent of the future timber crop is £568 per hectare – as discovered previously.

Either treatment of inflation may be used, but predicted monetary values must be used in conjunction with a monetary rate of discount, while purchasing power units are used with a real rate of discount.

In practice it is impossible to predict changes in inflation and monetary interest rates over a forest rotation. Since the two tend to fluctuate in tandem, especially in the long term, the real interest rate (representing approximately the difference between them) is much more stable. Thus it is easier to relate future revenues to the current purchasing power of the £ – that is, to project costs and revenues on the basis of current prices – and to discount at the real discount rate. Price increases are included only if they are 'real': that is if they are increasing *in relation to the prices of goods generally*. The 'real' approach is used throughout this book.

Technically, the real rate of discount is

$$(1 + m)/(1 + i) - 1 \qquad\qquad (7.6)$$

where m is the money interest rate
i is the inflation rate.

Choice of discount rate

Table 7.2 shows how much the discount rate would affect the value of forestry, so it is crucial that the rate is chosen correctly. For forest managers, however, unquestioning application of the rate handed down from above is expected in comparisons of cash flow over time. If a monetary rate of interest is charged to an enterprise, or if a particular return is expected on its shares, or if it has available clearly defined monetary interest-earning opportunities, profitability calculations use these rates – suitably adjusted for inflation. State forest enterprises may be charged, in practice or as an accounting exercise, a 'real' rate of interest defined by government, and appraisals are undertaken at this rate.

In fact choice of discount rate – both the concept on which it is based and the figure representing the concept – has excited enormous debate among economists, not least because of its implications for future generations. The whole question is re-opened in chapter 29.

Criteria for assessing profitability when costs and revenues occur at different points in time are discussed in chapter 11. The next chapters take up two costing problems which have a time dimension, and therefore could not be properly treated earlier: costing of machinery, and choice of forest roading and harvesting systems.

8 The Accounting Cost of Forest Machinery

With progressive mechanization of forest operations, especially logging, the cost of machines becomes ever more important, and may dominate the economics of an operation. Purchase of machinery is an investment, whose pay-off is spread over several years: this complicates methods of costing.

In many countries animals still provide the power for logging. But the principles involved in costing the capital represented by trained animals are not different from those applying to inanimate machines, although the use of animals is constrained by demands of humane treatment. For elephants, with a working life of fifty years, the problem of comparing time periods is even more prominent than for a mechanical device which is unlikely to serve longer than ten years.

The machinery used in every forest operation can be costed from first principles, but it is convenient if a cost for a given machine (usually per hour) is available. Chapter 8 examines methods used to provide such a standard cost; chapter 9 considers whether this standard cost truly represents the cost to an enterprise of using a machine.

Running costs of an operation

Machine costs conventionally comprise capital costs (those associated with *investing* in machines) and running costs (those associated with *operating* them). Repair and maintenance may be treated as a capital item (particularly major, infrequent overhauls) or as a running cost (particularly preventative maintenance) or as a separate category.

Running costs are straightforward. Fuel cost per hour assumes that the machine is working at a 'normal' rate in average conditions. Lubricant cost is often approximated as 20% of fuel cost.

Since machine and operator form an inseparable unit as far as useful output is concerned, the running cost of large machines often includes the

Plate II Elephant as capital: harvesting in India
(Photo: Gary Kerr)

labour cost of operating them. Piecework is advantageous in promoting high rates of output, but in the event of machine breakdown the operator may revert to a less remunerative plain time. Oncost is added to direct payment.

Tax and insurance recur infrequently, but can nonetheless be allocated hourly. They are fixed in the short term, but payment can be suspended if the machine is not used for a prolonged period.

Capital costs of machinery

Capital cost can be assessed by rule of thumb. For example, as

$$\frac{2.5 \times \text{purchase price}}{\text{hours of working life of machine}} \tag{8.1}$$

This is very rough and ready, particularly considering how large the purchase price may be. Besides, such a rule must be based on generalization of more detailed calculations (the figure 2.5 is empirical rather than theoretical). If these calculations are simple, it is worth improving accuracy by using a more specific method.

The calculation has two stages:

(a) definition of capital cost
(b) its allocation over the units of work (hours, or output achieved).

The conventional components of capital cost are *depreciation* and interest. Depreciation represents the loss in value of a machine over its working life – the purchase price less its resale (or scrap) value. Interest is paid (actually or notionally) on the remaining capital value after depreciation has been deducted.

A value of depreciation may be required for taxation or valuation purposes: the full range of methods for allocating depreciation is discussed in Openshaw (1980). In costing machinery for managerial purposes total depreciation is often distributed evenly over the machine's working life. Thus if purchase price is £70 000 and resale price after six years is £10 000, depreciation is £10 000 per year.

Calculation of appropriate interest is more problematical. If money has been borrowed to buy the machine, the interest rate should be that charged by the financing institution, whereas if purchase has been financed with the enterprise's own funds, the correct rate is the rate that could have been earned by alternative uses of the funds. Money interest rates should be adjusted for inflation (see equation (7.6)). In the ensuing examples purchase is treated as bank-financed: the principles are not different for internally financed purchases.

At the beginning of the machine's life the capital value is its purchase price: at the end of its working life the capital value equals resale price. Over this time, interest is due on whatever part of capital value is unrepaid. It is now relevant not only what total depreciation is, but how it is allocated over time.

'Straight-line' depreciation is debited continuously and uniformly through the machine's life (figure 8.1a). The average unrepaid capital $(\bar{K})$ over the machine's life is then the arithmetic mean of purchase price (P) and resale value (R).

$$\bar{K} = \frac{P + R}{2} \tag{8.2}$$

Using the figures above and a 10% interest rate, interest is £4000 per year.

An alternative is to depreciate in lump sums after each year. This gives a stepped profile for unrepaid capital (figure 8.1b) yielding an average capital over the machine's life of

$$\frac{(P - R) \times (N + 1)}{2N} + R \qquad (8.3)$$

with an interest payment of £4500.

However, since the machine begins to pay for itself immediately, and since machines are charged hourly rather than yearly, there is no justification for postponing depreciation till the end of each year.

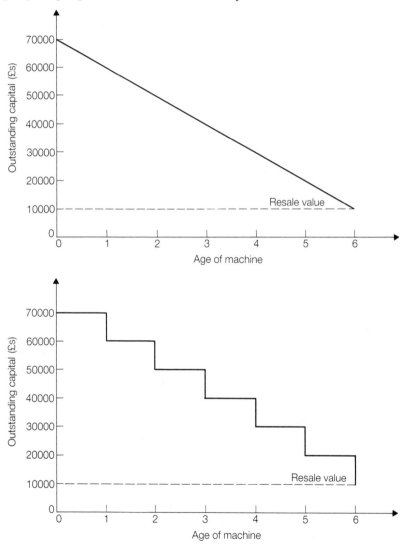

Figure 8.1 (a) straight-line depreciation
(b) stepped depreciation

Converting all these figures into a cost per unit output requires estimation of yearly work done by the machine. This in turn depends on working practices, and on *availability, utilization* and rate of output for the machine.

Working practices

If the labour force is willing and able to work two shifts a day, 365 days a year, more work per year is achieved than if one shift is worked, with weekends and public holidays omitted. Because large capital charges are assumed to accumulate regardless of whether the machine is working, the working day may be extended, and modern machines may have spotlights for night working.

Availability

However, allowances for preventative maintenance and repairs may mean that machines are available for about 75% of the working week. On this basis, 1500 hours availability per year with one-shift working may be reasonable, and an hourly charge for the above machine would be

$$\frac{\pounds 10\,000 + \pounds 4000}{1500} = \pounds 9.33$$

In costing a unit of production – such as a cubic metre of timber extracted to roadside – further allowance is made for:

Utilization

This is the proportion of time that a technically available machine is actually producing output. If a machine spends 8% of its working day travelling from depot to work site, 10% idle while the operator takes lunch and drink breaks and 5% waiting for fellers to trim and cross-cut enough produce for it to extract, then its capital cost per *working* hour is

$$\frac{\pounds 9.33}{100\% - (8\% + 10\% + 5\%)} = \pounds 12.12$$

Rate of output

If, further, the machine extracts 10 m³ of timber per hour when actually working, the capital cost per cubic metre = $\pounds 12.12/10 = \pounds 1.21$.

The other cost items already mentioned must also be included in the overall unit cost for a given operation. Examples appear in the next two chapters.

Is the capital charge adequate?

The difficulty in choosing among depreciation conventions is that depreciation represents an 'invisible' accounting item corresponding to no real cash flow. Even with loan-financed purchases, repayment of the loan depends less on calculated accounting charge than on cash-flow elsewhere within the enterprise or earnings achieved by the machine. The only fixed cash flows are outlay on purchase, and resale value. Nor is interest in practice charged constantly through life on the *average* outstanding loan, but in each short time period on the *actual* outstanding loan.

The key question is, does the charge determined above suffice to repay the loan by the end of the machine's working life? Take the total capital charge of £14 000 per year calculated above, equivalent to repaying at £269.23 per week. At the same time the bank adds interest weekly at 0.18346% per week (which compounds to 10% per year). After six years repayment, and remission of the resale price, a debt of £779 is still outstanding – not a huge sum, but it would have been larger if machine life was longer or interest rate higher. The error lies in basing interest on the average capital of £40 000. This is insufficient to pay interest on the initial £70 000. Thus the outstanding loan declines more slowly than straight-line depreciation indicates (figure 8.2). It only declines rapidly near the end of the machine's life, when it is too late to restore the deficit accumulated in early life. Over the whole period, the average outstanding loan, and therefore the average interest due, is clearly greater than is given by straight-line depreciation. Stepped depreciation could be seen as a crude attempt to adjust the interest charge upwards to allow for this. Unfortunately, depending on rate of interest, machine life and period between repayments, this method may either understate or overstate the due interest.

Depreciation, interest and discounted output

The problem can be redefined thus. The machine must pay for itself over its working life. The periodic charge must therefore suffice to clear the initial loan plus interest, once the resale price has been received. In this charge, the distinction between depreciation and interest can be dropped: the bank is concerned with cash repayments, not the accounting headings under which they are made. For capital purchase financed by the enterprise itself, an equivalent sum is needed, which balances revenues forgone in alternative investments.

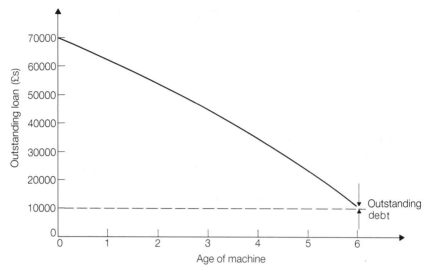

Figure 8.2 Actual unrepaid loan

The machine breaks even if the sum of discounted repayments equals the sum of discounted costs. Considering purchase and resale value only, the net discounted cost for the machine is

$$£70\,000 - £10\,000/1.10^6 = £64\,355 \qquad (8.4)$$

Let the annual repayment be A. Then the discounted sum of repayments, *allocated to the middle of each of the six years* of the machine's life is

$$A \times \left(\frac{1}{1.1^{0.5}} + \frac{1}{1.1^{1.5}} + \frac{1}{1.1^{2.5}} + \frac{1}{1.1^{3.5}} + \frac{1}{1.1^{4.5}} + \frac{1}{1.1^{5.5}} \right)$$
$$= A \times 4.568 \qquad (8.5)$$

Setting (8.4) equal to (8.5) gives

$$A = £64\,355/4.568 = £14\,088.$$

The weekly equivalent is £270.93 and the hourly charge £9.39.

If this repayment is made continuously, the loan is completely paid off at the end of the machine's life.

More generally, hourly charge is

$$G = \frac{\sum\limits_{t=0}^{t=T} C_t/(1 + r)^t}{\sum\limits_{t=1}^{t=T} H_t/(1 + r)^{t-0.5}} \qquad (8.6)$$

where C_t is cost at time t (resale being a negative cost)
   t is a time variable
   T is the machine's life in years
   H_t is the number of hours worked during year t.

The denominator of equation (8.6) may be termed the *summed discounted hours worked*. The discounting of hours worked reflects the judgement that the discounted value of hourly contribution to enterprise profit is greater in early than in late life of the machine. The adoption of this costing method may be acceptable in Islamic and Marxist economies using time preference rate discounting.

Strictly the formulation should discount working hours continuously as they occur. This can be achieved by the continuous discounting formula (7.4b), which distributes working hours over the whole year:

$$\text{Summed discounted hours worked} = \frac{H}{\rho} \times \left(1 - \frac{1}{(1 + r)^T}\right) \qquad (8.7)$$

A final possible modification of (8.6) is to replace H_t by U_t, the units of output achieved in year t, thus allowing variation in efficiency of output during the machine's life. This, however, is only useful when the machine performs one kind of job, in uniform terrain and forest conditions.

Discounted output versus conventional methods

The advantage of discounting methods is not so much their accuracy, but their avoidance of uncheckable or inconsistent assumptions about depreciation and interest payments. They can, moreover, provide scope to include other problematic items. In particular, maintenance expenditures, which rarely have an even profile through the life of the machine, can be discounted from the time when they are expected to occur: for example, the cost of a new engine can be attributed to halfway through the expected life. This is more satisfactory than charging such major and irregular items, unrealistically, at an average rate.

Furthermore, formula (8.6) can accommodate varying annual output from the machine. This allows that the machine may only achieve moderate utilization in its first year, when teething problems occur; will be heavily utilized in its middle years; will then show declining output as progressively more curative maintenance is needed; finally perhaps showing only sporadic output in a reserve capacity during its obsolescence.

Most of these features are illustrated by the Indian elephant. Its initial cost is that of capture or purchase, followed by a period of training. During its life it actually appreciates in value, and thus may represent a sound investment in its own right. Full-grown males earn revenue from participation in temple ceremonies; suitably discounted, these partly offset initial cost. When the elephant dies, its 'scrap' value is the ivory in the case of the male, but against this must be set the cost of burial. Veterinary bills and care of the elephant by its mahout (operator) represent repair and maintenance expenditure, and food is the fuel cost. While the elephant learns its job, output (cubic metres extracted in given time) builds up steadily, then maintains a high level for some decades until the elephant ages, finally to be retired either for humanitarian reasons or because the *additional* cost of food required during a working day is greater than the value of output achieved. Thereafter social constraints decree that the elephant should be kept in comfort. Availability is conditioned by illness, and in the case of males by the two-month annual 'musht', during which hormonal changes make the elephant unmanageable.

These irregular but very relevant factors would entirely defeat conventional accounting methods, but they are taken in the stride of the discounted output method. This method, however, is not normal accounting practice, and organization procedures may demand use of less accurate and flexible systems.

Applications of machine costings

The above methods may be used for

(a) setting a machine-hire charge (with a mark-up for profit);
(b) costing a job to decide if it is worth doing – see the conversion example in chapter 9;
(c) comparing different operational methods, such as labour and capital intensive harvesting, as below.

The most expensive phase of harvesting is often felling and debranching. In table 8.1 the cost of a mechanical harvester is calculated (in dollars) using equation (8.6). Purchase price is $320 000 and resale value $50 000. The four annual costs are allotted to half-years.

$$320\,000 + \frac{80\,000}{1.04^{0.5}} + \frac{70\,000}{1.04^{1.5}} + \frac{80\,000}{1.04^{2.5}} + \frac{90\,000}{1.04^{3.5}} - \frac{50\,000}{1.04^4}$$

$$= 572\,691$$

Table 8.1 Choice of harvesting technology

Item	Harvester 4%	Harvester 20%	Chainsaw 4%	Chainsaw 20%
Machine	63.89	76.24	0.62	0.66
Fuel and oil	5.00	5.00	1.50	1.50
Operator	10.00	0.60	9.00	0.54
Oncost	6.00	0.25	6.00	0.25
Totals	84.89	82.09	17.12	2.95
Output (m³/hr)	23	23	1.6	1.6
Cost/m³	3.69	3.57	10.70	1.84

The hours of split-shift working are discounted as in equation (8.5)

$$\frac{2200}{1.04^{0.5}} + \frac{2500}{1.04^{1.5}} + \frac{2600}{1.04^{2.5}} + \frac{2400}{1.04^{3.5}} = 8964$$

Cost per hour is $63.89. A similar costing is applied to the more labour-intensive chainsaw, and the costings are repeated at a 20% discount rate.

The figures in the 4% columns of table 8.1 represent conditions in a technically advanced country, with high wages. The 20% columns represent a developing country with low wages but high interest rates. Despite the instinct that the best affordable technology should always be used, the labour-intensive method is here more economical per unit output for the conditions of a developing country.

9 The Economic Cost of Forest Machinery

The costings in chapter 8 assumed that every cost item was variable (machines could be purchased, labour could be hired, fuels were available) and that some defined average rate of work in average conditions would be achieved. These costings are appropriate in deciding matters like mechanization policy, or whether purchase of a particular machine is justifiable.

However, rates and conditions are often *not* average, nor can factors of production be acquired immediately. In deciding whether to use an already-purchased machine for a particular job, how hard that machine should be worked, or which job a machine should be used for, a different costing is appropriate.

Choice and change in machine use

One of the forest's extraction tractors may have broken down. Or a natural disaster may require widespread salvage harvesting. The cost per hour of an extra machine is irrelevant if machines are unavailable at short notice, or not worth purchasing as short-term stop-gaps. When there are more jobs than machines available to tackle them, decisions concern which operations should receive priority, which delayed, and which abandoned.

The option may also exist of using available machinery harder. The operator of a broken-down tractor might take a second shift on a functioning tractor. All machines and operators could work several hours overtime per week to complete salvage fellings quickly.

By contrast, restrictive weather conditions or abnormal age-class structure may cause periods when available work does not occupy all machines. The options are then to undertake operations (such as felling 'non-commercial' species) which would not normally be worthwhile; to undertake operations before due time; or to leave machinery idle.

Chapter 19 outlines a method for deciding which operations to delay or advance when resources and work-load do not match. The remaining choice concerns how much use should be made of machines. What additional costs are incurred by using a machine for an hour, rather than leaving it idle? These changes appear to be:

(a) consumption of fuel and oil;
(b) payment of piecework rather than plain time rate (if those are the respective wages when the machine is and is not working);
(c) maintenance and repair due to wear and tear in use;
(d) shortening of life.

*Un*changed appear to be:

(e) labour oncost;
(f) vehicle tax and insurance;
(g) interest charges;
(i) depreciation caused and maintenance required by the ravages of time.

To cost the changes embodied in (a) and (b) requires no new techniques. Items (c) and (d), however, provide problems not so far confronted, particularly the nature of depreciation. Forest machines work in gruelling conditions. Wear of tyres and hydraulic systems occurs through traversing rocky ground and entanglement with tree snags, while engine and transmission suffer through the torque needed to move over steep, rough or boggy terrain. Even shearing of structural members may occur.

Passing time causes loss of value in two ways. Physical deterioration occurs through rusting and perishing, particularly if the machine is ill-protected. Economic obsolescence occurs through technological innovation which eventually leads to the machine giving higher unit costs than a replacement, despite being in physically good condition.

In the working conditions of forestry, use is more important than time in causing depreciation, repair and maintenance in machines. By contrast, for forest buildings time is the chief cause of deterioration. For forest roads both time and use are important.

Advance and delay of machine costs

Take the machine costed in chapter 8, which is to be replaced by a machine of similar cost and capability at six-year intervals. For simplicity, assume that maintenance is charged as a running cost. The net discounted cost of purchase and periodic replacement is

([purchase price] − [discounted resale price]) × [multiplier for perpetual series]

Plate III Forwarder under stress: use under forest conditions greatly accelerates depreciation
(Photo: Forestry Commission)

$$= \left(£70\ 000 - \frac{£10\ 000}{(1+r)^6} \right) \times \frac{(1+r)^6}{(1+r)^6 - 1}$$

$= £147\ 764$ when $r = 10\%$.

If purchase is postponed one year, this sum is discounted one year more:

$$£147\ 764/1.10 = £134\ 331$$

The saving by postponing purchase for a year is therefore

$$£147\ 764 - £134\ 331 = £13\ 433$$

Since a working hour is $1/1500$ of a working year, postponing purchase for one working hour saves

$$£147\ 764 - £147\ 764/1.10^{1/1500} = £9.38$$

Interestingly, this is almost exactly the hourly cost calculated by equation (8.6).

But reconsider the costing just *after* purchase of the machine for £70 000. The discounted *future* costs are now reduced by £70 000 to £77 764. Postponing use of the machine for a working hour delays the discounted cost of a perpetual series of replacements by 1/1500 of a working year, a saving of

$$£77\ 764 - £77\ 764/1.10^{1/1500} = £4.94$$

Obversely, this is also the cost of using an otherwise-idle machine for an hour. Over the machine's life, the cost of an hour's use increases steadily as time of replacement approaches, peaking at £8.75 immediately before replacement.

Two refinements may be added. If, say, 25% of depreciation is actually due to time, use of the machine for an hour only shortens working life by 0.75 hours, or 0.75/1500 of a working year. Cost of use now varies from £3.71 to £6.57.

Secondly, this method of costing can include regular and irregular repair and maintenance costs, as in table 9.1. The discounted value of this cash flow plus a perpetual series of replacement machines is £255 927, giving a cost per hour's use before purchase of £16.26. Once the machine has been purchased, the profile of cost for an hour's use (figure 9.1) ranges from £8.87 to £11.73. Discount rates of 0%, 5%, 10% and 20% have been used.

The higher the discount rate, the more variable the cost of use: costs are lower early on, and higher late on. These results are not intuitively obvious within the framework of conventional capital costing. The discounting-of-delay method, however, provides an intelligible explanation: in a discounting context, a cost delayed is equivalent to a saved cost, but a delayed cost represents a less significant saving, the further into the future when the delay occurs: thus cost rises as major expenditures are approached.

Table 9.1 Discounted cost – normal working

Item	Year	Cost	Discounted cost
Purchase	0	£70 000	£70 000
Overhaul	1, 2, 4, 5	£1 000	£3 039
Replace engine etc	3	£10 000	£7 513
Resale	6	−£10 000	−£5 645
Repair	Continual	£6 000/year	£27 417
Maintenance and movement	Continual	£2 000/year	£9 139
Total			£111 463

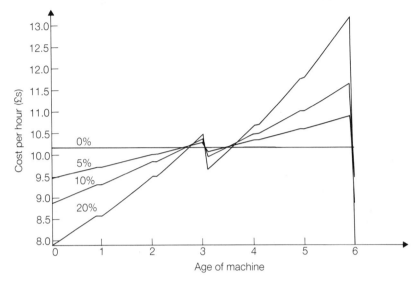

Figure 9.1 Hourly cost of machine use

It is instructive to compare the economic cost of using idle machines with that of using idle labour or animals. Use of 'living capital' in an ergonomically correct way may actually improve its condition. Bad working practice (such as poor lifting posture) or inadequate attention to health and safety (for example, in regard to chainsaw vibration) brings forward 'repair costs' (sickness pay) and 'replacement costs' (compensation and training of recruited labour), but these items should be minimized rather than budgeted for. Thus the cost of idle labour on plain time may be zero.

Two-shift costing

If a work programme is being increased, the practical possibilities may be two-shift working, or buying an extra machine. Techniques already presented can be used to evaluate the alternatives. Let two-shift working double usage to 3000 hours per year, maintenance being carried out on rest days only. If 75% of depreciation was formerly due to use, depreciation with two-shift working is at

$$75\% \times 2 + 25\% = 175\%$$

of the previous rate: expenditures either increase by 75%, or occur after 100%/175% = 0.571 of the original time. Table 9.2 embodies these changes.

Table 9.2 Discounted cost – two-shift working

Item	Year	Cost	Discounted cost
Overhaul	0.57, 1.14, 2.29, 2.86	£1 000	£3 409
Replace engine etc.	1.71	£10 000	£8 496
Resale	3.43	−£10 000	−£7 211
Repair	Continual	£10 500/year	£30 720
Maintenance and movement	Continual	£3 500/year	£10 240
Replacement	3.43	£70 000	£50 480
Total			£96 134

For a machine already purchased, the first £70 000 outlay occurs at replacement.

Capitalized cost in perpetuity is £344 746. As there are now 3000 working hours in the working year, and depreciation is 150%/175% = 85.7% due to use, the machine cost per hour just after purchase is

$$£344\ 746 - £344\ 746/1.10^{0.857/3000} = £9.38$$

Under the same assumptions, single-shift working costs £8.86 per hour, and a new machine would cost £16.26. The *average* hourly cost, £12.56, compares quite unfavourably with that of double-shift working. However, table 9.3 shows that savings by double-shifts are highly dependent on discount rate and depreciation. If these savings exceed additional costs (like extra payment for unsocial working hours plus keeping maintenance staff on standby), then two-shift working is economical.

Table 9.3 Savings (£s) through two-shift working

Time in life of existing machine	Depreciation % due to use	DISCOUNT RATE		
		0%	3%	10%
After replacement	75	1.71	2.14	3.17
	90	0.68	1.10	2.12
	100	0	0.44	1.40
Before replacement	75	1.71	2.08	2.99
	90	0.68	1.08	2.07
	100	0	0.44	1.40

Optimal replacement time

The best time to replace a machine is not, as so far assumed, technically determined. A machine should be replaced when its unit output cost exceeds that of a replacement machine. If a machine of similar performance and cost is the replacement, the machine life giving lowest average cost is optimal. Declining output due to reduced performance and increasing repair and maintenance costs eventually cause average cost to rise.

Replacement by a different system is more complex. Take a new forwarder, costing £22.22 per hour, and a skidder costing £17.75 per hour on the basis described above. These figures are relevant to the question 'should the skidder be replaced by another skidder or by a forwarder at the end of its useful life?'

There is, however, another question: 'should a skidder be replaced by a forwarder *before* the end of its useful life?' The relevant machine cost here is the outlay incurred by prolonging skidder life. This might be continual repair and maintenance costs of £8000 per year, and an expected reduction in resale price from £16 000 to £12 000 (discounted value = £10 909) over the year. The cost of retaining the skidder one year is thus (£8000 + £16 000 − £10 909) = £13 091. With 1200 hours worked per year, hourly cost is only £10.91. The options of immediate forwarder purchase and continued skidder use are compared in table 9.4. Tax and insurance are ignored. The forwarder's high availability and output favour it over a new skidder. But the fact that the old skidder's major cost is sunk makes it more economical, until its cost rises or output falls.

Optimal replacement time is further discussed in Murchison and Nautiyal (1971) and Mills and Tufts (1985).

Table 9.4 Costing for replacement (£s)

Item	Forwarder	New skidder	Old skidder
Machine cost	22.22	17.75	10.91
Operator plus oncost	7.00	7.00	7.00
Fuel	2.50	2.00	2.00
Total	31.72	26.75	19.91
m³/hour	12	8	8
Cost/m³	2.64	3.34	2.49

Differential working costs

Depreciation is affected not only by *whether* the machine is used, but by *how* it is used. Take an agricultural tractor used occasionally to power a portable circular saw, which converts roundwood to fence posts. The hourly accounting charge is calculated from the following:

Purchase and modification		£14 000
Annual repair and maintenance		£1 000
Resale value		nil
Life in years	15	
Hours worked per year	1000	
Discount rate	10%	
Discounted cost per discounted hour = £2.75.		

To resolve whether it is worth undertaking primary processing requires a fuller set of costs and revenues.

Value/m³ at roadside unprocessed	£14
Value/m³ at roadside processed	£22
Value added/m³	£8
Capital cost/hr of tractor	£2.75
Fuel and oil cost/hr	£0.50
Tax and insurance/hr	£0.30
Capital cost/hr of saw	£0.50
Labour cost/hr	£2.50
plus piecework equivalent to 50%	£1.25
Oncost @ 80% basic labour cost	£2.00
Total cost/hr	£9.80

If 1 m³ is processed per hour, value added apparently fails to cover costs. However, a different result emerges if both labour and machinery would otherwise be idle. Their opportunity cost is zero, since use in this operation does not withdraw them from other revenue-earning activities. Tax and insurance do not change. Fuel and oil costs vary with the operation. Piecework represents additional financial outlay if processing is undertaken, but labour oncost and the plain time element of pay remain unchanged. Thus total variable cost is £0.50 + £1.25 = £1.75/m³ and the operation is profitable.

However, true cost lies somewhere between the above extremes. With a work load of 1000 hours per year, an hour's use of the tractor brings forward the future cost stream by up to 0.001 years. With (say) 25% of depreciation allocated to time, the capital cost midway through the 15-year working life is £1.39; if all other costs are included, it is not worth processing.

But the tractor normally works under rather severe conditions. By contrast, in static use powering the circular saw, depreciation is slower. The depreciation rate might split as follows:

(a) time-based   25%
(b) working under sawing conditions   25%
(c) extra due to heavy use   50%

The tractor's life would be based on all three elements as embodied in its regular role. In its conversion role, however, only (a) and (b) are embodied, while only (b) actually varies with use. Thus the future cost stream is brought forward by only 0.25 × 0.001 years by an hour's use in this role. The consequent hourly cost is £0.46. Such a reduction from the accounting charge makes the operation clearly worthwhile.

The cost of skidder extraction

The above calculations assumed that an occasional use was being costed, so that the machine's life-span was determined by depreciation in its regular role. If there are two (or more) major roles with different depreciation rates, the calculation becomes more complex, since both machine life and timing of repairs and replacement depend on the proportions of the two roles.

Skidder extraction comprises six distinct phases:

1   especially in salvage or ill-organized fellings, chokering involves much effort in dragging winch cables and fixing chokers – the skidder itself, however, is stationary, the engine is idling and depreciation is negligible;

2   movement from stump to roadside entails maximum torque, strain in cables and battering to framework and tyres;

3   movement along roads imposes less stress on the machine, though torque remains high;

4   unchokering involves little depreciation;

5&6 are return journeys corresponding to 3 and 2. Absence of a load reduces machine stress, though higher running speed mitigates the difference – for decision-making purposes, the phases may be collapsed to three, whose putative depreciation rates are shown as a proportion of the maximum:

(a) terminal time (1 and 4)   25%
(b) in-forest movement (2 and 6) 100%
(c) road movement (3 and 5)   75%

Take a skidder operating over a mean in-forest distance of 250 m and a mean road movement distance of 50 m. Mean pole size is 0.4 m³, the mean load 4 m³, and the rate of extraction 8 m³ per hour over a working year of 1200 hours. Under these conditions, the proportions of phases are:

>terminal time   65%
>in-forest movement   30%
>road movement   5%

The relevant costs are:

>Purchase price   £60 000
>Major refit at year 5   £20 000
>Resale at year 9   £8 000
>Annual repair and maintenance   £8 000

With a 5% discount rate, continuously discounted capital costs are £128 786 while discounted output is 69 927 m³. The capital cost per cubic metre is £1.84.

Now consider the time (in minutes) per cubic metre over other distances. Terminal and road movement time are estimated at 5.25 minutes per cubic metre. However, in-forest movement time increases with extraction distance. The greater the percentage of in-forest movement, the greater the depreciation: mean distances greater than 250 m increase depreciation, while shorter distances reduce it. These factors are summarized in table 9.5. Depreciation rates clearly deviate very significantly from the average.

Table 9.5 Variation in depreciation rates

Distance (metres)	In-forest time	Total time	In-forest time (%)	Depreciation (% maximum)	Relative depreciation
50	0.45	5.70	7.9	34.2	68.4
100	0.90	6.15	14.6	39.0	78.0
250	2.25	7.50	30.0	50.0	100.0
500	4.50	9.75	46.2	61.5	123.1
1000	9.00	14.25	63.2	73.7	147.4

Limits of extraction

Small trees use a greater proportion of terminal time than large ones. In table 9.6, 20% of terminal time is taken to be independent of pole number, with an additional 8% for each of the 10 poles in a normal load. Increasing the number of poles to 15 thus increases terminal time by 40%. Fuel and oil costs averaging £2/hr are taken as proportional to depreciation rate. The figures represent the variation (in £s) of conventional from real cost, positive values representing conventional overcosting, and negative ones conventional undercosting.

The errors are quite sufficient to cause wrong setting of extraction limits (of size and distance). Small trees close to roadside may erroneously be considered submarginal, while larger ones at a long distance are inadvertently harvested at net cost.

Table 9.6 Miscosting of skidder extraction

Distance (metres)	MEAN VOLUME (cubic metres)			
	0.1	0.4	0.7	1.0
50	1.94	0.46	0.25	0.16
100	1.83	0.34	0.13	0.05
250	1.49	0	−0.21	−0.30
500	0.92	−0.57	−0.79	−0.87
1000	−0.23	−1.72	−1.93	−2.02

How widespread a problem?

Such inaccuracies arise only when depreciation rates differ, either between two or more roles for a machine, or between two or more phases within a given role. Thus specialized machines such as harvesters and processors are only affected by different terrain and forest conditions.

Machines which can efficiently fulfil more than one role tend to be inexpensive. The prime forestry example is the chainsaw, used for felling, debranching or cross-cutting, in low pruning, thinning or clearfall. However, depreciation costs of the chainsaw are only pence per hour, and the possible improvement of decisions too small to warrant differential costing.

Among extraction machines, cable systems repeat the skidder's pattern, with high movement depreciation and low terminal depreciation. Significant repair time is due to cable breakage. The greater the length of cable, the greater the rate of breakage per minute under a given load, and the greater the number of minutes spent under load. Cable repair cost is thus proportional to the *square* of cable length: increasing extraction distance from 250 metres to 500 metres quadruples this element of depreciation. Conventional capital costing

(a) understates the cost of long extraction distances;
(b) understates the cost of large log sizes;
(c) overstates the cost of set-up, and of small logs: this militates particularly against use in thinning, where mean tree size is small and low volume gives high set-up cost per cubic metre.

The forwarder case is less clearcut. Cross-country travel, heavily laden, imposes heavy depreciation penalties on engine, transmission, tyres and chassis. On the other hand, terminal time consists largely of loading and unloading, with severe stresses on hydraulic system and major demands on the engine. Consequently true cost may be roughly proportional to overall extraction time.

Conclusion

Costing of forest machines has been described at some length, because of the shortcomings of conventional costing techniques and the large proportion of total expenditure devoted to forest machinery. Given that use-based depreciation is the greatest single cost in many forest operations, it seems appropriate to give it careful consideration.

Very different costing techniques from those advocated here are used in most forests. In respect of mechanization policy, these techniques will not err seriously. However, the costing applied to machines with marked variability in rates of depreciation between operational roles or phases may give major errors.

No conventional method gives the real cost of varying a machine's rate of utilization, whether by using an idle machine during normal working hours, or by increasing its work-load to two shifts. Discrepancies between conventional and actual costs suffice to cause many wrong decisions. The economic cost of using an idle machine or of intensifying use of an existing machine always lies below the normal accounting charge, largely through exclusion of time-based depreciation. Use of a machine may therefore be justified even when the charge required to cover costs over its lifetime exceeds the revenue gained (or cost saved) by its use. On the other hand, the economic charge for use of machines always exceeds zero. The fact that a machine can generate some small revenue does not justify using it. There is a widespread intuition that it is imperative to utilize an expensive machine to its full capacity. But if depreciation is largely a function of use, then it is *using* the machine, rather than *owning* it, that incurs most of the cost.

It cannot be emphasized too strongly that the most sophisticated evaluation techniques are useless without sound work study data. The costings in this chapter cannot be more accurate than the figures for machine availability, utilization and rate of output. What a machine is theoretically capable of when in first-class order, with a fit, alert, trained and motivated operator working under ideal conditions of terrain, crop and weather is not relevant, given that these conditions are rarely found in combination. The field measurement of performance must be the starting-point for any realistic costing of a machine's output.

10 Choice of Roading and Harvesting System

Unless forests are densely criss-crossed by public highways, even an untarred forest road system entails heavy expenditure: UK construction costs in 1987 ranged up to £40 000/km. Roading is an investment: costs incurred in building roads save future inspection, tending, protection and harvesting costs. Usage of roads fluctuates from year to year, and, given periodic maintenance outlays, may continue over several cycles of production without overall deterioration. These features magnify the problems of cost accounting by methods involving interest; hence the calculations in this chapter are cast in discounting terms.

For a road system intended for use in perpetuity, capitalized cost is

$$R = C + M/r \qquad (10.1)$$

where C is construction cost
  M is maintenance cost charged yearly after construction

If only costs of the current rotation or exploitation programme are considered

$$R = C + (1 - 1/(1 + r)^T) \times M/r \qquad (10.2)$$

where T is the last year of maintenance costs (e.g. the last year of the rotation)

A variable profile of maintenance costs, for example major regrading after each thinning, can be accommodated by discounting each year's cost separately.

The usual assumption is that roads will be maintained to a constant standard, preventative and remedial maintenance offsetting deterioration. It is often implicit that such deterioration is a function of time rather than use, which partly it is, especially in extreme climates. Even without use, roads are damaged by rainstorms, baking and cracking, and frost-heave. But whether these conditions exist or not, heavy use accelerates deterioration.

Extraction method

Extraction and roading costs are interdependent. The harvesting method which gives the least cost may depend on the road system, existing or potential, and volume to be harvested. For example, conventional logging of a plantation isolated by distance or difficult terrain from public roads might need a forest road costing $100 000. With a volume of 2000 m³, helicopter extraction, at an excess cost of $30/m³, would be cheaper than roads (costing $50/m³). With a volume of 4000 m³, however, road cost is only $25/m³, and conventional logging is cheaper.

If the choice is between animal and machine power, a short haul to a dense existing road network favours animal power, but tractors, which do not tire over long extraction distances, better suit a lightly roaded forest (figure 10.1). Because of differences in movement speed and depreciation characteristics (see chapter 9) a dense network also favours skidders, while a sparse network favours forwarders.

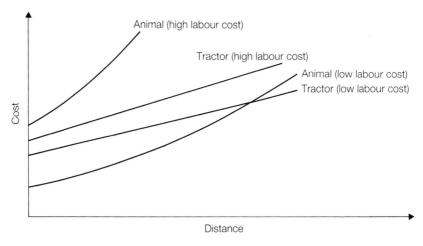

Figure 10.1 Animal vs tractor extraction

Examples of capital versus labour intensive systems are given in chapters 8 and 36.

Variation in terrain may mean that a boundary has to be fixed between two extraction methods. For example, there may be an area of easy ground suitable for forwarder extraction between a road and an increasingly steep and rocky slope where ultimately only cable extraction is feasible. The cost of setting up the cable system must be incurred anyway if the steep slope is to be extracted: it is irrelevant to fixing the boundary. The boundary should therefore be set where the *marginal* cost of forwarder extraction has risen to equal the *marginal* cost of cable extraction.

Each extraction method and road system has an optimal pattern of timber movement. Uphill extraction may be technically feasible, but may involve reduced loads or slower speeds, and faster depreciation. The boundary between downhill and uphill extraction zones should be set where extraction costs are equal in either direction.

$$X_u \times C_u = X_d \times C_d$$

$$\therefore \ X_u/X_d = C_d/C_u \tag{10.3}$$

where X is the limiting extraction distance
  C is extraction cost per m³ per km
  u, d are subscripts for uphill and downhill

Optimal density of roading system

Short average extraction distances and consequent low costs are achieved only through heavy road expenditure. Conversely, minimizing road expenditure gives large average extraction distances and costs. In all but the most uniform terrain and crops, the cost-minimizing balance between roading and extraction cost is impossible to define precisely, but a calculated optimal density of roads gives a useful planning guideline.

Take a system in which roads run parallel 1 km apart, a density of 1 km/ 100 ha. The cost of extracting timber to a representative 1 km length of road is the product of:

1 cost of moving unit volume of timber over unit distance;
2 mean extraction distance;
3 volume per hectare to be extracted;
4 number of hectares serviced by each kilometre of road.

1 This is established from hourly costs and work study data on rate of output. The relevant time is only the *in-forest movement* element of the extraction cycle: time spent loading, unloading, turning around and moving along roads is unaffected by road density, so is irrelevant. Unladen return to the felling area is faster, unless extraction is mostly downhill.
2 If two-way extraction is feasible, the limit of extraction is 0.5 km either

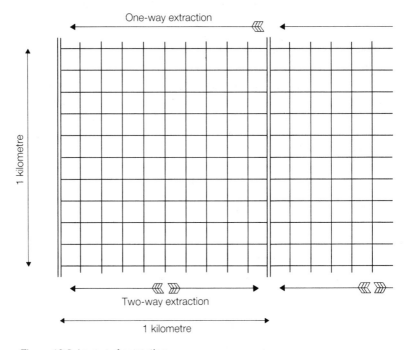

Figure 10.2 Layout of extraction
One square = 1 ha

side of the road. Unless the crop varies systematically in volume with distance from road, mean extraction distance is 0.25 km. For one-way extraction on steep slopes, maximum distance is 1 km, and mean, 0.5 km. Note that:

(a) in rough terrain with one-way extraction, return may be by ascending roads, at lower cost, the extraction equipment then descending back into the stand;

(b) the rougher the terrain, the greater the number and size of deviations needed to avoid boulders, stumps, cliffs, bogs and watercourses – this can be embraced in an 'indirectness factor', reckoned as 1.3 for tractors in average conditions, and 1.1 (due to the angle of extraction lines to the road) for cable systems (Rowan, 1976).

3 Exploitable volume per hectare is a mean for the area being roaded. The road may serve during several cycles of cutting (for example from first thinning to clearfelling, or from clearance of a natural crop through several rotations of a successor plantation).

4 Irrespective of whether extraction is one-way or two-way, each kilometre of road in figure 10.2 receives the production of 100 ha.

For an immediate clearfelling, movement cost is

$$(1) \times (2) \times (3) \times (4)$$

$$\text{or } H \times (M \times I) \times V \times A \tag{10.4}$$

where I is the indirectness factor

With several cycles of cutting (either in a thinned even-aged crop, or with regular felling of an uneven-aged one), movement costs at each cutting are separately discounted, usually to the time of road construction, then summed. Table 10.1 shows discounted costs for a sequence of volume removals per hectare, with a movement cost of £1.60/m³/km, mean extraction distance 0.25 km, indirectness factor of 1.25, a 5% discount rate and road construction at year 23 in the life of the plantation.

In general, total discounted extraction costs

$$
\begin{aligned}
&= \sum_{t=D}^{t=T} \frac{(H \times M \times I \times V_t \times A)}{(1+r)^t} \\
&= \sum_{t=D}^{t=T} \frac{V_t}{(1+r)^t} \times H \times M \times I \times A
\end{aligned}
\tag{10.5}
$$

where D, T are delays from road construction to first and last fellings.

Table 10.1 Discounted movement cost

Age	Volume	Cost	Discounted cost
25	50	25	22.7
30	50	25	17.8
35	50	25	13.9
40	70	35	15.3
50	400	200	53.6
Total	620	310	123.3

The summation in expression (10.5) may be termed the 'summed discounted volume' or SDV of the crop. It need not be given any conceptual meaning: it is simply a computational convenience.

Suppose the density of roads were increased to Y km/km². This would reduce both mean extraction distance and the number of hectares extracted to each kilometre of road. Modifying expression (10.4), total movement cost per kilometre of road is

$$H \times 0.25/Y \times I \times 100/Y \times SDV = H \times 25/Y^2 \times I \times SDV$$

while cost per square kilometre of forest is

$$H \times 25/Y^2 \times I \times SDV \times Y = H \times 25/Y \times I \times SDV \qquad (10.6a)$$

For one-way extraction, with mean extraction distance 0.5 km, the equivalent is

$$H \times 50/Y \times I \times SDV \qquad (10.6b)$$

In both cases road cost per square kilometre of forest is $R \times Y$.

So far a 'perfect' road system has been considered, in which roads run parallel at even spacing. In practice, the road system is inefficient due to

(a) connecting roads
(b) zigzagging e.g. to climb hills
(c) physical constraints on location e.g. bridging points, extreme slopes, which lead to uneven spacing
(d) roads through gaps in the forest cover, which do not provide a destination point for cross-country extraction.

The inefficiency factor, W, cannot be assessed from road configuration. It may be estimated by measuring length of roads, area of forest served, and mean extraction distance based on shortest distance to road from a random sample of points within the forest.

$$W \text{ is then} = 4 \times \bar{D} \times L/A \qquad (10.7)$$

where $\bar{D}$ = mean extraction distance
   L = length of road
   A = area of forest (if $\bar{D}$ is in km, A is in km^2)

A value of 1.35 is reasonable. Higher values arise in difficult terrain and where the road network is ill-distributed. Lower values occur in flat terrain where an approximation to the ideal pattern is achieved.

There are two ways of looking at inefficiency: for a given road density, mean extraction distances increase; or to achieve a given mean extraction distance, a greater road density is required. The first view is more useful. Thus summed road and movement cost per square kilometre is

$R \times Y + H \times 25/Y \times I \times \mathrm{SDV} \times W$ for two-way extraction (10.8)

From this, a cost-minimizing road density Y^* can be found either by trial and error, or by calculus (setting the first differential of the cost function equal to 0 and solving for Y). This yields the optimal density as

$Y^* = \sqrt{(H \times 25 \times I \times \mathrm{SDV} \times W/R)}$ for two-way extraction (10.9a)

$Y^* = \sqrt{(H \times 50 \times I \times \mathrm{SDV} \times W/R)}$ for one-way extraction (10.9b)

Note the terms that appear in (10.9a) and (10.9b) and those that do not. Greater movement cost, indirectness factor, discounted volume per hectare and inefficiency factor increase densities, while greater roading cost reduces them. Optimal density is *not* a function of the value per cubic metre of timber (unless value is significantly degraded during movement). For long-term harvesting programmes, the discount rate also has an important effect, via SDV, on optimal density, as table 10.2 (movement plus road cost) shows. While road construction costs are immediate, savings in movement cost are spread over a long period; a high discount rate reduces the relative significance of saved movement cost.

Historically, extraction technology has improved more rapidly than road construction technology, reducing its relative cost. If this trend continues, lower densities than those based on constant movement cost should be built.

Table 10.2 Illustrative figures for road-plus-movement cost
          * indicates minimum cost

Density	DISCOUNT RATE					
	2%	4%	6%	8%	10%	12%
0.50	36 079	29 507	24 986	21 839	19 620	18 038
0.60	32 541	27 064	23 297	20 674	18 825	*17 506
0.70	30 399	25 705	22 476	*20 227	*18 643	17 512
0.80	29 130	25 023	*22 197	20 230	18 844	17 855
0.90	28 444	*24 792	22 281	20 532	19 300	18 421
1.00	*28 164	24 878	22 618	21 044	19 935	19 144

Further considerations with optimal density

A greater density of roads than calculated above is indicated by:

(a) reduced wear and tear (and hence maintenance cost) per kilometre if less timber is extracted over each kilometre (Price, 1986);

(b) a higher rate of depreciation of the extraction machinery during movement as compared with terminal time, as in the case of skidders and cables;

(c) convenience of access for management and protective purposes;

(d) value of fire-check lines;

(e) benefits of drainage to the adjacent crop;

(f) reduced extraction damage.

A lower density is indicated by:

(g) opportunity cost of land occupied by roads, especially if semi-mature trees are felled to make road-lines;

(h) risk from wind penetrating the crop;

(i) crop disturbance during road-building.

There seems little evidence on the relative magnitude of these effects. They are probably small compared with the factors already quantified.

A denser road system might in theory have a lower inefficiency factor (a smaller proportion of connecting roads, especially in easy terrain): or the factor might be higher (greater proportional variation in road spacing due to terrain constraints). Variability of W with Y would invalidate the optimizing equations (10.9a) and (10.9b), but in practice little variation is observed.

The optimal spacing between set-ups of a cable extraction system is closely similar to the optimal road density problem, the cost of road being replaced by the cost of set-up, extraction to roadside by sideways movement to cableway. In practice, spacing tends to be set by technical considerations.

Variation of optimal density within forests

While a general optimal density guideline can be calculated for a forest, the exact figure varies wherever the determining factors vary. In difficult terrain, both roading and movement costs increase, the overall implication (see equations (10.9a) and (10.9b)) being neutral to density. However, if roading inefficiency and movement indirectness factors also increase in difficult terrain, optimal density increases too.

Probably the most significant variation within forests is the SDV. Less productive stands either yield less volume, or yield given volume over a delayed production cycle, reducing SDVs and justifying fewer roads. Hence road systems should fan out if there is a downward trend of productivity away from the point of entry to the forest: this is quite plausible where, for example, productivity declines with increasing elevation.

Returning to the harvesting problem in chapter 6, it might appear that road density would increase, the longer the transport distance from the harbour and the shorter the economic extraction distance. This is a false instinct: the optimal density does not vary with transportation distance as such. However, in a variable crop longer hauls reduce the volume per hectare worth harvesting (see table 6.1): again the effect would be a fanning of roads.

Optimal road systems in practice

Several practical factors prevent achievement of algebraic and geometric optima.

1 An optimal spacing of 1 km is meaningless if the maximum range of a cable system is only 0.4 km.
2 Topography may only permit certain lines for roads, *not* at the theoretical optimal spacing.
3 In a forest of irregular shape there may be more efficient road patterns than a regular grid.
4 The finite breadth of a rectangular forest permits only certain quantal road spacings: e.g. in a forest 1.5 km broad, one road can be inserted with an extraction limit of 0.75 km, or two roads with an extraction limit of 0.375 km and so on.

Fortunately, as table 10.2 shows, the total cost of roads and extraction is almost constant over a range of densities, so that these practical considerations need not oblige a much greater cost than is incurred by the theoretical optimum. In practice, the theoretical calculations can be used to form an idea of the desirable density, on the basis of which two or three feasible options can be designed, with one perhaps having a rather greater, another a rather smaller than ideal density.

Take a natural forest occupying two adjoining ridges 2 km apart. (This topographic configuration could be repeated laterally without changing the basic problem.) The river in the intervening valley is too deep and rocky to be crossed by harvesting tractors. Two-way extraction is possible, but reduced loads are extracted uphill. One-direction direct movement costs per cubic metre per kilometre are:

downhill, loaded   0.6:   uphill, loaded   1.0
downhill, unloaded   0.6:   uphill, unloaded   0.8

Volume of timber is 400 m^3/ha. A movement indirectness factor of 1.3 and a roading inefficiency factor of 1.35 are estimated. Road cost per kilometre is £22 000 on ridges, £28 000 on slopes and £25 000 by riverside.

Theoretical optimization cannot take exact account of the various movement and road costs, since the relative amount of each type cannot be established until the location of roads is known. Unweighted mean figures are used to estimate an optimum.

The transect in figure 10.3a results from attempting to impose the optimum on the forest. The river prevents the two-way extraction assumed in the optimizing formula, so this result is theoretical. Three alternative systems, at less and more than the theoretical density, are given in figures 10.3b, 10.3c and 10.3d. The positioning of roads on the slope in 10.3c accords with equation (10.3), as do mean extraction distance and cost. Summed road and movement cost per square kilometre is calculated using equation (10.8) – see table 10.3.

There is little to choose between 10.3b and 10.3c. Layout 10.3d has the advantage of all downhill extraction, but it combines the long roads of 10.3c with the long extraction distance of 10.3b.

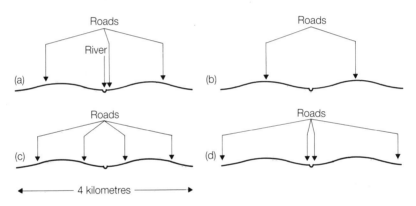

Figure 10.3 Alternative road layouts

Table 10.3 Costing of alternative road layouts

	(a) 'Optimum'	(b) Two roads at ridges	(c) Four roads on slopes	(d) Four roads by rivers
Road density	1.026	0.675	1.350	1.350
Road cost/km^2	25 650	14 850	37 800	33 750
Extr.cost/m^3/km	1.5	1.6	1.49	1.4
Extr.distance	0.346	0.5	≈0.25	0.5
Extr.cost/km^2	25 650	41 600	19 400	36 400
Total cost	51 300	56 450	57 200	70 150

The standard of road systems

Not all roads need be of the highest or same standard. One option is to build all roads, at low density, to a standard capable of taking the largest permissible lorries, and to accept long extraction distances. Alternatively, a single arterial road can be serviced by a dense network of tractor tracks which, although constructed to a cheap specification, nonetheless allow faster movement with less wear and tear per kilometre than occurs cross-country. A third option is to build a moderate density of roads suitable for medium-sized lorries, with a shorter total extraction distance, mostly cross-country. Smaller lorries have a greater cost per tonne-kilometre, so this option is expensive over long hauls. Multiple transfers (for example, skidder to four-wheel-drive truck to articulated lorry) are also expensive.

Where forest roads form an important proportion of the haul, road standard significantly affects time and hence cost of haulage (Groves *et al.*, 1987).

The complexity of the problem can be addressed by programming methods (see Buongiorno and Gilless, 1987). As with optimal density formulations, however, the irregularities of forests will probably require modification of the idealized guideline solution. An alternative approach is to cost several very different networks, then several variants of the cheapest network.

Choice of harvesting method revisited

When the best practical roading system has been designed, extraction method may be re-evaluated. If density differs greatly from expected, a method other than the provisional one may give the least cost. Whenever more than one technically feasible and reasonably cost-effective method is available, therefore, an optimal road planning exercise should be undertaken for each, the overall harvesting system giving least cost being chosen.

11 Criteria of Profitability in Forest Investment

The previous three chapters used interest and discounting to compare cash flows and output occurring at different times. The aim was only to quantify and minimize costs. When revenues and costs at different times are compared, a criterion of *profitability* (surplus of revenue over cost) is needed. This chapter describes some possible criteria, and their relative merits in assessing forest investments.

A profitability criterion must indicate:

1 *whether* an investment is profitable or not (the *acceptability* criterion);
2 *how* relatively profitable each of several incompatible or competing investments is (the *selection* criterion).

Non-discounting criteria

Maximum forest rent has been widely used in European forests, especially those with near-normal age-class structure. Forest rent is defined as

$$\frac{\sum_{t=0}^{t=T} R_t - \sum_{t=0}^{t=T} C_t}{T} \tag{11.1}$$

where R_t, C_t are revenue and cost at any time t
T is the length of the complete production cycle or rotation.

It is the *mean annual net revenue* over the rotation. If this value is positive, the investment is acceptable. Where a choice must be made, for example between different rotation lengths, or in applying funds to different plantation schemes, the course of action with highest forest rent is selected.

The forest rent criterion makes no distinction between revenues and costs occurring at different times: a thousand francs or a cubic metre of timber after a hundred years is as valuable as a thousand francs or a cubic metre of timber now.

The *payback period* criterion requires that projects *eventually* repay invested monies. The most desirable course of action is that which pays back in the shortest time. Table 11.1 compares A, a low-cost rapid exploitation of only the prime species in a mixed forest with B, a slower, more systematic removal of all commercial species.

Table 11.1 Cash flows and payback period

	INVESTMENT A		INVESTMENT B	
Time	Cash flow	Cumulative cash flow	Cash flow	Cumulative cash flow
0	−100 000	−100 000	−250 000	−250 000
1	50 000	−50 000		−250 000
2	50 000	0	150 000	−100 000
3	25 000	25 000	150 000	50 000
4		25 000	150 000	200 000

The criterion does consider timing of costs and revenues, giving greater weight to early than to late cash flows. All revenues before the investment is paid off are treated equally: all revenues after that date are ignored, no matter how large. Thus A is preferred, despite B's ultimately greater profits.

This yields curious results in forestry. Take a 40–year non-thin rotation for sawlogs. After 39 years it has paid back none of the original investment: after 40 years it has paid back the investment several-fold. Its payback period is 40 years, longer than the physical or economic life of many investments: forestry projects in the temperate zone would rarely be preferred to other investments under this criterion.

Furthermore, in comparing rotation lengths, a 30–year rotation producing nothing but pulpwood, which only just pays its investment costs, is preferred to the sawlog rotation, despite the latter having revenues several times greater. By contrast, at age 30 forgoing immediate revenue from the pulp crop is an investment with a payback period of only 10 years before the sawlog crop is harvested. And *then* the payback period of leaving the sawlog crop to become a slightly larger sawlog crop would only be a year (or a day, or a second). Thus, using the payback period criterion, no forests would be planted in the temperate zone, but those that *were* planted would always be grown on for another year until net physical growth ceased!

Since interest is not involved, the payback period is an acceptable measure of economic efficiency in strict Islamic and Marxist economies (see Sobik, 1982). Curiously, a form which adds interest periodically is also helpful in highly capitalist economies where cash flow constraints give priority to rapid clearance of debt. But this criterion is potentially very misleading in forestry.

Criteria using rate of return concepts

Investments can be ranked by their first year rate of return: that is, the net revenue in their first year of operation divided by the initial sum invested. Considered respectively as the rate of profit or the efficiency of the investment, this might be admissible in Islamic or Marxist economies as a *selection* criterion between investments. First year rate of return may also determine whether an investment should be made, by comparison with some standard rate: as that rate is normally a rate of interest, Islam and Marxism may exclude it as an *acceptability* criterion.

Certain forest investments could be judged on this basis. Investment in car parks or forest accommodation yields a return in the first year. The criterion could determine which among several potential recreation developments should be financed. It could also be adapted to judge which maturing crops should be allowed to remain, and which felled (the 'rate of return' here being annual value increment divided by current value).

Many investments, however, take some years to reach a maximum revenue. An alternative criterion is thus the *peak rate of return*: the highest net revenue in any year of the investment's life divided by the initial sum invested.

First year rate of return repeats, even more extremely, the short-term focus of the payback period criterion: only net revenue in the first year is relevant. Investment A, with 50% first year rate of return, would again be chosen. The peak rate of return, by contrast, regards only the *magnitude* of net revenue, not its timing. Investment B, with 60% peak rate of return, would be favoured. Both criteria assume that a single year's performance reflects average returns, but neither includes duration of returns, or their variability.

For plantations, with their long and irregular production cycle, these single-year rates give bizarre results. Under the first year rate of return rule, no silviculture would be undertaken, whereas under the peak rate of return rule plantations – capable of returning several thousand per cent of the initial investment in the year of clearfelling – would be a prime investment in every nation!

The average rate of return (mean annual revenue divided by initial investment) is better, favouring B at 45% against 42% for A. It fails to take any account of timing or character of cash flow, however.

Profit after interest

One way to include both magnitude and timing of all revenues and costs is to calculate profit after compound interest has been paid on loans.

$$[\text{profit}] = [\text{revenue}] - [\text{cost}] \times (1 + [\text{interest rate}])^{[\text{loan period}]}$$

This criterion penalizes long delay of revenues, increasingly the longer they are delayed, but allows that a large revenue, long-delayed, may be preferable to a small, short-term revenue.

Profit after interest produces results which are intuitively acceptable in silvicultural decision-making: once rates of interest are adjusted for inflation, some silvicultural practices seem profitable, others appear unprofitable. It is adequate as a criterion of whether a forest investment is acceptable.

However, as a selection criterion it is deficient, because the point in time at which profit after interest accrues depends on the duration of the investment. Take the choice, shown in table 11.2, between *sugi* (red cedar) with a 30–year rotation, and *hinoki* (cypress) requiring 40 years.

Table 11.2 Profit after interest and species choice

	Cost	Revenue	Cost plus interest	Profit
Sugi	400 000	2 400 000	1 728 800	671 200
Hinoki	400 000	4 000 000	2 816 000	1 184 000

At 5% interest, both species are profitable. *Sugi* yields a smaller profit, but does so earlier. Just as one cannot compare revenues accruing at different times, so these profits cannot be directly compared. It could be assumed that the profit of *sugi* was reinvested at 5% up to year 40, giving a pay-off of ¥1 093 000: *hinoki* still yields slightly more profit. But the comparison remains unbalanced, because *sugi* uses the site for 30 years, whereas *hinoki* occupies it for 40 years. Four successive rotations of *sugi* may legitimately be compared with three successive rotations of *hinoki*. *Sugi* now gives a slightly greater accumulated profit after interest (¥70 300 000) than *hinoki* (¥68 200 000) after 120 years of site occupation.

Optimal rotation calculations involve even more tedious comparisons, between (say) 15 veneer log rotations of 140 years and 14 of 150 years! Apart from the effort needed for such calculations, the results are difficult to interpret in present-day terms. If the difference in profit after 2100 years is $50 000, is it even worth the effort of making a decision?

Net present value

The usefulness of discounting to simplify problems with interest calculation has already been shown. It also provides a more satisfactory criterion of profitability than the methods so far discussed. The sum of all revenues, suitably discounted, minus the sum of all costs, suitably discounted, is variously known as net present value (NPV), net discounted revenue, net present worth, and net discounted cash flow. Formally it may be expressed as

$$\sum_{t=0}^{t=T} \frac{R_t}{(1 + r)^t} - \sum_{t=0}^{t=T} \frac{C_t}{(1 + r)^t} \qquad (11.2)$$

where R_t, C_t are revenue and cost at time t
T is the length of the production cycle or rotation.

In the simplest case, there is only one cost and one revenue. Applying equations (7.2) and (7.5) to the *sugi/hinoki* example, and discounting at 5% gives table 11.3.

Table 11.3 Net present value and species choice

	Discounted revenue	less cost	for 120 years	in perpetuity
Sugi	555 300	155 300	201 500	202 100
Hinoki	568 200	168 200	195 500	196 000

The absolute magnitudes of discounted figures are much less than profit after interest figures for the same investments. (The PV of a difference in profit of $50 000 after 2100 years for the 140 and 150 year veneer rotations is a minuscule fraction of a cent). The important point, however, is that they yield the same decision: any investment profitable after interest has positive NPV; both criteria always select the same investment as the *most* profitable from a given group. Also the *ratio* of NPV to profit after interest is the same for each investment.

The choice between the two criteria is thus a matter of convenience. NPV has the following advantages.

1 The result, being a present equivalent of future values, means more to decision-makers whose perspective is from the present than profit after

interest accruing in the distant future (and, in forestry, often beyond decision-makers' own lifetime).

2 The year zero (t_0) provides an obvious datum to which revenues and costs of all investments can be discounted and compared: there is no such common datum for profit after interest.

3 As equations (7.3) and (7.5) show, perpetual streams of cost and revenue have a finite NPV. This is not so with profit after interest.

4 The criterion is widely used by forestry and business enterprises, by financial institutions, governments and international development agencies, all of whom may require NPV calculations before funds are allocated.

5 *Provided* that discounting is based on time preference, not rates of interest, the criterion can be applied in strict Islamic and Marxist economies.

6 Most English-language literature of forestry economics is cast in discounting terms.

Detailed application of NPV to forestry means:

(a)   accepting isolated investments for which NPV is positive;

(b)   from a group of compatible investments selecting in order of highest NPV;

(c)   from a group of incompatible or interactive investments, increasing investment to the point where incremental discounted revenue equals incremental discounted cost (provided that incremental discounted revenue is falling relative to incremental discounted cost).

The normal forest fallacy

It is often stated that compound interest and discounting are only relevant when a nation is building up its forest resource, and that once a normal age-class structure has been established they can be ignored (Garfitt, 1986). The argument is that costs of replanting can be borne by revenues from felling, which normally leaves a substantial net revenue; nothing is now owing on the re-established crop; no interest accumulates during the rotation. Conversely revenues need not be discounted, as their role is to bear the contemporary costs of the next rotation.

This account fails to recognize the two separate decisions at the time of clearfelling: the decision to cash the asset represented by the standing crop, and the decision to replant. The first decision having been taken, it remains open to replant or not to replant. If the land is not replanted, then no successor crop will materialize. If the replanting investment is made, revenues will accrue, *but only after the lapse of the rotation*. The decision does not differ qualitatively from the decision to afforest previously open land: in both cases NPV is the revenues of the current rotation discounted from the appropriate point in the rotation, less discounted costs of the current rotation.

The introduction of uneven-aged crops and natural regeneration does not weaken this argument. In these cases, additional costs or delayed revenues are incurred during regeneration, with the explicit objective of gaining revenues from the *subsequent*, not the *current* crop. Again, the investment only matures when the subsequent crop is felled.

Admittedly, if custom or ordinance, or protective or environmental objectives oblige replanting, then the cost of replanting becomes an inseparable concomitant of revenues from the preceding felling, and profitability is correctly assessed by deducting those costs from the revenues just realized. It is then 'worth' replanting. But to say that replanting is the most profitable option when it is the *only* option is not very startling. Whenever the option of not replanting exists, the question is 'what changes as a result of replanting?' Whatever else *results* from replanting, it cannot be revenue from a crop already felled and sold.

NPV and benefit–cost ratio with limited funds

Both profit after interest and NPV assume that investment funds which can earn the going rate are available without restriction. Ability to pay the market price of borrowing money is deemed a sufficient test. Thus a plantation with NPV at 5% of £1000, earned by investing £2000, is more profitable than one using less intensive silviculture yielding NPV of £800 from investment of £1000.

But if funds are limited, even when they can earn the going rate, £2000 could be invested in *two* low-intensity plantations yielding a combined NPV of 2 × £800 = £1600. In these circumstances NPV incorrectly favours the intensive investment. A more efficient allocation of limited funds is achieved by using NPV per £ invested, or benefit–cost ratio (BCR).

BCR is the PV of revenues or benefits, divided by the PV of costs. Investments are acceptable if benefit–cost ratio exceeds unity. This always gives the same result as accepting investments whose NPV is positive:

if PVR/PVC > 1, then PVR > PVC, and PVR − PVC > 0.

However, NPV and BCR may not give the same *ranking* of investments competing for funds. Ranking may also differ between NPV per £ invested and BCR if not all costs arise in year 0. Consider the three investments in table 11.4 (costs and revenues have been discounted).

Table 11.4 NPV, BCR and project choice

	A	B	C
Planting cost year 0	1000	500	500
Cleaning and pruning cost year 7	500	300	—
Revenue year 20	5000	2800	2000
NPV	3500	2000	1500
BCR	3.3	3.5	4
NPV per initial £ invested	3.5	4	3

Whether NPV per £ invested or BCR is correct depends on whether future costs come under the same constraint as present ones. If so, BCR is correct: if only initial funds are limited, NPV per initial £ invested is correct.

When both land and funds are limited, choice must be made between incompatible investments on a given hectare, a problem treated in chapter 19.

When constraints exist on funds in many time periods, linear programming is an appropriate tool for selecting investments. The large number of constraints makes problem formulation more cumbersome, and the objective is now to maximize global NPV, but in essentials the process does not differ from that outlined in chapter 5.

In the absence of discounting, the number of profitable investments increases and the need for other means of rationing funds is more acute. Ranking forestry investments by *forest rent per franc invested* would be appropriate.

Internal rate of return

The internal rate of return (IRR) is the rate of discount which makes discounted cost equal to discounted revenue (or NPV = 0). In calculating IRR, no account is taken of market rates of interest or time preference rates: the IRR refers exclusively to the investment's *internal* ability to generate a rate of return. IRR is the maximum interest rate charged on investment funds at which an investment could break even.

For cash flows with one cost and one revenue, IRR may be calculated algebraically. Suppose a crop of *Gmelina arborea* is grown on a 10–year rotation for pulpwood. Investment costs are 1000 naira, and revenues 5000 naira per hectare. By definition:

Discounted revenues = (discounted) costs
$$5000/(1 + IRR)^{10} = 1000/(1 + IRR)^0 = 1000$$

Rearranging, we have

$$(1 + IRR)^{10} = 5000/1000 = 5$$

$$\therefore\ 1 + IRR = {}^{10}\sqrt{5}$$

$$\therefore\ IRR = 17.46\%$$

Equations can be compiled for the IRR of complex cash flows in a forest with frequent management expenditures and periodic thinning revenues. However, it is usually simpler to find IRR by trial and error. The process for the *Gmelina* example is shown in table 11.5. Not many steps are required to reach the right answer. An alternative method is to plot NPVs for a few discount rates, e.g. 10%, 15% and 20%. (The result of a rather more complex graphical approach is shown in figure 11.1 below.) The intercept(s) where NPV = 0 is the IRR.

Table 11.5 IRR calculation by trial and error

Discount rate	NPV	Comment
10.00	928	NPV exceeds zero: try a higher rate
20.00	−192	NPV less than zero: try a lower rate
15.00	236	IRR about midway between 15% and 20%
17.00	40	IRR much nearer 17% than 20%
17.50	−3	Try slightly lower rate
17.45	1	Just up a tiny bit!
17.46	0	This is the IRR

An isolated investment is accepted if its IRR exceeds some cut-off point, usually the prevailing rate of interest. IRR normally accepts and rejects the same set of investments as NPV or BCR.

Among compatible investments, the IRR criterion selects investments in descending order of IRR. If the budget does not suffice to fund all profitable investments, IRR tends to select projects with a shorter repayment period than NPV per £ invested.

Among incompatible investments, the investment with highest IRR is selected. This, however, raises a problem also encountered with BCR: an investment may be selected that does very little with a piece of land, but does it very efficiently. The do-nothing course of action on a piece of land which is generating a revenue without investment has an indefinitely large IRR or BCR, so no alternative can do better! Incremental criteria (see chapter 19) circumvent this problem, investment being intensified until either

(a) funds are all utilized, or

(b) IRR from the incremental investment falls below the prevailing interest rate. In this case the optimal intensity of investment is the same as that given by NPV.

It is sometimes claimed that IRR, BCR and NPV give the same selection among investments. There is no theoretical reason to suppose this will be true, and endless examples can be given where it is untrue. One such example, and further discussion of the criteria listed above, appears in chapter 18.

The IRR criterion is familiar in business circles, and is favoured because it promotes the fastest return from limited funds. Like BCR but unlike NPV, it does not favour projects with large initial investment or long occupation of a site. As a selection criterion, it also obviates the problem of choosing a discount rate. Since funding of desirable investments may depend on them showing an acceptable IRR, forest managers should at least know how to calculate it for an investment which they wish to implement. However, there are two important objections in the forestry context to selecting projects by IRR.

1 *The multiple roots problem*

IRR solves the equation NPV = 0. Many equations have more than one solution: for example, reconsider the algebraic solution of the *Gmelina arborea* problem above. One step of the solution sets $1 + IRR = \sqrt[10]{5} = 1.1746$. But -1.1746 is also the tenth root of 5, giving an IRR of -217.46%.

In this case the negative answer is invalid. However, when cash flows fluctuate between cost and revenue, there may be many solutions, some positive, some negative, some unreal, none obviously wrong: there is potentially one solution for each time the cash flow changes from cost to revenue or back again. Figure 11.1 illustrates the IRR for a forest exploitation project. Initial roading costs $1 000 000. Logging yields $2 500 000 in the first year, and $250 000 in years 2 and 3. Clearance of non-commercial species and preparation for agricultural use costs $5 000 000 in year 4. Agricultural net revenues are $500 000 for the next 12 years, whereafter fertility is exhausted. Meanwhile the annual value of yield from the natural forest, $50 000, is forgone in perpetuity.

IRRs exist at 2.45%, 11.61%, 59.48% and 107.35%. Below 2.45%, cash flow is dominated by opportunity cost; from 2.45% to 11.61%, by revenues from agriculture; from 11.61% to 59.48%, by the cost of clearance; from 59.48% to 107.35%, by logging revenues; above 107.35%, by roading cost. Which of the multiple solutions should be adopted? The temptation exists to select as the 'relevant' rate of return the one which confirms the evaluator's

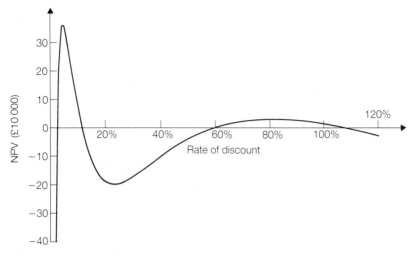

Figure 11.1 Multiple IRRs

intuition or self-interest. But no one IRR is in fact any more relevant than any other.

It is sometimes alleged that multiple roots are rare in practice: on the contrary, they are inevitable in exploitation investments which have indefinitely prolonged opportunity costs.

2 *The inappropriate discount rate problem*

Consider an exploitation project which yields net revenue of Rs1 million at the end of every year from the first to the tenth. After that time, the forest cover has been removed entirely, in consequence of which catastrophic flooding and erosion cause losses estimated at Rs1000 million. The IRR of this outrageous project (there is only one) is + 99.4%.

The explanation is simple and dreadful: the large future costs must be reduced to the same magnitude as the modest early revenues. This can only be done by discounting very rapidly. In fact, if the scale of damage had been greater, the IRR would have been higher, and the investment would have appeared even more desirable! In seeking a solution to the equation, the criterion has adopted a discount rate related to neither the rate of return available on reinvestment (see Schallau and Wirth, 1980) nor the importance of events 10 years hence.

The effect is greatest when costs occur late in a project's life, and hence produces the most anomalous results for exploitation projects with adverse long-term effects.

While this example is rather extreme, it is by no means idiosyncratic. The problem is found, less dramatically, in any IRR calculation. IRR is only the solution of an equation, and leaving mere equations to determine the weight to place on future events is a grave abrogation of human responsibilities.

Economists are often accused of being equivocal in their recommendations. Here is an exception. This particular economist's advice to those about to judge a forest investment by its IRR is: DON'T!

Sum of discounted consumption flows

For completeness, the attention of those with a philosophical bent is drawn to the sum of discounted consumption flows criterion advanced by Kula (1981) and subsequently applied to forestry decisions (Kula, 1986). In attempting to deal with the ethical issues of discounting, this criterion produces both logical impasses and bizarre results (Price, 1984c, 1987c).

12 Risk and Uncertainty in Forest Investment

To this point it has been assumed that the results of decisions – the physical consequences, costs and revenues – are known when those decisions are taken: in decision-making jargon, the approach has been *deterministic*. But if one thing is certain (apart from death and taxes) it is that the future will always be uncertain.

For foresters, this pervasive problem is exacerbated by timber's long production cycle. Farmers look ahead only a few months to the harvesting of crops; industrial investors seek a return within a few years; but foresters' efforts reach fruition only after decades, or even centuries. The range of uncontrollable and unpredictable factors operating over a forest rotation presents so horrifying a prospect that many foresters ignore them altogether. This is inexcusable and irresponsible. In many countries a wealth of research data allows quite reliable prediction of the physical condition of crops. There are sophisticated techniques, some of which are reviewed in chapter 35, whereby the trend of relevant economic and political variables can be predicted.

However, all forecasting is imperfect. What is needed is a technique which allows a rational approach to forestry decisions whose results are unsure.

The terminology of risk and uncertainty

Concise discussion of the subject needs some terms to be defined.

State of nature   The condition of some factor in the natural, economic or political environment over which decision-makers have no control, e.g. rainfall, world timber prices, income tax rates.

Strategy   What has hitherto been called a course of action, controlled by decision-makers and adopted in response to risk or uncertainty, e.g. planting a species tolerant of low rainfall, taking out insurance against fire, doing nothing.

Outcome   The predicted result of a strategy in a given state of nature, e.g. if we plant *Pinus caribaea* [strategy] and there is a prolonged drought [state of nature] the crop will fail [outcome].

Four different positions on a spectrum of knowledge may be distinguished.

Ignorance   We know nothing.

Uncertainty   We know the range of relevant states of nature, and therefore what outcomes are possible, but not the relative probabilities of each state of nature.

Risk   This is distinguished from uncertainty by knowledge of the probability of each state of nature. For example, both experience and reason suggest that a tossed coin will land in a 'heads' state of nature in 50% or 0.5 of all circumstances, and 'tails' in the remaining 0.5 of cases. Treating future circumstances as risky rather than uncertain needs either:

(a) actuarial data (historical evidence) on how often events of a particular kind (states of nature) occurred, and how severe the consequences were for forests (outcomes) – this is the normal basis for insurance against, for example, fire damage; or

(b) a mathematical model of the system good enough to give accurate forecasts.

Certainty   We know which state of nature will eventuate, and precisely what the outcome of a strategy will be.

While perfect certainty is unknown on earth, perfect ignorance is also rare (if it exists, there is no basis for rational decision-making). It may be unpredictable whether rainfall in the coming year will be 1000 mm rather than 800 mm; records may not indicate whether the former figure is more likely than the latter; but some rain will certainly fall, and it is unlikely to exceed 2000 mm.

In practice therefore most decision-making occurs under risk or uncertainty. Situations vary only in the exactness of our knowledge about the future.

The risks and uncertainties facing forestry have five main sources.

1 The natural environment. The major hazards are climatic (especially extreme events such as droughts, floods, lightning strikes or hurricanes) and biotic (attacks by insects, fungal or viral pathogens or browsing animals).

2 Technological advances. For example, who would have expected helicopters to provide a means of harvesting an isolated plantation when it was established 100 years ago?

3 Human factors, such as arson or accidental fires, illicit felling and illegal encroachment.

4 The markets in which forestry buys and sells, particularly markets for timber and labour. Markets are subject to unexpected surges and collapses, to unexplained fluctuations, to cycles of expansion and recession, and to general trends, which change their character in the long term.

5 The political milieu. Within a temperate forest rotation many governments come and go, wars are fought, political theories come to prominence and pass into oblivion, tax regimes are mooted, discussed, implemented and superseded, national forest services are set up, expanded, curbed or privatized.

Given these factors, it is surprising that forestry has continued as steadily as it has, with outcomes perhaps not quite as decision-makers intended, but close enough for them or their successors to review the decisions without particular regrets. This underlines the robustness to which evolution has conditioned forests, the versatility of their products in use, and the realization, vague though it may be, of the need for a stable political background for forestry. Nonetheless, there are no grounds for complacency: better decision-making methods could often have been employed.

Rational decisions under uncertainty

The first need under uncertainty is to assemble known facts in an informative way. Take a decision to establish plantations with an associated sawmill on one of three islands lying along a hurricane track. One island has a topography affording good shelter from hurricanes but the soils are poor. Another is exposed but offers rapid growth. A third is intermediate in characteristics. Two states of nature are hypothesized (that a hurricane will, or will not occur during the vulnerable latter half of the rotation). The information is summarized in table 12.1. The outcomes for each of the three planting strategies have been calculated in NPV terms ($million).

This constitutes a *sensitivity analysis* of the alternatives, showing how outcomes vary with different states of nature. If St Starts had the greatest NPV even with a hurricane, mere tabulation of information would indicate the decision, but in this case the correct choice is not obvious. Various criteria have been devised to assist.

Table 12.1 Data for decision-making under uncertainty

	STRATEGY		
State of nature	St Fitts	St Starts	Ambigua
With hurricane	5	−2	2
Without hurricane	8	16	10

Wald's maximim criterion

Wald (1950) suggested that decision-makers should adopt the strategy giving the best outcome in the worst circumstances which could affect that strategy. The worst state of nature is the same for each strategy – occurrence of a hurricane – giving St Fitts the best outcome. Wald's criterion is pessimistic: it expects the worst.

The maximax criterion

By contrast, this selects the strategy of best outcome in the best state of nature (St Starts). Its pointed optimism seems to invite disaster, and the criterion is not often formally applied, though the happy-go-lucky implement it under its informal alias of hoping for the best.

Savage's minimax regret criterion

Savage's proposal (1951) is more complex. Decision-makers are presumed averse to regrets about decisions which in the event appear misguided. To avert needless distress, the criterion guides them towards the strategy for which the maximum regret that could be felt is smaller than for any other strategy. Table 12.2 is a regret matrix.

Should there be a hurricane, and St Fitts had been chosen, there would be no regret about choice of strategy. But without a hurricane, the NPV would

Table 12.2 The minimax regret criterion

	STRATEGY		
State of nature	St Fitts	St Starts	Ambigua
With hurricane	0	*7	3
Without hurricane	*8	0	*6

be only $8 million rather than the $16 million which could have been obtained, had St Starts been selected. The margin between what was actually obtained and what might at best have been obtained *in that state of nature* is a measure of regret: in this case $8 million. Other figures in the matrix are derived in the same way. Under no state of nature is Ambigua the best choice, but, because Ambigua performs moderately in all states, the maximum value for regret (starred for each strategy) is lower than for any other island, and Ambigua is selected. The criterion seeks a balance between the optimism implicit in seeking the best return, and the pessimism of avoiding bad outcomes.

Laplace's equal probability criterion

This considers that, if nothing is known about probabilities, each state of nature should be assumed equally likely: there is a 50% chance that there will be a hurricane, and a 50% chance that there will not.

Here a new piece of terminology is needed: *mean expected value* is the mean outcome for a given strategy under the whole range of states of nature, each outcome being weighted by its probability. Thus mean expected value of the St Fitts investment is a 50% probability of $5 million (equivalent to $2.5 million) plus a 50% probability of $8 million (equivalent to $4 million) making $6.5 million in all. On the same basis, mean expected values for St Starts and Ambigua are $7 million and $6 million. This criterion selects St Starts.

Which criterion?

These rules have not been described with the intention of commending them, but to illustrate the difficulty of devising sensible criteria for uncertainty. The example showed four criteria giving three different answers, leaving decision-makers in the same doubt as before analysis began. Choosing the criterion according to decision-makers' propensities to optimism or pessimism is little better than giving them licence to choose projects intuitively: indeed it is worse in that it permits prejudiced judgement under the guise of objectivity.

Apart from the conflicting indications, each criterion is defective in failing to use all the data. Wald's criterion ignores the possibility that the worst may not happen. Savage is more comprehensive, but, in selecting Ambigua, neglects the fact that regret will be felt here, whatever the state of nature. Laplace uses all the figures in the matrix, but, in assuming that a hurricane is as likely as no hurricane, takes no account of existing evidence on the real frequency of hurricanes.

Situations where absolutely no assessment of probabilities can be made are actually rare. In absence of historical records or validated models, it is better to estimate probabilities subjectively than to assign probabilities by some arbitrary rule, or to ignore some states of nature.

This philosophy underlies the view that uncertainty is not really distinct from risk: there are not four discrete states of knowledge, but a continuum from virtual ignorance to virtual certainty. In almost any situation an attempt can be made to quantify probabilities. Experts and non-experts alike have some feeling for the likelihood of events: a proposal to use Laplace's equal probability assumption is often challenged and refined by someone who had lately claimed that nothing worthwhile could be stated about probabilities. A modified Laplace criterion is the basis of modern treatment of risk.

Risk and mean expected value

Suppose climatic records reveal that in periods of 20 years (the expected crop rotation) the probability of a hurricane is 0.6. Outcomes must be weighted by this probability rather than Laplace's 0.5. The probability of no hurricane is, necessarily, 0.4.

The steps of the decision process can be laid out formally thus.

1 Classify strategies and states of nature.
2 Determine the probability of each state of nature, from records, system simulation, consultation with experts or local people, or informed guesswork.
3 Determine the outcome of each strategy under each state of nature, and enter it in a decision matrix.
4 *For each strategy*, sum for all states of nature

   [probability of state of nature] × [outcome under that state of nature].

5 This sum is the mean expected value of the strategy: the strategy with the highest sum is selected.

These steps can be identified in the final *probabilistic* evaluation of the hurricane example, given in table 12.3.

All available information has now been incorporated in the decision to plant on St Fitts. In retrospect (should no hurricane happen) the decision may be regretted, but without hindsight no better can be done.

Quantifying risk aversion

The above process is precise, almost clinical, and something psychological may seem to be missing. At its most extreme, it suggests that a small land-owner with total wealth of £100 000 should treat a 50% probability of

Table 12.3 Mean expected value

State of nature	STRATEGY		
	St Fitts	St Starts	Ambigua
With hurricane $p = 0.6$	$5 \times 0.6 = 3.0$	$-2 \times 0.6 = -1.2$	$2 \times 0.6 = 1.2$
Without hurricane $p = 0.4$	$8 \times 0.4 = 3.2$	$16 \times 0.4 = 6.4$	$10 \times 0.4 = 4.0$
Mean expected value	6.2	5.2	5.2

gaining a further £100 000 as exactly counter-balancing a 50% probability of losing the £100 000 already possessed. History is replete with examples of land-owners who have indeed depauperated themselves by gambling. But such risks are not usually taken by rational decision-makers, because an unstated objective of most economic organizations is survival.

Less dramatically, the opprobrium (from Treasury, shareholders, colleagues) incurred by a year of negligible profits weighs more heavily than the euphoria that would follow doubling of annual profits: forestry on the whole is a conservative profession. And, less dramatically still, an investment that offered a guaranteed NPV of £X would be preferred by most decision-makers to one offering only a *mean expected value* of £X.

In other words decision-makers tend to be risk-averse. Part of this aversion is a logical response to the factors just outlined; part stems from human craving for certainty; part relates to such personal matters as the relative promotion prospects of a manager who makes no bad mistakes and one who balances dismal failures with spectacular triumphs.

Simply avoiding risky investments leads to sacrifice of much potential good: most worthwhile innovations in history can be traced to someone's willingness to risk departing from the 'safe' choice. This is as true of silvicultural innovation as of the fruits of the Reformation and the Industrial Revolution. What is required is some means of penalizing risky investment without actually prohibiting it.

A common practice is adding a 'risk premium' to the discount rate used in NPV calculations for risky projects (Chang, Foster, 1980). In providing a more stringent criterion, however, this device also distorts the relative magnitude of immediate and future cash flows. Often revenues do become less certain the further into the future that revenues accrue, but:

(a) not all risks increase over time (fire risks to plantations are often greatest early in a plantation's life, when much inflammable ground vegetation persists);

(b) where risks do increase through time, it is not always in the exponential way of compound interest (wind instability may not be a problem for 30–40 years, but increase dramatically thereafter);

(c) market and political uncertainty is not sufficient reason for discounting, since it may entail outcomes better as well as worse than expected;

(d) a higher discount rate need not penalize investments at all. Take the project of Cutandrun Logging Inc. described in table 12.4. Adding a 5% risk premium actually makes the project acceptable.

A better 'stringency' measure is to require a greater NPV per £ invested for risky than for risk-free investments. This does not distort relative discounted cash flows at different points in time.

Table 12.4 Effect of adding a 5% risk premium to discount rate

Operation	Year	Cash flow	PV @ 10%	PV @ 15%
Construct road	0	−300 000	−300 000	−300 000
Exploit forest	1, 2, 3, 4, 5	200 000/year	758 157	670 431
Reinstatement	6	−850 000	−479 803	−367 478
NPV			−21 646	2 953

Mean expected utility

Income and wealth measured in currency units are like other economic commodities: when scarce they are highly valued. The value of an additional unit decreases as quantity increases, till a state of satiation is reached where extreme affluence precludes further expenditure from yielding measurable increase of happiness: thus millionaires are forced into philanthropy as a desperate last resort. The phenomenon is referred to as the *diminishing marginal utility of income*. It has great significance in economics, and will appear in several other contexts.

Each unit added to profit has diminishing marginal utility to the individual or enterprise, while each unit of decrease in profit (or increase in loss) has successively *increasing* marginal disutility. Thus units of decrease in profit are individually more significant than units of increase, and a given probability of a given monetary loss is not balanced in value by an equal probability of the same monetary gain (see figure 12.1).

Consider a decision on whether a not-very-wealthy farmer should purchase an all-aged woodland, at a price of £100 000, in the uncertain months before an election. The Socialist Union, which is given a 45%

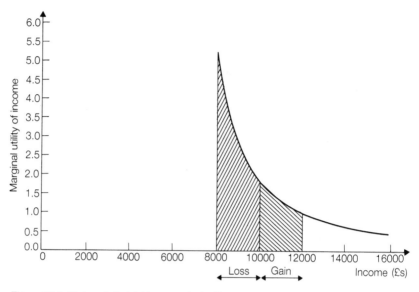

Figure 12.1 Risk and diminishing marginal utility

probability of winning the election, is committed to extend income tax to include forest products: the National Democrats would retain favourable tax treatment.

The farmer's present post-tax income is £10 000. Purchase of the woodland would be wholly financed by a bank loan on which 8% interest in real terms would be paid. The woodland is expected to yield an annual income of £10 000, on which the tax rate would be 40% in the event of a socialist victory. The decision matrix is given in table 12.5.

In terms of mean expected *cash* value, the investment seems just worthwhile. But examine figure 12.1, which shows the respective gain and loss of utility as compared with the no-purchase strategy: areas under the curve are proportional to utility changes. The loss of utility following a socialist victory is clearly greater than the gain of utility following an NDP victory; the difference outweighs the slightly greater probability of an NDP victory. The woodland should not be bought. If necessary a numerical estimation of mean expected *utility* change could be made from figure 12.1, or from an algebraic formulation of utility of income (see equation (28.2)).

An element of risk aversion is also attributable to the disbenefit of worry over a risky investment. This element is independent of actual outcome: even if the investment succeeds, past worries cannot be nullified by subsequent events. A combined estimate of disutility of worry and diminishing marginal utility can be made by asking decision-makers to select an investment with

Table 12.5 Political risks and decision-making

State of nature	Purchase woodland (£s)	No purchase (£s)
Socialist victory		
Present income	10 000	
Woodland income	6 000	
Bank interest	−8 000	
Net income	8 000 × 45% = 3 600	
		10 000
NDP victory		
Present income	10 000	
Woodland income	10 000	
Bank interest	−8 000	
Net income	12 000 × 55% = 6 600	
Mean expected value	10 200	10 000

certain outcome which they consider as valuable as a given risky investment (see Weston and Brigham, 1979). This forces a more conscious quantification upon decision-makers, but has little other advantage.

Strategies for risk avoidance

Assiduous avoidance of risk may lead an individual land-owner or manager to eschew all risky investments, even though these are often the source of greatest profit and social advance. But, as chapter 34 shows, the risks for the individual and for the state of investing or failing to invest in forestry are very different. It is pertinent to ask, therefore, whether there are ways of abating the risks of desirable investments.

An obvious and familiar strategy is to adopt risky investments but to insure against the risk. Fire insurance by woodland owners is particularly sensible, enormous losses being possible, but not sufficiently probable to make insurance premiums prohibitive. Many countries also have good enough historical records to allow realistic premiums to be set.

Suppose the mean value of insured plantations is £2000/ha, the total area insured 100 000 ha, the probability of a given hectare being destroyed in one year is 0.1% and the cost of providing insurance services 25% of the sums paid out. On average 100 ha will be destroyed each year and the annual cost of fire damage will be £200 000, or £2/ha. The total cost of insurance will be £200 000 + 25% = £250 000, and the premium per hectare £2.50. In pure monetary terms, then, the mean expected value of an insurance strategy is normally less than the mean expected value of bearing the risk. Nor does insurance itself reduce aggregate risk: it simply pools the risks of so many individuals that it is unlikely that a large proportion of insured properties will suffer major loss in any year. A charge is naturally made for administering this pooled risk. But avoiding the possibility of disastrous loss makes the service charge worth paying for most individuals.

Within large forestry organizations (a major processing corporation with its own plantations, the state forest department), the service charge is avoided by pooling risks internally. In any year no more than a small proportion of total plantation area is burnt, and the cost of bearing the loss involved is less than the insurance premium in most years. Even in a bad year, the losses will not reduce organization profits by a large percentage, so the marginal utility factor operates only weakly.

A similar result could be achieved if many small land-owners entered a form of collective ownership under which each had a share in every separate wood. The total destruction of one wood would not then be a disaster as it would under individual ownership. However, the legal and economic problems of managing such a scheme are such that individual ownership plus fire insurance continues to be the preferred strategy.

One silvicultural disadvantage of insurance is that it reduces the incentive to deploy physical strategies against fire, such as maintenance of fire-breaks and fire-ponds. Hence insurance may be conditional on a certain level of protective treatment, or a higher premium may be charged for plantations whose layout and management puts them at undue risk.

In general, information on climatic and biotic risks is less available, and insurance is less common.

Linked risks and diversification

Fire outbreaks tend to be isolated, and, while the weather of a particular year may make most plantations in a region particularly vulnerable, it is rare for a large proportion of the crop to be destroyed. The same cannot be said of market risks. During the early 1980s technological and market changes, resulting in the shutdown of much pulping capacity, affected the profitability of forestry throughout Britain. Similarly, changes in tax laws can seriously compromise the profitability of all private forests.

More than most enterprises, forestry has flexibility to respond to such changes. Sawlogs can, regretfully, be cut up for firewood. The product can be stored 'on the hoof', continuing to put on increment, until market conditions or tax laws improve. A high proportion of growing stock can be pre-emptively liquidated, leaving increment little affected. But some risks may be linked for all wood products, over a time period too long to be survived without cutting. Climatic changes (Kauppi, 1987) could affect both productivity and timber price, worldwide and for centuries.

The appropriate response to such linked risks, by enterprises large enough to afford it, is diversification of the investment portfolio (Mills, 1988): funds are placed not only in forestry but in many other activities (agriculture, housing, manufacture of leisure goods) that are unlikely to be susceptible to the same risks. An ideal arrangement is to divide investment between enterprises in which risks are negatively related – that is, a particularly bad outcome in one is usually associated with a particularly good outcome in another. For example, some oil companies have recently invested in energy forestry: should oil supplies fail in the long term, the prospects of forestry as a renewable energy source are improved. Unfortunately, however, for the small land-owner, diversification of the enterprise in search of reduced risk loses scale economies, and may raise costs to an unacceptable level.

Multiple risks and multiple strategies

Risks, like other troubles, do not come one at a time. A plantation on Ambigua might survive a hurricane, with expected NPV $2 million, only to face collapse of sawtimber prices. Such outcomes are best evaluated by a branching diagram, which represents the probability of various combined events, leading to a range of outcomes (see figure 12.2).

The value of any cash flow is now modified by two sets of probabilities. In 60% of cases there is a hurricane, and in 25% of those cases (60% × 25% = 15%) there is a discounted revenue of $4 million, with mean expected value $600 000. Generally, the mean expected value of a cash flow is its face value, multiplied by each probability on the branches leading to that cash flow. Table 12.6 compiles mean expected value for all outcomes, in $million.

It may be possible to take decisions during the life of the crop, in the light of emerging risks. If, for example, by mid-rotation the regional saw-timber market is in decline, clearfelling early for pulp might be contemplated. This not only makes the best of available markets, but also pre-empts any hurricane damage.

As such delayed decisions give an opportunity to avoid the worst outcomes, they improve mean expected value, compared with a situation where plans could not be modified. It is, therefore, desirable to work backwards through decisions, assuming that the best decision will be taken in the light of knowledge at each point in time. Figure 12.3 shows part of a simple decision-tree. Readers may wish to complete it, and consider whether the choice of island for the project is now changed.

Aversion to bad outcomes leads decision-makers to think of risk only as undesirable variation in states of nature. While 'abnormal' climatic and biological factors are generally adverse, markets may often prove better than expected. In such cases, the kind of adaptive decision-making outlined above is again useful: for example, a crop intended for pulp may be grown on

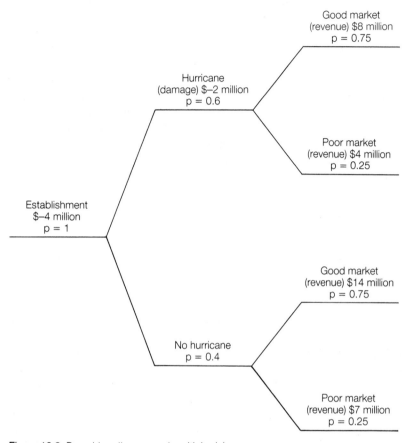

Figure 12.2 Branching diagram and multiple risk

Table 12.6 Climatic and market risk combined

Event	Discounted cash flow	Probability	Weighted value
Establish	−4	1	−4
Repair hurricane damage	−2	0.6	−1.2
Revenues:			
Hurricane			
bad market	4	0.6 × 0.25	0.6
good market	8	0.6 × 0.75	3.6
No hurricane			
bad market	7	0.4 × 0.25	0.7
good market	14	0.4 × 0.75	4.2
Mean expected value			3.9

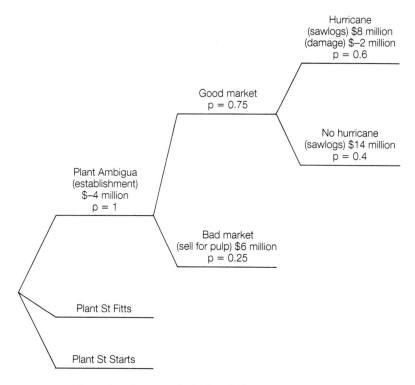

Figure 12.3 Branching diagram and adaptive strategy

in an improving sawlog market. The possibility of such adaptation increases the mean expected value of strategies which are potentially flexible.

Covering all possible states of nature and strategies becomes extra-ordinarily complex. Yet silvicultural investments usually do involve multiple decisions, multiple variables and, very often, multiple risks. Part II of this book moves on to elements of these complex decisions. Risk is sometimes explicitly considered: sometimes the text focuses on other complications, but it must constantly be remembered that forestry outcomes are almost never certain.

Part II   The Economics of Silviculture

13 The Optimal Forest Rotation

Silviculture is intervention in ecosystems so as to modify the yield of woody species in a desired way. But from the economic viewpoint silviculture means making and implementing a set of interrelated investment decisions. For the simplest silvicultural system, the set of decisions is small: at minimum, a decision whether to plant a crop on a given site, plus one on when to fell it for a given market. Normally, however, the decision-tree is more complex. Chronologically, the decisions may be represented as in figure 13.1.

Most elements of this decision-tree are interactive: for example the cost of thinning depends on whether a plantation has been low-pruned to facilitate inspection and harvesting; but whether any pruning at all is worthwhile depends on whether there is a premium on knot-free timber, which in turn depends on whether thinning is designed for quality markets.

Therefore no decision can be taken in isolation, but each is made given certain assumptions about other elements in the decision-tree: decisions on rotation are made for a given species treated under a given thinning regime, while species choice is made with some idea of rotation and end use in mind.

Planning and prediction

In the following chapters such decisions will be examined from an economic viewpoint, and largely in a long-term planning context. The starting point is either an area of open land which could be planted, or a forest to be brought under management by whatever seems the most desirable method, including felling and starting again. Such decisions have the following features:

(a) all technically feasible options may be considered and all silvicultural factors are variable (though site factors are fixed);

(b) all factors of production and markets are variable: the time-span is such that input or output constraints are not binding.

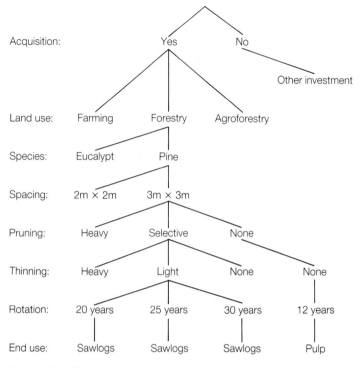

Figure 13.1 Silvicultural decision-tree

Every planned determination of optimal treatments depends not only on some estimate of the crop's production profile but also on predicted prices many years in the future. Since these predictions (even if only projections of current prices) are rather uncertain, the point of long-range planning might be questioned. After all, the decision on thinning regime need not be made, in some cases, for 30 years, while the optimal rotation for slow-growing species under certain criteria may not be reached for two hundred years.

There are three purposes behind long-term planning:

1 Interactions mean that decisions to be implemented many years hence influence decisions to be taken now. For example, a decision not to thin would favour wide initial spacing.

2 Operational planning and particularly production forecasting require some working hypothesis about how long the crop will stand before yield (by size and quality classes) is taken from it.

3 A rational decision about whether to purchase a forest, or land for

afforestation, can only be made if some idea of silvicultural treatment has been formulated.

These important purposes justify efforts to approximate an optimal regime long before all its details are implemented. Inevitably circumstances will differ from those predicted, and some unexpected events will require the original decision to be modified. Sometimes factors of production and markets impose no limitations on making this change, and the new decision simply revises the old one, using updated information. Where constraints operate, the decision techniques discussed in chapter 19 should be applied.

Data and decisions

One function of economists is to predict costs and revenues per unit of input and output. It is *not* their function to determine the *number* of units entailed in each option. Input units are the responsibility of the work study team and output units of mensurationists. Economists are often blamed for the inadequacy of their data–base, but these other specialists are implicated too.

Data, for example on the effect of different thinning regimes on size categories of produce, are notoriously difficult to obtain, since, unlike in the agricultural production cycle, experimental or field observation may need decades to produce results. Where there have been no long-term observations, translocation of results obtained elsewhere (as for exotic species in tropical plantations) is tempting but perilous. Even where a long silvicultural tradition exists, the results of radically new regimes may be difficult to predict. Computerized stand modelling allows the probable results of untried silvicultures to be reproduced in seconds, but the possibility of some crucial factor being absent from the model limits the reliability of results.

The need for practical testing of new regimes and the long time taken for tests to mature both point to the urgency of setting up valid experiments. But part of the validity of the experiment is to be treated in a manner typical of a commercial operation, and there is a danger that plots are either too small or too carefully tended to be representative.

The optimal rotation

As with exploitation decisions, so in silviculture, decision-making is best undertaken in reverse chronological order. When some hypothesis about end uses has been formulated, the desirable rotation length can be considered for each species suitable for that use. When rotation length is known, thinning and tending regimes can be decided. Only when the most profitable regime for each species has been determined can choice of species be made. And only then can it be resolved whether it is worth acquiring or retaining the land for forestry at all. The decision-process resembles a knock-out sporting contest in which the best regime in each pool goes forward to the next round, with forestry's 'finalist' meeting the most profitable option among alternative land uses in the last round – this often taking the form of competitive bidding for land.

The meaning of optimal rotation depends on objectives. The ecologist's optimum comprises the complete cycle of growth, maturity, death and decay. Silvicultural rotations relate to natural regeneration. Biomass rotations seek maximum mean annual increment, while technical optima require timber to be grown to a specification for a particular end use.

The financially optimal rotation is not *in opposition* to these concepts: on the contrary, the above factors are important influences on financial rotations. But economic appraisal entails balancing these and several other relevant factors:

(a) volume growth pattern

(b) crop price–size relationship

(c) trends in 'real' price of timber

(d) discount rate

(e) value of land

(f) climatic and other risks to crop survival or growth.

There are two distinct approaches to combining these factors in assessing optimal rotation.

1 The 'total' approach aggregates predicted costs and revenues of various rotations and selects the rotation of highest NPV, IRR, forest rent, etc. This approach is normal in planning rotations.

2 The 'incremental' (or less accurately 'marginal') approach regards extension of rotation as an investment decision: by leaving the crop standing, one effectively reinvests its current sale value in order to realize greater value in future. One may either compare the NPV of the crop kept for one or a few more years with its current value, or divide the rate of value increase by the current value: this latter figure, representing the current rate of return on the crop, is called the *indicating percent*. The incremental approach is particularly useful in day-to-day decision-making. Examples appear in chapters 15, 17 and 19 and later in this chapter.

The individual effects of the factors are as follows.

Volume growth pattern

Light-demanding or pioneer species accumulate volume rapidly at first, and reach a growth peak early, after which increment declines. Hence *percentage* increase in volume per year falls dramatically, soon dropping below the required rate of return: in terms of volume increment, it is not worth prolonging the rotation. Shade-bearing or climax species grow slowly at first and only gradually build up to peak annual increment. Hence increment percent remains above the required rate of return longer than for a light-demanding species of equal overall productivity.

Price–size relationship

The price–size relationship for individual trees may be stepped if there are distinct markets for different size categories of timber. Unless the crop is very uniform, however, the trees step up into a new volume category over a protracted time-period. Hence the relationship between *mean* value per cubic metre and *mean* tree volume is generally smooth rather than stepped.

Increase in price per cubic metre raises the rate of return represented by current crop increment: if volume increment percent is 3% and the price per cubic metre for the crop is increasing by 1.5% for each percentage point increase in tree volume, the indicating percent is:

$$\frac{[\text{new volume}] \times [\text{new price/m}^3] - [\text{old volume}] \times [\text{old price/m}^3]}{[\text{old volume}] \times [\text{old price/m}^3]}$$

$$\frac{(100\% + 3\%) \times V \times (100\% + 3 \times 1.5\%) \times P - V \times P}{V \times P} = 0.07635 \text{ or } 7.635\%$$

Adding volume increment percent (3%) to price increment percent (4.5%) gives indicating percent approximately.

An initial rapid increase in price per cubic metre up to a price plateau gives fast fall-off in price increment percent and short rotations, while prolonged, steady increase favours long rotations. If there is a technically optimal tree size, mean tree price will surge upward as most of the crop moves into this category, and the optimal rotation is likely to come soon after. By contrast, if there are technical limits to the size of tree that can be harvested or processed, a dip in mean tree price signals that the optimal rotation has been exceeded.

Real price of timber

There is some evidence that timber prices have increased historically somewhat faster than prices of goods in general (Barnett and Morse, 1963), particularly in countries running down an originally abundant natural forest resource. If so, trees are an investment similar to art masterpieces or rare stamps (except that trees do grow in volume and quality as well). Historic trends, of course, are less relevant than predicted ones (see chapter 35). The faster the predicted increase in real price, the more prolonged the planned rotation.

Apart from trends, there are short-term price movements due to cycles in economic activity, climatic or political constraints on timber supplies, or local demand factors such as the start of a major construction project. Cutting to take advantage of temporary high prices (price-responsive cutting) may be better than waiting till the planned end of rotation. On the other hand an expectation of improving markets (say a new sawmill is to be built in the locality) may justify prolonging the planned rotation.

Discount rate

The lower the discount rate, the further the indicating percent can fall before extending the rotation ceases to be a worthwhile investment. Low discount rates usually lengthen rotations.

Land value

If forest land is rented temporarily, short rotations curtail rent payments. The higher the rental, the sooner the value increment of the crop, less rent, drops below the sum needed to achieve an acceptable indicating percent; hence the shorter the rotation. If the land is owned, but could be sold for another purpose, the higher its price, the greater the loss by postponing sale. If the land is permanently dedicated to forestry, shorter rotations allow a successor crop to utilize the land earlier. The more productive the land, the greater the profitability of successor crops, and the greater the urgency to replace the existing crop. High timber prices likewise shorten rotations, possibly to less than the rotation of maximum volume production. Thus a one-off price rise may actually reduce sustained timber supply, a perverse conclusion which has occasioned some excitement among forest economists (Johansson and Löfgren, 1985). Obversely, silvicultural factors, like delay of regeneration, which reduce profit, prolong rotations.

Risk to the crop

Recurrent risks to trees include fire, wind, illicit human felling and any biotic agent that degrades the timber. In the face of such risks the crop may be felled early to pre-empt damage (see chapter 17). Biotic agents which kill the crop but leave the timber undamaged do not curtail the *economic* rotation in the same way: indeed, because of the reduced land value factor, the economic rotation is actually longer. However, in evaluating a particular species, or planning timber supplies, the possibility of premature harvest of a dead crop must be included.

All these factors apply equally to uneven-aged crops, which, if felling is in large groups, can be regarded as a collection of small even-aged stands. However, greater harvesting costs may somewhat lengthen rotation. Where age groups are intimately mixed, rotation determination must include the effect of removal on releasing neighbouring trees from competition. As these trees may themselves be felled within a few years, discounting has a lesser effect on the value of this 'replacement crop'. In these circumstances, the rotation decision has much in common with the thinning decisions discussed in chapter 15. For further discussion, see Chang (1981) and Shahwahid (1985).

Rotation of maximum NPV

Most of these factors are subsumed in an NPV for each potential rotation. Tables 13.1 to 13.3, for clarity of example, refer to a single non-thin rotation of a fast-growing species. Planting costs are 50 000 shillings. Revenues and NPVs are in thousands of shillings. Several discount rates are used. Rotation of maximum NPV (which may mean minimum loss) is starred.

Table 13.1 Optimal single rotation and NPV

Rotation	Revenue	NPV @ 4%	NPV @ 8%	NPV @ 12%	NPV @ 16%
9	80	6.2	−10.0	−21.2	−29.0
12	150	43.7	9.6	−11.5	*−24.7
15	230	77.7	22.5	*−8.0	−25.2
18	310	103.0	27.6	−9.7	−28.6
21	410	129.9	*31.4	−12.1	−31.8
24	500	145.1	28.8	−17.1	−35.8
27	580	*151.2	22.6	−22.8	−39.5
30	650	150.4	14.6	−28.3	−42.4
33	710	144.6	6.0	−33.1	−44.7
36	760	135.2	−2.4	−37.1	−46.8

Table 13.1 shows the following:

1 Discounting terminates the rotation while revenue is still growing rapidly.
2 The lower the discount rate, the longer the rotation.
3 NPVs of rotations a few years shorter or longer than optimal are not much less than that of the optimum. This gives some flexibility of rotation length, for example if there are constraints on the rate at which a large even-aged forest can be harvested.

The value of successor crops can be included by applying the periodic discount formula (7.5) to each rotation length; with a 24–year rotation, for example, clearfelling occurs at 24, 48, 72, etc. years. From table 13.2 these additional points emerge:

4 Optimal rotation for crops with positive NPV is reduced by including successor rotations.
5 Optimal rotations increase for crops with negative NPV: when NPVs are negative, there is advantage in delaying the successor crop (a cost discounted is a cost reduced). If there is no obligation to replant the crop, the cost can be avoided altogether, and the optimal rotation is that for a single production cycle.
6 At moderate to high discount rates, successor rotations have little effect on NPV or optimal rotation.

Table 13.2 Optima for a perpetual series of rotations

Rotation	Revenue	NPV @ 4%	NPV @ 8%	NPV @ 12%	NPV @ 16%
9	80	20.9	−20.0	−33.1	−39.3
12	150	116.4	15.9	−15.5	−29.7
15	230	174.7	32.9	*−9.8	*−28.2
18	310	203.5	36.8	−11.1	−30.7
21	410	231.5	*39.2	−13.3	−33.3
24	500	*237.9	34.3	−18.3	−36.9
27	580	231.4	25.8	−23.9	−40.2
30	650	217.5	16.2	−29.3	−42.9
33	710	199.2	6.5	−33.9	−45.0
36	760	178.7	−2.6	−37.8	−46.6

Other criteria

For those who believe in these criteria, rotations of maximum forest rent and maximum IRR can also be determined. Finally, if natural regeneration provides the first and successor crops immediately and at no cost, the present value of a perpetual series of revenues (PVR_∞) is as in the last two columns of table 13.3. Table 13.3 shows that:

7 The rotation of maximum forest rent (equation 11.1) is much shorter than the single rotation of greatest net revenue, which has not been reached at the longest rotation considered. The value of successor crops is the most important factor curtailing rotations under this criterion.

8 The rotation of maximum IRR resembles rotations of maximum NPV at moderate discount rates. IRR of successor crops is the same as that of the first crop. Only if land purchase is included as an initial cost do successors increase IRR and thus shorten optimal rotation.

9 Free (or cheap) re-establishment increases the profitability of replacing the current crop with successors. Hence rotations giving maximum PVR_∞ are shorter than those giving maximum NPV_∞. Generally, factors which increase profit shorten rotations.

10 IRR cannot be calculated when there are no establishment costs to set equal to discounted revenues: the IRR of all rotations is infinite – this is another defect of IRR.

As chapter 11 indicated, neither payback period nor peak rate of return criteria gives a sensible optimal rotation. The first year rate of return method resembles the incremental method outlined above.

Table 13.3 Other criteria and optimal rotation

Rotation	Revenue	Forest rent	IRR	PVR_∞ @ 4%	PVR_∞ @ 8%
9	80	3.3	5.36	189.0	80.1
12	150	8.3	9.59	249.6	98.8
15	230	12.0	*10.71	287.2	*105.9
18	310	14.4	10.67	302.2	103.5
21	410	17.1	10.54	*320.6	101.6
24	500	18.8	10.07	319.8	93.6
27	580	19.6	9.50	308.0	83.0
30	650	*20.0	8.93	289.7	71.7
33	710	*20.0	8.37	268.1	60.8
36	760	19.7	7.85	244.9	50.8

Annual management costs do not affect optimal rotation under either forest rent or NPV_∞ criteria. These costs are fairly constant with respect to rotation. Thus the PV of a perpetual succession of management costs is unaffected by rotation and has no bearing on the choice. Management costs reduce optimal single rotations, since short rotations have smaller total management costs. By contrast, management costs increase the rotation of maximum IRR: the greater the costs, the lower the IRR, and the less heavily the returns of long rotations are discounted.

These results may appear bewildering, but inexorable logic underlies them, and they are perfectly general, irrespective of discount rate or rotation. The reader is advised to understand the inexorable logic, rather than to memorize the bewildering results.

The incremental method

While the above computations set the norm for rotation lengths, there are circumstances where the method is inappropriate, and the incremental method proves valuable.

In the example summarized in table 13.4, local prices have risen temporarily due to a three-year construction project. The question is whether an immature crop should be felled now at the premium price, raising £3800/ha, or undergo the two remaining thinnings (the first at the premium price) and be clearfelled at the originally scheduled time. All previous costs and thinning revenues are irrelevant, but there is advantage in early re-establishment of successor crops with NPV_∞ per hectare of £800 at 3% and £250 at 4%. At 3% it is worth continuing the rotation; at 4% the decision is marginal; at any higher rate immediate felling is preferable.

Table 13.4 The incremental method and a transient market

Operation	Year	Value	NPV @ 3%	NPV @ 4%
Clearfelling	0	3800	3800	3800
Next crops	0		800	250
Total (fell now)			4600	4050
OR				
First thinning	0	800	800	800
Second thinning	5	700	604	575
Clearfelling	10	3700	2753	2500
Next crops @ 3%	10	800	595	
Next crops @ 4%	10	250		169
Total (delay 10 years)			4752	4044

The second example concerns replacement of a crop which is ill-adapted to site – a frequent occurrence during the first rotation of plantations, when experience of site conditions is limited. The figures are for unthinned Norway spruce with productivity 6 m³/ha/year, to be replaced by a thinnable Sitka spruce crop whose expected productivity is 14 m³/ha/year. At each age the questions are: what is the NPV of the crop felled five years hence, plus a perpetual series of Sitka spruce rotations beginning thereafter; is it greater than the NPV of the crop felled now plus a perpetual series of Sitka spruce rotations beginning immediately? The crop should be felled when the latter quantity exceeds the former:

$$R_t + \text{NPV}_{SS} > \frac{R_{t+5} + \text{NPV}_{SS}}{(1+r)^5}$$

where R_{t+5}, R_t are revenues respectively in 5 years and immediately
NPV_{SS} is the NPV of a perpetual series of Sitka spruce rotations.

The values are shown in table 13.5 for several different ages, preceded by values for Norway spruce alone. A 5% discount rate is used, making $(1+r)^5 = 1.276$. Values in £s are taken from Forestry Commission (1983).

Surprisingly, given the disparate productivity, it is worth keeping the Norway spruce crop till age 65, almost its own optimal rotation. The explanations are that the costs of this crop are sunk, whereas those for the successor are yet to be incurred, and that this crop has already grown part-way towards a valuable size, whereas the successor needs 20 years even to become salable. This result is normal, though at low discount rates the superior productivity of the successor crop has more weight. Even at the outset of the rotation, when the unproductive crop has made little progress towards commercial size, the cost of clearing and replacing it may outweigh

Table 13.5 The incremental method and crop replacement

Age	R_t	$R_{t+5}/1.276$	$R_t + NPV_{ss}$	$(R_{t+5} + NPV_{ss})/1.276$
35	−623	−149	−402	24
40	−190	226	31	399
45	288	656	509	829
50	837	1170	1058	1343
55	1493	1742	1714	1915
60	2223	2354	2444	2527
65	3004	2956	3225	3129
70	3773			

the revenue advantage of a more productive crop, under moderate discount rates.

The intuition of most foresters would be that crop replacement should occur at the earliest opportunity. A little economics not only refutes what seems an intuitively sensible conclusion, but also reveals why the conclusion is less sensible than it seems.

The replacement crop need not be a forestry one either. A similar set of calculations could be used to determine the optimal time to fell a crop to make way for another land use.

The incremental approach has numerous applications: in anticipating the effects of thinning and fertilizing on rotation length; in determining appropriate strategies when various hazards threaten crop survival; in setting priorities when not all desirable courses of action can be undertaken.

Private finances and the felling decision

Different perceptions of prices, different discount rates, different targets, mean that silvicultural decisions by individual land-owners differ from those of large organizations, even in the same circumstances and when the same criteria are applied. Rotations may be influenced by the need to find large cash sums at short notice. Woodlands are often used as a sort of bank, withdrawals being made for family crisis or celebration, or to fund new investments. The timing of these requirements is, of course, unrelated to crop age, which means major fellings are often not at the optimal time, conventionally measured.

Another rather unpredictable factor is price-responsive cutting. Temporarily high prices encourage additional cutting by large organizations. But for individuals using woodlands as a bank, high prices mean less volume need be sold to raise a given sum. The diminishing marginal utility of income (see chapter 12) also gives an incentive to smooth out annual cash flows by over-cutting at times of low prices, and reducing fellings when prices are high. This 'perverse' supply response may amplify fluctuations in timber availability, since shortages cause high prices, which reduce felling and aggravate the shortage.

If, however, land-owners have alternative investments available, it is rational to cut more at times of high prices and to invest surplus cash outside the forestry enterprise. Funds are withdrawn from this alternative investment, rather than from the forest, when prices are low. This response alleviates price fluctuations.

Taxes and grants affect the private profitability of forestry, which in turn affects optimal rotation – especially under the maximum IRR criterion. Table 13.6 shows part of table 13.3, recomputed with a grant or tax relief covering 80% of the 50 000 shillings establishment cost. By contrast,

Table 13.6 Effect of grant on IRR and optimal rotation

Rotation	Revenue	IRR (no grant)	IRR (with grant)
9	80	5.36	*25.99
12	150	9.59	25.32
15	230	*10.71	23.25

taxation of forest income without tax relief on costs reduces profits and extends rotations. Taxation also reduces the post-tax rate of return on alternative investments. The consequent reduction of discount rate adopted by individuals could significantly extend rotations. But, perversely, higher taxes increase marginal utility of forest income and could increase cutting.

Taxes on wealth give an incentive to be less wealthy! Curtailing rotations by a few years can dramatically reduce the cash value of woodlands. Taking figures from table 13.1, the mean capital value over a 24–year rotation is about 180 000 shillings, while that over a 21–year rotation is about 140 000 shillings. The taxable sum is reduced by 22%, and progressive tax rates might make the reduction in tax burden even greater. Yet the NPV_∞ of the shorter rotation is only 2.7% less. An annual wealth tax on plantations is not only difficult to assess, but substantially affects profit-maximizing silviculture.

14 Spacing and Thinning: Quality, Quantity, Timing

Chapter 13 examined *how long* trees should be grown. This chapter turns to *how many* trees should be grown: the number initially planted (the spacing decision) and the number removed during the rotation (the thinning decision).

Spacing

The closer the spacing of trees in a plantation, the greater the cost of establishment. But the relationship is not simple. Some costs are proportional to tree numbers: those of growing or purchasing seedlings, planting them, and applying individual protection against insects, fungi, weeds or browsers.

Other costs depend on the planting layout. If the same pattern (say square or equilateral triangle) is maintained, the number of planting lines increases as the *square root* of plant numbers. A square pattern with 2.5 m by 2.5 m spacing gives 1600 plants and 40 planting lines on a square of 1 ha, but at 2 m by 2 m spacing there are 2500 plants and 50 planting lines. Plant numbers increase by 56%, but total length of planting line only by 25%. The affected costs are those of creating cultivation lines (ploughing or mechanical weed clearance) and those of planters traversing the lines during planting. The same applies to subsequent treatments given along planting lines. On the other hand, if greater numbers are achieved simply by planting closer *within* lines, the cost of lines is fixed with respect to numbers.

Yet other costs are constant with tree number, including those of land acquisition and whole-crop protection or improvement operations, such as fencing or aerial application of fertilizers or herbicides. Such costs are irrelevant to spacing.

To maximize revenue, optimal spacing is sometimes (as in fuelwood plantations) simply a matter of maximizing volume production. Too wide a spacing causes long delay in canopy closure, with interim loss of increment:

on the other hand too much congestion may reduce increment in light-demanding species. Between these extremes, there is normally a range of spacings over which total volume production on a given rotation varies little.

Wide spacing also affects timber quality, although the exact influence is varied and controversial. Diverse views are expressed by Grah (1960), Fenton and Dick (1972), Cown (1974), Brazier (1977), Bunn (1981) and Sheikh and Raza-ul-Haq (1982).

(a) Greater light intensity low in the canopy promotes heavy side branching, entailing either strength degrade from knots, or expenditure on early pruning if quality timber is to be produced.

(b) As volume and height increment are little affected by spacing, diameter increment of individual trees must be greater for wider-spaced crops. This in turn gives greater bole taper, with potentially more difficult handling and processing, and lower recovery rates for saw-timber or veneers.

(c) The effect of fast diameter growth on wood properties arises by differences through time in the kind of wood formed. In ring porous species like oaks, fast growth gives more latewood, with greater density and strength. In species like spruces with light latewood, density decreases with fast growth, and poor working quality and dimensional instability may ensue. In species where seasonal differences are slight, diameter growth rate has little apparent effect on quality.

In close-spaced plantations, better early site utilization yields a greater proportion of weaker juvenile wood on a given *rotation,* whereas a wide-spaced plantation may have somewhat more juvenile wood in trees of given *size*.

(d) Low planting density allows less scope for selection, possibly forcing acceptance of trees of poor form or low vigour simply to retain complete canopy. This factor is less important with genetically uniform material and careful establishment.

Narrow initial spacing may therefore, though not invariably, lead to a better price *for trees of given size*.

But the rapid individual volume growth associated with wide spacing has advantages. At a given age trees are bigger: first thinnings may be sold at profit rather than loss; a greater proportion of final fellings will be in the large sawlog category. Where rotation length is constrained by factors like susceptibility of tall trees to wind or snow damage, or where fire or other risks favour a short rotation, a larger mean tree size at final felling is the most likely result of wider spacing.

Alternatively, faster individual growth can be encashed by achieving a given tree size sooner: wider spacing effectively shrinks the time scale of individual tree growth. The value of a shorter production period in a discounting context should be clear. The balance among these factors is represented in figure 14.1. Note particularly:

(a) Fixed establishment costs plus uniform cost per additional tree give linear increase in total cost with tree numbers.

(b) With non-discounting criteria, the dominant factor is maximum long-term revenue. The greater the numbers per hectare, the fuller the site utilization and, for some species and regimes, the better the timber quality. Thus maximum profit from a single rotation (the point of maximum difference between total revenue and total cost) is achieved with large numbers of trees per hectare. Even over a perpetual series of rotations, growing many individual trees slowly to large size normally yields the maximum forest rent. However, if trees are grown on limited rotations regardless of spacing, wide spacing is advantageous even with low discount rates, since mean tree size at removal is invariably greater, and so, therefore, price per cubic metre.

(c) With moderate discount rates, the long waiting period counts against slow-grown, close-spaced trees. Even on a single rotation, this factor eventually outweighs site utilization and quality effects (Wardle, 1967).

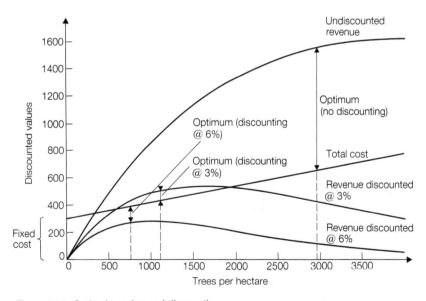

Figure 14.1 Optimal spacing and discounting

(d) Above a critical discount rate, there is no tree number on which profit can be made: either the fixed costs of establishment cannot be paid by the revenues, or the decline in quality and site utilization with wide spacing cannot be compensated by sufficiently rapid tree growth.

Apart from the discount rate, the other crucial factor affecting optimal spacing is existence or absence of a well-developed market for quality timber. In countries with a wealth of slow-grown timber from natural forests (Canada), or a tradition of silviculture for high quality (France), there is usually a market premium for trees which grow slowly. Where silviculture has recently evolved around fast-growing plantations (UK) or where end uses do not require 'quality' (firewood-dependent countries) wood-using industries are less likely to recognize and make good use of quality timber: a premium may be obtained, if at all, only by vigorous marketing.

Blanking

In time, tree numbers per hectare may prove less than ideal (through unexpectedly high mortality), greater than ideal (through too-copious natural regeneration) or just wrong (through change in silvicultural policy). Blanking is intended to correct insufficient numbers. Whether it is worth doing depends on how great the shortfall is and the pattern of gaps in the crop (Busby and Grayson, 1981). The costs, like those of initial establishment, comprise a fixed element (inspecting and traversing the site), and an incremental element per tree actually planted. If only a few replacements are needed, the fixed element gives high average cost per replacement, and the operation is unlikely to be worthwhile (figure 14.2).

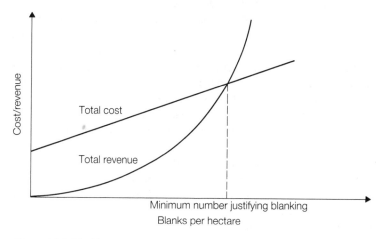

Figure 14.2 Blanking

If losses are scattered sparsely, it is also unlikely to be worth blanking: the period to canopy closure, over which significant site utilization is forgone, is short, and replacements may be shaded out by older competitors. Indeed, scattered failure of a proportion of trees having low inherent vigour or poor site adaptation may beneficially reduce expenditure on precommercial thinning.

On the other hand, if losses occur in groups, full site utilization may never be achieved, the probability of replacements being shaded out is reduced, and successful blanking could prove profitable. As group losses may reflect an unfavourable micro-site, rather than random chance, the cause of failure should be established. If the site is unsuitable, blanking may simply involve wasting money twice over; the operation should be assessed probabilistically (see chapter 17).

Because of high fixed costs and the risk of inherent reasons for failure, blanking normally costs more per tree than initial establishment. Where initial establishment is only marginally profitable, it may not even be worth assessing the scale of losses. The exception is when large initial protective and site improvement expenditures are still effective, yet, being past costs, have become irrelevant to the profitability of blanking.

Respacing and precommercial thinning

If too many trees become established, a proportion may be removed early in the crop life. Such excess may be caused by unexpected natural regeneration, changing ideas on optimal spacing, or by a deliberate attempt to provide scope for early selection of desirable trees. The arguments for respacing resemble those surrounding initial crop espacement, except that incremental costs are now incurred for each tree *removed from* the crop, rather for each *additional tree planted* (Edwards and Grayson, 1979).

Respacing is not clearly distinct, either, from precommercial thinning (thinning at net cost). Philosophically, chronologically and budget-wise, respacing is part of establishment, whereas precommercial thinning is part of harvesting. Ecologically, respacing precedes crop competition. Technically, the two operations often use different tools. From an economist's viewpoint, respacing is an operation whose discounted cost per hectare increases with age (as the stand becomes denser and the removed trees more difficult to cut) whereas the discounted net cost of precommercial thinning declines with age (as it is longer postponed, and as the value of sub-marginal trees comes closer to paying the cost of harvesting).

From the decision-making point of view, it does not matter where respacing ends and precommercial thinning begins. Both are investments in improved long-term revenue from the crop.

Thinning

Like initial spacing, thinning is concerned with the number of trees over which crop increment is distributed, and hence with individual tree increment and its effects on timing and quality of yield. But thinning is altogether more complex, both because it may entail removal of salable volume and because there are several thinning variables to consider – frequency, intensity, type, method and timing. Moreover, all these variables interact, making thinning potentially the most difficult and interesting element of silviculture.

Traditional European silvicultural systems considered the advantages of thinning unequivocal.

(a)   In purely biological terms, it allows removal of less efficient photo-synthesizers, increasing mean productivity in the current rotation, and genetic quality for subsequent rotations.

(b)   It pre-empts or cures check in light-demanding species.

(c)   It avoids waste by harvesting suppressed trees before decay begins.

(d)   It promotes stand hygiene by removing dead and dying trees which are potential centres for insect and fungal damage, and by allowing freer air circulation.

(e)   Economically, it permits early removal of ill-formed trees, especially coarsely branched dominants, thus concentrating increment on high-quality trees (and again improving genetic quality).

(f)   It also normally concentrates increment on trees at the upper end of the size spectrum, which, provided the trees have good form, yields the best price per cubic metre added.

(g)   It returns revenue early in the rotation, vital in a discounting context, as well as bringing forward the time when final crop trees (whose volume growth is accelerated by reduced competition) reach a given target size. Early revenue also reduces the capital on which tax is paid.

(h)   It gives scope to utilize excess labour, meet market contracts or generate flexible cash flow before the crop reaches economic maturity: this is particularly important when a plantation pro-gramme is being built up, and little mature forest exists.

(i)   It allows easier access into the stand for management inspection (and also, where relevant, for recreational use).

Unsurprisingly, in the face of this formidable list, the wisdom of thinning was rarely questioned. The disadvantages are rather more subtle.

(j)   Intervention in the crop may have malign effects: breaking up the canopy may render the stand more vulnerable to wind; harvesting may cause physical damage to and initiate biological deterioration in the remaining trees; soil compaction by extraction equipment may depress increment (cf. (d) above).

(k)   Early selective removal of poor-quality or small trees may occur at net cost. Thus, far from providing early returns, thinning may increase investment in the crop, requiring considerably enhanced later revenues to justify it (cf. (c), (e) and (g) above).

(l)   This argument is reinforced if the forest is still unroaded, or the roads are in disrepair, since thinnings can then be sold only if access is provided. Building a road system for thinnings, rather than waiting till the crop is mature, brings forward a major expenditure, whose discounted cost is thereby increased. Even without discounting, additional road maintenance costs are incurred over the interim period.

(m) Irrespective of tree size, thinning is less susceptible than clearfelling to use of high-output work methods and mechanized harvesting.

(n)   While increment is itself more valuable if applied to already-large trees, such increment *may do little to enhance the value of the volume to which it is added*, since large trees may already have reached the plateau of the price–size relationship. Hence there may be a case for retaining the smallest trees in the crop so that their value may be enhanced, rather than taking them out as low-value thinnings (cf. (f) above). This is discussed in chapter 15.

The balance of arguments

Arguments (k) (l) and (m), and to some extent (j), can be partly mitigated by thinning to waste, that is leaving felled trees on the ground or simply poisoning unwanted trees, thus reducing crown and root competition without incurring all harvesting costs. On the other hand, not all advantages of thinning are achieved thereby, particularly those associated with stand hygiene.

The opposition between these groups of arguments means that no general case for or against thinning can be made, nor for any particular form of the operation. A particular thinning regime is only justified by a favourable balance of results achieved in particular circumstances. That balance cannot be evaluated purely in silvicultural terms: a 'silviculturally optimal regime' can in fact only be decided by prejudice or intuition.

Economics offers two approaches to determining an optimal thinning regime. The experimental approach examines the timing and volumes of out-turn under various regimes, combining them with prices for each product category and with operational costs. The regime with highest NPV (or other measure of profit) is adopted.

The problem with this approach is its specificity: it cannot produce general prescriptions. Moreover, because it depends on experimental results, the value of different regimes can only be assessed after a long period of stand growth. The alternative is an analytical approach, which seeks relationships for stand growth and prices, on the basis of which models can be developed. While these models, like any others, *are* simplifications of reality, they can deliver results rapidly, and at least indicate regimes which might be tested experimentally.

The next chapter uses such models extensively. But it is important to remember that they are simplifications. Furthermore, they refer to particular circumstances, and do not yield universally applicable results.

15 Spacing and Thinning: Managing the Variables

Because there are many dimensions to treatment of tree numbers during the rotation, it is sometimes difficult to grasp the significance of individual elements in thinning regimes. This chapter attempts to introduce the elements of decision-making little by little. It works towards a regime that emerges logically, though not very traditionally, from the conditions of much plantation forestry in the northern temperate zone.

Frequency and method: cost vs selectivity

Optimal frequency and most profitable method of thinning both depend on the balance between efficiency in photosynthesis and efficiency of operations – between land productivity and labour productivity. Biologically, the ideal is extreme flexibility: trees are marked for removal whenever and wherever their increment can be advantageously reallocated to trees of superior vigour and form. At the same time, creation of large gaps in the canopy, which reduce site utilization, is avoided.

Unfortunately, repeated inspection and marking is expensive in skilled labour. Each time a harvesting team is deployed costs money, particularly if it entails setting up cables, or arranging a separate timber sale. Frequent thinning gives ideal allocation of increment, but loses scale economies. For high-quality or fast-growing crops, or where wages are low, cash advantage lies in ideal allocation of increment, and frequent thinning is optimal. In practice, however, not much is lost by a frequency somewhat different from optimal, and for operational convenience or to ensure a steady work-load a uniform thinning cycle may be adopted throughout a management unit containing variable crops.

A similar conflict exists spatially. Ideally trees are individually marked for removal (selective thinning) wherever increment can be better used by neighbours. Such a method, however, entails inspection and marking costs (Raymond, 1985) and may require low pruning of the crop to expedite this.

To avoid these costs and facilitate extraction, thinning methods may be adopted which remove trees in some systematic pattern, for example, one row in four. Unfortunately, all selectivity is thereby lost: some badly formed trees are left in the crop, some of high vigour are removed. Compromise may be sought in two ways.

1 Intermediate methods involve selectivity within systematic rules, such as:
   (a) favouring the best tree in a square of nine;
   (b) moving along a line of trees and removing the poorer of each pair;
   (c) taking out one in four rows plus trees of bad form which are thereby made accessible.
2 Mixed methods entail a change, usually from systematic to selective methods, during the thinning period.

Although intermediate and mixed methods seek the best of both worlds (achieving selectivity and low cost), there is no theoretical reason why they will not fall between two stools (achieving neither effectively).

As well as crop quality and level of labour costs, the discount rate is important in balancing selectivity and cost. Thinning costs are incurred immediately, whereas the advantages accrue over the remaining rotation, often to the final crop trees. Hence low discount rates favour frequent selective thinning, while high discount rates penalize its delayed returns. Table 15.1 shows the increase in discounted revenue from a selective thinning which enhances the value increment of final crop trees by £10 per year over the remaining rotation. At high discount rates, the best pay-off from selectivity is achieved over quite a short period. Mixed systems are sensible in this context, the higher costs of selection being accepted only late in the thinning period.

Table 15.1 Benefits of improved value increment

Delay till felling (years)	DISCOUNT RATE				
	1%	3%	5%	7%	10%
5	47.57	43.13	39.18	35.65	31.05
10	90.53	74.41	61.39	50.83	38.55
20	163.91	110.74	75.38	51.68	29.73
30	222.58	123.60	69.41	39.41	17.19
40	268.66	122.62	56.82	26.71	8.84

Method and type: which tree?

Thinning type refers to the category of tree – dominant, co-dominant, sub-dominant or suppressed – removed in thinning. Selective thinning normally removes an explicit target category. Systematic thinning also has implications for thinning type, since harvesting, say, every fourth row leads to trees in all dominance classes being removed.

Where thinning is selective, the case for removing trees of low vigour, small size and poor form might seem unequivocal. Thus far, such trees may have fulfilled some role in keeping boles of better trees straight and branch-free. Once serious competition between trees begins, however, advantage lies in giving more growing space to better trees. Such thinning also improves the stand's genetic quality.

It is always desirable to favour trees of superior inherent vigour: the case is less clear for favouring trees which are well-formed, or merely large. Taking together points (f) and (n) from pages 147–8, it can be seen that applying an extra cubic metre need not enhance the value of large trees more than that of smaller ones. Figure 15.1 shows the value increase attained by applying an extra cubic metre to various tree sizes.

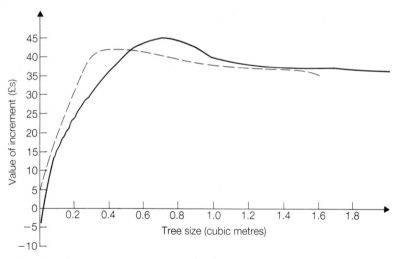

Figure 15.1 (a) solid line – value of marginal increment
(b) dashed line – value of several size classes of increment

Increment adds little value to small trees. Indeed, very small trees may become a greater liability, the greater volume to be removed at cost more than offsetting the better price per cubic metre. However, the largest trees may not be the most profitable recipients of increment either, if they reach a plateau where growth no longer much improves value per cubic metre. Trees needing a little growth to reach a plateau make best use of increment.

Price–size relationships vary over time, and between countries and species. This variation results in markedly different profiles for value of increment. Where there are lucrative markets for special size categories, or a stepped price–size relationship, a roller-coaster profile may result, with erratic implications for thinning type.

This analysis of value of increment can also include varying photosynthetic efficiency. It is plausible that large trees are large because they are efficient utilizers of a given amount of growing room and light. Suppose there is an exponential relationship, such that, say, trees of 0.6 m³ have 25% greater photosynthetic efficiency than those of 0.3 m³: the benefit of extra growing space then increases continuously with tree size, except for a slight dip as shown in figure 15.2.

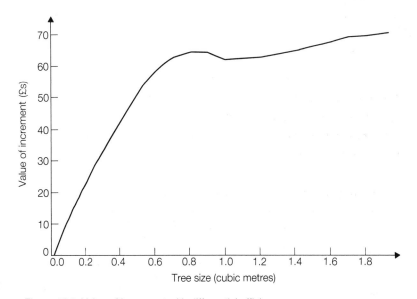

Figure 15.2 Value of increment with differential efficiency

However, large size might also result from favourable early site conditions, or an aggressive branching and rooting habit. In the former case figure 15.1 is more realistic than figure 15.2. Trees which grow rapidly by suppressing neighbours and annexing their portion of growing space are not desirable plantation trees (Cannell, 1979). If they also show coarse branching habit, they are among the early targets for removal in 'silvicultural' thinning.

The ideal tree for retention in selective thinning thus has inherent photo-synthetic efficiency, good form and moderate to large size (though local prices may modify this). Under non-discounting criteria, thinning type needs no further consideration.

Discounting and thinning type

But under discounting criteria the 'early return' function of thinning complicates matters. There is, for example, a period when small trees are sub-marginal, so that harvesting them increases investment in the crop, whereas harvesting bigger trees produces early revenue.

This immediate cash advantage of removing large trees persists into the post-commercial thinning period. In the long term, given increment increases crop revenue more if applied to large rather than small trees. But discounting makes that delayed advantage less significant, compared with the immediate advantage of harvesting large rather than small trees in thinnings.

Further generalizations are indicated in table 15.2, which uses:

(a) the 1987 price–size relationship for conifers in Great Britain
(b) equal photosynthetic efficiency of all size classes
(c) equally desirable form for all size classes
(d) repeated thinning removing approximately 50% of increment
(e) a 5% discount rate.

Table 15.2 Benefits of retaining different tree sizes

Tree size	DELAY UNTIL TREE IS FELLED (years)				
	10	20	30	40	80
0.01	1.06	3.48	6.94	10.90	24.41
0.03	3.89	9.33	14.71	19.48	31.47
0.05	5.96	12.36	18.23	23.62	29.24
0.12	8.67	17.04	24.61	29.72	21.49
0.20	10.73	20.66	27.03	26.76	16.05
0.40	13.88	20.33	20.50	18.51	7.26
1.00	7.09	8.60	7.70	5.60	−5.64

The figures represent the value of *retaining* 1 m³ in trees of various sizes for various periods during thinning. 'Value' means the difference between the trees' current worth and their discounted future worth. Expected future size is based on the increased increment resulting from thinning to favour trees of that size.

This table suggests that:

1 If the rotation is constrained to last (say) another 40 years, the ideal target tree has modest size. The smallest trees do not reach valuable size within the prescribed rotation. The largest trees, on the other hand, are already on the price plateau, and volume increment hardly adds enough value to offset the effect of discounting.

2 If the choice lies between trees retained for a shorter period – say 10 years, until third thinning, the ideal tree size for retention is much larger – probably the largest at that time.

3 If the rotation can be prolonged indefinitely, the ideal tree is much smaller, though its discounted value increment is little more than that of modest-sized trees on *their* optimal rotation.

4 Large trees reach their optimal rotation as individuals much earlier than small ones. Beyond it, these trees lose discounted value, so should be removed irrespective of the value increment of trees with which they are competing. Thus, even when small trees have low vigour or poor quality, they represent a more profitable target for further increment in late thinning.

5 Recalculation of the table shows that the higher the discount rate, the greater the advantage of removing large, well-formed trees early in the rotation, and favouring low-value trees.

6 Lack of selectivity for size in thinning is not always very disadvantageous.

The argument applies to trees of poor form too. Increment is less valuable on them, but the advantage of removing well-formed trees immediately may outweigh this. The results for two trees of equal size and increment, but different quality, are shown in table 15.3. However, it is always better to retain good trees when their indicating percent exceeds that of poor trees (unless they have passed optimal rotation).

Table 15.3 Benefits of retaining different tree qualities

	Value now	and in 5 years	discounted @ 6%
Poor tree	$10	$14	$10.46
Good tree	$15	$20	$14.95
Poor tree now + good tree later			$24.95
Good tree now + poor tree later			$25.46

These prescriptions are at odds with traditional thinning. There is, however, nothing new about them in an economic context, high-grading of the best stems in a natural crop having been practised since time immemorial.

Timing, intensity and non-thin regimes

The factors relevant to thinning type also affect timing of first thinning. Whatever the shape of the value-of-increment profile, some combinations of tree size and quality offer greater addition to total revenue than others: there is advantage in thinning as soon as such trees suffer competition from less desirable recipients of increment.

However, several complicating factors may favour a delay.

(a) Death and loss of lower branches make better working conditions.

(b) Where no roads exist, delay of construction is advantageous; even without discounting, it avoids intermediate maintenance costs, permits more increment by trees standing on the road line and gives scope for roads to be planned with a better idea of final extraction technology.

(c) Removal of small thinnings may represent an early cost, whereas increased crop revenue is not fully realized till the end of the rotation. Even after thinnings become salable, delay makes them more valuable per cubic metre, an advantage realized immediately thinning is undertaken.

There are also additional factors against delay.

(d) Delayed thinning creates large gaps in the canopy, possibly making the crop vulnerable to wind.

(e) In light-demanding crops, delay exacerbates the loss of increment due to retaining trees of low inherent vigour.

(f) Other objectives of thinning (like promotion of hygiene) are best pursued by early thinning.

As with thinning type, no reliable intuitive balancing of these factors can be achieved: quantification is needed. Suppose for simplicity that 3000 trees share equally an increment of 10 m^3 per year; that thinning at age 15 would remove 1500 trees of 0.05 m^3 ($\equiv$ 75 m^3), while delayed thinning at age 16 would remove 1406 trees of 0.0533 m^3 ($\equiv$ 75 m^3). Clearfelling at age 40 removes 325 m^3, tree size being 325/1500 = 0.217 m^3 and 325/1594 = 0.204 m^3 for immediate and delayed thinning respectively. Revenues discounted to year 15 at 5% are shown in table 15.4.

Table 15.4 Immediate versus delayed thinning

Age	Tree size	Price/m³	Volume	Discount factor	NPV
15	0.05	−1.04	75	1	−78
40	0.217	12.97	325	0.295	1243
Total (immediate thinning)					1165
or					
16	0.0533	−0.69	75	0.952	−49
40	0.204	12.37	325	0.295	1186
Total (delayed thinning)					1137

This simplified case shows clear advantage in immediate thinning, although thinnings are below salable size. Even the cost of advancing road construction to extract the thinnings (say £250–£250/1.05 = £12 per hectare) is insufficient to favour delay. This result does, however, vary with size class, price–size relationship and growth characteristics of the stand. Calculations for a wide range of conditions (Price, 1987b, 1988b) gave the following conclusions.

1 It is generally advantageous to start thinning once serious competition begins, even when competing trees are sub-marginal.

2 There are exceptions:

(a) Trees are suppressed. They no longer compete with desirable trees. Removal should be delayed, both to reduce discounted cost, and to increase the probability of natural removal by decay.

(b) Road costs are high. Delay of this cost is a significant advantage of delayed thinning in poorly roaded plantations. Difficult (mountainous or boggy) terrain favours delayed thinning.

(c) The price–size curve rises very steeply to a plateau. The large benefit of applying increment to small trees, coupled with the short time lapse until this increment is realized in delayed thinning, favours delay, even of post-commercial thinning in plantations already roaded.

(d) The crop has low productivity, with expected long rotation. The long time-lapse until benefits of early thinning are realized favours delay.

3 High discount rates favour delayed thinning of precommercial sizes.

4 With no price differential between tree sizes, thinning should begin when the value of bringing forward thinning revenue equals the cost of bringing forward road costs (or when thinnings are salable, in a roaded forest).

Conclusions favouring precommercial thinning of uneven-aged stands have also been reached (Speechly and Helms, 1985).

If thinning is delayed at the traditional time of first thinning, indefinite delay – a non-thin regime – might be considered. On one hand, sudden and major intervention in the canopy late in the rotation may fatally predispose the crop to wind damage. On the other, near the end of the rotation the benefits to the final crop of thinning come sooner (less effect of discounting); this may eventually favour thinning. A particular advantage of not thinning is that the entire rotation's production is harvested at one time, with maximum operational economies and scope for high-output machines (harvesters and processors).

Thus, according to circumstances, immediate, delayed, or no thinning may each prove economically optimal.

All the silvicultural effects of thinning are emphasized by increased intensity of thinning. However, since extraction routes must exist if thinnings are to be harvested at all, the advantage of delayed roading does not affect intensity: once thinning begins, it is normally beneficial to increase intensity at least to the point where site utilization or timber quality start to suffer. How much *further beyond* this point thinning should be intensified raises again the arguments about optimal spacing, with the additional factor that more intense thinning yields greater net revenues (or net costs if pre-commercial). High discount rates favour intense thinning with its tendency to bring forward all revenues but to reduce total long-term revenue: high premiums for quality timber favour a lighter regime.

The interaction of spacing, thinning and rotation length

It has been shown that duration of the remaining rotation can affect decisions on thinning type and intensity, and indeed on whether to thin at all. But thinning itself has effects on optimal rotation, some of which are shared by wide spacing. The more intense the thinning, the greater the indicated adjustment of rotation.

1 A checked stand has low indicating percent. If the indicating percent is less than the discount rate, the crop should be felled. Similarly, under non-discounting criteria the crop is probably earning less net annual income than a replacement crop. By removing check, thinning improves the performance of such crops, and prolongs the period over which they earn respectively a

better rate of interest than an alternative investment, or a better net annual income than an alternative crop.

2 Heavy thinning and wide spacing compress the physiological time-scale of individual tree growth. A tree with little competition reaches its maximum mean annual increment earlier than one grown in a crowded stand. In that optimal rotation is related to volume production profile, heavy thinning tends to shorten rotations.

3 Effects also arise from the price–size relationship. The percentage rate of price increase is

$$\frac{dP/dT}{P} = \frac{dP/dV \times dV/dT}{P}$$

dP/dV is the gradient of the price–size curve. A thinned crop normally has larger trees, so dP/dV is smaller, given a decreasing price–size gradient. dV/dT is the rate of individual tree increment. As thinning increases individual increment, this term is larger for thinned crops. P is the current price per cubic metre. Past thinning normally increases this.

Combining these effects, regular past thinning is likely to reduce dP/dV and increase P enough to outweigh effects on dV/dT: the tendency is to shorten rotations. By contrast, thinning initiated late in the rotation chiefly increases dV/dT, which prolongs rotations. This assumes normal thinning. The 'creaming' thinning type described earlier may reduce volume increment and price per cubic metre, and the price–size factors act differently.

4 In a discounting context, an important aspect of thinning is reduction of investment in the crop, and therefore of the value increment required to give an acceptable indicating percent.

In different terms, the discount factor at 5% over a five-year thinning cycle is 0.7835. Suppose a crop's current value per hectare is £4000 and the expected value of increment over five years is £1000. The discounted value of £5000 five years hence is £3918, and it would be better to take £4000 by clearfelling. But if thinning reduces standing value to £3000 without affecting value increment, the discounted value of £4000 five years hence is £3134, and it is worth waiting rather than clearing the remaining 3000 poundsworth of the crop.

Whichever way this effect is viewed, it tends to prolong rotations. (Wealth taxes also penalize high standing value, and under them thinning prolongs rotations.)

5 The economic purpose of thinning is to increase NPV of each rotation (or IRR or other criterion). As chapter 13 showed, the higher the NPV of successor crops, the greater the urgency to end the current rotation. Hence

thinning the *next* rotation reduces the *current* one, though the effect is small. The increase of IRR by thinning raises the implicit discount rate, which tends significantly to shorten rotations under this criterion.

6 Where thinning makes a crop more unstable to wind, premature felling to pre-empt damage may be considered (see chapter 17).

Under moderate discount rates, factor 4 dominates these arguments, and optimal thinned rotations normally exceed optimal non-thin rotations (by about five years in Britain, at a 5% rate). This contrasts with the effect of wide spacing, which shortens rotations: spacing does not affect factor 4, and factors 2 and 3, both shortening rotations with wide spacing, dominate.

Under non-discounting criteria, factor 4 is irrelevant, so that, for shade-bearers at least, factors 2 and 3 shorten a thinned rotation. For light-demanders, on the other hand, factor 1 may prove decisive: removal of check by thinning may be the only way to justify prolonging the rotation.

More complex modelling of the interaction of thinning and rotation is described by Kao and Brodie (1980).

It is little use to know that thinning extends or reduces rotations, if one does not know whether the margin of change is one year or fifty. But the magnitude of change, as well as its direction, depends greatly on discount rate and local circumstances, which must be given before a prescription is offered.

Constructing a regime for tree numbers

It may be helpful to summarize what economic criteria imply for optimal spacing and thinning regimes, because of marked differences from the prescription evolved in Europe and transplanted around the world. On the basis of the arguments and calculations presented, the features of a regime maximizing NPV at 5% might be as follows. (Similar results might apply to tropical crops, higher discount rates offsetting faster growth rates.)

1 If trees have uniform quality and vigour, and if the quality effects of wide spacing are unimportant, the ideal initial spacing is sufficiently wide that competition between trees becomes serious only when the discounted sale value of first thinnings just covers the cost of establishing those trees. If seedlings are variable or if quick canopy closure is desired, incremental cost of planting more trees should be compared with incremental discounted revenue from improved selectivity or higher-quality timber.

2 Irrespective of initial spacing, thinning is generally justified, even at a cost, once serious competition begins between trees, unless

(a) roads are particularly expensive to construct, or

(b) site productivity is low, with expected long production cycle, or

(c) tree size is uniform, or

(d) discount rate is high.

The case for thinning is emphatic if delay entails loss of increment, or use of growing space by poor-quality trees.

Unless the smallest trees use growing space as efficiently as larger ones, they are not valuable recipients of increment. These, therefore, along with larger trees of poor form, should provide first thinnings, which should be heavy. Suppressed trees can be left unless removal is needed for hygiene or operational convenience.

3 By second thinning it may be unclear whether trees for retention should be dominants or vigorous co-dominants. The absence of decisive advantage to any particular thinning type means that systematic thinning can be preferred for its cost advantage, as can cutting for ephemeral markets.

4 As the rotation proceeds, the advantage shifts further towards retaining relatively small trees, particularly for shade-bearing species whose co-dominants respond well to release. Even major reduction of crop increment does not change this conclusion, since it is based on the fact that large trees reach optimal rotation earlier than small ones. Thus the later stages of the rotation are characterized by removal of the largest remaining trees at each thinning. The best pay-off from thinning comes by enhancing increment on trees destined for removal soon. Selective thinning should therefore favour the largest of the trees to be retained – because they are the next thinnings, not because they are the final crop.

5 Such a regime has no tidy and clearly defined rotation end. (It may suggest images of a wasteland from which sporadic spindly sub-dominants mournfully protrude, though in a genetically uniform shade-bearing crop this need not be the result.) As successive cohorts of large trees approach individual maturity and are felled, the question may be neither whether there are still trees earning an acceptable indicating percent, nor whether the site is being fully utilized, but whether there is anything better to replace the crop. Under moderate discount rates the profitability of successor crops is only a weak argument for ending the current rotation.

Where soil and climate favour fast growth to valuable sizes, discounting has less effect on the value of final crop trees, and early, heavy thinning regimes designed to promote their increment are logical. The greater value of successor crops also militates against allowing small, poorly formed trees to occupy growing space, after the large ones have been felled. Much the same arguments as outlined above, therefore, lead (in different circumstances) to the high-intensity regimes followed in the southern temperate zone (Fenton and Sutton, 1968).

Economics and tradition

In traditional silviculture, many of the above suggestions are inconceivable. Nevertheless, the picture is instructive, if only in showing the pervasive and unexpected results of ruthlessly applying discounting to silviculture. Although the model is simplified, an analytical approach to thinning economics highlights possibilities about which the experimental approach supplies no information.

Silviculturists will be relieved to know that low discount rates in the models described confirm traditional practice: early, frequent and moderate low thinning, regardless of price–size relationships, crop productivity or high roading costs.

16 Crop Improvement in Managed Stands

Crop improvement is straightforward investment: resources are devoted to operations which increase volume, quality or earliness of crop yield. While the list of such operations is endless, the same principles always apply. They will be illustrated by two treatments of the crop – pruning and fertilizing – one treatment of the site – irrigation – and one investment in future crops – research and development.

Grants and tax concessions to promote forest investment may alleviate crop improvement expenditures, while taxation may reduce revenues. Grants given for a particular operation simply affect whether or not it is worthwhile. Grants proportional to costs, or tax rebates on expenditure, also affect the optimal intensity of operations such as fertilizing. The effect varies from country to country and time to time, and no attempt is made here to cover specific cases.

Pruning

When timber is used structurally or decoratively, large knots, particularly dead ones, are a serious defect. Pruning and close tree spacing are alternative strategies to reduce knottiness. Economically, the advantages of pruning over close spacing are:

(a) time interval between investment and improved revenue is reduced, both because wider spacing (with faster individual tree growth) can be used, and because pruning is done later in the rotation;

(b) the treatment is applied only to selected stems, when final crop trees can be identified;

(c) there is more flexibility in timing for pruning than for planting – pruning can use surplus labour at slack times, the financial cost being the difference between plain time and piecework rates.

(d) the operation is under finer control of the forester.

However, not all the quality benefits of narrow spacing are achieved. Pruning only gives a worthwhile premium to trees suitable for higher-quality use – veneers and constructional/decorative grade saw-timber. In practice uncertainty exists about future markets and probable growth pattern of trees. Thus, while the best trees in a crop may be almost certain to obtain a clearwood premium, and the worst certain not to, intermediate trees may or may not attain the premium.

Incremental cost and revenue per tree pruned are illustrated in figure 16.1a. The first trees pruned have large size and good form. As the numbers pruned increase, cost per tree declines slowly as lesser trees, with smaller branches, are drawn into the operation. Mean expected incremental revenue declines more rapidly than incremental cost: the premium applies to a smaller volume per tree, and there is diminishing probability of the premium being attained at all. Consider a premium for clear timber of £7 per cubic metre. If the largest trees in the crop are likely to attain a bottom log volume of 0.8 m³, with an estimated 90% probability of achieving the premium, the mean expected incremental revenue from pruning each such tree is

$$£7 \times 0.8 \times 0.90 = £5.04$$

For trees expected to produce a log of 0.35 m³ with an estimated 40% probability of achieving the premium, mean expected incremental revenue is only

$$£7 \times 0.35 \times 0.40 = £0.98$$

The exact profile of incremental revenue (figure 16.1a) depends not only on the relationship between expected size and probability of achieving the premium, but on the distribution of tree sizes. However, the result is general: the optimal number to prune per hectare is at the point where incremental revenue equals incremental cost.

Also shown is incremental revenue discounted over an illustrative 35–year interval between pruning and final felling, at 5% and 10%. Although this period is shorter than the rotation, discounting dramatically reduces incremental revenues, by factors of 5.52 and 28.10 respectively. The consequence is a major reduction in the number of trees worth pruning at 5%, while no pruning at all can be justified at 10%. This result is representative of the effect of discounting on crop improvement: progressive reduction in intensity as discount rate rises, culminating in total abandonment of operations.

A different approach to the same problem is to calculate compound

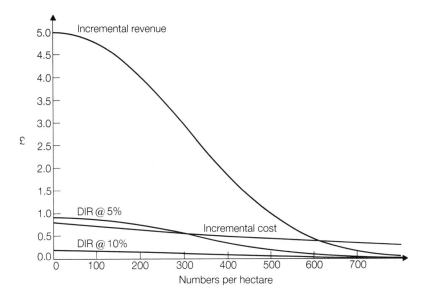

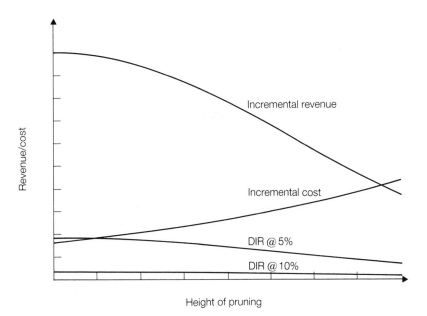

Figure 16.1 Pruning economics:
(a) numbers of trees
(b) height of pruning
DIR means discounted incremental revenue

interest on pruning cost, and hence what premium, or what probability of achieving it, would be needed to cover the cost.

The decision on how high to prune (figure 16.1b) has the same outcome. The higher pruning goes, the less likely is it that that length of stem will enter a premium market and the smaller the volume per metre run of stem. However, incremental cost of pruning increases up the tree, as higher climbing or less manageable pruning tools become necessary. Incremental revenue may be discontinuous if sawlogs are grown for a particular dimension market, say 6-m lengths. The optimum occurs then at one of a few discrete lengths.

Discounting criteria are one reason for abandoning or severely curtailing pruning in some countries. Another is the increasing cost of labour in relation to timber values, since attempts to mechanize pruning have not been very successful. The reduced number of trees pruned per hectare brings its own problems, since fixed costs of selecting and finding marked trees then inflate average cost, jeopardizing the remaining operations.

Pruning and premium price

Once pruning becomes unusual, the premium itself may wither. When high-quality stems are rarely available, the costs of searching a crop for pruned trees, differentiating a market strategy and setting up a production run for a quality product are not justified by the small volume of output to which a premium applies. Mechanization of wood processing with high throughput of uniform (often mediocre quality) material has exacerbated this factor. The situation then facing timber growers is known as 'the prisoner's dilemma': few foresters grow high-quality trees, because buyers offer no premium; buyers offer no premium, because insufficient volume is available to make the product profitable. It is in nobody's interest to make the first move, in everyone's to wait for someone else to do so, and nothing changes. Resolving this situation needs concerted action by some body representing the mutual interests of growers and buyers.

This lamentable situation contrasts with the high-intensity pruning regime followed for Monterey pine in New Zealand (Fenton and Sutton, 1968). Early selective thinning, often to waste, is undertaken in widely spaced rows, and the remaining trees are pruned heavily. Pruning is repeated frequently, and on a good site a clear 6–m sawlog is achieved in 25–30 years. This regime has been compiled with an economic return in mind. Favourable growing conditions allow a short rotation. This advantage is enhanced by giving maximum light to final crop trees, the tendency to coarse branching being circumvented by the uncompromising pruning regime. A target (export) market has been identified and developed, so that a premium is paid for a quality product available in bulk. The predominance

Plate IV Pruning in New Zealand: drastic, but economic
(Photo: Terry Thomas)

of this product avoids the costs of search and selection for target trees and allows high systematization of pruning. While pruning costs are high, the short rotation reduces the effect of discounting on incremental revenue. High revenue is assured by the marketing programme, which in turn is made economic by the scale of production. The IRR on silvicultural investment is up to 12%.

A moral might be drawn: while focusing on the detail of incremental cost and revenue in decision-making, one should not forget that sometimes the greatest profits are achieved by a bold step which combines big changes in several related variables. Not every country has spare land of the productivity that allows such a regime to be so profitable, but parallel development of silviculture and marketing is always worth considering.

Low pruning

The pruning of low branches, while a first step towards knot-free timber, is an operation with separate objectives, primarily to improve access to the crop. It aids inspection so that crop growth may be assessed and treatment determined. In young crops it is needed before selective thinning, to permit both marking, and access by the harvesting gang. There is a bonus in reduced time in removing side-branches after trees have been felled.

Other benefits include improving the appearance of the stand and permitting prospective purchasers of standing timber to assess timber volume and quality more accurately. These effects may attract improved bids for purchase of the forest or the parcel of timber respectively.

The economic essence of low pruning is that it involves immediate costs in a labour-intensive operation (which does, however, represent a very flexible use of surplus labour) in order to reduce later costs, improve later revenues or perhaps to permit future operations that would otherwise be infeasible. The higher the discount rate, the less likely is low pruning to be worthwhile. The operation is most easily justified where growth is fast, or where other economic factors favour selective thinning.

Once low pruning is discontinued, early selective thinning is often ruled out too, and sometimes a non-thin regime ensues. Economic decisions on low pruning and on thinning method should be taken jointly. As with selective thinning, compromise regimes, where every other lane between tree rows is debranched, may offer the best of both worlds, or fall between two stools: yet another case which can be resolved only by work-study and price data.

The effects of crop fertilization

Forests often grow on infertile sites whither they have been confined or banished by competition from agriculture. Trees have low requirements of mineral nutrients by comparison with agricultural crops of equal productivity, but their growth is often improved by fertilizing. On some sites it may be essential for successful establishment.

Like thinning, fertilizing regimes include many interacting variables: method; intensity; timing; choice of target crop. Like thinning, it affects subtle and contentious qualitative as well as obvious quantitative factors – many of which are common to the two operations. Like thinning, it has complex interactions with rotation.

Fertilizing accelerates *crop growth* (cf. thinning, which accelerates *individual* tree growth). Faster growth may be encashed as greater volume yield on a given rotation, or as earlier yield of the same volume, or as a mixture. The factors determining the effect of fertilizing on optimal rotation bear point-by-point comparison with those for thinning.

1 Increasing the growth rate by fertilizing in mid-rotation, like releasing from check, increases indicating percent and prolongs the rotation. However, regular fertilizing also increases standing volume, so the overall effect is neutral to indicating percent.

2 Earlier culmination of mean annual increment for a more productive crop shortens rotation.

3 Past fertilizing increases size and therefore price per cubic metre of the current crop; the price–size gradient would normally be reduced; together these factors lower the percentage rate of price increase with volume. However, faster individual tree growth accelerates movement up the price–size curve. The net effect probably shortens rotations for crops fertilized regularly, but prolongs it if fertilization begins late in the rotation.

4 Unlike thinning, which normally reduces the investment represented by crop standing value, fertilizing normally increases it, so that greater value increment is required to maintain indicating percent.

5 To the extent that fertilizing increases NPV or IRR, it advances the time when it is profitable to replace the current crop by successors.

6 Unlike thinning, fertilizing markedly increases height growth. If wind stability is a problem, the crop reaches a vulnerable height earlier, the greater the intensity of fertilizing.

Some arguments relating to thinning and rotation length have counterparts in fertilizing. But factor 4, which crucially swings the balance towards prolonged rotation for thinned stands, is rather equivocal for fertilization. Factor 1 prolongs rotations only for late fertilizing, while factor 6, where applicable, probably shortens it more for fertilizing than for thinning. Thus regularly fertilized crops probably have shorter rotations, as contrasted with regularly thinned crops, or crops fertilized late in life, whose rotations are normally longer.

Fertilizing in itself accelerates both height and diameter growth, so need not change geometry and taper of trees. However, fast crop growth, like wide spacing, gives wide growth rings, with possible effects on density, strength and dimensional stability. The importance of these depends on markets. If the crop is wide-spaced, unselectively and heavily thinned, and unpruned, the end use will probably be low-value anyway: no further price penalty may apply to weak and light timber. If this is the general silviculture of the region, then the absence of a market premium for prime timber is a further reason to ignore ring width as an economic feature. Fertilizing is more usually associated with mass production silviculture than with growing for quality markets.

Intensity and technique of fertilization

At a given time, for a given fertilizer and crop, the decisions are how much fertilizer to apply, and by what method? Fertilizer shows what both biologists and economists call diminishing returns. A light application, say

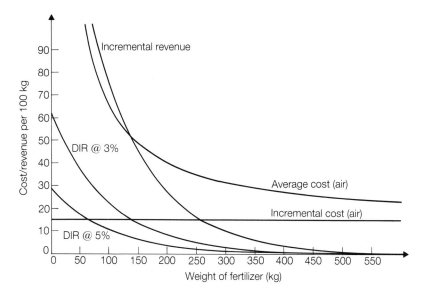

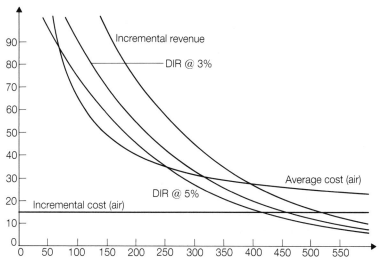

Figure 16.2 Fertilizer economics
(a) (top) young crops
(b) (bottom) near-mature crops
Left-hand graphs are for aerial application, right-hand ones for hand appplication
DIR means discounted incremental revenue

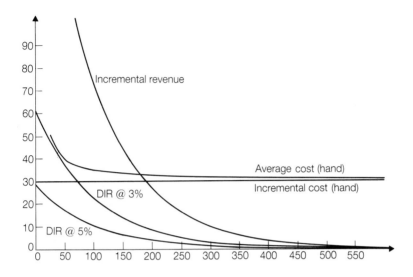

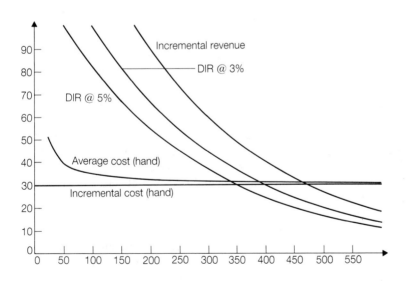

100 kg/ha, may stimulate growth markedly. Application of an extra 100 kg/ha induces less response. With successive additions a point is reached where factors other than shortage of that particular nutrient are limiting, and no more growth can be stimulated: incremental revenue is zero. Incremental revenue may even be negative, if excessive fertilizer is toxic.

Cost of application comprises fixed and variable portions. With hand application most of the cost – the fertilizer itself and carrying it into the crop – is variable with intensity of application. For mechanical application, particularly by air, there is a substantial fixed cost *per hectare* in traversing the site, and a further indivisible cost for the whole operation: setting it up, moving equipment to site and even possibly providing a landing for helicopter or plane. There are scale economies in treating several contiguous sites together, and all the fine detail of which crops to treat, how and when, must be interpreted with this in mind. Once the fixed costs of mechanical application have been undertaken, the incremental costs of increased weight of application tend to be lower than for hand application.

Discounted incremental revenue from increasing application is affected not only by species and site conditions, but the stage of crop growth. At establishment, planted crops are far from utilizing the whole site, so can only use a small application. The delay till harvesting of enhanced increment is long and the effect of discounting commensurately severe. Incremental discounted revenue is thus small, falling off rapidly with increased application. By contrast, older crops utilizing the whole site show much larger incremental discounted revenue from a given growth response, and maintain that response to higher applications. Figures 16.2a and 16.2b illustrate the two situations.

Optimal application is lower to young crops than to old ones. Also, owing to the high fixed costs of aerial application, hand application gives smaller average cost at this low intensity. By contrast, at the greater intensity indicated in figure 16.2b, aerial application is probably cheaper. Intensity and method cannot be independently determined.

As shown by incremental discounted revenue at 3%, the optimal application in given physical circumstances is higher, the lower the discount rate. The instinct that fertilizing shortens rotations and therefore is favoured by a high discount rate is false: incremental revenues of fertilizing are always greater under low than high discount rates.

The biologically ideal frequency of fertilizing, as of thinning, is continuous, maintaining nutrient status at a permanently optimal level against the effects of leaching and tree uptake. As with thinning, however, the substantial fixed costs of the operation militate against repeating it often; a compromise is to use a slow-release fertilizer. A form of fertilizer which releases nutrients to the crop over the whole rotation would not, however, be economic, since none of the cost could be discounted.

Priorities for fertilizer application

For tree physiologists, fertilizer should be applied to crops whose need, as indexed by poor growth, is greatest. Economists have a different view. Firstly, a fast-growing crop often occupies a site where soil or climate or both are favourable (Davies, 1980). Such a crop is more likely to be limited by nutrient status than one which is slow-growing because of water-logging or low temperature. Thus a greater increase in yield may be achieved by applying fertilizer to a crop which is *already* fast-growing. Secondly, the optimal rotation for a fast-growing crop is shorter, the revenue expected earlier, and the effect of discounting reduced. Moreover, a greater proportion of increased volume is on trees with high value per cubic metre of increment. The overall effect is demonstrated in figure 16.3 by discounted revenue figures for several different yield (productivity) classes of Sitka spruce, compiled from Forestry Commission (1983).

These illustrate the shorter optimal rotation of higher yield class (or more intensively fertilized) crops. They also show that the difference in maximum PVR between yield classes 16 and 20 (£586) is greater than that between yield classes 6 and 12 (£537). Boosting the slow-growing crop by 6 m³/ha/year increases profitability less than boosting the fast-growing one by 4 m³/ha/year. The value of fertilizing a fast-growing crop is greater, even if its response is poorer. In the words of St Matthew's Gospel, 'to them that have, it shall be given'.

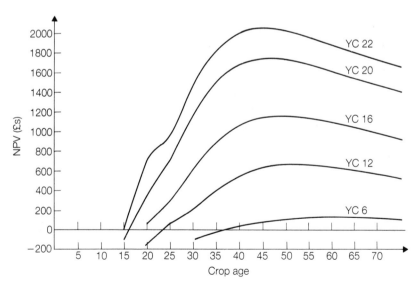

Figure 16.3 Effect on NPV of enhancing productivity
YC is a measure of productivity

It may further be concluded that with a limited amount of fertilizer, or a limited budget, crops nearing full rotation age should be favoured, rather than those for which the pay-off lies perhaps 30 or 40 years ahead (Sar and Crane, 1984). But late fertilizing, by advancing the clearfelling date and the size of final-crop tree, itself improves the NPV of early fertilizing.

Crop improvement and the allowable cut effect

Fertilization or other crop improvements increase expected future yield. If a sustained yield constraint exists in a mixed-aged forest, this means that mature stands formerly scheduled for future felling can be felled immediately, their supply being replaced by the fertilized crop. Thus it appears that fertilization can have an immediate pay-off, with very high IRR and NPV.

This so-called allowable cut effect has been the subject of much controversy (Schweitzer, Sassaman and Schallau, 1972; Teeguarden, 1973). It is a valid argument, given the constraint and the existence of a mature crop. However, the constraint implies that

$$R_T/(1 + r)^T > R_0 \qquad (16.1)$$

where R_T is the revenue obtainable by selling the 'reserved volume' after T years

R_0 is the revenue obtainable by selling it now.

If this condition did not hold, the constraint would be a 'bad thing' for profitability.

If fertilizing has positive NPV under the allowable cut effect, then

$$R_0 > C_0 \qquad (16.2)$$

where C_0 is the cost of fertilizing.

Combining (16.1) and (16.2) gives

$$R_T/(1 + r)^T > C_0$$

which is to say that fertilizing is profitable without invoking the allowable cut effect.

Site amendment

Drainage and other site improvements are undertaken, not just for the current crop, but for its successors, so benefits in perpetuity must be included. As shown in table 16.1, an irrigation system built in mid-rotation doubles growth rate of a semi-mature crop and its successors, halving the time scale of future yields. Cash flows are in rupees, the discount rate is 8%, and the decision is made just after first thinning.

Table 16.1 Benefits of site amelioration

		NO IRRIGATION		WITH IRRIGATION	
Operation	Cash flow	Years ahead	PV	Years ahead	PV
Thinning 2	20 000	8	10 805	4	14 701
Felling	80 000	16	23 351	8	43 222
Replanting	−9 000	16	−2 627	8	−4 862
Thinning 1	10 000	32	852	16	2 919
NPV			32 381		55 980

This sequence of cash flows is repeated in perpetuity, every 32 years for the unirrigated crop and every 16 years for the irrigated one. The multiplier for periodic cash flows (equation (7.5)) can be applied, giving NPV$_\infty$s of Rs35 397 and Rs79 056. The difference, Rs43 659, is the maximum worth spending per hectare on construction and maintenance of the irrigation system.

The indefinite sequence of increased revenues resulting from a single expenditure beguiles many foresters into believing that such an investment must eventually be profitable. Clearly, however, even if beneficial effects are maintained in perpetuity, the incremental PVR from all crops is a finite sum, not much larger than that of a single cycle with discount rates above 10%.

Similarly, treatments of the current crop which permanently impair site productivity for successor crops incur no serious loss of discounted revenues (Routledge, 1987). Ruthless exploitation of the site's every utilizable ion is often entirely justified under discounting criteria. But, even among forestry organizations which manage the *crop* to such criteria, there is a reluctance to adopt such indications for the *site*: it is part of foresters' instinct for sustainability.

No judgement is now offered as to whether the economists or the foresters are right. Chapter 29 re-examines the question of discounting, within a broad context of natural resource management.

Investment in research and development

Of all investments, research on improving forest crops is the longest in maturing, especially that in tree breeding. There is not only the time-lapse of the current rotation (and longer delay for succeeding ones) but also the delay in completing basic research, developing results on a commercial scale, and, in the case of tree breeding, carrying the crop to seed production or bulking up vegetative propagules.

Normal discounting criteria show such research projects in unfavourable light. Grayson (1987) contrasts an estimated IRR of 9% from a set of forestry research projects with 30–70% from agricultural research. The low rate of commercial return means much of this research is undertaken in the public sector, by universities or the state forest service. In the latter case their unprofitability may be concealed by classifying them as 'overheads', a stratagem meeting the requirements of accountants, but not satisfying economists. Economists ask, not 'can current profits of this organization cover the cost of research?', but 'do mean expected increases in future revenue resulting from this research exceed its cost?'.

Better returns are available in research with relatively rapid pay-off. For example Talbert et al. (1985) report potential post-tax IRR of 17–19% from seed improvement (for a short-rotation crop), while Westgate (1986) considered a containerized seedling project earned at least 37% (through early cost-saving).

The pay-off from *prospective* research is harder to estimate. Economic uncertainty exists, not only about the magnitude of gains, but about the time-lapse before they are realized.

17   Crop Protection

While crop improvement aims to increase revenue above the baseline provided by non-intervention, crop protection aims to avoid revenue being reduced *below* this baseline by damaging agents, physical, biotic or human. Given that avoiding loss of revenue is equivalent to gaining revenue, evaluation of crop protection does not differ from that of crop improvement. However, protection characteristically deals with probabilistic situations. It is certain neither that protective measures will be completely effective, nor that without protection the crop would be completely destroyed – or even attacked and damaged at all.

The probabilistic nature of forest protection is complicated by the long time period. Farmers apply protective measures for one growing season, perhaps only during the flight period of an insect pest. For foresters the possibility of attack is repeated, sometimes daily, sometimes yearly, usually with changing probability over time as a crop's vulnerability diminishes or increases.

This chapter first considers conceptual aspects of protective strategies, then various possible sequences of attack, then how economic analysis of each may most readily be accomplished.

Protection strategies and their outcomes

Strategies to protect the crop can be classified as initial, recurrent or terminal. An initial strategy is implemented at establishment or initiation of management, and lasts till felling (or even through several rotations). Examples are selecting a species resistant to a particular pathogen, fencing against browsers and making fire-breaks in the crop. A terminal strategy ends the rotation when a threat to the crop, as by storm damage, becomes sufficiently great. Recurrent strategies, like spraying against insect pests, are applied during the life of the crop, and are designed for immediate effect:

there may be a period over which the treatment shows some, but declining, efficacy, whereafter it is re-applied.

Terminal and recurrent protection may be either pre-emptive (felling before the crop reaches a height susceptible to wind; maintaining a high population of insect-eating birds) or responsive (felling when a significant proportion of the crop has blown over; spraying with insecticide if defoliation occurs). Initial strategies are always pre-emptive, though they may be adopted responsively for a replacement crop if a young plantation is wiped out.

The ideal outcome of a protective strategy is survival, intact, of the crop to its desired rotation. The antithesis is complete destruction of merchantable value, or complete failure of a crop to establish. However, most protection decisions have less starkly contrasted outcomes. An unprotected crop may establish partially, giving delayed canopy closure and less scope for selection, but still producing worthwhile volume. A fire which kills the crop may, nonetheless, permit salvage of valuable timber. A defoliating insect attack may retard crop growth in the year of occurrence only, or debilitate the crop for some years, or leave it more vulnerable to subsequent defoliation or to other damaging agents.

On the other hand, protection might only reduce the scale of damage, or even make no difference. The cost of protection is part of the mean expected value of protective strategies, and the worst possible outcome is complete failure despite expensive protection.

Survival through establishment

Many agents – bud weevils, root-rotting fungi, browsers and frost – threaten establishment of young crops. The decisions required are *whether* to protect the crop, and *how* to protect it (where there is a choice of methods). If all methods are equally effective, it should first be decided *how*, then *whether*. If there are differences in effectiveness, it should be decided whether each method is worth applying, then which method – if any – has the greatest mean expected value.

The best method of protection against browsers depends, among other factors, on the scales of the plantation and of management control. For large areas under unified management, control of the browser population may confine damage to an acceptably small proportion of the crop, with sacrifice of some area for population management purposes. The browsers themselves, wild or domesticated, probably represent an economic resource in themselves, and the objectives of the forest enterprise may include exploitation of this value.

In small to moderate-sized plantations, where sufficient population control cannot, for legal or economic reasons, be exercised, choice lies between fencing browsers out of the whole regeneration area, or protecting individual trees. Fencing demonstrates classic scale economies, overall cost increasing as the square root of the area enclosed. Thus individual tree protection only becomes economic for small or very irregular plantings, or for very wide spacings, as in traditional coppice-with-standards silviculture (see figure 17.1). Fencing may, however, be ineffective on too large an area: if small browsers penetrate the fence, they may be difficult to eradicate from a large enclosure.

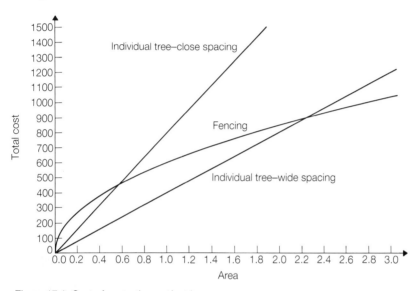

Figure 17.1 Cost of protection against browsers

Cumulative conditional probability and establishment

Local experience may indicate the overall probability of establishment of a given species on a given site in the face of some recurrent climatic problem, such as frost or drought. With a new site or species, however, it may be necessary to use climatic records and compile a probability of survival on the basis of known behaviour of the species elsewhere. This requires use of *cumulative conditional probability*.

It might seem that, if there is a 10% probability of a spring frost severe enough to kill the young crop, then after 10 years death is certain! However, probabilities do not interact like this. Firstly, as the crop gains height and robustness it becomes less susceptible to damage. Secondly, the crop can only be killed in the second year if it has survived the first year. The sequence of possible events is depicted in figure 17.2.

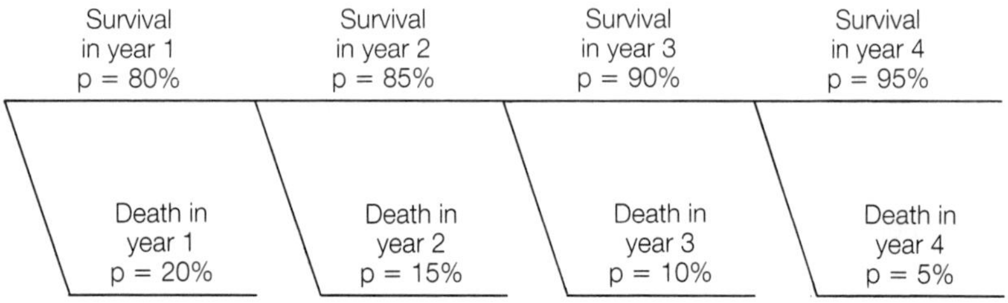

Survival in year 1 p = 80%	Survival in year 2 p = 85%	Survival in year 3 p = 90%	Survival in year 4 p = 95%
Death in year 1 p = 20%	Death in year 2 p = 15%	Death in year 3 p = 10%	Death in year 4 p = 5%

Figure 17.2 Cumulative risk of crop failure

In 80% of cases, the crop survives its first year. *Out of those 80% of cases*, the crop is killed in its second year in 15%: 15% of 80% = 12%. A total of 20% + 12% = 32% of cases are killed in the first two years. Of the remaining 68% of cases, 10% (= 6.8%) are killed in the third year. On the same basis, 3.06% are killed in the fourth year. And 95% × 90% × 85% × 80% = 58.14% of all cases successfully establish. The mean expected value of planting the crop is the probability of survival multiplied by the value of the outcome, a discounted revenue of £1000 per hectare, giving mean expected value of £581, less the £400 per hectare establishment cost = £181.

On the same site, a frost-hardy provenance might have half the probability of death in each of the four establishment years, a £400 planting cost and a discounted revenue, conditional on survival, of £800 per hectare. The cumulative conditional probability of survival is 77.11%. The net mean expected value of this strategy is £217, higher than that of the susceptible provenance.

The analysis is, however, incomplete. Suppose a crop is killed: what follows? The site might be abandoned for forestry, but this would be irrational, given that the mean expected NPV of replanting is positive. Moreover, if the second planting fails, foresters can hope to be lucky the third time; or a fourth or fifth time. After successful completion of a rotation, the cycle repeats in perpetuity.

The mean expected NPV of planting replacement or successor crops, when it occurs, equals that of planting in the first place. But this value must be discounted for some period, depending on when the crop is killed. M is the mean expected NPV of planting and (where necessary) replanting, for a perpetual series of rotations, and n is the number of years of frost risk.

$$M = \begin{bmatrix} \text{probability} \\ \text{of success} \end{bmatrix} \times \left(\begin{bmatrix} \text{PVR of} \\ \text{success} \end{bmatrix} + \begin{bmatrix} \text{discounted NPV}_\infty \\ \text{of successor crops} \end{bmatrix} \right) - \begin{bmatrix} \text{establishment} \\ \text{cost} \end{bmatrix}$$

$$+ \sum_{t=1}^{t=n} \begin{bmatrix} \text{probability} \\ \text{of failure} \\ \text{in year } t \end{bmatrix} \times \begin{bmatrix} \text{NPV}_\infty \text{ of} \\ \text{replacement} \\ \text{crops} \end{bmatrix} \times \begin{bmatrix} \text{discount} \\ \text{factor for} \\ t \text{ years} \end{bmatrix} \qquad (17.1)$$

$$= 0.5814 \times \left(1000 + \frac{M}{1.05^{50}}\right) - 400 + \frac{0.2 \times M}{1.05} + \frac{0.12 \times M}{1.05^2} + \frac{0.068 \times M}{1.05^3}$$

$$+ \frac{0.0306 \times M}{1.05^4}$$

Rearranging, $(1-0.4339) \times M = 181.4$

$\therefore M = £320$

By the same process, mean expected NPV of planting the frost-tolerant provenance is £300: provenance choice is reversed.

Under non-discounting criteria, full site utilization is important, and the delay caused by establishment failure may be significant. Mean delay of establishment, $\bar{D}$ is

$$\sum_{t=1}^{t=n} \begin{bmatrix} \text{probability} \\ \text{of failure} \\ \text{after } t \text{ years} \end{bmatrix} \times \left(\begin{bmatrix} \text{immediate} \\ \text{delay} \end{bmatrix} + \begin{bmatrix} \text{mean delay} \\ \text{for replanted} \\ \text{crop} \end{bmatrix} \right) \qquad (17.2)$$

For the frost-sensitive provenance this gives

$$\bar{D} = 0.2 \times (1 + \bar{D}) + 0.12 \times (2 + \bar{D}) + 0.068 \times (3 + \bar{D}) + 0.0306 \times (4 + \bar{D})$$

$$\therefore \bar{D} \times (1-(0.2 + 0.12 + 0.068 + 0.0306)) = 0.2 + 0.24 + 0.204 + 0.1224$$
$$= 0.7664$$

$$\therefore \bar{D} = 1.32$$

For the frost-tolerant provenance $\bar{D} = 0.57$

In table 17.1 mean expected establishment cost has been calculated by a version of equation (17.1) which omits discounting and successor crops. While risk reduces net revenue for the frost-sensitive provenance by 3.8%, forest rent is reduced by 6.3% because of delayed establishment. Nonetheless, the greater productivity of the frost-sensitive provenance makes it unequivocally superior under the forest rent criterion.

Such indirect effects of crop failure are, unfortunately, a regular feature of crop protection decisions. But these decisions are very suitable for computer models, and facilities to aid the forest manager are becoming more widely available.

Table 17.1 Choice of crop using forest rent

	FROST-SENSITIVE		FROST-TOLERANT	
Item	Risk-free	Risky	Risk-free	Risky
Establishment	£400	£688	£400	£519
Revenue	£8000	£8000	£6400	£6400
Net revenue	£7600	£7312	£6000	£5881
Rotation	50	51.32	50	50.57
Forest rent	£152	£142.48	£120	£116

When to stop protecting?

Removing annual weeds is a recurrent strategy. The question is not *whether* it should be done but *until when* it should be done.

Recurrent strategies have numerous theoretical permutations: for example, if weeding is unnecessary after the sixth year, it is still feasible to weed or not weed in each of six years, giving 2^6 = 64 possible weeding strategies. It is, fortunately, easy to reduce these strategies. The probability of a planted crop surviving its first year without weeding is very small on fertile sites. Thereafter the probability of crop loss declines dramatically. Wherever such decline occurs, sensible strategies entail weeding for a certain period, then stopping.

The correct approach is to work backwards from year 6, using equations like (17.1). Table 17.2 shows the relevant data for a crop with planting cost Rs4000 and PVR at 10% of Rs11 000 on a 25–year rotation. Replanting would be done in the year following failure or harvest.

Table 17.2 When to stop weeding?

Year	Probability of loss[a]	Probability of survival[b]	Weed cost	Discounted weed cost	Summed cost[c]	M[d]
6	0	1.0	150	85	5258	6268
5	0.01	0.99	200	124	5173	6274
4	0.04	0.950	250	171	5049	6073
3	0.2	0.760	300	225	4878	—
2	0.65	0.266	350	289	4653	—
1	0.98	0.005	400	364	4364	—

Notes: [a] Probability of loss in the following year if the crop survives through that year. [b] Cumulative probability of survival to full rotation if weeding is done up to and including that year. [c] Planting cost, plus discounted weeding costs up to that year. [d] Value of weeding up to and including that year.

As an example, M for weeding through to year 5 is given by

$$M = 0.99 \times 11\,000 + \frac{0.99 \times M}{1.1^{26}} - 5173 + \frac{0.01 \times M}{1.1^6}$$

It is only necessary to calculate as far back as year 4: it will obviously be worth weeding in earlier years.

Strategies are more complex for removing woody perennials, which may relieve competition for more than one year.

Alternatively, weeding decisions may be treated deterministically. Not weeding in years 1 and 2 causes crop failure; not weeding in year 3 leads to sporadic establishment with NPV = Rs3000; not weeding in year 4 results in patchy failure, with NPV = Rs4500; not weeding in year 5 gives an almost-complete crop with NPV = Rs5500; weeding for five or six years gives perfect establishment with NPV = Rs5800.

Such treatment simplifies the decision. But the fundamental question is: what changes as a result of not weeding? Is there a probability of complete failure, or certainty of a less successful crop? The answer lies in the dynamics of plant growth: it is the job of silviculturists to answer it. Economists merely devise the correct analytical method for each circumstance.

Recurrent protection against growth retarders

Certain insect pests do not normally kill healthy trees, but reduce increment in the year of attack. The effect may be slightly reduced yield, or slightly delayed time of felling. Consider a non-thin crop yielding $10 000 per hectare at 40 years, followed by crops with expected NPV at 5% of $400. If defoliation occurs in any year, current annual increment is halved, and all subsequent operations to that crop are delayed half a year.

The pre-emptive strategy is to spray the crop at a susceptible stage of the insect's life-cycle, at sufficient intensity to prevent the insect population reaching levels which threaten defoliation. The strategy has a deterministic result: known expenditures are made on protection, and the crop gives known revenue at the expected time. The responsive strategy is to spray, at higher intensity, only when defoliation becomes apparent. This strategy has higher financial outlay and forgone discounted revenue, but it is deployed only infrequently.

In any one year the costs of the two strategies can be compared. Let pre-emptive spraying cost $30 per hectare and responsive spraying $100 per hectare, and let the probability of defoliation without pre-emptive spraying be 0.10. At age t the mean expected cost of having to spray, plus delayed discounted revenue and NPV of successor crops, is

$$0.10 \times \frac{\$10\,400}{1.05^{40-t}} \times \left(1 - \frac{1}{1.05^{0.5}}\right) + 0.10 \times \$100 = \frac{\$25.06}{1.05^{40-t}} + \$10$$

As figure 17.3 shows, by age 36 this cost equals the $30 of pre-emptive spraying, which becomes the better strategy for the last four years of the crop's life. Before then the delayed NPV is too distant to outweigh the extra cost of pre-emptive spraying.

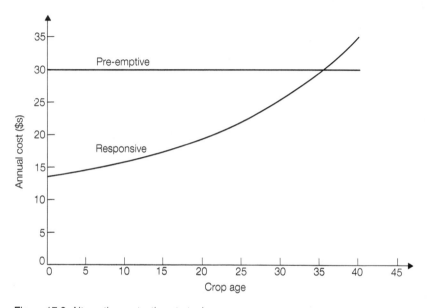

Figure 17.3 Alternative protection strategies

Again, however, there are complications. During each year of the pre-emptive strategy NPV is reduced by an annual $30 (appropriately discounted); with the responsive strategy, expected rotation is prolonged by 0.10 year per remaining year of the strategy. Reduced NPV alters the optimal changeover time between strategies somewhat.

Nor are the effects of spraying confined to the year of application. Even non-persistent insecticides affect insect populations for two or three years, whereafter the probability of defoliation builds up steadily. Populations of predators and parasites may also be reduced, commuting biological control. Decisions about protective treatment in these circumstances require a more complex model than is presented here.

Premature termination of rotation

The incremental method described in chapter 13 can be used in designing terminal strategies under risk.

Damaging events may recur at discrete intervals: for example, fire may be a problem only during a short dry season, or when neighbouring farmers traditionally burn off crop residues or woody vegetation. In Hong Kong fires occur most often at an annual festival when fire-balloons are released.

When risk is spread continuously over time but terminal strategies are reconsidered at discrete intervals, it is usually a good approximation to assume that damage, if it occurs, does so halfway through the interval (Price, 1981c). Consider the felling decision when there is risk of storm damage. If the crop blows down, its net value is reduced through:

(a) increased working costs in disorganized fallen timber;
(b) physical damage to the stem if trees have been snapped;
(c) with widespread damage, depression of market price by the glut of timber;
(d) greater replanting cost.

Plate V Windthrow: reduced revenue and increased cost in prospect
(Photo: Forestry Commission)

The discount rate is 5% and current crop value is £4000. (If thinning is intended, this figure should be the difference in value between thinning the crop and clearfelling it.) Let value rise linearly to £5500 over five years, if the crop remains standing. NPV_∞ of more stable successor crops is £500. The probability of the stand blowing over in the next five years is 30%. Windblown timber has average net value 75% of standing timber. Windblow increases replanting cost by £50. Mean expected PV, if the crop is left, is

$$\frac{£5500 + £500}{1.05^5} \times 0.70 + \frac{£4750 \times 0.75 + £500 - £50}{1.05^{2.5}} \times 0.30 = £4356$$

The current value of the crop and its successors is £4500. Thus the crop should be felled now. This conclusion contrasts with the preferred strategy without risk, when the PVR of felling in five years time is £4701.

Initial strategies and repeated risk

At the end of the rotation, it might seem time to bid adieu to the economics of protection. Not so. Only after decisions have been taken on optimal rotation under risk can initial strategies to reduce risk be evaluated. Extending the wind damage example, consider the value of protective strategies such as draining to encourage deep rooting. Figure 17.4 represents the assessed probabilities of the crop blowing down in each of several five-year periods. If the crop is still standing at the end of each five-year period, thinning revenues are obtained. Structurally identical branching diagrams could be drawn for plantations susceptible to fire, devastating insect attack or any event which would unavoidably end the rotation.

Establishment cost is £300 (£50 extra following windblow). Mean expected PVR for one rotation is compiled in table 17.3. Premature termination of the rotation allows re-establishment of a perpetual series of successors, with $NPV_\infty = M$. Multiplying M by probabilities and discount

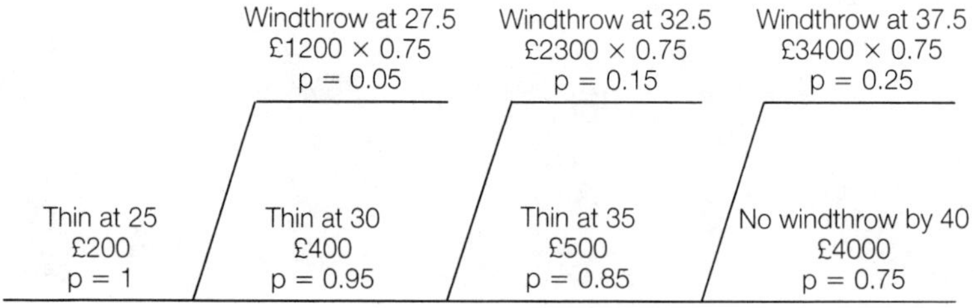

Figure 17.4 Branching diagram for wind-susceptible crop

Table 17.3 Mean expected value under repeated risk

Event	Time	Revenue	Probability	Discount factor	MEV
Thin	25	200	1	0.295	59
Windthrow	27.5	1200 × 0.75	0.05	0.261	12
Thin	30	400	0.95	0.231	88
Windthrow	32.5	2300 × 0.75	0.95 × 0.15	0.205	50
Thin	35	500	0.95 × 0.85	0.181	73
Windthrow	37.5	3400 × 0.75	0.95 × 0.85 × 0.25	0.160	83
Felling	40	4000	0.95 × 0.85 × 0.75	0.142	344
Total					£709

factors for each time period and summing for all time periods produces a modified equation (17.1).

$$M = £709 - £300 + (0.0131 + 0.0292 + 0.0323) \times (M - £50) + 0.0860 \times M$$

$$\therefore M = £482$$

The NPV_∞ of crops assured of standing till age 40 is £594, so it is worth spending at least £(594 − 482) = £112 to ensure stability. As optimal risk-free rotation would be longer and more lucrative, it may be worth spending more.

Recurrent protection in all-aged forests

So far attention has focused on protection of individual stands, the protection regime varying through stages of the stand's life; this is appropriate in intensively managed plantations of even-aged crops. In extensive all-aged forests, however, protection is usually applied, recurrently, on a large scale at a constant level over time. The traditional economic objective of such protection is to minimize cost (of protection) plus loss (by damage). It is, however, more in keeping with other examples in this book to maximize NPV_∞; this also avoids the problem of defining a datum of profit from which loss is measured. (The mathematics used to resolve the problem is somewhat more strenuous than that required elsewhere in this book, and timid readers may proceed from the definition of the problem direct to figure 17.5.)

Take the case of a forest susceptible to fire, which may occur at any time of year, and which may start in, or spread into, stands of any age-class with equal probability. Fires are devastating, leaving no salvageable timber.

The constancy of the risk makes the continuous form of discounting appropriate (equation (7.2b); a parallel formulation expresses the probability of a stand reaching a given age. If any given hectare is burnt on average every P years, the continuous probability of fire, π, is $1/P$. The probability of a crop surviving to rotation age T is $e^{-\pi T}$. The mean expected value, $M1$, of a rotation about to be established is

$$R \times e^{-\pi T} \times e^{-\rho T} - C = R \times e^{-(\pi + \rho)T} - C$$

where R is the revenue at time T
ρ is the continuous discount rate
C is establishment cost.

To this must be added the values of replacement crops (following fire) and successor crops (following harvest) as in equation (17.1). However, unlike in (17.1), replacement does not occur at one of a few discrete times, but at any time during the rotation. The mean expected value of replacements is the sum for all times of

$$M1 \;\times\; \begin{bmatrix} \text{probability of} \\ \text{loss of a crop} \\ \text{at time } t \end{bmatrix} \;\times\; \begin{bmatrix} \text{probability} \\ \text{of survival} \\ \text{till } t \end{bmatrix} \;\times\; \begin{bmatrix} \text{discount} \\ \text{factor for} \\ t \text{ years} \end{bmatrix}$$

The summation can be expressed algebraically as follows (those unfamiliar with calculus must take the results on trust):

$$M1 \times \pi \times \int_{t=0}^{t=T} e^{-\pi t} \times e^{-\rho t}\, dt$$

$$= M1 \times \pi \times \frac{1 - e^{-(\pi + \rho)T}}{(\pi + \rho)}$$

Because most crops in an all-aged forest are already established (artificially or naturally) it is convenient to redefine NPV_∞ as M2, with establishment cost occurring for the first time after harvest or fire loss.

$$M2 = \begin{bmatrix} \text{discounted MEV of this} \\ \text{crop plus successors} \end{bmatrix} + \begin{bmatrix} \text{discounted MEV} \\ \text{of replacements} \end{bmatrix}$$

$$= (R + M2 - C) \times e^{-(\pi + \rho)T} + (M2 - C) \times \pi \times \frac{1 - e^{-(\pi + \rho)T}}{(\pi + \rho)}$$

As in previous examples, this formula can be solved for $M2$ by rearrangement.

Now take an all-aged forest. The discounted mean expected value of replacements (the second part of the expression above) is unaffected by the age of the current crop. The value of the current crop of age t and its successors, however, is greater for crops nearing full rotation: the period of discounting and probability of burning are both less, giving value:

$$(R + M2 - C) \times e^{-(\pi + \rho)(T-t)}$$

Because of periodic fires, age-classes are progressively less frequent, the probability density being

$$\frac{e^{-\pi t}}{\int_{t=0}^{t=T} e^{-\pi t}\, dt} = \frac{\pi \times e^{-\pi t}}{1 - e^{-\pi T}}$$

Multiplying probability by value, integrating over ages 0 to T and adding the value of replacement crops gives mean value per hectare as:

$$(R + M2 - C) \times \pi \; \frac{(e^{\rho T} - 1)}{e^{(\rho + \pi)T} \times (1 - e^{-\pi T})} \; + (M2 - C) \times \pi \times \frac{1 - e^{-(\rho + \pi)T}}{(\rho + \pi)}$$

Reducing the probability of fire increases the cost of protection; there will normally be diminishing returns to protection expenditure, until perfect

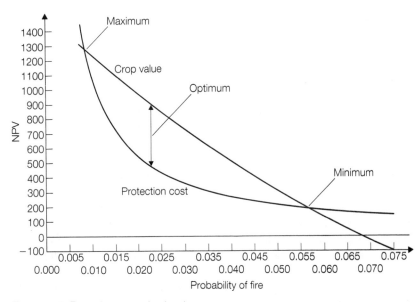

Figure 17.5 Extensive protection levels

protection becomes indefinitely costly. Figure 17.5 shows NPV_∞ gained and protection costs incurred by reduced fire probability. It indicates minimum and maximum levels at which protection is worthwhile, as well as optimal protection.

Repeating the calculations for different rotations provides an alternative way to optimize premature felling. The calculations show that:

(a) longer rotations have a higher optimal level of protection, as fire destroys a greater value;

(b) greater levels of risk produce shorter optimal rotations.

Complications arise when there are thinning revenues; when probability of burning varies with age; and when burnt timber has salvage value. Provided a mathematical expression of these factors is available, however, they can be incorporated in equations of similar structure to those above.

Variability of outcomes

In all the above examples, outcomes are weighted simply by probabilities to obtain mean expected value. Individual forest owners are interested also in how big the likely variation in actual outcomes is. Simulation models, in which mishaps to crops and their successors occur randomly, give such information (Buongiorno and Gilless, 1987).

Interacting risks

Although account has been taken of a particular risk repeated over time, the effect of one damaging agent on the optimal protective strategy against another agent has not been considered. The problems cannot be tackled separately: one damaging agent reduces the mean expected value of the crop, and this reduced mean expected value is the outcome of protecting successfully against every other damaging agent. One agent may also render the crop more susceptible to another.

Often one agent presents the key protection problem, acting in dramatic and discrete blows, against which heroic protective measures may prevail. All other agents act by scattered, sporadic, but economically irremediable attrition, which is lumped into a general figure for loss of potential productivity – say 10% less revenue than could be expected for a crop reaching full rotation undamaged. Indeed, the 'normal' increment of plantations, and particularly natural forests, is what is left after many mildly damaging agents have taken their 'cut'.

Specific strategies may be designed against two or more major damaging agents. Simultaneous evaluation of protection is obstructed by the numerous combinations of strategies and states of nature. An iterative approach is more practical, the value of successfully protecting against the second agent depending on the crop's value under attack by the first. On this basis, mean expected values of strategies against the second are evaluated. The optimal strategy yields the mean expected value fed into an evaluation of protection against the first, the process being repeated until a stable combined strategy has been derived. A computer package, or at least a structured format, is desirable in concluding these tedious and error-prone calculations correctly.

When market and political risks of forestry are added to those of climate, insects, fungi and malign human intervention, the profitability of forestry may appear in serious jeopardy. Indeed, the ultimate response to overwhelming odds is to abandon silviculture altogether. Foresters may regard this last resort as an admission of incompetence or lack of resolve: economists see it simply as rational and profit-maximizing decision-making. Zero profits may be preferable to either an unprotected crop which suffers heavy losses, or a crop which reaches fruitful maturity only by excessive outlay on protection.

18 Choice among Silvicultural Regimes

Individual components of a silvicultural regime have now been considered: initial spacing, protection and tending of the growing crop and removal of timber over the rotation. These components interact, so that one dimension of a regime cannot be optimized without reference to the others. When one dimension (for example, rotation length) has been optimized for given values of the other dimensions, then each other dimension (initial espacement, thinning, protective treatment, fertilizing) must be reassessed. The new value taken by each factor becomes part of the changed context of each other one. Thus compilation of an economically optimal regime is a long and tedious process, which cannot realistically be undertaken experimentally. Economists must continually resort to assumptions about stand growth if a new regime is to be designed. The task is complicated by spatial and temporal price variation, which affects not just profitability of the enterprise, but the nature of the profit-maximizing regime: a greater distance to markets, for example, reduces optimal tree numbers, application of fertilizer and duration of protective expenditures.

The silvicultural variables discussed have been more or less continuous ones. The decision has been how far to move along a scale: which tree size to favour in thinning, when to make a pre-emptive clearfelling and so on. This chapter turns to discrete choices between different regimes, each optimized in its own terms. These constitute the Great Debates of silviculture, which rouse passions and prompt dogmatic statements about physical effects. Economists are not qualified as such to evaluate these statements, but merely to point out the economic consequences if they are true.

Even-aged versus uneven-aged forestry

Many advantages claimed for uneven-aged stands are environmental (better wildlife habitat, more attractive landscape, greater recreation potential). Where these claims are valid (and a contrary view can sometimes be defended), the beneficial effects may be evaluated as in chapters 24–26. The following cash advantages have been cited:

(a) increased yield in a given period, due to better site utilization (there being no period when the site is sparsely occupied, by small trees);

(b) better timber due to more even ring width and smaller proportion of weak juvenile wood;

(c) reduced susceptibility to storms through mutual support of many sizes of tree;

(d) improvement of site by reduced soil insolation;

(e) more interesting work conditions, giving higher output by management and workers.

Cash disadvantages are:

(f) difficult, small-scale working (particularly harvesting), with higher unit costs;

(g) more *dispersed* working, increasing transportation costs;

(h) time taken to create an uneven-aged system.

To create uneven-aged structure by afforestation entails an opportunity cost, in that planting of some land is delayed for a period up to the whole rotation. Equally, conversion of an even-aged stand entails felling some trees before optimal rotation and leaving others to become financially over-mature. It is also costly to convert uneven-aged forests to even-aged (Haight, 1987), as it entails keeping the oldest age-class far beyond its optimal rotation, or clearing younger trees before theirs, or both.

The opportunity costs can be abated by spreading conversion over several rotations, so that no tree is ever felled *much* too early or late. However, the advantages of conversion are then very long delayed.

Since the benefits of conversion are possibly marginal and certainly long-term, since costs are unavoidably immediate, any substantial discount rate makes maintaining the *status quo* the profit-maximizing course of action. One potential exception exists: if it is more profitable to remove the largest trees in mid-rotation thinnings, the ensuing gaps can be regenerated immediately; as successive age-classes reach their individual optimal size they too are felled and an uneven-aged successor crop automatically arises in their stead. Given that the remaining trees in general have low vigour, natural regeneration will not provide a desirable successor. Which leads to the next Great Debate.

Natural versus artificial regeneration

The effects of natural rather than artificial regeneration are:

(a) low initial cost (unless fanatical efforts are made to prepare a seed-bed);

(b) possible higher tending costs, as regeneration rarely has ideal density or systematic spacing;

(c) probable delay in establishment, because regeneration comes either too slowly, or too densely – a period of intense competition ensuing during which most increment accrues on stems that will not be harvested;

(d) reduced final revenue, both because genetic quality is less controlled than with artificial planting, and because the desired species gives incomplete site cover;

(e) opportunity costs of retaining seed trees past optimal rotation.

Given the association of natural regeneration with traditional silviculture, and of artificial planting with modern technologies, the effect of discounting is surprising. The greater importance of complete site utilization and high-quality timber under low discount rates justifies the heavier investment of artificial regeneration, where these long-term benefits are expected. Loss of useful production during regeneration also has greater weight. By contrast, high discount rates give less weight to long-term revenue, and the short-term cost-saving of natural regeneration dominates; high labour and plant costs relative to timber prices have the same effect. Delayed establishment is not so important under high discount rates: the effect of delay falls largely on clearfelling revenues, which have less relative significance at high rates.

These generalizations assume that rational decisions are taken about natural regeneration, which could cost more in ground preparation, tending and opportunity cost than the entire artificial planting process (Sunda and Lowry, 1975). Near the climatic limits of species, where seed years are unpredictable, the evaluation becomes probabilistic. Table 18.1 shows the PVR for a veneer oak crop plus NPV_∞ for a perpetual series of planted successors. Immediate costless establishment would give NPV_∞ £7500 at a 2% discount rate. Artificial establishment costing £1500 per hectare has NPV_∞ £6000. Total NPV for natural regeneration is given by summing costs (£400, plus £80 per year) during the delay, and subtracting them from PVR. Opportunity cost of retaining seed trees is ignored.

NPV of the naturally regenerated crop falls quickly below that of the artificial one. The critical probability of a seed year, which must be exceeded to justify natural regeneration, is

$$p = \frac{(1 + r) \times C + r \times (I + V - A)}{(1 + r) \times V - (I + V - A)} = 0.1805 \text{ in this case} \qquad (18.1)$$

where C is annual cost of maintaining the seed-bed
       I is initial cost of natural regeneration
       V is PVR + NPV$_\infty$
       A is the cost of artificial regeneration.

Table 18.1 Value of natural regeneration

Delay period (years)	PVR + NPV$_\infty$	Initial cost	Extra discounted cost	ΣNPV
None	7500	480	0	7020
1	7353		78	6795
2	7209		77	6573
3	7067		75	6357
4	6929		74	6144
5	6793		72	5936
6	6660		71	5732

Short-rotation crops

Coppicing is another traditional silvicultural system whose relative performance improves under high discount rates, short rotations and costless regrowth being the keys.

Other means of abbreviating the rotation include bulk energy plantations (whose low product value can be partly offset by highly mechanized harvesting); and early and intensive thinning, sometimes to waste, which produces timber of sawlog size on perhaps half the normal rotation. Such regimes are described by Moore and Wilson (1970), Cannell (1980) and Gogate (1983). The relatively short investment period justifies heavy application of fertilizers, pesticides and other inputs, even though the crop often commands a low unit price.

Growing small ornamental trees (particularly Christmas trees, on which Foster and Cote (1970) report IRRs up to 55%), has a quite opposite philosophy, quality of tree being paramount and timber volume irrelevant.

For highly profitable short-rotation crops, it is important to calculate NPV of a perpetual series of rotations, or to use forest rent rather than profit on a single rotation. Short-rotation crops produce not only *early* return, but also *more frequent* return. These separate attributes need separate treatment.

Discounting allows for earliness: on a prime site, Douglas fir with a 45–year rotation might achieve NPV £2500 at 5%. Norway spruce on an eight-year rotation for Christmas trees might have comparable NPV. Frequency of return is allowed for by using equation (7.5), which gives NPV_∞ £2813 for Douglas fir, but £7736 for Norway spruce.

Coppice management is often complicated by loss of vigour over several cutting cycles. Optimal rotation involves simultaneous determination of length of cycle and number of cycles before replanting (Medema and Lyon, 1985). Low discount rates favour more frequent replanting, to maximize production.

Species choice

A perpetual series of rotations may also affect species choice for conventional markets, when rotation lengths differ substantially and when low discount rates are used. At high discount rates successor rotations only affect species choice when the margin of profit between species is anyway rather small.

The discount rate bears too on choice between quantity and quality. The advantage of high-yielding plantation genera (*Pinus*, *Eucalyptus*, *Gmelina*) is not so much larger yield per rotation, but shorter rotations. They often produce bulk cellulose into relatively well-supplied markets, so command low unit price. Slow-growing species may make up in price per cubic metre what they lack in yield. In table 18.2, intermediate costs and revenues are ignored for simplicity. Cash flows are in rupees. The discount rate is 4%.

Judged by net revenue of one rotation or forest rent, teak is clearly preferable. The NPV of one rotation of teak also greatly exceeds that of eucalypt. Including successor rotations favours eucalypt marginally. Higher discount rates favour eucalypt even more: for example at 6% its NPV_∞ is Rs110 602 while that of teak is Rs58 312.

Table 18.2 Criteria and species choice

Species	Mean increment	Rotation	Price	Revenue	Discounted revenue
Teak	8	50	3000	1 200 000	168 855
Eucalypt	20	12	500	120 000	74 952

	Cost	Net revenue	Forest rent	NPV	NPV_∞
Teak	10 000	1 190 000	23 800	158 855	184 868
Eucalypt	4 000	116 000	9 667	70 952	189 001

Plate VI Black walnut in Illinois, USA: very high revenues but only after 100 years.
(Photo: USDA Forest Service, Forest Products Laboratory)

Market risks may also influence species choice. Species traditionally accepted for established industrial processes offer the safest return. New species, whose silviculture and adaptability to site are little known, are further handicapped by uncertain reception from timber buyers. Even superior-quality timber only commands a premium if it is *perceived* by processing industries as superior, and is available in sufficient quantities to justify investment in research, marketing and the fixed costs of setting up an appropriate production line.

Thus a species of mediocre yield and timber-quality may remain the norm for planting. This does not demonstrate absence of acumen among timber growers or processors. On the contrary, it is entirely rational for each individual to take the safe, well-tried choice, and to leave others to risk financial disaster by experimenting: even if the mean expected income of changing to a new species exceeds that of continuing with the old species, the mean expected *utility* of an experimental strategy would be low for anyone with a substantial proportion of wealth invested in forestry. There are parallels with the 'prisoner's dilemma' encountered in pruning: some corporate response is needed to overcome inertia.

Monocultures, mosaics and mixes

As well as identifying species suited to sites and markets, foresters must decide in what pattern to grow them: as a monoculture throughout a forest; in a mosaic where appropriate species are allocated to different site types; or as intimate mixtures where each stand contains individuals of more than one species. The silvicultural rationale of mixtures is beneficial interaction between trees of different species; of mosaics, beneficial matching of species to site; of monocultures, consistency of treatment.

Monocultures achieve maximum scale economies in marketing and application of a uniform regime. They do not meet requirements for diverse kinds of timber, but there is no need for them to do so: different forests can achieve economies by each specializing in whatever species grows well in representative conditions, and still contribute to regional diversity. There may even be a case for regional specialization, or for some penalties to be accepted in a *national* monoculture, if scale economies in research, technical development and processing are thereby achieved.

Mosaics lose some scale economies by broadening the technical and marketing expertise required within one administrative unit, but provide the same ease of stand management as monocultures. Intimate mixtures, though involving no greater variety of species within administrative units than mosaics, present management problems within the stand throughout the rotation. Different establishment requirements may obstruct mechanized ground preparation and retard planting; differential growth rates may cause premature suppression of one component of the mixture (with alternative dangers of becoming a pure crop, or engaging unreasonable costs and loss of potential revenue in efforts to preserve mixed status). Thinning regimes may differ between species, and the desirability of maintaining mixed character constrains choice of thinnings. Substantial differences in growth pattern may cause one or all component species to be felled otherwise than at optimal rotation. Harvesting and marketing may be rendered more costly by the need to separate products by species as well as size.

There are compensating advantages. Mixtures exploit a site more fully if, for example, the components root in different zones. Species interaction may be beneficial, as when one component is a nitrogen-fixer, or a water-tolerant species whose roots ameliorate the site for a more productive but less tolerant partner. Differences in vigour may be deliberately exploited in self-thinning mixtures: a sacrificial pioneer species is suppressed in a more reliable pattern, at a more predictable date, than is produced by variable vigour within a pure planting of the final crop species.

The rationale of mosaics is quite different: matching the most productive species to each site. There is a strong intuition among silviculturists that each species has an 'ideal' site, and that where such a site exists it is imperative to plant that species. But it is not axiomatic that yield is maximized by variety. For economists, the relevant point is that each site has an 'ideal' (= most profitable) species, and one species may be ideal for every site in a given forest.

Unless severely limited by seedling supplies, the local manager should not be solving a linear programming problem in which the constraints are areas to be planted with various species; the activities, sites with various potential for each species; the objective function, maximization of volume output. This is sometimes the problem at regional level, but the solution may as easily lie in diversity *between* forests as in diversity *within* them.

Risk and planting pattern

Intimate mixtures might be expected to give maximum risk insurance. Transmission of narrow-spectrum pests and diseases is retarded. Strategically-located lines of less combustible species help to limit fires. Ecological diversity – of age as well as species – may moderate insect population explosions by maintaining a better pest–predator balance.

Mixtures also adapt better to damaging events. Consider two species, each susceptible to its own utterly lethal insect pest, which has a 20% probability of attacking during the susceptible pre-commercial phase. Each species costs $1200/ha to establish and has PVR of $2500/ha if it survives to maturity.

A 2-ha monoculture of either species has mean expected revenue

$$= 2 \times \$2500 \times 0.80 = \$4000.$$

A mosaic of both species, planted on two separate hectares, has aggregate mean expected revenue

$$\$2500 \times 0.80 + \$2500 \times 0.80 = \$4000$$

On the other hand, a 2-ha mixed stand has a cumulative probability of total elimination of

$$0.20 \times 0.20 = 0.04$$

The probability of both species surviving is

$$0.80 \times 0.80 = 0.64$$

with mean expected revenue

$$2 \times \$2500 \times 0.64 = \$3200$$

The remaining state of nature (only one species wiped out) has, by subtraction, probability 0.32. The surviving component of an intimate mix would probably utilize the growing space vacated, and the incident would have a self-thinning character. Given that the killed trees have no salable value, and that increment might be more valuable if concentrated onto fewer trees, the attack could actually enhance NPV. If not, the contribution to mean expected revenue is

$$2 \times \$2500 \times 0.32 = \$1600$$

and the overall mean expected revenue, $4800, better than monoculture or mosaic.

In cash terms there is nothing to choose between monoculture and mosaic. In utility terms, however, the mosaic is preferable for risk-averse land-owners: the monoculture has a 20% chance of making a loss, the mosaic only 4%.

A parallel case is that of market risks, though quantification is rather speculative. By the time of first thinning, the distinctive future markets for two very different species (a broadleaf/conifer mixture perhaps) are easier to predict, and thinning can favour whichever species shows the better prospect, or remove the species whose market has collapsed. A mosaic *would* leave part of the crop unable to adapt to the best market. A monoculture *might* leave all the crop in this state. Again, for any risk-averse owner, possible utility gains from planting solely the 'right' species do not balance possible utility losses from choosing the 'wrong' one.

Risk-avoidance is less relevant to large organizations with diverse interests, and certainly does not constitute a case for mosaics within every forest of the national forest service. In the latter case the 'risk' of growing one species per forest lies in the *greater probability* of having to relocate half the region's harvesting operations if one market collapses.

Naturally, high discount rates, high labour costs and low timber prices all discriminate against the long-term advantages of the mixture, and emphasize the early scale economies of monoculture.

Choice of treatment in semi-natural forest

Natural stands are often uneven-aged species mixtures with low pro-ductivity. Silviculture often changes these characteristics, trading zero growing costs and low risk-proneness for low harvesting costs and greater productivity.

Optimal intensity of forestry depends on the profitability criterion chosen, as the following example illustrates. Five treatments are defined in table 18.3 for a forest type covering 1 million hectares. Intermediate management costs and revenues are ignored. Cash flows are in naira per hectare. Treatments III, IV and V will be repeated in perpetuity.

Table 18.4 shows profitability under various criteria. Also shown are values for some *incremental investments*: III→IV means 'undertake treatment IV instead of treatment III'. Values for each criterion are calculated for *increments* of cost and of revenue between III and IV.

Table 18.3 Options for forest treatment

Treatment	Description	Cash flow	Time
I	Build rough road	−50	0
	Light felling for local needs	50	1 − ∞
II	Build heavy-duty road	−500	0
	Log commercial species	750	1, 2, 3
	Light felling for local needs	50	1 − ∞
III	As II plus enrichment planting in gaps	−150	0
	Harvest planted trees	18 000	55
IV	Build heavy-duty road	−500	0
	Log commercial species	750	1, 2, 3
	Clear and plant *Gmelina*	−1 000	0
	Harvest *Gmelina*	12 000	20
V	Build heavy-duty road	−500	0
	Log commercial species	750	1, 2, 3
	Clear and establish *Terminalia*	−1 250	0
	Harvest *Terminalia*	120 000	55

Table 18.4 Treatments and criteria: BCR here means 'net future benefits divided by first-year costs'

Treatment	NPV_∞ @ 6%	BCR @ 6%	IRR (%)
I	783	16.67	100.00
II	2338	5.68	150.45
III	2943	5.53	110.75
IV	5489	4.66	27.43
V	5276	4.01	15.32
I → II	1555	4.46	156.83
II → III	605	5.03	9.09
III → IV	2546	4.00	11.86 and −3.25
IV → V	−213	0.15	5.85

IRR selects the treatment (II) with quickest returns; BCR selects the treatment (I) with best long-term value for initial investment. Both favour exploitative intensification, progressively through the whole forest area, before any silviculture is undertaken. NPV selects a silvicultural treatment (IV), which gives the best long-term revenue from the land.

The appropriate criterion depends on circumstances. If land is scarce and funds which earn 6% freely available, NPV is correct. Adopting intensifications for which incremental IRR exceeds the ruling discount rate (6%), or for which incremental BCR exceeds unity, gives the same selection as NPV (treatment IV).

If cash is limited in the short term and natural forest land is abundant, the BCR, picking less-intensive treatments, seems to offer the best answer (Earl, 1973), the discounted revenue per naira invested in treatment I being almost three times that for treatment II.

Given the arguments listed in chapter 11 and foresters' instincts against rapid exploitation, there seems little merit in choosing treatments of greatest IRR. But suppose that, following initial investment of 1 million naira, all forest profits (and no other funds) would be devoted to forest investment: what would be the fastest way to bring the whole forest area to treatment IV?

The answer is, by initially adopting the fast-profit treatment II favoured by IRR. This generates enough funds to establish treatment IV or V over the forest area within seven years, whereas it takes nine years using the annual income from the 'efficient' treatment I, and 40 years using finance from treatment IV itself. Provided there are no late costs in exploitation, provided funds are ploughed back into silviculture, and provided material production from the forest is the dominant goal, selection by IRR gives the most efficient development path. But these are important provisos, rarely if ever met.

Of course management of semi-natural forest systems raises many other economic and political problems: the ethics of irreversibility; the evaluation of gene resources; distributional aspects of local subsistence use of forests; control of exploitation of common property. Parts III and IV discuss these issues.

Economic influences on silvicultural trends

It may be helpful at this point to review trends of silviculture through time and through stages of economic development.

At first the forest resource suffices for the human population. But that population is growing, and awakened expectations of material improvement create demand for increasing consumption per head. In this phase of severely restricted investment funds and abundant land, the IRR criterion apparently meets the needs of circumstances, selecting investments that give the fastest build-up of funds and so create maximum scope for future intensive forest management, and for other national investments.

If development goes well and the need to mine forest wealth abates while some forest yet remains, there may follow a phase in which foresters luxuriate within the generous bounds allowed by the normal forest fallacy (chapter 11). Forest land is limited, so must be used productively, but it also generates a cash surplus which seems to refute the notion of scarce investment funds. Discounting vanishes and intensity of silvicultural investment increases: it is acceptable to spend a mark as long as it eventually returns a mark. In this phase, many foresters in Europe and North America are still enrapt.

There may follow a period (particularly if deforestation has occurred) in which industrial development competes with forestry for investment funds: the relevance of NPV is mooted, disputed, and adopted (often under protest) by forest managers. The effect of discounting is pervasive. Spacings of trees and of roads are widened, thinnings made more intense, improvement and protection are neglected, rotations curtailed.

Contemporary with these changes, rising labour costs cause rationalization – discontinuance of labour-intensive operations – and mechanization – increasing the importance of scale economies. The result is reduction in husbandry applied to individual trees, extra investment coming, if at all, through treatments like aerial spraying which can be applied at low unit cost to large areas. A reduced palette of species is usual. Extensive natural forest changes to extensive artificial forest, via an intensive intermediary.

Another way to view development is as a change from a phase when land, labour and wood are abundant and investment funds scarce, through one in which labour and investment funds are abundant and land and wood are treated as scarce, to one in which land and wood are treated as abundant and labour and investment funds are treated as scarce.

But some seers envisage a further phase, when the relative abundance of labour and scarcity of wood in a heavily populated and increasingly automated world will restore the place of husbandry and high land productivity. Such a forecast is controversial: chapter 31 reviews it.

Nor are the described processes inevitable. Revenues from high-IRR projects do not invariably finance silvicultural improvement, as many forest services know to their cost. Net revenues generated by quick-yielding exploitation projects either accrue largely to agencies outside the country, or are frittered away on ill-conceived prestige investments and trivial consumption for the rich (Westoby, 1987). In the development jargon, the forest economy does not reach take-off point (where further international aid and expertise are superfluous): it reaches the end of the runway (with no more resources to exploit). And all too often the national economy remains with it, wheels stuck in the morass of international indebtedness, lacking even the natural resources which were once both its richness and the reason for its downfall.

This dismal picture is partly a matter of politics, partly of misconceived and misapplied economic criteria. In the real world of finite runways, profounder criteria of worth than NPV and BCR and, particularly, IRR are needed. Such criteria are discussed in Part III.

19 Silvicultural and Harvesting Priorities

This review of silvicultural economics has so far assumed that forest managers can attend to one stand at a time. Although the interaction of all silvicultural variables for that stand must be considered, the stand itself is viewed apart from the rest of the forest. The economically ideal silviculture for the stand is determined on the assumption that managers can implement this ideal.

Yet forests cannot in practice be managed like this. As chapter 5 noted, the available markets and factors of production may not allow all stands to have ideal treatment at the ideal time. Moreover forests with a history of mismanagement or no management may contain numerous neglected stands, which are so far from the ideal that many years must elapse before that state is approached: constraints simply do not allow faster conversion. At other times an embarrassing superfluity of factors and markets may arise, exerting pressure to do *more* silviculture, *earlier* than had been planned. Management targets like normal forest structure or sustained yield further constrain how much (or little) felling or planting can be done in one year.

In these constrained circumstances, compatible courses of action cannot be considered in isolation, nor is maximization of NPV per hectare an adequate criterion of choice. The question is, can any economic criterion improve on intuitive choice among competing priorities for silvicultural attention?

Choice and initiation of management

Chapter 18 considered choice among treatments of previously unmanaged high forest, focusing on the individual hectare. With limited funds, however, treatment of one area affects that of other areas. Choosing by maximum NPV per hectare leads to extravagant intensification of an elite area, starving the remaining areas of funds. Efficient use of funds is shown by BCR: values for the projects in table 18.3 are reproduced in table 19.1.

Table 19.1 Incremental BCR from one level of treatment to another

	FROM TREATMENT LEVEL				
	0	I	II	III	IV
To treatment level					
I	16.67				
II	5.68	(4.46)			
III	5.53	4.60	(5.03)		
IV	4.66			4.00	
V	4.01				0.15

The first column of ratios shows an orderly reduction of BCR with increasing intensity (such a progression does not always happen). Funds should first be allocated to treatment I. Once funding of treatment I has been approved for the whole forest, however, further investments can only be incremental ones. In a planning context, an incremental investment like II→III does not mean 'convert a hectare of treatment II to treatment III', but 'schedule a hectare for treatment III instead of treatment II'. The diagonal of table 19.1 represents incremental BCRs of successive steps of intensification: II→III clearly gives a better return per additional naira invested than I→II. But II→III cannot be adopted unless funding for I→II has already been allocated. As I→III is also superior to I→II, any surplus funds from treatment I should be used to intensify directly from treatment I to treatment III, with no areas of treatment II.

Forestry investments on other land types also compete for funds, for example planting acacias in the semi-arid northern region, with BCR of 4.5. It is rational to intensify forest management to treatment III before allocating funds to acacias. Despite the 4.66 ratio for treatment IV, *incremental BCR* for III→IV (4.00) is less than that of the acacias, which are the next best use of funds.

The general procedure for allocating limited funds is:

1 For each forest type arrange treatments in ascending intensity.
2 Calculate BCR for each increment of intensity and tabulate it as above.
3 Starting with the most intensive investment in each table, delete any ratio which is lower than the ratio *diagonally below it and to the right*.
4 Replace the deleted ratio by the ratio for *two* increments of intensity, *below and in the same column*.

5 Delete the ratio *horizontally right* of the new ratio.
6 Repeat, until the remaining ratios decrease with increasing intensity.
7 Allocate funds among all forest types in descending order of incremental BCR, until either funds are exhausted, or remaining investments have BCR less than one.

If quantifiable constraints exist on funds in several time periods, the above procedure must be expanded into linear programming format.

Timber-growing for a target

A similar procedure applies when the aim is growing a product, like sawlogs, at least cost. The relevant efficiency ratio is minimum discounted cost per cubic metre, which is helpful in, say, choosing between expensive but productive land and cheap but low-yielding land. Again, however, incremental cost per incremental cubic metre should be calculated for intensification strategies like fertilizing.

The cost of delay

The situation in table 19.1 is static, in that natural forest and savanna ecosystems are taken to be in equilibrium. Choosing priorities becomes more complex when the forest changes if treatment is delayed. This is normal in managed forests.

When operations cannot be undertaken at the ideal time, loss of profit is incurred. For example, a few years beyond optimal rotation, NPV begins to decline rapidly: there is a *cost of delay* (an opportunity cost) in postponing clearfelling much beyond optimal rotation. Where constraints operate, this cost of delay cannot be avoided in all stands.

To make meaningful comparisons among costs of delay, some reference period of delay must be defined: obviously a long delay entails greater costs than a short one. Calculations in this chapter all refer to a year's delay. Being precise, the cost of delay is the yearly rate of change of NPV at an instant in time; readers who think in calculus terms will envisage the first differential of NPV with respect to time; those who prefer a graphical analogue could visualize the gradient of the tangent to the NPV versus time curve. For practical purposes it can be regarded as the value of the crop and the discounted value of its successors *this* year minus the discounted value of the crop and its successors next year. The discount rate naturally affects the cost of delay – and even whether delay is a cost at all.

Take two crops that ideally should be felled immediately. One is a 5-ha block of slow-growing pine, long past optimal rotation, standing at 250 m^3/

Table 19.2 Cost of delay in harvesting

Stand	Revenue now	Revenue next year	Discounted revenue next year	Cost of delay
Pine	2990	3080	2933	57
Fir	5640	5850	5571	69

ha. It has not yet been felled because the road system has only just reached it. The other crop is barely over-mature fir, 400 m³/ha on a highly productive 20-ha site. Table 19.2 gives the pertinent cash values.

If the objective is to maximize NPV at 5% of the whole forest, within the constraint of a small felling gang, it seems that total cost of delay is minimized by tackling first those stands whose discounted value is declining most rapidly (those with the highest cost of delay). The figures apparently favour felling the fir first. Another instinct is that the fir has a large differential in its favour, since there are 20 ha of it, with a total cost of delay of £1380, whereas that for the pine is only £285.

These intuitive reponses are incorrect, because both erroneously assume that the *period* of delay is the same for both crops – if the fir is felled first, then felling of the pine will be delayed for, say, two years; if the pine is felled first, then felling of the fir will also be delayed for two years. Clearly this is not so. In the first place there are more hectares of fir to fell before the pine can be tackled; in the second place there are more cubic metres of fir per hectare. For both reasons, clearing the fir will take longer than clearing the pine, and this has implications for period of delay.

Let the work gang harvest 25 m³ per day, and let there be 200 full days per year suitable for harvesting. It will take 50 days = 0.25 working year to harvest the pine, and 320 days = 1.6 working years to harvest the fir. Table 19.3 shows timing and cost of delay under the two harvesting schedules. The appraisal now favours felling the pine first.

The urgency index ratio

The scheduling procedure above gives the right decision (felling the pine first) and the correct margin (£111) by which this is better than felling the fir first. But it is time-consuming and tedious, firstly because a schedule for all relevant operations must be prepared, secondly because, as the operations to be scheduled proliferate, so the permutations of ordering increase exceedingly. This renders the procedure impossible beyond a very

Table 19.3 Alternative harvesting schedules

Schedule	Period (years)	Mean delay (years)	Cost of delay/ha/year	Area (ha)	Overall cost of delay
Fir harvest	0–1.6	0.8	69	20	1104
Pine harvest	1.6–1.85	1.725	57	5	492
Total					1596
Pine harvest	0–0.25	0.125	57	5	36
Fir harvest	0.25–1.85	1.05	69	20	1449
Total					1485

few operations: the permutations of ordering for 55 stands are 1.270×10^{73}, more than the number of atoms in the universe!

Fortunately, there is an effective short-cut. The feature favouring pine in the above example was the rapidity of felling, a result of the small factor input needed. Priority should be given to operations where the constrained factor of production avoids delay efficiently – an analogue of BCR. To put it simply, if operation B requires twice as much labour per hectare as operation A, then only 0.5 ha of B can be treated while 1 ha of A is treated. Thus the cost of delay *per hectare* of B must be halved before it can be compared with the cost of delay per hectare of A. The appropriate index of efficiency is

$$\frac{[\text{cost of delay (per year) avoided, per hectare}]}{[\text{input of constrained factor per hectare needed to avoid delay}]}$$

This may be termed the *urgency index ratio* (UIR) of the operation. Applying this criterion to the pine and fir example, we obtain values of 5.7 for pine and 4.3 for fir. Thus pine gets priority, as before.

The units of UIR depend on how factor input is measured: in this case gang-days is the suggested measure, and UIR has units of £s per gang-day. Its interpretation is the saved cost of delay, per gang-day, of applying the gang to that operation this year rather than next. Provided UIR is calculated in the same units for all operations to be undertaken by a particular gang, it gives the relative urgency of each operation. The most profitable schedule is to undertake operations in descending order of UIR. There is no implication that the delay of other operations will be a year, or any other particular time. There is no need to schedule each remaining operation, nor even to consider if a constraint exists in the next time period: the task is to assess immediate priorities. Sufficient unto the day are the complexities thereof. Next year the calculations can be repeated.

UIRs can be given for any forest operation whose cost of delay and factor requirement are calculable.

1   The cost of delay in salvaging dead timber is greater than for living crops, because there is no increment to offset the effect of discounting – on the contrary, insects or fungi may cause progressive degradation.

2   Delay of thinning not only postpones yield from the crop, but leads to unsatisfactory allocation of increment to trees.

3   Delay in applying protective treatment may be very costly if it entails high probability of serious crop damage.

4   Delay in planting postpones the NPV of the whole crop; since the planting season may be short, delay of a few days sometimes results in establishment being delayed by a whole year.

Other constraints

The constraint need not be labour. Take the choice between planting a fertile site where regular thinning is expected, at 2 m × 2 m spacing, and an exposed site where, because of the risk of wind damage, thinning is proscribed and planting will be at 3 m × 3 m spacing. Respective NPVs are £1300 and £700/ha, giving costs of delay per hectare of

$$£1300 - £1300/1.05 = £62 \text{ and } £700 - £700/1.05 = £33$$

There is a shortage of seedlings. Since 2500 plants per hectare are needed for the first site and only 1111 for the second, UIRs for the two sites are

$$£62/2500 = 0.025 \text{ and } £33/1111 = 0.030.$$

Seen another way, 10 000 plants suffice for 4 ha of the first site, saving a £248 cost of delay, or 9 ha of the second, saving £297.

In harvesting, the constraint may be availability of markets. If, for example the only accessible sawmill has annual capacity for 5000 m³ of sawlogs, UIR is

$$\frac{[\text{cost of delay per hectare}]}{[\text{cubic metres of saw-timber per hectare}]}$$

Harvesting operations are ranked by UIR, and enough are scheduled to produce 5000 m³.

So far comparisons have only been made between operations of one kind. This is proper when, for example, specialized machines are used, or workers form discrete harvesting, silvicultural and maintenance gangs. In small forests, however, and particularly farm woodlands, workers may be used for any operation. Cost of delay and UIR per hectare can still be calculated; UIR shows priorities for operations.

Intuitive means of choosing priorities between such disparate operations as planting, thinning, salvaging fire-killed young crops and felling over-mature timber are unreliable (Gray and Price, unpubl.). Yet a few simple economic calculations give foresters an unambiguous list, as table 19.4 illustrates. All figures are per hectare. The discount rate is 4%.

I   Plant open land with a crop with NPV_∞ £1000.
II Remove £400 of thinnings; delay of thinning retards crop development by 0.25 year; NPV to present of current and successor crops is £4000.
III Clearfell crop worth £10 000; indicating percent is 3%.
IV As III, plus immediate replacement by a crop of NPV_∞ £1400.

Part of cost of delay in felling is attributable to delayed re-establishment of successor crops. The UIR of felling and replanting is the summed costs of delay for felling and replanting, divided by the summed work-days to undertake both operations (*not* the sum of UIRs for the two operations). However, as discussed in chapter 11, felling need not entail replanting; hence UIR for simply felling should be included too. As felling-and-replanting has a higher UIR than felling, areas should be replanted as they are felled. If UIR for felling were higher, all felling should be done before any replanting.

Development of the forest means that priorities change over time: clearfelled areas may become heavily overgrown, increasing the labour requirement for planting and reducing UIR; light-demanding trees reach a stage where thinning is needed to avoid check; older crops pass optimal rotation; susceptible crops are killed and need to be salvaged. Thus UIRs should be recalculated periodically, giving a new list of priorities.

Too much of a good thing

The UIR concept is adaptable to many different situations. Sometimes, for example, the problem is not lack of factors or markets, but excess in relation to the intended programme: this often happens in forests of irregular age-class structure. Rather than leaving workers idle, it may be worth undertaking some operations before the ideal time. The objective is to mini-mize total cost of advancing operations. Cost of delay is avoided by doing as *many* operations as are compatible with the constraint: by contrast, now one

Table 19.4 Urgency index ratios for diverse operations

Operation	NPV now	NPV next year	Cost of delay	Work-days	UIR
I	1000	1000/1.04	38.46	10	3.85
II	400 + 4000	$400/1.04 + 4000/1.04^{0.25}$	54.41	5	10.88
III	10 000	$10\,000 \times 1.03/1.04$	96.15	50	1.92
IV	10 000 + 1400	$10\,000 \times 1.03/1.04 + 1400/1.04$	150.00	64	2.34

tries to do as *few* operations, or to *put off* as many operations as possible, given the constraint. The rule is to select by lowest value of the ratio

$$\frac{[\text{cost per hectare of bringing forward the operation}]}{[\text{units of constrained factor in or product from one hectare of the operation}]}$$

It makes no sense to consider the cost of advancing the operation by a year. It is brought forward from whatever its ideal time is, to now.

Frequently, to encourage establishment of new processing industries, the state forest service, or a consortium of private growers, guarantees a supply during the early years. If this input is a low value category, such as pulpwood, supplying the guaranteed amount may involve sacrificing timber that could otherwise find a higher-valued market. Table 19.5 shows standing volume expected from 'representative' non-thin stands at various ages. NPV per hectare at 5% of successor crops is £200 and the optimal rotation, yielding standing value £4000, is 45 years.

Table 19.5 Least-cost means of premature harvest

Age	Opportunity cost	Less offset	Volume	Opportunity cost/m^3 (net)	Extra harvest	Total cost/m^3
20	1240	1040	60	17.34	3.50	20.84
25	1583	1383	180	7.68	2.40	10.08
30	2020	1820	280	6.50	1.60	8.10
35	2578	2378	370	6.43	0.95	7.38
40	3291	3091	440	7.02	0.40	7.42
45	4200	4000	500	8.00	0	8.00

The problem is to decide which age classes should be felled to fulfil the guarantee, while minimizing the opportunity cost of premature felling. If guaranteed volume is V and the contract price P, a revenue of $V \times P$ is made from the contract, irrespective of which age-classes the volume is obtained from. Since revenue does not change, it is irrelevant to choice of strategy; extra harvesting costs, however, are incurred for smaller trees. Revenues from felling before 45 are also irrelevant, since the options are either to put timber into the guaranteed supply at the fixed price, or to grow the trees to 45 years. The opportunity cost is hence £4000 plus £200 for successor crops at 45, discounted to the current stand age. There is an offsetting NPV of £200 for successor crops planted immediately after felling. These factors are gathered in table 19.5.

The third column is the net opportunity cost of bringing forward felling to fulfil the guarantee. The lowest value in the last column gives the least-cost method of supplying a cubic metre, and the best felling strategy.

The result (ages 35, 40, 45, 30, 25, 20) is not the steady progression that might be expected. The advantage of early felling is that forgone revenue is long-delayed and therefore heavily discounted; the advantage of late felling is that it supplies a large volume per hectare to the contract. The late middle ages offer the best of both worlds.

Value of relieving a constraint

The problem of priorities arises through shortages of factors or markets. The problem can be side-stepped if these constraints are relieved. Long-term shortages can be eliminated by recruiting and training more labour, and short-term problems can be alleviated by hiring contractors, or paying the existing work-force for overtime. To assess the value of bringing forward overdue work programmes requires a provisional work programme by year and month to be drawn up. UIR calculations fix the order of work; compiling the programme is then a matter of assessing the time required for each job.

The value of hiring a contractor is the sum of two changes:

(a) the value of advancing the job undertaken by the contractor from its current position in the list of priorities to the immediate future;
(b) the value of the forest's own work-force tackling earlier the urgent jobs with lower priority than the one allocated to the contractor.

Table 19.6 shows alternative schedules. Costs of delay include those of successor crops.

The combined value of bringing forward all urgent jobs until harvesting is back on schedule is £28 000. If hiring the contractor costs less than this, then the contractor should be hired. No saving of wages to the forest's own workers should be included, unless overtime is avoided or the work-force will eventually lapse from piecework to plain time at an earlier date. The work-force must be paid anyway: the advantage of hiring the contractor lies in bringing subsequent events forward in time.

What about forest rent?

UIR is based on cost of delay for that perpetual series of events provisionally planned for a site. There is obviously also a cost of delay under the forest rent criterion when mature crops are allowed to rot, when stands lose increment for want of thinning and when plantable land is left to grow weeds.

Table 19.6 Effect of contractor-hire on harvest schedule

Job	Cost of delay/year	Time (years)	Total cost of delay
Without contractor			
Fell fir stands	8 000	0–1	4 000
Fell spruce stands	12 000	1–3	24 000
Thin larch stands	6 000	3–4	21 000
Fell pine stands	2 000	4–5	9 000
Total			58 000
With contractor			
Contract-fell spruce stands	12 000	0–2	12 000
Fell fir stands	8 000	0–1	4 000
Thin larch stands	6 000	1–2	9 000
Fell pine stands	2 000	2–3	5 000
Total			30 000

Two kinds of cost can be distinguished.

1 There are actual losses, confined to a definite time-period, whereafter nothing changes, as when delayed thinning reduces revenue over the originally defined rotation.
2 There is a delay in the forest rotation, as when planting is postponed till the next season. The cost is mean annual net revenue multiplied by period of delay.

Some delayed operations embrace an element of both. Delay of clearing fallen trees entails direct loss through degradation of timber. It also incurs delayed establishment of the successor rotation.

This slightly different concept of cost of delay apart, UIR can be applied equally well when discounting is not done.

Linear programming and harvest scheduling

When there are two or more constraints on a given set of operations, linear programming is needed. However, it is as well to check that at least two constraints are *binding:* that is, both in practice limit rate of working. Felling teams and extraction machinery are both needed to perform harvesting operations, but often it is lack of one rather than the other that restricts output at all harvesting sites.

The example in table 19.7 has two operating constraints. After a fire, three stand types are to be cleared. Inputs and dollar values are per hectare. Degrade of value at 4% per year is expected; the discount rate is 5%. Six chainsaw hours are available for each skidder hour. The objective function is to minimize global cost of delay. Relevant basic solutions are given in table 19.8.

Table 19.7 Harvesting options with two constraints

Stand type	Chainsaw hours	Skidder hours	Stand value	Cost of delay
A	200	50	5000	429
B	320	40	6000	514
C	400	50	8000	686

Table 19.8 Basic solutions and shadow prices

AREA PER HOUR			SHADOW PRICE		
Type A	Type B	Type C	Chainsaw	Skidder	UIR
0.01	0.0125	—	1.1675	4.31	10.715
0.01	—	0.01	1.285	3.44	11.15
—	0.01875	—	1.6063	—	9.6375
—	—	0.015	1.715	—	10.29

The best combination of activities is 0.01 ha per skidder hour of A and C. If type C is finished first, 0.01 ha of A and 0.0125 ha of B per hour is the next combination. If A is finished first, all resources should be devoted to C before any of B is tackled.

Linear programming models have been built to schedule harvesting and regeneration for whole regions, given a constraint of regularly supplying fixed markets, or building up supply as new processing capacity comes on stream, or achieving a regular sequence of age classes within each forest. Johnson and Scheurman (1977) survey these models. Rather than explicitly using cost of delay and UIR concepts, these models incorporate estimates of volume available in different future times. Generally, they are broader in their scope in time and space than the UIR examples presented here, but less finely tuned to local circumstances.

With increasing availability of on-line computing in forest offices, such models will be increasingly available to local managers, though the larger versions will be confined to high-level decision-making. There is neither the prospect nor the need for managers to understand the mechanisms by which linear programming algorithms are solved, but it is desirable that they should know how to formulate a problem in terms intelligible to the computer. At forest level, calculating cost of delay and factor requirement per hectare may remain the manager's own responsibility. Once these and the sizes of the constraints are known, a linear programming package will quickly determine an optimal schedule of priorities.

Tailpiece

The traditional world of forestry economics was free of constraints: anything could be transacted at any time at a market price. The modern world of linear programming is equally extreme, based on invariable constraints. In grey reality, markets and inputs have flexibility, to a limited extent and at additional cost. A linear programming solution should never be accepted without inspecting the shadow price of constraints, to check whether they are unreasonably high, and if so whether they can be alleviated at reasonable cost. Table 19.8 shows shadow prices per hour of skidder and chainsaw which represent the value of avoiding a year's delay in undertaking operations. A schedule like table 19.6 is needed before the overall value of acquiring extra factors can be judged.

20 The Economics of Mixed Land Use

The institutions and organization of land tenure do not always coincide with rational divisions of land use. In rich agricultural holdings which foresters could not afford, there are nonetheless pockets of steep, stony or marshy ground where woodland has, by design or default, become the land use. Similarly, within expanses of low-grade forest land there are areas of deeper soil capable of providing good grazing or even an arable crop, and land too exposed or rocky for anything but primary conservation use.

Considering forestry in conjunction with other land uses reproduces some aspects of the discussion of monocultures, mosaics and mixtures in chapter 18. Forestry or agriculture may after all be the best use for the entire land unit; variation of site or the advantage of diversified enterprises may favour interspersed single uses; or the benefits of interaction between individual plants may favour intimate mingling of annual and woody species for a range of purposes. Much has been said recently about the advantages of multiple and integrated land use and about agroforestry, not all logical or based on sound experimentation. This chapter discusses the costs and benefits claimed for these options.

Mosaics and margins of land use

If land uses are interspersed, a criterion is needed to fix the boundary between them. Sometimes a physical feature, such as a sharp change of slope or a river, marks an obvious changeover. More usually, conditions change gradually and no boundary can be visually recognized. In such cases it may be possible to plot estimated NPV against some variable representing site conditions. In Britain elevation markedly affects profitability of timber (Price and Dale, 1982) and arable crops, but has less influence on sheep grazing. The result is plotted in figure 20.1.

Profits should only include incremental costs and revenues of *extending* each enterprise by one hectare. The cost of land is irrelevant, being a sunk

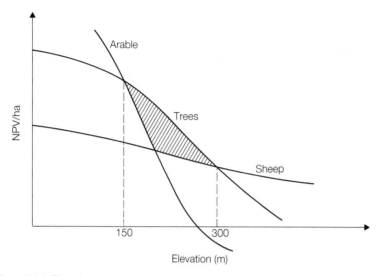

Figure 20.1 Elevation and land use
Shaded area represents added profit of including forestry in the land use
mixture

cost common to both enterprises. The cost of an access bridge for timber lorries is irrelevant, being unchanged by extending the forest by a hectare. The cost of sheep shearing and dipping facilities is irrelevant, being fixed within wide limits of flock size. The cost of the fence-line separating sheep from trees is irrelevant if its length is the same, regardless of how high up the slope it is erected. All these are fixed costs with respect to placing the boundary.

In some cases, however, the fence-line increases in length, the further upslope it is placed. Figure 20.2 shows a land-holding in a semi-circular valley-head. At r metres from the focus of the semi-circle, the separating fence has length $(2 + \pi)r$. Extending r by 1 metre increases the fence by $(2 + \pi)$, and encloses an extra

$$\pi r \text{ m}^2 = 0.0001 \, \pi r \text{ ha}$$

Thus at a fencing cost of £2/m it costs

$$£2 \times (2 + \pi)/(0.0001 \, \pi r) = £32\,732/r \text{ per ha}$$

for additional fencing to extend the forest upslope. For reasonable values of r, this is not negligible, especially if the fence needs periodic replacement.

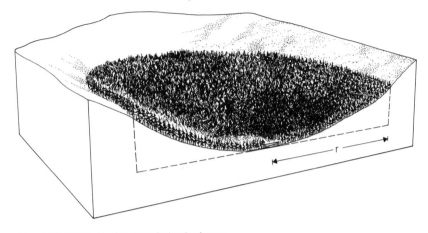

Figure 20.2 Fencing for a semi-circular forest

A geometrically similar effect is exposure at the forest edge. Strong winds, especially cold or ice- or salt-laden ones, severely reduce tree growth within, say, 50 m of the forest edge. The loss in increment may reduce NPV by £500 per hectare. For the valley-head forest, this loss is about £25 000/r per extra hectare, and could materially influence the tree-line. If, however, a forest lies along 10 km of a uniform valley-slope, only 100 m of extra edge at each end of the forest is created by extending a further 100 m upslope, giving a total extra exposed area of

$$2 \times 100 \times 50/10\ 000 = 1\ \text{ha} \equiv \text{£}500\ \text{loss}$$

Since the gain is 100 ha, the loss per hectare is insignificant.

Outward expansion of forest area increases roading costs as the system is extended further upslope. Afforesting enclaves of farmland or unproductive wet or rocky patches within the forest area affects road cost quite differently. These areas must be traversed (or circumvented) whether the land is forested or not. Only if the whole road system can be shortened by realignment to avoid those areas is there any incremental road cost in afforesting the enclaves. If the road system is already there, its construction is a past cost and should not influence the positioning of boundaries.

Even the straightforward incremental costs of establishment, tending, protecting and harvesting may be reduced from average costs where scale economies exist.

Not all agricultural costs are direct ones either. Afforesting a piece of low-lying grazing land which provides an early flush of spring growth may not just deny the direct grazing value of that sward, but make it impossible to keep a sufficient flock to utilize summer grazings fully.

The variability of cost depends so much on the lie of the land that only general guidance can be given on how an extension of forest should be assessed. As always, the individual manager should look at the area in question and ask: *what changes* with extension along this particular front? Naturally, the discount rate is all-important in fixing the boundary between forestry, with its prolonged maturation period, and farming – or almost anything else – with its much faster returns.

Benefits and costs of mosaics

Mere existence of areas where incremental net revenue of farming exceeds that of timber-growing and *vice versa* does not justify a mosaic of land uses. Farming and forestry require their own special expertise, traditions and equipment. Unmodified agricultural tractors are not robust enough for timber harvesting in rough terrain, while a forest enterprise does not have the buildings and enclosures needed for intensive stock farming. There are fixed costs attached to each enterprise. In terms of figure 20.1, unless the differences in incremental NPV between elevations of 150 m and 300 m (shaded area) exceed the fixed costs of establishing a forestry enterprise, profit is maximized by wholly agricultural use. Equally, an enclave of fields within the forest is not worthwhile unless the difference in NPV between grazing and timber-growing on that area exceeds the cost of fencing the enclave.

Lack of expertise and special equipment may be overcome by forming co-operatives with sufficient aggregate forest area to justify acquiring both. However, some extra fixed costs are endemic to a mixed enterprise.

On the other hand, mixed enterprises have economic advantages. What was said of market risks and forest mosaics is true with greater force of mosaics of wood-producing and other enterprises. However different the timbers of two tree species may be, there is some correlation between their price movements. On the other hand, timber prices may well be low when food prices are high. Some insurance against uncertain times is also provided by the increased self-sufficiency of a mixed holding – food, fuel and constructional materials all being available internally. The different cash flow characteristics of the two enterprises gives a flexibility not attainable by one in isolation. For farmers, a woodland is a source of income and a place to work when agriculture is depressed, but can be left untouched for some years when agriculture is thriving. For foresters, an agricultural element offers income in the early years of a plantation.

The different financial characteristics also allow farmers to raise money for agricultural improvement by selling land to forestry (or by using woodland as loan collateral). Since poor-quality land acceptable to forestry may be surplus to the agricultural enterprise, farmers can thus increase winter and spring grazing potential of valley-bottom land, which may be the limiting factor on stock numbers, without reducing usable summer grazings.

The selling-off strategy concentrates land management with individuals and agencies already possessing the requisite skills and equipment. There is a danger, however, in the ensuing separation of management (Mutch and Hutchison, 1980). For example, in the early life of plantations, it is mostly in forestry's interest to maintain fences excluding browsers. But once the vulnerable parts of trees are above browsing height and ground vegetation has been suppressed by canopy closure, the benefits of keeping stock out of plantations lie with the agricultural enterprise. Unless contractual obligations are rigidly specified, separated management poses formidable problems.

Integrated land use

The financial model has so far been essentially competitive, land being allocated to that use whose NPV exceeds that of rival claimants. The case for land use mosaics depends essentially on variation in productive capacity – the mosaic of land quality itself – or on the flexibility of diversified cash flow. Integrated land use implies something more than this: increase in revenues or reduction in costs consequent on joint pursuit of two or more enterprises.

Beneficial biophysical interactions may exist at boundaries. The most-often-mentioned are shelter and shade provided by forests to agricultural crops and animals. For animals these offer reduction in mortality and body-weight loss; stock tend to congregate behind shelterbelts in bad weather, facilitating gathering if need be. For crops, reduced windspeed reduces transpiration, hence increasing the period when stomata remain open and photosynthesis can occur. Lower windspeeds reduce evaporation from reservoirs, suggesting benefit from integrated forest/water catchment management.

The extent of forest justifiable by the sheltering effect is, however, limited. Once enough shelter has been created for all the animals, there are no incremental benefits from extending the area, which may make stock harder to find. A minimum-sized shelterbelt produces little good timber, because exposure depresses tree growth and quality. Moreover, the benefits of shelter are not unequivocal. Shading of crops and root competition may decrease aggregate agricultural production in temperate latitudes, where sunlight is frequently the factor limiting photosynthesis. Even the benefits to stock farming may be diminished by rapid spread of disease and incidence of starvation in the crowded, overgrazed conditions leeward of the belt.

Tree belts designed to flight birds for sport shooting have clear rental value – which readers may interpret in light of their own value system. Less controversial are the benefits of trees in screening unsightly farm buildings and recreational facilities, and creating variety of landscape and edge-habitat for wildlife. But even these benefits have negative counterparts: blocking views otherwise visible from the recreation facilities, harbouring predators of small farm animals, and creating problems for controlled agricultural burning.

An integrated holding may also benefit from complementarity between factors of production in forestry and agriculture, especially if activity peaks in agricultural and forestry calendars do not coincide. Workers who might otherwise be idle can alternate between the enterprises. As chapter 9 made clear, however, the benefits of utilizing machinery more fully would be rather small, even when the same machines can be used in farming and forestry.

Shared costs

Fencing not only separates vulnerable trees from stock, but also assists grazing management. But consider an 81–ha block of land divided into nine sections, shown in figure 20.3a–c. The NPV per hectare of uncontrolled grazing is £600, that of controlled grazing is £1000, that of forestry is £800, while the capitalized cost of a permanent fence is £5/m.

On the existing holding (figure 20.3a), only a 3600 m boundary fence is erected, and NPV is

$$81 \times £600 - 3600 \times £5 = £30\ 600$$

By erecting a further 3600 m of internal fencing, NPV could be increased to

$$81 \times £1000 - 7200 \times £5 = £45\ 000$$

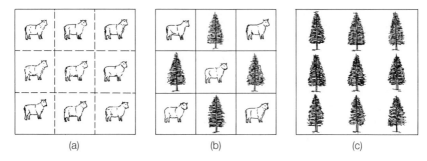

| (a) | (b) | (c) |

Figure 20.3 Alternative land allocations

As the farmer lacks cash to erect the fences, a compromise is to sell the 36 ha shown in (b) for forestry, with total value

$$36 \times £800 + 45 \times £1000 - 7200 \times £5 = £37\ 800$$

Arrangement (b) is ideal for grazing management, giving a central enclosure from which gates lead into four satellite enclosures. Increased intensity of stocking almost compensates for loss of area. Each grazing area now gives higher NPV per hectare than forestry, and no improvement on this pattern by further conversion to forestry seems possible. However, in (c) all the land is in forestry. Internal fences are unnecessary, and NPV is

$$81 \times £800 - 3600 \times £5 = £46\ 800$$

On the other hand, had the NPV of controlled grazing been £1200 per hectare, arrangement (a) plus internal fences would have given NPV £61 200, (b) would have given £46 800, and (c) would also give £46 800.

Experiment with figures for grazing and forestry NPVs and for fencing costs confirms that under no combination of figures does the benefit of fences for controlled grazing justify integrated land use. Where a mosaic of site types favours interspersed forestry and grazing, the fencing required to separate land uses has beneficial spin-off for grazing management; this spin-off may tip the balance in favour of the mosaic. Where financial or political constraints prevent complete conversion to forestry, partial conversion may represent the best feasible option. But it is these factors themselves, rather than the benefits of fencing, that favour mixed use.

Similarly, roads provided for forest harvesting give the farming enterprise benefits of access: enclosures previously unreachable with heavy equipment can be cultivated and fertilized. If the NPV of pastures so improved exceeds that of forestry, which in turn exceeds that of unimproved pasture, a maximum NPV for a holding seems to be achieved with mixed land use.

But consider a series of bridges built to take a forest road to a remote area earmarked for agricultural improvement (figure 20.4). Without the bridges improvement cannot occur. Since NPV of improved grazing exceeds that of forestry, all land beyond the last bridge goes to grazing. Thus the bridge serves grazing alone. If the NPV of grazing *after* paying for the bridge is less than that of forestry, then forestry should occupy the land. Grazing cannot be made more profitable by transferring engineering cost to the forestry account. If, however, grazing can pay for the bridge and still outperform forestry, it should also occupy the land on the forest side of the bridge. The argument can be pursued backwards, bridge by bridge, till the forest component of the land holding is eliminated. Again a mixture of land uses is only justified by different site types: for example, a forest road up a steep

Figure 20.4 Roads as shared infrastructure

hillside may provide incidental access to improvable grazings on the plateau above.

Moreover, a forest road network would ideally be built only at time of first thinning; but, if pasture improvement is to compensate for loss of land to forestry, access roads must be constructed before planting begins. If roads would have been constructed at age 25 for forestry purposes, but are put in at age 0 to service agriculture, the cost of advancing construction at a 5% discount rate is

$$£X - £X/1.05^{25} = £0.705X$$

Thus 70.5% of construction cost should be allocated to agriculture.

The arguments over shared infrastructure have been reviewed in detail because they are often urged rather uncritically. The arguments have no standing in themselves. They may, however, sometimes be valid subsidiary arguments when diversity of land or political factors favour mosaics.

Multiple land use

Producing several products on one plot of land has intuitive appeal in countries where land shortage is severe. However, total production or NPV does not automatically increase simply because coextensive land uses occupy a site. One might as well argue that a pint pot can be made to contain a quart of salad dressing because one pint is vinegar and another pint is oil.

Multiple land use is analogous to mixtures of tree species; the economic arguments favouring it resemble those reviewed in chapter 18.

1 *The uses exploit different levels or different attributes of the site*

Under tropical light intensities, a complete tree canopy still allows substantial light to be utilized by ground-level annual crops; rooting zones may differ; different nutrients may be limiting on woody and agricultural crops. Uses such as recreation require the spatial rather than the biological resources of the forest and can be conducted below a complete canopy. Contrariwise, electricity transmission lines can be suspended above the canopy of a short-rotation crop without significantly reducing light levels.

2 *The cycle of forest growth normally includes periods when trees are not fully utilizing the site*

The taungya system exploits the availability of light and growing space in the period before canopy closure. Agricultural crops are established between rows of trees. The forest generally benefits, as the cultivators effectively provide free weeding in exchange for short-term use of the land. This may crucially affect the profitability of tree growing (Nwonwu, 1987). Similarly

Plate VII Agroforestry in Chile: maximizing use of the resource
(Photo: Terry Thomas)

systems developed in New Zealand and Chile combine an initial period during which hay crops are taken from between widely spaced rows with an intermediate stage when stock graze under the still-incomplete canopy and a final stage in which only trees occupy the site (Borough, 1979). Grazing may be a cheap way of checking weed competition.

In the annual cycle, spring grazing may be rich under deciduous trees, especially those late in leafing. The combination brings the additional benefit of effective winter shelter for stock.

3 *Certain plants assist the growth of others*

The best-documented examples are leguminous crops. Clover or lupins, for example, sometimes help to establish tree crops on very infertile sites, though if this is their only purpose the mixture is not genuine multiple use. In other cases intermixing of plants may combat insect and fungal damage.

4 *Mixed land uses could conceivably reduce the need for labour or other management inputs*

A traditional management example is the practice of releasing pigs into regenerating oak woodland. Foraging for acorns by pigs reduces the need for mechanical cultivation. The art of successfully deploying this system lies in removing the pigs from the forest before all the acorns have been eaten! Shade-trees may improve productivity of farm workers (Hoekstra, 1987).

The cases quoted all embody some specific reason for expecting advantage from multiple use. There are also clear cases where uses compete directly for the same limiting resource. In many climatic conditions interception by trees of rainwater creates direct and proportional opposition between the interests of forestry and water catchment. And for much of a tree crop's life the only way of significantly increasing food or forage under the canopy is to reduce the growing space available to trees.

Worse than that, interactions between trees and other uses can be actively detrimental. Some agroforestry experiments report root damage and loss of height increment caused by sheep, while fleeces became contaminated with spruce twigs and needles (Adams, 1986). Recreation within forests has similar potential to damage the site by excessive trampling and by accidental or deliberate abuse of the trees themselves. Spread of fires from camp-sites and smokers is another hazard. Where multiple uses do co-exist, it is often only by virtue of additional management expenditures. Indeed, greater management input is characteristic of multiple use systems.

Showing that some tree planting on farmland, or opening forest for grazing, improves profitability does not constitute a complete case for agroforestry: it may be better to change land use completely.

This suggests, not that multiple use is a bad thing, but that there are 'multiple problems of multiple use' (Zivnuska, 1961). Experience and experimental evidence are needed in identifying amenable sites and suitable systems for practice of multiple use. Because of the incidence of management costs, and the variability of product values, data on physical productivity are insufficient in selecting the most efficient system. Riitters, Brodie and Hann (1982) show that according to discount rate and relative prices, trees alone, grazing alone or a mixture may all be optimal.

As with land use mosaics, multiple cropping reduces risk (Blandon, 1985). The question then is, can this benefit be most efficiently achieved by intimately mixing plants (and other sources of revenue) or by apportioning the land-holding into suitable sites for exclusive use by each of several crops or enterprises? However, the flexibility of mixed crops to adapt to changing economic circumstances is always an argument for intimate mixtures.

21 Forest Valuation and Land Acquisition

The ultimate economic question about commercial forestry (or about a mixed holding which includes woodland) is 'what is it worth?' Much unnecessary mystique surrounds forest valuation: the subject involves no more than discounted cash flow principles.

A given physical asset does not have the same value to everyone. This is partly because objectives differ – only aesthetically sensitive buyers will pay a premium for attractive woodland – partly because perceptions differ – for example in expectations of timber prices – and partly because circumstances differ – as when marginal tax rate affects the advantage of woodland ownership.

The desired value depends also on the purpose of valuation. Owners may wish a high valuation when:

(a) seeking compensation for woodlands compulsorily purchased or destroyed by third parties;
(b) negotiating with potential purchasers;
(c) trying to impress friends;
(d) establishing value as loan collateral.

By contrast, a low valuation is wanted when:

(e) tax liability is assessed;
(f) negotiating with potential sellers.

An unbiased value is desirable when:

(g) deciding whether to buy or sell;
(h) insurance is being arranged.

Apart from the variability inherent in interpretation of such matters as the appropriate discount rate, flexibility in valuation exists because there are three ways of valuing a property: from its historic cost of creation; at its present market value; through its expected contribution to future revenues and benefits. Only in a perfectly functioning market do all three coincide.

Present sale value

Where there are frequent transactions involving rather similar properties, a clear idea of market price for that type of property can be formed. For example, estate agents know that a particular type of house in a given town has a basic price, with credits and debits given for special attractive or detrimental features. The constant turnover of such properties checks the accuracy of the pricing process.

However, when transactions are infrequent, or a property has unique characteristics, no clear market value can be determined. The market price lies somewhere between the lowest price the seller will accept and the highest price any potential buyer will pay. When the lowest acceptable price exceeds the highest offered price, no transaction occurs. Otherwise, sale price depends on the relative bargaining strength of seller and buyer: if there are many potential buyers the price is likely to be high; if there is only one buyer and the seller urgently needs cash the price is likely to be low.

Sellers and buyers in such markets need guidance on what value may reasonably be placed on the property. Sellers usually consider the past cash flow of the property, while buyers are more concerned with future cash flows.

Historic cost

Land is a gift of nature – or rather at some point in the past it was annexed without payment. Nonetheless, the current owner of a property often has either paid cash for it, or inherited it with some idea of what it was worth at that time. At the simplest, the owner will not wish to sell the property for less than that, after some mark-up for inflation. If expenditures have been incurred in improving the property, these too may be incorporated in the base price. If the property is simply an amenity – for example a woodland used for shooting only – there may be no further considerations. If, however, the property is an investment, the owner may add compound interest on costs incurred, deducting from the base price any revenues accruing since purchase, also with compound interest. In table 21.1 negative years indicate a date in the past.

The figures should either be actual cash transactions adjusted upward for inflation (or compounded at a *monetary* rate of interest) or, in absence of

Table 21.1 Historic cost valuation

Item	Year	Cash flow £	Cash flow compounded @ 5% £
Land purchase	−10	−10 000	−16 289
Sale of timber	−9	+7 500	+11 635
Replanting	−7	−2 500	−3 518
Weeding	−6	−500	−670
Weeding	−5	−350	−447
Christmas tree sale	−2	+500	+551
Total			−8 738

sufficiently detailed records, a present-day cash flow for an equivalent operation. To recover the net historic loss on cash flow, the base price must be £8738.

Expectation value

As far as purchasers are concerned, past costs are sunk costs, nor are past revenues theirs to spend. Attention focuses on future expectations of profit or pleasure that the property affords: they want a discounted predicted cash flow from existing and successor crops. Nothing more than NPV calculation is involved, but, unlike in comparison of silvicultural options, where only relative magnitudes matter, here absolute values are needed and the time when the valuation is made is vital. For example, a no-thin, extensive-management wood, expected to yield $5000 at year 40, has expectation value of $1157 at the age of 10 years, but $3918 at 35 years with a 5% discount rate. The entire future cash flow must be considered, including NPV of replacement crops, as exemplified by table 21.2.

A new factor in this cash flow is periodic general management costs. There may be no large operations in a stand between completion of establishment and the beginning of harvesting. However, more or less regular expenditures may occur on inspecting the crop for signs of ill-health, assessment of growth for yield planning purposes, surveillance during the fire season, maintenance of the road and drainage system, and so on. Although small, such expenditures mount up, even after discounting. Management costs do not change markedly between silvicultural options (or if they do, the variation is rarely quantified reliably). They can be regarded as pre-committed costs if silviculture is to be undertaken at all, and were thus irrelevant to the silvicultural decisions examined in chapters 13–18. But

Table 21.2 Expectation valuation

Item	Year	Cash flow $	Cash flow discounted @ 5% $
Purchase of property	0		
Final thinning	3	20 000	17 277
Clearfelling	8	90 000	60 916
NPV successor crops (or land sale price)	10	10 000	6 139
Less capitalized value of annual $500 cost			−10 000
Maximum purchase price			74 332

they are part of forest ownership, and must be included as a debit against forest value.

Expectation values should normally be calculated separately for stands of different productivity and age, and aggregated in a global valuation. 'Property averages' are unacceptably inaccurate. However, the whole may be worth more (or less) than the sum of the parts, if, for example, the forest has well- (or ill-)balanced age-structure. It may also have extra value if it complements the wood supplies or land resource of a particular buyer: 'cash flow' in this context means 'addition to total enterprise cash flow'.

'True' value

Where valuations differ, which is the 'true' value? Market price may be difficult to identify, and in any case depends on attitudes of sellers and buyers. Historic cost is, as far as purchasers are concerned, an irremediable sunk cost. If sellers are rational, they too should regard past costs as irrelevant. A $1 000 000 historic cost of creating a property has no present consequence, if no purchaser will pay more than $500 000. If, further, no better price is likely to be offered in future, the seller should cut losses and accept the best offered price.

Two roles remain for historic cost:

1 to explain or respond to irrational behaviour – for example, so that a purchaser can offer a price just sufficient to prove acceptable to a seller;
2 to ensure fairness when a property is compulsorily purchased.

Treatment of infrastructure

A valuation may be given for roads, bridges and buildings in a forest, sometimes via historic cost, sometimes via present cost of constructing an equivalent standard of infrastructure. There is, however, no justification for these procedures. The present price of equivalent infrastructure is only relevant for movable items, such as prefabricated buildings, which have a resale value. As for historic cost, the arguments already presented apply. The value of a road system does not lie in its costliness, which may result from poor design and planning. Nor is a road more valuable because it was put in too early, and thus incurred compound interest for twenty unnecessary years. The value of such infrastructure generally lies in its ability to contribute to future profitability, a value subsumed in the expectation value of crops. For example, the price bid for standing timber in a forest depends on the accessibility of the stand. To include both a premium on timber for its accessibility and a value for the road which gives that accessibility is double-counting. On the other hand, if the necessary infrastructure does *not* exist, the discounted future cost of providing it is a debit against expectation value.

The historic cost approach also has practical disadvantages. It is common for young plantations to be valued via historic cost, while older plantations in the same property are valued at expectation value. The cost of a road serving both could be allocated on the basis of relative areas of young and old plantations. But the road has greater value for old plantations, due to be harvested soon, than to young plantations, for which the road will provide benefits only in the distant future.

Similarly, infrastructure such as offices and depot facilities is necessary to realize the expectation value of crops. The (discounted) cost of any such infrastructure still to be built is a debit against forest value. However, ownership of other forest holdings in the locality may enable some potential purchasers to avoid these costs and so offer a better price.

Existing commercial recreation facilities should be valued at the discounted stream of net revenues expected from their rental. *Potential* for such rentals, and the cost of planning and installing them, may also enter valuations.

Taxation and other personal circumstances

When existing or expected tax and grant arrangements assist forestry, a valuation specific to a given person or agency should include their influence on cash flow. Investors with high marginal tax rates may claim more tax relief on costs, and may pay more tax on revenue than those with low marginal rates. Depending on the precise arrangements, plantable land may be more or less valuable to them.

Similarly, individuals with low time preference rate give more emphasis to long-delayed revenues, so value a young woodland relatively highly. These differences of circumstance and perception allow mutual advantage in land sales.

Accounting

The objectives of accounting and those of managerial economics differ, although they use a common data set. Accounts attempt to portray the financial situation *as it is*: economics asks 'what changes?' when the situation is *altered*.

Accounting is a separate subject, and there is little point in trying to do it justice in a corner of an economics text. However, estate accounts are clearly an important part of forest valuation, not so much as records of historic costs and revenues, but for what they suggest about future cash flows.

The extraordinary length of forestry's production cycle means that:

(a) annual income and expenditure accounts are of interest only if they are detailed enough to indicate operational costs – they are no guide to long-term profitability;

(b) change in stock valuation is unusually important, and unusually ambivalent given the overlap of forestry's productive capital and its product;

(c) revaluation to allow for inflation over long periods is crucial.

Nothing better illustrates the pitfalls of valuing a forest from its accounts than the revaluation in 1972 of the British Forestry Commission's assets to a level on which a 3% return could be achieved (Forestry Commission, 1974). There were reasons for this stratagem, but the ensuing accounting value bears little resemblance to commercial value.

For a full review, see Openshaw (1980).

Competition, acquisition and allocation

Land use decision-making reaches its climax in the competition to acquire land. Each use has its costs and revenues, including different continual management costs and infrastructural needs. The use affording the greatest profit has the greatest scope to bid a high price when the land is for sale, so the market mechanism tends to channel land to its highest-profit use. On common, customary or state-controlled land, allocation need not follow the market, yet profitability of alternative uses is often an important argument.

In calculating forestry's bid, every cost of setting up a forestry enterprise – the road system giving access to the forest boundary, the offices, the depot – every cost that will become a sunk cost or an unallocated overhead in relation to later and more detailed decisions – all should be deducted from the summed discounted profits of individual hectares. Should trees already be growing on the site, they enter the computation as discussed above. Assuming that the freehold of the land is sought, then the NPV for the enterprise in perpetuity represents the maximum that could be paid for the land without long-term loss on the transaction.

The competitiveness of forestry at a particular location depends not only on physical conditions (as shown in figure 20.1) but on distance to markets. In an early model of land allocation, von Thünen (1875) showed that land uses should arrange themselves around market centres so that the land use whose product per hectare had the highest transport cost per kilometre should locate closest to the centres. In the same way, figure 20.1 shows the land uses most sensitive to changing physical conditions occupying the most favourable sites.

Within an 'isolated state' (a market system not trading with the rest of the world) even the least productive land uses have their place: as competition reduces the land area available to them, so their products become scarcer and more valuable, increasing their profitability to a competitive level. In practice, nevertheless, forestry shows up as an anomaly within von Thünen's system. Despite high physical yields and transport cost per hectare, silviculture seems to be consigned not only to low-quality land (which it withstands better than arable crops) but to the furthest zone from markets. This process initially results from forest land being valued for its exploitation potential and as a source of agricultural land, timber supplies merely being harvested at the closest location. Later, when incipient timber shortages encourage replanting, it may be that *discounted* transport costs per hectare are too small to let forestry bid a sufficient premium for land near centres.

Once imports become possible, the uncompetitiveness of a land use can no longer be redeemed by the increasing scarcity of its product. Thus there is no guarantee that the NPV of forestry will exceed the asking price for land – or even exceed zero – anywhere within a nation. Despite Sedjo's optimistic appraisal of plantations (1984), the sad fact is that in the northern temperate zone, where forest is so often pushed onto poor and inhospitable sites by the more competitive agriculture, the forest investment is at best marginally profitable under normal criteria. Even in the tropics, where high growth rates and low labour costs give better returns, these advantages are often nullified respectively by high discount rates and high transport and infrastructure costs. No amount of rhetoric against the soulless concerns of economists, no specious arguments about normal forests and compound interest, no covert devices to relocate costs to the end of the rotation, can change that all-too-pervasive fact. Foresters may not want to hear it, but it is what economists have to say.

Yet economists too have their doubts about the meaning of profitability as a measure of performance, particularly for land uses of such duration and with so many environmental and social implications as forestry. Part III of this book turns to matters other than strict profitability, and to the techniques which have been devised by economists to bring them into the economic calculus.

Part III   Social Valuation of Forestry

22 Profit and Welfare

Up to this point profit-maximization has been taken as the objective of decision-making. This objective may be adopted because it has been set by a superior power, or because it seems the only way to commercial survival, or because it is 'normal'.

The time has come, however, to examine the credentials of profit-maximization. The aim is not to praise or to execrate the profit motive *as such* – it is a mere manifestation of self-interest, and deserves no debate. Instead its *effects* are considered in an economy where each individual pursues profit (as producer) and satisfaction (as consumer).

Three distinct beliefs can be adopted.

1 Profit-maximization tends (with unimportant exceptions) to secure the greatest possible benefit to those within an economic system.
2 Profit-maximization harnesses humankind's worst selfish instincts, producing wealth for a few and immiseration for many.
3 Profit-maximization promotes efficient production of desired consumer goods, but fails to account for all impacts of economic activity, and cannot alone assure the best outcome from that activity.

The first two are expressions of political dogma, though selective evidence can be presented in favour of each. Rigorous application by governments of the first belief tends to produce evidence supporting the second: the second leaves a need for alternative means of decision-making, examples of which include ruthless monomaniac dictatorship and ineffectual group consensus. This text adopts the third belief. The present chapter attempts to identify specific strengths and deficiencies of a market mechanism driven by the profit motive; the remaining chapters of Part III explore how forest managers might remedy the deficiencies.

What does profit measure?

Profit is revenue (a good thing) minus cost (a bad thing), and therefore has been taken provisionally as a measure of net improvement. However, profit is a *proportionate* measure of net improvement only if:

(a) benefit of production is proportional to price and quantity of goods produced;
(b) loss of benefit incurred by using factors of production is proportional to the price and quantity of factors used;
(c) benefit and loss of benefit are measured on the same scale.

These are exacting requirements, but if any of them fails the arithmetic of profitability does not correspond to calculations of social good.

Suppose, as a working hypothesis, that consumers seek value for money – they purchase the combination of goods and services giving the maximum satisfaction obtainable within their income. Table 22.1 represents the purchases that an individual might make in a given time period, and the marginal utility of two forest products. Marginal utility is measured in some arbitrary unit (*utils* appear in the literature); it diminishes with increasing consumption.

How should an individual spend a budget of 50p? Best value for money is achieved by purchasing items which give greatest marginal utility per penny expended. Hence the first purchase is a kilogramme of firewood, next a second kilogramme of firewood, while in equal third place come the third kilogramme of firewood and a metre of building poles. At this point the budget is exhausted, and no rearrangement of purchases can yield greater utility.

Table 22.1 Price and marginal utility

FIREWOOD (price = 10p/kg)			BUILDING POLES (price = 20p/m)		
Quantity	Marginal utility	Marginal utility/penny	Quantity	Marginal utility	Marginal utility/penny
1	100	10	1	50	2.5
2	45	4.5	2	30	1.5
3	25	2.5	3	20	1
4	10	1	4	14	0.7
5	5	0.5	5	10	0.5
6	2	0.2	6	8	0.4

If the budget increases to £1, the purchases increase to include a fourth kilogramme of firewood and two further metres of building poles. If it increases to £1.50, total purchases increase to five kilogrammes of firewood and five metres of building poles.

At the 50p budget level, marginal utility of a kilogramme of firewood is 25 utils, and its price 10p; marginal utility of a metre of building poles is 50 utils, and its price 20p. The ratio of marginal utilities is

$$25 \text{ utils} : 50 \text{ utils} = 1 : 2$$

The ratio of prices is

$$10 \text{ pence} : 20 \text{ pence} = 1 : 2$$

Marginal utilities are in the same ratio as prices. At the two higher budget levels the same result emerges.

The implications are crucial. If purchasers seek value for money, and pursue this objective rationally, their *willingness to pay for* (= price of) a product is a proportionate measure of the extra value that product has for them. If the argument is true for firewood and building poles, it must hold for firewood and paper, firewood and food, food and entertainment, and for anything readily available at a market price.

Furthermore, if two additional units of a product are produced, then marginal utility can be created for two such consumers, with twice as much benefit. Thus price of product multiplied by quantity produced is a proportionate measure of utility created, provided that the addition to production is not so large as substantially to depress price. Price multiplied by quantity produced is also the revenue generated by production.

Now consider cost. An extra unit of some factor of production, say a worker, can be made available to forestry by using up one more unit in total, or by diverting the unit from alternative use. A worker is effectively a one-person firm, producing a single product: hours of work (see figure 22.1). The marginal revenue per hour is the price of labour (wage rate). This, like other prices, can usually be deemed constant across the feasible range of output by the 'firm'. The marginal cost of producing another hour's work is an opportunity cost (the forgone value of an hour's leisure) plus a possible disbenefit (the dissatisfaction of working). Optimal output is Q^* hours of work; below this, the wage is worth more than the opportunity cost of leisure time: above it the wage is worth less. The 'price' of leisure is the monetary wage forgone in order to enjoy it.

Workers, in deciding how many hours to work, effectively choose between purchasing leisure (by forgoing an hour's wage) and purchasing goods (which an hour's wage could buy). Take a purchaser of firewood and

Figure 22.1 Wage–leisure trade-off

building poles who is also a worker. It is rational to work until the ratio between marginal utilities of leisure and of firewood equals the ratio between prices of leisure (wage) and of firewood. Price is therefore a proportionate measure of factor cost, on the same utility scale as is used for benefit.

Alternatively, workers may be withdrawn from another enterprise in the economy, causing an opportunity cost. In a competitive economy, the wage represents what employers are willing to pay for an hour of services, and that, at maximum, is the extra revenue which an hour's work would produce for the employer. If the wage is less, profits are increased by buying more hours of work. Eventually the increasing value of scarce leisure time raises the wage at which workers will render services, or the decreasing efficiency of production reduces the contribution of the worker to revenues, until the two reach equality. Contrariwise, if the wage exceeds contribution to revenues, the profit-maximizing employer reduces the hours of work offered until again equality of wage and contribution to revenue is achieved.

This contribution to revenue is, of course, the price of the goods, multiplied by the extra units produced in an hour's work. And that in turn is a proportionate measure of the marginal utility of those goods. The cost to the economy of diverting workers from producing them is the forgone marginal utility of those goods, of which the wage is thus a proportionate measure.

If revenue is a proportionate measure of marginal utility created (as shown) and cost is a proportionate measure of marginal utility forgone (as shown) and if the constant of proportionality is the same for revenue and cost (as shown), then profit measures net marginal utility created.

Policy and project implications

While the above argument is a considerable simplification (Winch (1972) gives a fuller account), the complete argument consists of similar additional stages. For example, profit-maximizing producers, choosing the cheapest production technology for a given good, also minimize the cost to the economy of a particular quantity of production; those who bid most to buy land are those anticipating greatest profits from its use, who in turn can produce either the greatest utility from a hectare by given factor input or a given utility with least expenditure on (= opportunity cost of) other factors.

The profit/welfare argument has implications at policy and project levels. Additions to profit represent additions to welfare. When producers can do no more to increase profits, the economy has reached the highest level of welfare attainable with the available resources. Therefore any government policy which interferes with the economy, or imposes prices other than those generated by the market, at best leaves welfare unchanged, but more probably reduces it.

If the government does actively enter the economy, for example by funding a state forest service, that service should imitate the behaviour of private producers. The profitability of a project is a proportionate measure of net utility gain: profit-maximization is the appropriate objective for state forest decision-makers, as for their private counterparts.

Deficiencies of profit-maximization

A theory so clean and neat and complete can hardly be valid in the tarnished, messy, fragmented real world. But it is essential, in understanding the limitations of profit-maximizing, to be clear about where the invalidity lies. If the theory is invalid at every point, a new basis for decision-making must be sought. But if it has identifiable and restricted defects, it may be more constructive to allow for those defects within some modified or constrained measure of *social* profitability.

Deficiencies are not hard to pinpoint. Firstly, not all products of an economy enter the market; they have no price, and cannot influence profitability. These so-called *externalities* may be good or bad. A forest may produce positive environmental effects, such as improved wildlife habitat.

But as this generates no revenue, profit-maximizing managers have no incentive to adopt silvicultural regimes favourable to wildlife: they would prefer an ecologically impoverishing monoculture even if it is only slightly more profitable than a richly diverse mixture. On the other hand a pulpmill pays nothing for the services of rivers and atmosphere into which it dumps pollutant by-products. The disbenefits thereby imposed are real, yet do not influence the costs perceived by mill managers. Even if pollution-abating technology is available at trivial cost, it is still more profitable to pollute the environment.

Hence not enough positive externalities are created, and too many negative externalities.

The national economy also has objectives outwith maximization of gross national product: balance of external trade and of the state budget, maximization of employment and minimization of inflation. It is not inevitable that individual pursuit of profit benefits these collective goals.

Where markets do exist, identifiable deviation from pure and perfect competition means that prices do not proportionately measure benefit or cost. If, for example a pulpmill has monopsony power (it is the only major buyer of small roundwood in the region), it may offer a lower price than the revenue gained from processing an extra unit. By so doing, it reduces costs of all wood purchased, and thereby increases profit. Thus it is sometimes claimed – though a cause is not always specified – that prices understate the marginal value of wood to the economy (especially if wood cannot be imported). The true value of forestry should include the excess profits generated in processing industries.

Governments themselves manipulate the price of foreign exchange and interfere with interest rates. They tax income, breaking the equality between what an hour of work costs the employer and what an hour of leisure is worth to workers. They make illegal the consumption of one harmful drug, while subsidizing medical services to provide other drugs which turn out no less harmful. Their motives for such intervention may be obscure, but for forest managers it means that not all prices are reliable indicators of value.

A particularly damaging weakness is apparent from the firewood and building poles example (table 22.1). For the purchaser with a 50p budget, a penny buys 2.5 utils of value: for the purchaser with £1.50, a penny buys only 0.5 utils. The value of production, therefore, depends not only on product price but on the income of the purchaser. Neither the free market (at policy level) nor profit-maximizing decisions (at project level) takes into account this matter of income distribution.

Distributional issues also intrude on the way the market mechanism treats future costs and revenues. The interest rate supposedly represents the relative values given to money present and money future. But when the chief beneficiaries of money future – future generations – cannot register willingness to pay in present markets, the validity of the relationship between price and utility is doubtful.

Finally, an effective market mechanism requires that everybody is knowledgeable and rational: that consumers know the prices of firewood and building poles, of paper, food and entertainment, the wages available in all employment open to them; that their decisions *in effect* are like the choices described between firewood and building poles, even if conscious tabulation of marginal utilities does not occur; that producers know their costs and revenues, and maximize profits.

Observers of humanity might argue that ignorance and irrationality also play their part; that producers follow tradition rather than present profit opportunities; that they have inadequate knowledge of cost structure in their enterprises; that personal advancement rather than pursuit of enterprise objectives rules decision-making; that the purchases of consumers and job commitments of workers are made impulsively, without fully considering alternatives; that advertisements condition the perception of goods' utility, as much as their real value; that in a free market system consumers choose drugs and gambling habits and life-styles that immiserate, impoverish and destroy their existence. All this is partially true. Yet economists contend, not that *every* decision conforms to the rationality model: but that decisions, on the whole, and with well-recognized exceptions, tend to increase rather than decrease profits of firms, and promote satisfaction rather than dis-satisfaction of consumers.

Elimination or amelioration of these defects is a matter of economic policy, in which forest policy may play some small part (as in relief of high regional unemployment). However, for forest managers the important requirement is to take decisions, *given* the defects as they are and as they are likely to become. This means taking cognisance of not only the defects of profit-maximizing in the forest itself, but also those defects which affect the economic context within which forestry is practised.

Alternative means of decision-making

The array of faults in the case for profit-maximizing should promote a search for alternative means of taking decisions. It is simply not possible to *avoid* taking decisions: even doing nothing is a selected course of inaction, and its consequences are as much the responsibility of decision-shirkers as are results obtained by their more decisive counterparts. The question really concerns how explicit the decision processes are.

There is advantage in formalizing decision processes, if only to allow other people to examine the basis of and comment upon decisions. It is more democratic, as well as confronting decision-makers with the real nature of decisions.

These arguments apply to private and corporate as well as state forests. Although profit-maximization remains the major private objective, it is increasingly pursued within a context of state surveillance, control and financial encouragement of forest activity. Socially responsible and responsive forestry also promotes community goodwill in a way that may ultimately enhance profits.

Chapter 23 examines some formal alternatives to the profit-maximizing criterion. Some take profit-maximizing as a basis, trying to retain its desirable features; others attempt to build from nothing a criterion to replace it. All methods accept the deficiencies of a pure profit-maximizing rule.

23 Decision-making with Multiple Objectives

Society has multiple objectives and multiple products, not all reflected in profits, but which should be incorporated in decision processes. This chapter discusses two kinds of process: those informing decision-makers about courses of action, and those embodying rules about which course of action should be chosen.

Non-profit objectives and forgone profit

Courses of action which promote environmental objectives often reduce profit: for example, extending rotations or harvesting small coupes to enhance forest landscape, planting low-yielding species to promote wildlife interest, or leaving areas unplanted for informal recreation.

Suppose a plantation of exotic species, currently 40 years old, has a present standing value of $6000 per hectare, and an optimal rotation of 50 years, yielding $11 000 per hectare. Successor crops would have NPV at 5% of $1500 per hectare. To landscape the surrounds of a new recreation facility, it is proposed to replace it immediately by indigenous trees with NPV at 5% of $-600 per hectare and an expected rotation of 120 years. The least error-prone way to calculate net forgone profit in perpetuity is as two alternative cash flows, as in table 23.1.

If a 5-ha area is so treated, total cost is $11 820. The result is more helpful if translated into a cost per unit of output. For instance, what is the cost of prolonging the rotation per car-load of visitors expected to enjoy it? Given that environmental benefits arise in perpetuity, the discounted output concept (see equation (8.5)) is useful. For example, the number of visits to the facility might be expected to build up as follows: year 1, 5000 visits; year 2, 8000 visits; year 3, 10 000; each year after, 10 000 visits.

Table 23.1 Opportunity cost of environmental management

Item	Commercial plan	Environmental plan
This crop NPV to year 40	$11 000/$1.05^{10}$ = $6753	$6000
Next crop NPV . . .	$1500	$-600
in perpetual series . . .	$1500 \times 1.05^{50}/(1.05^{50} - 1)$ = $1643	$-600 \times 1.05^{120}/(1.05^{120} - 1)$
		$-602
discounted to year 40	$1643/$1.05^{10}$ = $1009	$-602
This crop + successors	$6753 + $1009 = $7762	$6000 - $602 = $5398
Net forgone revenue	$7762 - $5398	= $2364

Summed discounted visits

$$= \frac{5000}{1.05^{0.5}} + \frac{8000}{1.05^{1.5}} + \frac{10\ 000}{1.05^{2.5}} + \frac{10\ 000/0.05}{1.05^{2.5}}$$

$$= 198\ 201\ \text{[discounted] visits}$$

(10 000/0.05 is the 'capitalized visits' from year 3 onward)

Net forgone profit in perpetuity ($11 820) divided by summed discounted visits in perpetuity gives cost per visit (6.0¢). Often such unit costs are so modest, or so enormous, that there is no difficulty in deciding whether the sacrifice of profit is worthwhile.

Where an inverse linear relationship exists between profit and non-profit output, the shadow prices produced by linear programming similarly indicate the profit lost by imposing non-profit targets.

Ordinal land use decision rules

Thus far this book has used cardinal numbers, on which normal arithmetic operations may legitimately be performed. The justification was that costs and revenues are proportional to losses and gains of benefit. If that justification is not accepted, ordinal numbers (first, second, last) may be used in decision rules: instead of cash flows being *summed*, one course of action is deemed *best* in one respect (perhaps at producing timber) while another is best in cost economy. (Schuster and Zuuring (1986) give further description of scales and the problems of manipulating and aggregating them.)

Take three alternative land use plans, with four products, shown in table 23.2. Two products are salable, but production is measured in tonnes per hectare per year. Recreation is measured in thousands of visits per year, wildlife as species of breeding bird. While these numbers are cardinal

Table 23.2 Performance under multiple objectives

Objective	Forest plan	Integration plan	Multiple land use plan
Timber	16	14	12
Food	1	6	6
Recreation	10	0	9
Wildlife	27	4	26

measures of *quantity*, they are not all cardinal measures of *value:* for example, not every species of breeding bird has equal conservation importance.

For a decision-maker who is also land-owner, intuitive overall preference among the plans may guide choice. Preference is in fact the most basic expression of quantification: the preferred plan is 'better' than any other.

But for a community, or a decision-maker acting on behalf of society, the difficulty is that not everybody agrees on the best plan. If, however, they agree on the order of importance of the objectives, decision-rules can be formulated. In table 23.3, Roman numerals indicate ordinal numbers, I meaning 'best' or 'most important' and so on. Cardinal measures of quantity are replaced by ordinal measures of value, the assumption being that, for example, *any* extra species of breeding bird improves attainment of the wildlife objective.

Table 23.3 Ordinal measures of performance

Objective	Objective rank	Forest plan	Integration plan	Multiple land use plan
Timber	II	I	II	III
Food	I	III	I=	I=
Recreation	IV	I	III	II
Wildlife	III	I	III	II

The 'dominant use' rule favours the plan which performs best under the most important objective, in this case food production. Integration and multiple land use plans perform equally well, so the second-ranked objective, timber production, is brought in. As integration outperforms multiple land use under this objective, it is selected.

Two objectives played no part in this decision. An alternative which corrects this omission may be termed the 'Olympic' rule: the best plan is the one gaining most 'gold medals' for best performance on each objective. Under this rule the forest plan (three 'golds') is chosen. If two plans achieved two 'golds' each, the best would be the plan with most 'silver' medals.

This system also has deficiencies. It ignores 'silver' and 'bronze' awards except when there are equal 'golds'. Some athletics meetings remedy this by giving 'placing points' for, say, the first four positions. This too has shortcomings, notably that it fails to reflect the 'margin of victory'. If placing points are I = 4, II = 2, III = 1, the forest plan scores 13 points, the integration plan 8 points, and the multiple land use plan 9 points. But the difference of one species of bird gives the forest plan a 2-point advantage over multiple land use, whereas a difference of 22 species gives multiple land use a single point advantage over integration.

Table 23.4 The goals-achievement matrix

Objective	Objective rank	Objective weight	Forest plan	Integration plan	Multiple land use plan
Timber	II	8	128	112	96
Food	I	10	10	60	60
Recreation	IV	3	30	0	27
Wildlife	III	6	162	24	156
Total			330	196	339

To reflect the 'margin of victory' factor needs cardinal numbers, where intervals, as well as rankings, have significance. Table 23.4 has been expanded to include a set of cardinal weights reflecting the assessed importance of each objective. Weights are consistent with ranks, but contain more information on relative magnitude.

The totals under each plan now represent a combined measure of value: the degree of achievement of each objective (from table 23.2) multiplied by the weight of that objective. The plan with the biggest total (multiple land use) is deemed best. This 'goals-achievement matrix' method is due to Hill (1968).

Multiple goal programming (see Buongiorno and Gilless, 1987) can replace goals achievement where 'plans' involve continuous variation of some forest feature to which achievement of objectives is mathematically related. Varying the objective weights generates plans with different degrees of achievement of objectives, and so allows decision-makers to examine the effect of the weights.

Goals achievement eliminates the worst deficiencies of ordinal methods. It includes all objectives and all performances, and allows for the 'margin of victory'. There are, however, snags.

1 Degree of achievement is measured on very diverse (and arbitrary) scales. Although wildlife is the third-ranked objective, it contributes the most to points totals, simply because achievement reaches higher numbers. Had timber and food production been measured in kilogrammes rather than in tonnes, the result would have been very different!

2 To avoid such bias, achievement could be measured on a 0–10 scale for each objective, or as a percentage of the performance achieved by the most successful plan (these would not necessarily give the same result). Even then it is unclear that moving one point up the scale means the same thing throughout the range. Is moving from 9 to 10 superfluous

gilding of the lily, or consummation of perfection? How does that compare with solid but unspectacular improvement from 5 to 6? For timber and food such intervals have constant meaning, but the value of an additional breeding species depends on its rarity.

3 Neither is the meaning of or method for deriving objective weights self-evident. If all members of a community contribute to weighting objectives, what prevents farmers from applying a weight of 1000 to food production? Even if each person is restricted to a total of (say) 27 points to be allocated to the objectives, it is still in the interest of the outdoor activities lobby to give all those points to timber production. (Readers may check that transferring the 3 recreation points to timber raises the forestry plan (best for recreation) to a 'winning' score of 348.)

4 If, to avoid such strategic behaviour or to simplify decision-processes, the power to weight objectives is vested in a group of decision-makers, weights may be biased by the narrow interests of that group.

Democracy does not help either. Suppose that the objective weights in table 23.4 reflect the votes of a population sharply demarcated into four groups, each person favouring one objective. Eight foresters would vote for forestry, as would three recreationists and six ornithologists, leaving farmers to distribute their ten votes between the integration and multiple land use plans – a big majority favouring the forestry plan. But again degree of preference counted for nothing.

The desiderata for numbers to be useful in decision-making are extremely restrictive. They should be:

(a) measured on a cardinal scale – a given interval represents the same additional value at every point on the scale;
(b) commensurable – every scale is numerically comparable with every other scale;
(c) truthful – weights express the true perceived importance of objectives, or the real degree to which they are attained;
(d) equitable – they embrace the interests of every affected party.

The difficulties of deriving such numbers from physical quantities or democratic processes show the market mechanism in more favourable light, and raise the question of whether useful values might, after all, be derived by modifying prices to allow for identified deficiencies. This is what cost–benefit analysis attempts.

Cost–benefit analysis

Cost–benefit analysis has been defined as an economic appraisal of the costs and benefits of alternative courses of action, whether those costs and benefits are marketed or not, to whomsoever they accrue, both in present and future time, the costs and benefits being measured as far as possible in a common unit of value. Far from being a modern technique, cost–benefit analysis originated in the nineteenth century (Dupuit, 1844; Pingle, 1978), as deficiencies of profit-maximization were pinpointed. The literature of the subject is largely concerned with correcting these deficiencies.

Cost–benefit analysis (CBA) is ambitious and all-embracing, attempting to aggregate costs and benefits of many kinds, to all people, in every generation. Its key distinguishing feature is its attempt to translate all costs and benefits (or all objectives) into a common (commensurable) unit of (cardinal) value. It is in this translation, while maintaining truthful and equitable representation of value, that technical problems arise. Given the definition, it would be unreasonable to oppose CBA in theory: the problem is, in practice can it be done?

Chapter 22 adopted utils as a common unit of value. Utils, however, are arbitrary, useful in theoretical welfare economics, but not directly measurable. The alternative is a unit related to money. After all, 'getting your moneysworth' is a commonly understood expression of value, and many costs and benefits of actions are directly measured in monetary terms. Most deficiencies of profit-maximizing arise from failure to measure the money value of certain effects, rather than from any shortcoming of money itself. Even apparently insuperable problems of valuing distribution effects and non-market costs and benefits in monetary terms are in fact susceptible to indirect solutions.

The numeraire

The unit of value in CBA is called the *numeraire*. It has units of whatever the convenient currency may be: US dollars, pounds sterling, Indian rupees, Kenyan shillings, Australian dollars, etc. But it is not enough to nominate the currency. The following must also be specified.

1 *The base year to which the purchasing power of this currency refers*

No currency has the same value as it had 25 years ago; one unit today represents much less purchasing power than it represented then. It is conventional, and convenient, to take the current year as the base year. In CBA, as in profitability calculations, prices for particular products should be taken as constant over time unless there is reason to expect them to increase faster or slower than those for commodities generally. Monetary interest rates must of course be adjusted for inflation.

2 *The convertibility of the currency*

Units of domestic currency may be freely convertible: or there may be a mark-up on foreign exchange. Most developing countries (and many developed ones) experience chronic shortages of foreign exchange which make hard currency in the hand worth more than its official domestic equivalent.

3 *The purpose (if any) to which the currency is committed*

During economic development, investment funds may be scarce for political and institutional reasons: a unit which the government is free to invest is more valuable to long-term social welfare than one committed to immediate consumption.

4 *Ownership of the currency*

CBA is usually undertaken by or for a government agency, and currency in government hands is normally considered more valuable than currency in the hands of the people. However, within that population greater importance may be given to an extra unit in the hands of poorer citizens.

While it is essential to use the same closely specified unit of value throughout the analysis, it is a matter of convenience how that unit is defined. Many manuals of CBA for developing countries use a numeraire defined in terms such as: 'the value at 1990 prices of uncommitted foreign exchange (or its official domestic equivalent) in the hands of the government'. It is, however, easier to develop understanding of CBA if the numeraire is 'the value *at present-day prices* of *domestic currency* used for *consumption* by citizens having the *mean income level* for the country': this is the normal numeraire of Part III.

To value the diverse objectives and effects of forestry in terms of this numeraire, CBA appeals to an economic dictum: 'the end of all economic activity is consumption'. The word 'end' has two-fold meaning: it suggests both the objective at which economic activity is aimed, and the final result of each economic act. 'Consumption' means 'use of goods and services to promote happiness', and could hardly be disputed as a reasonable objective.

The point is that creation of environmental amenity and job opportunities, the balancing of a nation's trade account, the redistribution of the nation's income are themselves unimportant. Even amassing 'uncommitted foreign exchange in the hands of the government' is itself but a means to an end. It is only as they tend to promote the happiness of the nation's citizens that these objectives are worthwhile: the job of CBA is to estimate as best it can their net beneficial effect.

Some economists claim that happiness is no part of their responsibility, and that cost–benefit analysts who dabble with such concepts tarnish their reputation as objective social scientists. Others consider that unless economists have something to say about happiness, they are not worth listening to. For economists in private forestry corporations the happiness of shareholders is pursued by profit-maximization: for economists working for national and international institutions the remit is wider, and it too should ultimately concern happiness.

Shadow pricing, cost–benefit style

Although consumption is the end of all economic activity, although changes in consumption are the basis for evaluating investments, such changes are not the immediate effect of all projects. When cost–benefit analysts ask 'what changes when this project is adopted?' they do not expect an immediate answer in terms of altered consumption, but rather a miscellany of changes including extra factors of production required, extra inter- mediate goods to be purchased and, in due course, extra goods available for sale or distribution by other means.

The large question of 'what is the forest investment worth?' can, therefore, be split into smaller questions: 'what changes when one unit of this factor of production is diverted into the project?'; 'what is expected to change when this forest produces timber?' For each factor of production and good, a miniature CBA in effect must be done, to establish how much additional consumption arises when one more unit becomes available, or what consumption is lost when one more unit is used up. The value of a factor or good so established is called its *shadow price*. Shadow prices in CBA play the same role as market prices in profitability calculations. The next task of a CBA methodology is to systematize calculation of shadow prices for the major goods and factors of production.

In developing economies particularly, a distinction is made between factors of production and goods whose availability affects trade, and those whose availability does not. (A third category *potentially traded* is some- times added.) A traded good is not simply a good that crosses national frontiers. For example, plantations in a remote region might produce elec- tricity supply poles for local use. As a result poles produced in another region would no longer be required, and could be exported. The locally used poles are hence treated as traded goods. By contrast, if an integrated rural development scheme produces a crop, such as coffee, on which there is an international export quota, no extra coffee can be exported from the country as a whole. The scheme merely displaces export of coffee produced elsewhere in the country: more coffee is consumed domestically, or is wasted. Coffee is untraded.

The test of whether a good is traded is: are there any changes in trade, and consequently net foreign exchange earnings, as a result of one more unit being produced, or used by the project? If not, the good is untraded. Untraded goods are usually either difficult to store and/or transport, or subject to trade restrictions.

The effect of using or producing a traded good is a change in available foreign exchange (see chapter 27).

Untraded goods

When an untraded good is used [produced], the consequences depend on price elasticities of supply and demand for the good. Take a requirement for electricity to run a sawmill, the only supply being from a small hydroelectric power scheme. Supply is totally inelastic in the medium term, since higher prices cannot make more water flow through the turbines. Extra units can only be supplied to the mill by reducing supply to other consumers. The shadow price is an opportunity cost – the value of electricity forgone by consumers who would otherwise have been supplied. Conversely, any change in upstream forest management which increased river-flow would be valued via increased electricity consumption. Change of consumption creates or removes *marginal social benefit*.

By contrast, take a good with very inelastic demand: salt is the textbook example. Although not an obvious input to forest production, it may be used to maintaining harvesting in countries where winter freeze-ups are combated by distributing salt on roads. Given inelastic demand and quite elastic supply, the overall effect is likely to be more salt production. This in turn incurs a *marginal social cost* as extra factors of production are mobilized.

These factors of production include traded goods (perhaps depreciating machinery), other untraded goods (such as electricity), labour, investment funds (if productive capacity is expanded), and land (meaning all natural resources). The untraded goods can be further costed according to whether they incur forgone marginal social benefit or additional marginal social cost, which itself can be broken down yet again. Natural resources are often in totally inelastic supply (like the river-flow for hydroelectric power): their commitment to a project automatically denies their use by other consumers, so forgone marginal social benefit is entailed.

Table 23.5   The basis for shadow pricing of fuelwood

Item	Cash value	Physical value
Landed cost of kerosene/litre	$0.228	
Taxes	MK0.22	
Marketing costs	MK0.22	
Marketing profits	MK0.12	
Calorific value of kerosene (Kcal/litre)		8000
Thermal efficiency of kerosene combustion		0.30
Calorific value of wood (Kcal/kg)		3500
Thermal efficiency of wood combustion		0.08
Air dry wood density (kg/m³)		525
Kerosene equivalent of 1 m³ wood $0.08 \times 3500 \times 525/(0.30 \times 8000) = 61.25$ litres		

The example in table 23.5 shows the CBA approach to pricing (Misomali, 1987). Fuelwood is extensively used in Malawi both for domestic cooking and in tobacco-curing. Under present policy it is supplied free or at a subsidized price (around 5 Malawian kwachas per solid cubic metre). At this price fuelwood plantations appear unprofitable.

However, additional fuelwood production reduces the need for imported kerosene, which gives a better basis for evaluation. Although the official exchange rate is $1 = MK1.68, the premium on foreign exchange means the shadow price of $1 is MK2.00 (see chapter 27). Taxes and profits are transfers, not resource costs. Thus the shadow price of 1 m³ of fuelwood is

$$(\$0.228 \times 2 + 0.22) \times 61.25 = MK41.41$$

More intensive analysis would have split marketing costs into labour and traded transportation inputs.

Alternatively, wood may replace animal dung for domestic heating (Newcombe, 1984). The dung is thus available as a fertilizer, the benefit being either:

(a) marginal social benefit of increased food production, or

(b) saved cost of equivalent artificial fertilizer (import cost plus internal costs).

The relevant value is the one representing the savings actually brought about by increased fuelwood supply.

At the end of the initial assessment, all inputs and products are reduced to the following categories: marginal social benefit (created or forgone); traded goods; labour; investment funds. The next few chapters describe how to derive shadow prices for each category.

Standard conversion factors

As well as the primary factors of production listed above, some composite inputs (especially transportation) are used in nearly all projects. To avoid duplication of effort, a *standard conversion factor* may be calculated, equal to the general ratio of shadow price to market price. Market cost in any particular project is multiplied by this factor to give shadow price.

Schools of thought in CBA

CBA is not an agreed body of techniques accepted by all practitioners. Differences in numeraire have been alluded to, but there are more fundamental divergences. Much of the literature falls into two categories. 'Environmental CBA', whose main concern is evaluating non-market costs and benefits, has been the major preoccupation in industrialized countries. 'Development CBA' concentrates on distortions of market prices and distributional issues, and has vital relevance to the Third World. None-theless, environmental effects of land use are now clearly global issues, while economic development has always been a priority for rural regions within rich countries. Both strands of CBA deal with matters of great importance to foresters everywhere.

Another distinction often made, but not often made clearly enough, is between economic CBA and social CBA. The two are not synonymous: in some ways they are diametrically opposed. Economic CBA deals with products: social CBA focuses on income. Social CBA absorbs distributional objectives into the numeraire: economic CBA separates efficiency and distributional objectives. Shadow prices in economic CBA are efficiency prices: those in social CBA are social prices.

Nonetheless, the two techniques have common data requirements, and, through much of the discussion of shadow pricing, can be treated together. Both are clearly distinct from so-called financial CBA, which is just another name for profitability assessment.

24 Valuing Changes in Consumption

Forestry projects exist to increase consumption, for shareholders, project workers, or citizens generally. Reduced consumption of some goods is also a likely result of factors of production being diverted into projects. Even when products are traded, or when monies accrue to government investment accounts, the ultimate concern of CBA is with how much consumption the foreign exchange earned or the capital laid down will generate in due course. If the satisfaction which consumption imparts is the end of all economic activity, a means of evaluating it is the chief requirement of CBA. This chapter examines general techniques for doing so; the two ensuing ones apply the techniques to evaluation of recreational, aesthetic and conservation benefits.

Willingness to pay and net social benefit

The willingness of consumers to pay the price of a product implies that they expect to derive satisfaction from consuming it. And, as the example of firewood and building poles in chapter 22 showed, rational choice means that willingness to pay the price is a proportionate measure of extra satisfaction expected from an additional unit of the product. In this respect profit-maximization effectively promotes welfare, and CBA simply takes on its desirable characteristics.

But willingness to pay is not the same thing as price, and in using willingness to pay CBA differs fundamentally from profit-maximization. Figure 24.1 shows a demand curve for firewood in a market serving poor urban-dwellers exclusively. The curve is shown as a straight line to simplify calculations. However, the conclusions would be valid for any demand curve with negative gradient.

The market price is 400 pesos, but as part of a social welfare programme the Forest Service intends to sell at a controlled price of 200 pesos. The demand curve indicates that sales will increase from 2000 to 3000 bags per

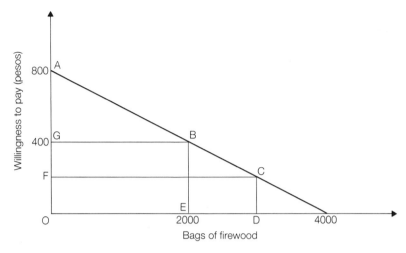

Figure 24.1 Urban demand for firewood

week. Only willingness to pay for *extra* consumption is relevant. The value of the 2000 bags which would be consumed anyway does not change as a result of the programme. But is the willingness to pay for the extra 1000 bags 400 pesos (original price) or 200 pesos (new price)? Actually it is neither. Only for the 2000th bag is 400 pesos the willingness to pay. Only for the 3000th bag is 200 pesos the willingness to pay. Between these limits, marginal utility diminishes as consumption increases, so that willingness to pay for the 2600th bag would be (from the graph) 280 pesos. Mean willingness to pay is 300 pesos per bag, and the total willingness to pay, 300 pesos × 1000 bags = 300 000 pesos.

Generally, total willingness to pay is area BCDE, that is *the area under the demand curve, between the limits of quantity consumed before and quantity consumed after the project*. Whenever consumption increases, mean willingness to pay is less than the pre-project price and more than the post-project price.

So much for benefits, as measured by willingness to pay. But how is this extra consumption made available? The supply of firewood is totally inelastic, owing to a sustained yield constraint. The shadow cost of firewood must, therefore, be the forgone marginal social benefit incurred because supplies are diverted from the other consumers – a relatively affluent group of rural farmers, whose demand curve for fuelwood forms figure 24.2.

At 400 pesos, 6000 bags were consumed. To make an extra 1000 bags available for urban sale, the Forest Service raises the rural price to 600 pesos. The benefit lost through forgone consumption is area IJKL, 500 000

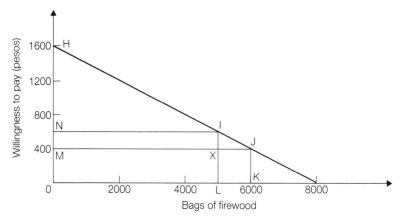

Figure 24.2 Rural demand for firewood

pesos. Net benefit is −200 000 pesos, indicating that the programme is not worthwhile.

Willingness to pay and distribution

However, redistribution of consumption – the main motive for this programme – has so far been ignored. Willingness to pay 100 pesos by the rich does not indicate the same value as willingness to pay 100 pesos by the poor: *willingness* to pay is conditioned by *ability* to pay as well as by perceived value of the purchases. There are two sharply divided views on how this fundamental problem should be tackled.

1 *The Pareto improvers*

Economic cost–benefit analysts justify direct use of willingness to pay by appealing to the notion of *potential compensated Pareto improvement*. Pareto was a welfare economist who attained fame by making the unremarkable proposition that if anyone is better off (happier) as a result of a change, and no-one worse off, the change is a good thing. One could hardly object to this: the problem is that most forestry projects leave some people worse off, perhaps because of reallocation of consumption (as above), or because they lose access to customary grazing land, or because they dislike the forest's appearance, or because they had hoped to borrow the funds now set aside for forestry. Note that it is not sufficient that *most* people should be better off: Pareto improvement requires that not a single individual is worse off.

To overcome this restrictive condition, the idea of *compensated* Pareto improvement was introduced. It is in the interest of project beneficiaries to bribe the losers from the project to withdraw their objections to it, rather than have the project lapse because it failed to meet the Pareto improvement criterion. In the firewood redistribution programme, the total willingness to pay of beneficiaries (300 000 pesos) is plainly insufficient to compensate the losers (who have lost 500 000 pesosworth of consumption). Again, the programme is not justified.

Suppose, however, that a land-owner discovers a mineral deposit worth $10 million under a forest. Exploiting that resource might deprive a forest-dwelling population of its livelihood (or, in an industrialized country, destroy a recreational amenity). The Pareto improvement criterion insists that no-one be made worse off: however, the land-owner would pay up to $10 million in compensation, if that was the only way to obtain political clearance for mineral exploitation. On being offered such compensation, the affected parties would probably find an acceptable alternative to the forest. Everyone could be made better off, and mineral exploitation would be uncontroversially good.

Unfortunately compensation is rarely paid to all losers when projects are implemented. This very practical problem is sidestepped by further modification of the criterion: rather than requiring that compensation should *actually* be paid, the *potential* compensated Pareto improvement criterion demands only that it should be *theoretically* possible for adequate compensation to be paid. Thus the potential compensated Pareto improvement criterion simply entails summing the willingness to pay of gainers (potential source of compensation) and deducting the willingness to accept compensation (or forgone willingness to pay) of losers. Under this dispensation, minerals could be exploited to supply a rich person's frivolous fancies and the forest-living population could starve: that would not matter, because *in theory* the forest-living population could have been paid enough compensation to establish them in an alternative livelihood. There can be no ethical justification for such a criterion

Proponents of economic CBA, however, say that ethical matters are for politicians, not economists, to decide. For example, a political constraint could be imposed, that projects would be unacceptable if they worsened income distribution: while this is laudable, in practice it is almost as difficult to find a project where there are no *poor* losers as to find one in which there are no losers at all.

It can be argued that, if distribution is not ideal, then the tax system should be modified to make it so. According to this view, *projects* should be selected for their economic efficiency: economic equity is achieved by selecting *policies*. Again, this viewpoint is impractical. In reality there are institutional constraints on reform of the tax system, and adopting suitable projects may be the easiest way to improve the welfare of the poor. Furthermore, some projects so alter income distribution that a tax system optimal before the project would have to be modified to neutralize the project's distributional effect.

2 The distribution weighters

The attempt to separate distributional issues from project evaluation is not satisfactory when projects and distribution are inextricably linked. *Social CBA* therefore explicitly evaluates distribution. It proceeds from the premise that money is worth more to poor than to rich consumers, and that willingness to pay should be weighted accordingly.

The first step is to establish who is advantaged, who disadvantaged, and by how much, as a result of a project, in terms of willingness to pay. The beneficiaries of the firewood programme obtain firewood worth 300 000 pesos, but to obtain it they forgo purchasing power (200 000 pesos) spent on the additional 1000 bags. They are thus better off by 100 000 pesos. The poor purchasers of the 2000 bags sold prior to the redistribution programme also benefit. They still buy these bags, but at 200 pesos less per bag, and are consequently better off by 400 000 pesos. Overall, the poor group is better off by 500 000 pesos.

The change can be interpreted in terms of figure 24.1. Before the programme, the poor consumed 2000 bags, for which total willingness to pay (ABEO) was 1 200 000 pesos, but for which they actually paid 800 000 pesos (GBEO). The difference between willingness to pay and actual payment (400 000 pesos) is called the *consumers' surplus*; it is represented by ABG. Willingness to pay, actual payment and consumers' surplus after implementation of the programme are respectively 1 500 000, 600 000 and 900 000 pesos, represented by ACDO, FCDO and ACF. The change in consumers' surplus is 500 000, represented by GBCF.

By contrast, the richer rural purchasers of firewood lose consumers' surplus of 1 100 000 pesos. This is composed of 500 000 pesos of lost firewood consumption (IJKL), a saving of 400 000 pesos on those units of firewood consumption (XJKL), but additional expenditure of 1 000 000 pesos on the 5000 bags of firewood still consumed (NIXM).

The Forest Service formerly sold 8000 bags at 400 pesos: now it sells 3000 bags at 200 pesos and 5000 bags at 600 pesos. The change in revenue is

$$(3000 \times 200 + 5000 \times 600) - 8000 \times 400 = + 400\ 000 \text{ pesos}$$

In effect, the government taxes consumption of firewood by the rich, and thereby more than offsets its subsidy to the poor. Any measure like this which changes the overall tax position should be evaluated by asking specifically 'who is advantaged, and who disadvantaged, and by how much?' Because pesos do not have the same value for all groups, changes in consumers' surplus cannot be compared without applying weights which reflect relative values: this is analogous to the need to apply discount factors to cash flows at different points in time before they can be added. Let the weight on the poor group's pesos be 2, that on the rich group's, 1, and the weight applicable to Forest Service revenues, 1.5. Table 24.1 summarizes the changes. The programme is now clearly worthwhile, and it is worthwhile because it achieves its objective of redistributing consumption.

Note that the unit of account is not pesos, but pesosworth, the reference worth of the peso being its value to the rural rich (with weighting 1). Pesosworth of value must be distinguished from pesos of finance.

An interesting sidelight on the real world is given if the urban poor, instead of consuming the additional 1000 bags of fuelwood, simply resell it to the rural rich at the old price of 400 pesos. By this transaction, the rural rich gain 100 000 pesos in consumers' surplus. The urban poor lose 300 000 pesos (willingness to pay for the 1000 bags), but gain 400 000 pesos in cash. Table 24.1 can now be rewritten as table 24.2.

Table 24.1 Distribution effect of firewood project

Economic group	Weight applied	Change in surplus	Weighted change in surplus
Urban poor	2	500 000	1 000 000
Rural rich	1	−1 100 000	−1 100 000
Forest Service	1.5	400 000	600 000
Total			+500 000

Table 24.2 Beneficial effect of firewood resale

Economic group	Weight applied	Change in surplus	Weighted change in surplus
Urban poor	2	600 000	1 200 000
Rural rich	1	−1 000 000	−1 000 000
Forest Service	1.5	400 000	600 000
Total			+800 000

The change from table 24.1 is an actual Pareto improvement: the urban poor and rural rich are better off, the Forest Service is no worse off. The overall change is better than simple redistribution of fuelwood. This underlines a point often made by economists, that it is better to redistribute income than to subsidize particular products. The government could have taxed the rich by 1 000 000 pesos and given 600 000 pesos to the poor, retaining 400 000 pesos for its own use. Institutional factors prevented this, so a physical redistribution programme was implemented instead. It is not necessarily bad for welfare if illegal resale produces the desired redistribution informally!

Where do weights come from?

Weights are crucial. If, for example, the weight to the urban poor was only 1.2, and that to the government only 1, then the total weighted change in surplus would have been $-100\ 000$ pesosworth.

Weights are also politically contentious. They reflect the importance given to groups within society: it is in every group's narrow interest to secure a high weight for itself and a low weight for everyone else.

Not everyone is persuaded of the validity of weighting either. One cannot argue from the single premise of the diminishing marginal utility of an individual's consumption to a higher weight on willingness to pay of the poor. For example, it is often asserted (usually by the rich) that the rich have great sensitivity which enables them to derive more satisfaction than the poor from consumption at any given level. Equally, it can be asserted that habitual spending brings a jaded palate and an inability to delight even in the basics of life. It can be argued that the rich are so by reason of meritorious industry, and that the poor are so through blameworthy indolence. Or equally, that riches are obtained by oppression and exploitation, and poverty brought about by working such long hours that the labour market is oversupplied and wages driven down.

If, however, sensitivity and deservingness are randomly associated with income (a supposition which neither theory nor experience refute) then *on average* the weight on a peso should be greater for the poor than for the rich. Thus those who wish to weight for sensitivity and deservingness must do so as a separate exercise.

Possible methods of deriving weights (see Weisbrod, 1972 for elaboration) are:

1 Governments simply dictate what weights should be used or are solicited to provide them by cost–benefit analysts. Unfortunately many politicians would not understand numerical weights, and if they did would assume they were part of a plot to supplant their functions (see chapter 32).

2 Weights are implied by past government choices among projects. Some redistributive projects could only rationally have been adopted if a weight in excess of (say) 3 was applied to a group. Others could only rationally have been rejected if a weight less than 4 was applied to the same group. Fortunate is the cost–benefit analyst who finds a government acting so consistently!

3 If the relationship between income and its marginal utility has been defined mathematically, the weight appropriate to a group's willingness to pay is proportional to the marginal utility of its income. The relationship is sometimes characterized as

$$MU_Y = a\,Y^{-n} \qquad (24.1)$$

where Y is income
   a is a constant
   $-n$ is the elasticity of marginal utility of income

Since only *relative* weights are important, a need not be known, but n, which determines how rapidly marginal utility of income diminishes, must be evaluated. Methods suggested for doing this include

(a) looking at responses to risks which involve a large range of possible incomes;

(b) examining trade-offs made between time and money (for example in journey-to-work decisions) by people at different income levels (Clark, 1973);

(c) comparing price and income elasticities of demand, the relationship implying elasticity of marginal utility of income (Fellner, 1967).

These methods provide an unbiased set of weights. Values suggested for n in the literature range from 0.5 to 3.

There is no means of avoiding weights, except in the rare case of an actual Pareto improvement. Whenever one group's gain is traded against another's loss, some kind of weight is given. 'No weight' in reality means 'equal weight': a peso is deemed equally valuable to everyone – a rather unlikely assumption. The debate is about how explicit, consistent and objective the weighting process should be.

Evaluation of non-market benefits and costs

Foresters often refer to environmental and social benefits of forestry as 'intangibles' or 'imponderables'. These are unhelpful terms, implying that such benefits are immune from sensible contemplation and discussion. Generally associated with this mentality is the opinion that it is unethical to evaluate such benefits economically. On the other hand some foresters still suggest that these benefits are rather peripheral to the main purpose of forestry (growing wood) and should not be dignified by monetary evaluation.

In fact the feature distinguishing these benefits from timber production is not that they are more ethically sacrosanct, or more ethereal, but that they do not enter markets, for reasons to do with conditions of production and consumption, rather than their reality or moral worth. The attempt to evaluate such benefits in monetary terms carries no implication that they should be sold commercially. The purpose of evaluation is to give them an appropriate emphasis in comparing courses of action. Evaluation may show them to add little to the case for forestry investment. If so, so.

Whole books have been written about evaluating non-market benefits and costs, and even on evaluating one particular type of cost or benefit. To this literature foresters have made no small contribution: Sinden and Worrell (1979) review the methods available systematically. A bare outline of possible bases for value, and some of their problems, is given below.

1 *Marketable products which arise elsewhere in the economic system*

CBA is concerned with benefits 'to whomsoever accruing'. Marketable effects generated for other consumers as a result of forestry are therefore relevant: for example, changes in crop yield caused by shelter effects. Depending on climate, and on whether total run-off or evenness of flow is more important, forests may increase or decrease usable run-off from water catchments. Where either the water itself or hydroelectricity is sold, resultant net revenue gained or lost can be computed. Barrow et al. (1986) have shown that the opportunity cost of lost water yield may be greater than net timber value on hydroelectric power catchments.

2 *Financial costs saved elsewhere*

The protective effects of forests, for example in checking avalanches, can sometimes be alternatively achieved by major engineering works. If the two methods are equally effective, the value of forests' services is the saved (shadow) costs of the engineering alternative. A value of £200 000 million has been suggested for the protective function of Swiss forests (Seymour and Girardet, 1986). The tacit assumption, not always valid, is that protection is so important that it must be achieved one way or another.

Conversely, forestry may impose financial costs. A technique due to Collett (1970) evaluates adverse hydrological effects. Let demand for water be rising at 1% per year from the current 100 million litres per day. Let existing reliable supply be 130 million litres per day. New reliable supply will be required when

$$100 \text{ million} \times 1.01^t = 130 \text{ million } (t = 26.367391 \text{ years ahead}).$$

Let afforestation increase total evaporative loss by 20% of 1000 mm rainfall = 0.2 m.

Spread over 1 ha, this gives $0.2 \times 100 \times 100$ m^3
= 2 000 000 litres per year
= 5476 litres per day, reducing reliable yield to 129 994 524 litres per day.

Hence new reliable supply will be required when

$$100 \text{ million} \times 1.01^t = 129\ 994\ 524\ (t = 26.363158 \text{ years ahead}).$$

Let the capital cost of the next reservoir be £5 000 000. If the discount rate is 5%, the discounted cost of this 26.367391 years ahead (no forest planted) is

$$\frac{£5\ 000\ 000}{1.05^{26.367391}} = £1\ 381\ 222$$

The discounted cost if 1 ha of forest is planted is

$$\frac{£5\ 000\ 000}{1.05^{26.363158}} = £1\ 381\ 507$$

Thus 1 ha of forest increases discounted cost of new water supply capacity by £285. Further hectares increase the cost more than proportionally, as the time of replacement is brought successively nearer. The costs of advancing a succession of added reservoirs should also, technically, be included.

Other imposed hydrological costs of forests may include liming to correct acidic run-off, and filtration to remove excess sediments caused by forest operations.

3   Price of similar products which are in fact marketed elsewhere

Recreation facilities offered free in the forest (perhaps because usage does not justify paying anyone to collect fees) may be sold commercially where use is heavier, and the commercial fee may be taken as a measure of benefit. It is, however, questionable whether the product in the forest (often quiet and informal) is the same as that sold commercially (often noisy and highly organized); the type of consumer (and therefore willingness to pay) may also differ greatly.

4   Voluntary subscriptions to causes or campaigns

Even when no market exists, conscientious consumers may voluntarily contribute money, both to general causes (such as the World Wildlife Fund) and to specific campaigns (like a legal battle to prevent an amenity woodland being felled). A difficulty lies in the uncertain nature of what consumers are actually 'buying'. 'Will you give £1 to save the giant panda's habitat?' is a rather deceptive question, implying that if one does give £1 the giant panda's habitat will be saved, and if one doesn't it won't. In fact the situation is probabilistic. If £1 is given to the campaign, the probability of saving the habitat may be 0.500 000; if it is not, the probability may be 0.499 999. If that difference of probability is worth £1 to an individual, the certainty of saving the habitat is worth £1 000 000! The matter is further complicated by the possibility of altruistic subscription, money being contributed, not to benefit the contributor, but to save the giant panda's habitat for all humanity (and pandadom!)

5   Questionnaires

CBA seeks people's willingness to pay for benefits, or willingness to accept compensation for tolerating disbenefits. The most straightforward way of finding out is to ask directly. The appealing simplicity of direct questions overlies a tangle of problems in perception and motivation, which may render this method unworkable. These are detailed in chapter 25. However, the method is worth considering as a first or last resort. Its directness, if nothing else, commends it.

6   Own judgement

Sparing themselves even the trouble of questioning the consumer, decision-makers or economists or those making legal judgments may ask how they *personally* value a benefit, or what compensation would induce *them* to accept a disbenefit. The result, multiplied by the expected number of consumers or sufferers, yields a global value. Despite the unfamiliarity of such questions, it is often only necessary to ask 'is it worth £100?' 'well, £1 then?' '£10?' to find at least an approximate value. Again, the technique should not be despised for its mere simplicity.

It holds very serious dangers, however: firstly, of atypical judgement (assessors may be more knowledgeable and have more refined tastes than, or different tastes from, the consumers on whose behalf the judgement is made); secondly, of biased judgement (assessors may have vested interests in a particular outcome, and this method grants licence to distort truth in favour of the desired outcome). On both grounds, foresters are not suitable people to make neutral and representative judgements about, say, the aesthetic value of productive woodlands.

7 *Accepted past costs*

Earlier generations of foresters recognized non-market benefits, even if there was then less pressure to evaluate them. Environmental improvements were made with some sacrifice of profit, either by financial outlay or through departure from profit-maximizing silviculture. Examples of such opportunity costs were given in chapter 23. These sacrifices would only have been rational if benefits exceeded costs, and a minimum level of benefits is therefore implied (Gregory, 1955).

Of all the methods of valuation, this can most readily be dismissed. The underlying assumption, that past decisions were right, can be guaranteed only if earlier managers had

(a) a prior conception of the monetary value of the benefit being promoted, and
(b) a reliable means of calculating profit forgone by the chosen course of action.

The second condition is not improbable, though the appropriate discount rate and hence the actual opportunity cost was probably different when the decision was taken. The first condition, however, raises the question of how earlier managers assessed non-market benefits. Was it, perchance, as the opportunity cost willingly accepted by some previous manager? And how was *that* decision made? Thus the accidents of history become embedded in the received scientific knowledge of a later age!

The best that can be said for this method is that, in conjunction with an independent present-day judgement, it may lead towards inter-generational consensus on the value of certain benefits.

8 *Associated expenditure*

Access to non-market benefits may require expenditure on marketable goods. A classic example is purchase of a particular house in order to obtain a good view. The better the view, the higher the house price, all else being equal. On a smaller scale, a complement of trees appropriate to the size of garden may be an important amenity, for which a substantial premium price is paid. By contrast a screen of trees on adjoining land may block a view and reduce market price.

Of course, many other factors affect house prices, and it might be considered impossible to disentangle the premium due to one favourable factor. However, estate agents make a living from such judgements, and economic researchers may replicate this expertise using multiple regression analysis.

The most widely used example of associated expenditure, however, is travel and accommodation costs incurred to gain access to countryside or wilderness recreation. This underlies a technique of major significance in forestry, treated in detail in the next chapter.

25 Recreation Evaluation

Over recent decades recreation has become an important product of forests in affluent nations, and is becoming increasingly so in countries like Malaysia whose income and urban population are growing rapidly.

Contemporary with the rising importance of recreation has come development of recreation economics. The two main strands relevant to forestry are tourist income generation (see chapter 33), and evaluation of consumers' surplus from informal recreation. This chapter aims to review the capabilities and limitations of evaluation techniques, rather than to describe their scope fully.

As so often in CBA, interest centres not on a single price, but on a *distribution* of willingness to pay. The two tasks of recreation economists are to plot this distribution for a particular site or facility, and to evaluate its managerial implications.

Questionnaires

Asking forest visitors how much they are willing to pay for their visit presents several problems.

1 *Hypothetical questions*

Where free access is usual, the question is strange or even sinister. People are accustomed to buying bread or renting accommodation, and their willingness to pay for these commodities is set in a framework of reasonable norms. There may be no such experiences or norms for informal recreation. It may not even be clear whether the questioner means 'willingness to pay for the whole experience' or 'willingness to pay for entry to site'.

Hostility could also condition the response. Free access may be a long-established right or tradition, and to pay for entry may be unthinkable. Any positive response is then seen as a breach of principle, even if there is clearly no intention of charging in practice. Thus individuals who value the site intensely, as well as those who care little about it, may give a zero response. Even in the absence of such emotions, it can be argued that the appropriate value of a free facility is the compensation required for giving up a visit, rather than willingness to pay for it. Hammack and Brown (1974) have shown that the former value may greatly exceed the latter.

2 *Interviewer bias*

To supply a framework of norms, interviewers may suggest a 'reasonable' fee and elicit visitors' responses to it; according to response, a higher or lower fee is then suggested, and eventually a maximum acceptable fee is defined. But it can readily be shown that visitors are greatly influenced by the first fee suggested (Boyle et al., 1985). If the initial suggestion was £10, £2 seems quite moderate, and might be accepted. But if the initial suggestion was 10 pence, £2 would seem extortionate and be rejected. Such biases can only be avoided by meticulous and scrupulous questionnaire design.

3 *Strategic response*

Even if visitors know their willingness to pay for a visit, they may not reveal it truthfully. Self-interest could cause bias in either direction. If they believe that the fee stated would actually be charged, self-interest dictates a low response. On the other hand, interviewers might hint that the survey aims to establish whether the site's recreation value justifies retaining public access, or whether the forest should be cleared for housing or agriculture. Respondents would then wish to emphasize the high value of recreation, and so exaggerate true willingness to pay. There is obvious merit in keeping the purpose of the questionnaire vague. If visitors cannot decide whether self-interest lies in exaggeration or understatement, they may tell the truth for lack of other guidelines!

Associated expenditure – household survey

Though entry to forests may be free, the recreation experience can generally only be obtained by spending money (probably) and time (certainly) on travel. If the forest is far from visitors' homes, there are costs of accommodation too. Specialized forms of recreation require further expenditure on clothing and equipment. Such expenditure is real rather than hypothetical; there are no strategic advantages in misrepresenting willingness to pay by making visits that are not worthwhile, or staying at home when a visit would yield net benefit. Hence expenditure data are a more reliable indicator of willingness to pay than responses to questionnaires.

Household surveys involve sampling the resident population to establish recreation habits – preferably past visits rather than projected ones. The advantage is that they build up a comprehensive picture of all recreational activity – indeed, they can be combined with broader social surveys. This is the correct approach when the subject of research is the consumers themselves and their pattern of consumption.

In evaluating a particular recreation site, however, or even a particular kind of recreation activity, household surveys provide an inefficient sampling frame. Many households contacted may never participate in forest recreation. Only a tiny fraction may ever visit the forest under investigation.

Associated expenditure – site survey

It is more efficient to interview visitors at the site itself, where every interview produces relevant data. Interviewers may ask directly about expenditure and about visitors' personal data, but the most basic analysis records only the visitor's home town and mode of transport to site. The remaining data can be compiled from other sources. Suppose a 1% sample of visits during a year yields the data in table 25.1. The relationship between costs and visits shows no obvious resemblance to a demand curve. However, if visits (say) per thousand population are plotted against cost, a more intelligible picture appears. Figure 25.1 shows demand curves for the recreational experience, for the given number of people over a given period.

Table 25.1 Data for the gross recreation demand curve

Home town	Cost of travel	Population	Sampled visits	Total visits	Visits/1000 population
Netherton	2.3	12 000	35	3500	292
Nexton	3.5	25 000	53	5300	212
Middleton	4.2	8 000	10	1000	125
Distanton	5.8	54 000	31	3100	57
Remoton	7.1	14 000	4	400	29

Statistical problems in compiling the demand curve

When the points of the demand curve lie in orderly fashion, the curve can be drawn by eye – though there may be problems in extrapolating it. Often, however, sampling errors and factors not included in the analysis produce a scatter of points, and the right shape and location for the line is not clear.

In any case, it is desirable to subject the curve to regression analysis, if for no other purpose, to determine whether the relationship depicted is likely to

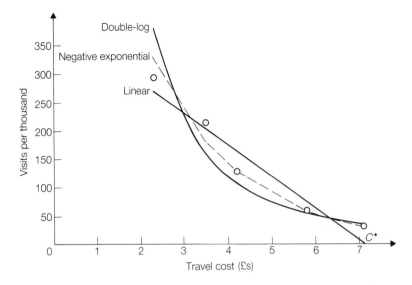

Figure 25.1 Different curve-fits for demand data

be real, or the result of a fluke. (Readers unfamiliar with regression analysis should either become familiar with it, or skip to the next section.)

What is the shape of the demand curve? a straight line? a negative exponential (with a given percentage decline in visits per thousand for each unit increase in cost)? a double-logarithmic curve (as often depicted in textbooks, approaching both price and quantity axes, but never crossing them)? The three shapes are superimposed in figure 25.1. All of them fit the points quite well. Regression analysis shows which shape explains most variation in visits per thousand.

However, before determining the shape empirically, consider the implications of each shape. The straight line cuts both axes, implying that at some quite small cost (C^* in figure 25.1) no-one would visit the forest. If the cost exceeded C^*, the graph suggests negative visits, which cannot be sensible. The double-logarithmic curve, on the other hand, suggests that if visits are free then an infinite number would be made in one year, which cannot be sensible either. (The double-logarithmic model also makes consumers' surplus infinitely valuable if price elasticity of demand ≥ -1.) The negative exponential model implies neither negative nor infinite visits. It predicts increasing visits at a negative price (if people were bribed to visit the site) but finite value for visits, both of which are sensible too. It has other technical advantages. Its equation is

$$V/P = a \times e^{-bC} \qquad (25.1)$$

where V/P is the visits per thousand population
  a and b are constants
  e is the base of natural logarithms
  C is return travel cost.

The regression is estimated by taking natural logarithms of both sides, giving

$$\log_e (V/P) = \log_e 1027.7 - 0.49796 \times C \qquad (25.2)$$

The relationship is highly significant: adjusted R^2 is 0.985 – markedly higher than for the other shapes.

Because of sampling error structure, and as a result of taking logarithms, not all data points are equally reliable. This problem of *heteroskedasticity* exists in many biological and social relationships, but is particularly important when data points are widely scattered. Treatment of this problem is detailed in Bowes and Loomis (1980), Christensen and Price (1982) and Price and Wan Sabri (unpubl.)

Demand for the recreation site

The demand curve derived above is for the recreation experience. It is analogous to the demand curve for finished wood products. As shown in chapter 2, however, most consumer expenditure on wood products pays for processing, transportation and harvesting. The value of timber in the forest is the residual value after all these costs have been deducted from final product price. If CBA aims to derive values for 'raw' recreation comparable with those of 'raw' timber, then the costs of obtaining the experience must similarly be deducted from overall willingness to pay for it. An experience valued at £3.50 obtained by spending £2.30 on transport has a net value of only £1.20: if an entrance fee higher than this were charged, the visit would not be worthwhile. As with firewood in chapter 24, the benefit to consumers is measured not as willingness to pay, but via consumers' surplus *after actual payment has been deducted*.

The most instructive approach to summing consumers' surplus for the site is to predict the response of visitors from various towns to various hypothetical entrance fees. For example, a £1 fee would raise the total cost of a visit from Nexton to £4.50. Substituting this price in equation (25.2) gives

$$\log_e (V/P) = \log_e 1027.7 - 0.49796 \times 4.5 = 4.6943$$

$$\therefore\ V/P = 109.32$$

Since population of Nexton = 25 000, total visits per year would be

$$25 \times 109.32 = 2733$$

Out of the 5300 annual visits from Nexton, 2733 impart a consumers' surplus of at least £1.

Repeating for other towns and other entrance fees gives table 25.2. The column totals of visits worth at least £Fee more than actual costs gives a demand curve (figure 25.2) for the site's whole catchment, showing residual willingness to pay over and above actual costs.

The demand curve does not reach the cost axis, but the area under it within the scope of the graph is about £25 000, this being the total consumers' surplus. Counting squares on graph paper is a simple but effective means of estimating area.

Table 25.2 Data for the net recreation demand curve

Town	Fee = 50p	Fee = £1	Fee = £2	Fee = £4	Fee = £10
Netherton	3059	2384	1449	535	27
Nexton	3506	2733	1661	614	31
Middleton	792	617	375	139	7
Distanton	2409	1878	1141	422	21
Remoton	327	255	155	57	3
Total	10 093	7867	4781	1767	89

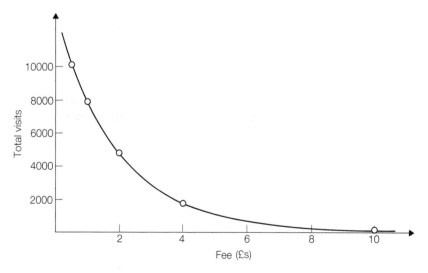

Figure 25.2 The net recreation demand curve

This elegant method, due to Clawson (1959), has since dominated informal outdoor recreation economics, being sufficiently straightforward for routine application by non-economists. The legitimacy of adding the dissimilar entities consumers' surplus and (say) timber revenues is sometimes questioned. The fact is, however, that the value of extra timber production is simply revenue to the forest owner: timber sales in one forest create little consumers' surplus (since willingness to pay for one more unit equals price). By contrast, the value of free recreation is simply consumers' surplus. These *are* the values, and they should be added.

Those familiar with calculus may consider further the negative exponential demand curve (other readers may proceed direct to the next section). Integrating the equation of the curve:

$$\int (V/P)\, dC = a \int e^{-bC}\, dC = a\,[e^{-bc}/-b]$$

Inserting limits C^* and ∞ gives

$$a\,[0 - (e^{-bC^*}/-b)] = a\,e^{-bC^*}/b$$

which is the consumers' surplus per thousand population for whom $C = C^*$. The number of visits per thousand population for whom $C = C^*$ is

$$a\,e^{-bC^*}$$

whence consumers' surplus per visit is

$$\frac{a\,e^{-bC^*}/b}{a\,e^{-bC^*}} = 1/b \text{ (for all values of } C) \qquad (25.3)$$

In this case $1/b = 1/0.49796 = 2.0082$

This remarkably compact result (Christensen, 1985) is another useful feature of the negative exponential. It gives an algebraic estimate of total consumers' surplus from the site as

[total visits] × [consumers' surplus per visit]

$$= 13\,300 \times \pounds2.0082 = \pounds26\,709$$

Complications in Clawson's analysis

Despite the straightforward appearance of the method, small complexities and uncertainties infiltrate it at every point. The underlying assumption of the method is that willingness to pay is uniformly distributed in the population of every town: for example, the 29 visits per thousand made from Remoton at a cost of £7.1 imply that 29 visits per thousand from Netherton are worth at least £7.1. This may not be so. The population of Netherton may be older and less active than that of Remoton; they may have less money to spend on travel (so distributional issues also arise). These socio-economic differences can in theory be circumvented by undertaking separate analyses for each socio-economic group, or by including socio-economic variables in the equation which predicts visits per thousand. Less easily dealt with are systematic biases: people may have settled at Netherton because they particularly enjoy forest recreation, and are willing to pay more than the citizens of Remoton for it.

Suppose there is a town called Nunton near Middleton, from which no visits are recorded at all. The absence of visits implies that *no-one* values forest recreation as highly as £4.2, just as the existence of visits from Middleton implies that some people *do*: the data are biased by omitting this. Nunton's resounding silence may be incorporated by putting Middleton and Nunton into one population grouping, with visits per thousand intermediate between that of the individual towns. If zero visits are explicitly recorded, logarithmic transformation in the regression analysis becomes impossible.

It is also assumed that visitors correctly perceive the cost of travel: many surveys have shown that this is not precisely true.

Cost per kilometre of travel to the forest varies according to mode: some visitors travel alone in expensive cars; others share the cost of a minibus, or come by bicycle. A separate analysis could be done for every travel mode, but data are usually insufficient to permit this, and mean travel costs are used instead.

The journey to the forest takes time, which has an opportunity cost. Many visitors to urban and urban fringe woodlands may have walked from home: time cost is then the only basis for a Clawson analysis. This cost could be estimated (Beesley, 1965) and added to the direct financial cost of travel. Alternatively, various hypothetical values could be used, the value providing the best fit of data to the demand equation being adopted (Common, 1973).

But the journey to the forest may itself be enjoyable: time spent on it is a benefit, and some consumers' surplus of the visit ought to be ascribed to the journey. This problem is magnified when other sites are visited during a trip to the forest, and becomes crucial when the forest constitutes one of many visits during a holiday. A technique of allocating benefits of multi-site holidays, and of incorporating multiple transport modes into one analysis, is described by Christensen et al. (1985).

The costs of time spent at the site, and of accommodation and subsistence in the vicinity, are the subject of disagreement, some authors contending that these costs indicate greater willingness to pay than is conventionally ascribed. However, as this extra indicated benefit is balanced by extra actual expenditure, consumers' surplus is not necessarily affected.

Consumers' surplus – in relation to what?

A recurring theme of this book has been the need to ask: what changes when a course of action is adopted? This treatment of recreation, however, has not yet considered any courses of action at all. Nothing changes: consumers' surplus just *exists*. Is it an absolute value? a value over-and-above something? the value lost if some (unspecified) change occurred? or created by planting the forest? Remarkably few recreation economists seem interested in answering these questions. Forest managers may affect consumers' surplus by:

(a) changing the availability or accessibility of a particular facility;
(b) changing the visual and biological character of a given location;
(c) regulating or redistributing the number of people using a site or series of sites, with consequences for congestion.

Changes (b) and (c) entail changing environmental quality, which is the subject of chapter 26.

The most dramatic change in availability of a facility is closing a forest to the public. This may result from a new use incompatible with recreation (for example, live-round military training or open-cast coal-mining), or from change from public to private ownership. It might seem that visitors then automatically lose their consumers' surplus (being denied the experience for which they were willing to pay, but saving their actual expenditure). However, the possibility exists (which surveys confirm as a majority preference) of substituting a visit to another recreation site. If this site has similar characteristics (another forest, perhaps) and is not much further distant, little consumers' surplus would be lost. A survey of what visitors regard as the next best alternative allows that loss to be estimated.

Failing detailed information, a reinterpretation of Clawson's analysis may be useful. If potential substitutes for the recreation site exist, it can be said that for V/P visits per thousand the net value of the forest site exceeds the consumers' surplus available at the substitute (or the substitute would have been visited instead).

[willingness to pay] − [cost] ⩾ [consumers' surplus from substitute]

This can be rewritten

[willingness to pay] − [consumers' surplus from substitute] ⩾ [cost]   (25.4)

That is to say the relationship recorded is one between cost and the visits per thousand population for whom its value *over and above the net value of the best alternative* exceeds cost. The consumers' surplus measured, therefore, is not an absolute figure, but an excess value over that of substitutes. It is precisely this excess which is lost when site closure forces the substitution to be made.

A roundabouts-and-swings factor apparently operates with substitutes. On one hand, by diverting some visits (particularly from distant centres) away from the site under evaluation, they cause underestimation of consumers' surplus; on the other, they ameliorate the effect of site closure by providing a better alternative to the site than merely staying at home.

This conclusion holds even if the quality of substitute differs from that of the forest site, *provided that recreation sites are randomly distributed in space* (Connolly and Price, unpubl.). If sites are clustered, visitors can divert to a nearby site with little loss, unless congestion effects are serious.

Unfortunately this convenient interpretation cannot be applied to evaluation of projected facilities (since potential visitors cannot be interviewed). Instead, recourse must be made to surveys of households and similar sites in the region, to establish how many visits might be diverted to the new facility (with saving in travel cost) and how many extra visits might be made (with positive consumers' surplus).

Time trends

Whereas the productivity of the site clearly constrains the profit obtainable from timber, the forest's recreation value can be enjoyed by an increasing number of consumers, until congestion becomes a problem. Thus the fast growth of outdoor recreation increases its value per hectare. But does consumers' surplus grow in proportion to visits? Or do extra visits have diminishing marginal utility? These questions are reconsidered in chapter 29.

Distribution

Participation in outdoor recreation, and expenditure per experience, is typically greatest in middle to upper income groups. Poorer groups, if they participate at all, use cheaper modes like buses and motor-cycles. After weighting, however, their consumers' surplus per visit may equal that of other groups. Low participation may also reflect lack of information about country recreation among impoverished central-city-dwellers. These factors enhance the economic case for locating forests for recreation purposes near urban areas and public transport routes therefrom.

Conclusions

Elegant and straightforward though it is, the Clawson method suffers defects whose cumulative effect is serious. Of these, the most serious is that it does not specify the course of action to which its value is relevant. No better method has yet been devised, however. Carefully applied, it gives an indication of the value of forest visits (usually in the range $1–$10), and forms a basis for evaluating environmental quality.

26 Evaluation of Environmental Quality

Scenic beauty and wildlife interest are two aspects of environmental quality much influenced by forest management decisions. From an economic viewpoint, they share many attributes; the same evaluative techniques are applicable to both.

Environmental quality may also be affected by the number of visitors to a recreation site. Some research results have cast doubt on whether congestion of recreation sites does detract from environmental quality. These results can however be explained in terms of extraneous variables (Heberlein and Shelby, 1977; Chambers and Price, 1986), and it is clear, certainly for some visitors and certainly above given threshold levels, that congestion degrades visitors' experience in the forest. Evaluation of congestion is complicated by the relationship between number and quality of visits, and by the availability of direct management measures to change the number of visitors, as well as the quality of the visit.

The decisions discussed so far have concerned changes in quantity supplied (of wood, water or recreation visits) to satisfy a given demand. This chapter addresses decisions which change the nature of the product supplied, with consequent shift of the entire demand curve. The difference is illustrated in figure 26.1.

Improvement in quality has two identifiable effects: more visits (*extra* visits having positive consumers' surplus) and increased willingness to pay (implying greater consumers' surplus) for visits taking place *already*. Neither can be evaluated without estimating the shift of the demand curve, which is the main preoccupation of this chapter.

Travel cost analysis and difference of quality

In theory the effect on demand of differences in environmental quality is easily determined. The travel cost method (chapter 25) is used to derive demand curves for a forest with a particular interesting mammal present

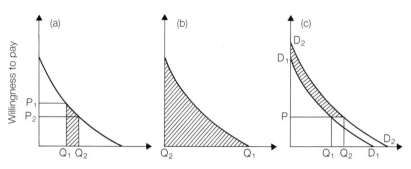

Figure 26.1 Kinds of change and willingness to pay
(a) increase in output
(b) loss of a site
(c) improved quality
Shaded area indicates change in willingness to pay

and for one without; for a forest of mixed indigenous tree species and for a monoculture of exotic conifers; for a forest which is crowded and for one which is not. The differences between demand curves are the demand curves for the difference of quality in each pair of cases: the demand curve for the mammal; the demand curve for natural forest structure; the demand curve for solitude.

In reality it is not so easy. The three complicating factors are

(a) the small difference of quality in relation to residual error in travel cost analysis,
(b) the difficulty of finding paired sites that differ in only one important feature,
(c) the interaction of features composing the perceived environment.

Factor (a) means simply that the real difference in demand for the sites is likely to be swamped by extraneous factors unless the visitor-catchments of the sites are similar in every respect, including the availability of potential substitute sites. This need for homogeneous catchments turns factor (b) to virtual impossibility. One must therefore settle for sites which differ in several respects, which exacerbates the problems of factor (c).

The value of an individual feature within an environment is not independent of other features. The subtle colour-tones of mixed woodland are less appreciated on a day of driving rain than on one of fresh breeze and sunshine. The grandeur of tall ancient conifers may be more fitting in a rocky wilderness than in a soft pastoral scene. Even if one could find rocky wildernesses identical except in respect of tall ancient conifers, the value ascribed to them in that setting could not be transplanted to other circumstances.

The perverse effect of even quite simple interactions *between* sites is well illustrated by the attempt to value uncongested conditions. A given site has higher imputed consumers' surplus per visit during congested public holidays than out of season. This is because at holiday time all sites are crowded, and crowd-sensitive visitors travel further to avoid the *worst* of the crowds. According to equation (25.4), travel cost analysis measures consumers' surplus over and above that available at alternative sites. Off season, alternative sites may be agreeably uncrowded: during holidays they are unbearably congested. As figure 26.2 makes clear, travel cost analysis shows only that the differential in favour of the remoter site increases in season, not that visitors travel further to find congestion!

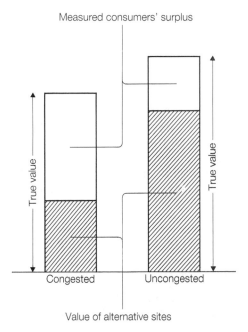

Figure 26.2 Measured and actual site value under congestion

Interaction of features within and between sites is so intricate that one could hardly combine them into a mathematical model for one location, let alone a region. Attempts to separate demands for individual components of environment by additive statistical techniques like multiple regression analysis are doomed from the outset. Incorporating interactive variables is statistically dubious because of the indefinitely large number of possible models (Price, 1976, 1978b). There is simply no way to circumvent this problem. Subjective judgement must be invoked. But it can be done systematically.

Questionnaires again

The effect of a specified change in a given environment is implied by what inhabitants or visitors say they would be willing to pay for it (or how much compensation would be needed for deterioration in the environment). The perils of questionnaires have already been discussed, but bias can be reduced.

The first requirement is to represent the change accurately. Words convey different things to different people. A photomontage (less prone to the rose-tinted-spectacles factor than an artist's impression) shows what changes are proposed. Some description of associated ecological change would be helpful, but the aim is to evaluate the *most probable* course of development, not to cordialize public relations with glossy pictures that imply unlikely superabundance of rare and picturesque creatures.

Next, the aim is to elicit a truthful response to this accurate representation. Despite the inherent risks of strategic response, Brookshire, Ives and Schulze (1976) argue that if respondents believe their stated willingness to pay will be averaged with everyone else's in determining an entry fee, there is no incentive to mis-state true willingness to pay to maintain quality natural environments.

Questions can be phrased according to circumstance. Where visitors are accustomed to paying for the environment, a simple cash value may be elicited.

'How many dollars would it be worth to you to see racoons in this forest?'

Within traditionally free-access sites, it is more acceptable to ask

'If the beauty of this site is presently rated at ten points, how many points would you rate it at if ... [here the change is specified and illustrated]?'.

Alternatively,

'Would you prefer

$$\left[\begin{array}{c}\text{a 50\% chance of keeping}\\ \text{this site as it is}\end{array}\right] + \left[\begin{array}{c}\text{a 50\% chance of}\\ \text{never seeing it again}\end{array}\right]$$

or

[certainty of keeping it, but with fewer species and a shorter rotation]?'

The latter question actually means 'is the present state of the forest more or less than twice as valuable as the forest after the proposed change', but it states the nature of the choice more forcefully.
Alternatively:

'Would you prefer to visit the site

[once without anyone else at all present] + [four times with it as crowded as this]

or

[five times with this moderate level of crowding]?'

[Different photomontages are shown to illustrate the alternatives].

These questions require (cardinal) evaluation of environment in its own terms. Perhaps surprisingly, visitors treat them seriously and give sensible answers. The advantages are that similar quantities are being compared; that the unacceptable taint of money is avoided; that it is difficult to perceive any strategic reason not to tell the truth. The problem remains of interpreting answers in terms of willingness to pay, but this deficiency can be made up by combining questionnaires with travel cost analysis. If mean willingness to pay of visitors is £2 when the site is in its current 10–point state, the mean willingness to pay should be £3 if the site is enhanced by 5 points. For more detailed analysis, the demand curve for the recreational experience can be expanded by 50% on the willingness to pay axis.

Not just quality

Part of environmental quality may be universally recognized, as in international lists of World Heritage sites. Satisfaction with a site may also be conditioned by cultural and personal factors. Depending on upbringing, education, personality and customary environment, a certain type of landscape may be perceived as restful or boring; a certain mammal may be regarded as wildlife or vermin. This mixture is reflected in willingness to pay for components of the environment, but it does constrain the transfer of values between countries, regions or even urban and rural areas. It also means that differentials of value are not constant through time, as customs, perceptions and norms change.

Familiarity with a particular place in a particular condition is an aspect of satisfaction which is distinct from general preference for a type of landscape or ecosystem. A desire for stability is something slightly different again. Commercial foresters are apt to dismiss the protests of the public over major changes during the rotational cycle: ('the people objecting to us felling this wood are the same people who objected to us planting it 50 years ago'). But love of the familiar and the seemingly-unchanging are not irrational, for most people dwell a little in the past and crave some stability.

These values are inaccessible to ordinary techniques of evaluation. People are most familiar with the environment closest to them: they do not express their love of it by willingness to pay large sums to visit it. Questionnaires on compensation for loss of the things which touch the whole of people's lives, understandably, elicit the most hostility, or may lead them to express the simple but inconvenient truth that no amount of money would compensate them for losing the things that best make life worth living.

Management of congestion

Because more experiences means congested experiences, feasible strategies in response to congestion are circumscribed. The problem is self-regulating in that excess of visitors so reduces site quality that the demand curve shifts down and fewer people come.

The equilibrium shown in figure 26.3, however, is not an economic optimum. At equilibrium, the marginal visit gives benefit equal to actual cost: it imparts no consumers' surplus. On the other hand, by increasing congestion, it imposes non-marginal disbenefits on all other visitors. Like other negative externalities, congestion is over-produced by a free market. Hence the case for regulation.

At this point managers face two intertwined questions: by *how much* should the number of visits be reduced? and by *what means?* Questionnaires of the type suggested above indicate the optimal level of use. A more difficult problem is to achieve this level. Excluding further entrants after a given number of visitors have arrived causes many wasted journeys to the site. Charging for entry may provoke ideological hostility. Yet the ethical case for selling the scarce resource of solitude is as strong as that for selling the scarce resource of timber. Being charged for entry is no more expensive to the visitor than paying for fruitless journeys, while being cheaper to the nation in physical transportation resources. Economically, charging is the best option. But if charging is politically unacceptable, consumers' surplus may be greater under free access, with attendant congestion, than under physical regulation, with unproductive use of travel resources. This is particularly so when demand for recreation is inelastic (Price, 1981a).

A second broad strategy is to increase capacity, either by opening new sites or by vegetation management to create the illusion of solitude. The costs of implementing this strategy may be greater, but there are benefits in both increased number and increased quality of experiences (Price, 1981b).

Thirdly, an attempt may be made to redistribute visitors within a particular site, or among a group of sites, by charging, persuasion or coercion. With sophisticated regulation of timing and route as in North

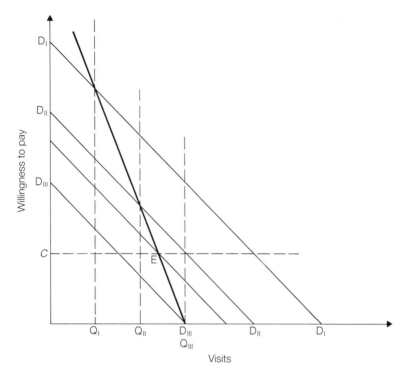

Figure 26.3 Supply and demand with congestion
The heavy line indicates feasible combinations of demand (D_I, D_{II}, D_{III}) and
quantity of visits (Q_I, Q_{II}, Q_{III}). E is the equilibrium number of visits at cost C.

American wilderness areas, 'trail encounters' can be significantly reduced
(Shechter and Lucas, 1978).

When visitors spread freely over a site, rather than following a prescribed
trail at a prescribed rate, the case for redistributing use is either that

(a) the relationship between satisfaction and crowding is highly convex-
to-origin, or that

(b) visitors are split between highly crowd-sensitive and totally crowd-
insensitive groups (Price, 1979).

Evidence for either condition is hard to find. With a given number of visitors
in a given number and size of forests, the optimal management is probably to
allow visitors to distribute themselves as they will, except when irreversible
ecological degradation results from intense visitor pressure. The question is
then one of investment: is the short-term disbenefit, probably slight, of

visitors being diverted from their preferred path justified by the long-term benefit of preserving that part of the site for all posterity? At a high enough discount rate, the answer would be no.

Visitor response to change

To evaluate change in environmental quality, managers must judge how visitors will respond. When adverse change occurs, or when site regulation is implemented, will they stay at home, go elsewhere, or just tolerate it? How many more visitors might there be if conditions improve? And will they simply divert from other, less attractive sites? To evaluate all possible consequences accurately requires an unobtainably complex model of the whole recreation system: forest managers must seek simplifications.

Fortunately, impact on environment of many day-to-day management actions is a small enough part of forest value that most visitors will keep coming with the same frequency. Their gross willingness to pay simply benefits, or suffers, in proportion to the change in quality and the proportion of the whole trip affected by it (figure 26.4). Whether the percentage change is assessed by interview, by foresters personally, or by experts is a matter of expediency and availability of resources.

If change is detrimental, and sufficiently major to divert some visits away from an area, the 'surplus-over-substitutes' interpretation of the Clawson analysis (equation (25.4)) estimates the loss of value for the visitors expected to adopt this strategy. Where sites are clustered, the overstatement of loss calculated by this method is partly offset by the additional congestion such diversion imposes.

For beneficial changes there is no satisfactory alternative to examining the system of sites. After the change has been implemented and come to maturity, the value given by travel cost analysis approximately reflects the contribution of the site to the value of the recreation system. Retrospective comparison with the former site value in theory indicates the value of the improvement. In practice the time-scale of improvement is likely to be such that other factors swamp the real effect of the change.

Physical use restriction is even less justifiable for systems of sites than for sites in isolation. The response may be a more-or-less haphazard journey in search of alternatives, creating congestion on roads and, eventually, at another site, transportation resources having been needlessly expended on the way. The more inelastic the demand for recreation, the more likely it is that attempts to frustrate that demand will have undesirable side-effects (Price, 1983a).

Remaining 60% of cardinal value   Net benefit from rest of visit

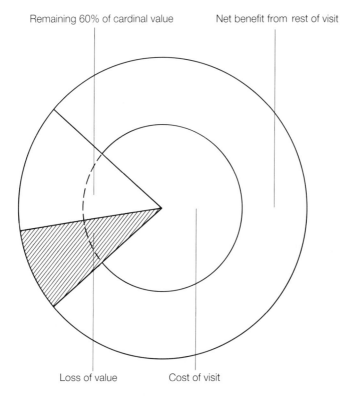

Loss of value   Cost of visit

Figure 26.4 Composition of gross benefit of a forest visit: the outer circle represents gross benefit; the inner circle represents cost; the left-hand sector represents the portion of visit value due to a given site, and its shaded portion the benefit lost through detrimental change (e.g. clearfelling)

Off-site values

Attention has so far been confined to the value enjoyed by forest visitors. For very high-quality landscape, and for very rare wildlife, substantial value is also derived by non-visitors. This *option demand,* as it is loosely called in the literature, has three components:

(a) knowledge (analogous to the peace of mind permitted by adequate insurance) that the site or species exists, should a visit ever be desired;
(b) pleasure due to the knowledge that other people *are* deriving direct satisfaction from the site or species;
(c) personal satisfaction derived from knowing that the site or species exists.

By definition, these values cannot be found by on-site interview. Household survey is very inefficient for specific sites, though for species enjoying the status of wildlife celebrities, like the giant panda, willingness to pay for their continued existence would be found in many households. Responses on emotive subjects like the value of endangered species are prone to upward bias, particularly as a fee is unlikely to be charged for those who do not visit reserves where the species survive.

The possibility of species extinction introduces the value of genetic conservation. The gene pool is valued, not just because it affords opportunities for wildlife study to future generations, but because material and marketable values may in due course be derived from it: breeding material for disease resistance or adaptation to extreme environments, species for use in biological control, providers of therapeutic drugs. In principle genetic material is salable, so could enter financial analysis. In practice the gene pool is regarded as a public property, and the recurrence of a particular gene in populations spread over numerous land holdings makes the market value of a few individuals very low (even when their desirable characteristics have been identified). The prisoner's dilemma recurs, with all individuals looking to every other individual to pursue public benefit, while themselves pursuing private profit. And there is little private profit in genetic conservation.

The public worth of the gene pool, and particularly of the contribution made by any particular patch of natural forest, is probabilistic: what is the chance of this hectare containing genetic material which

(a) has significant advantage over alternative material
(b) is not available from alternative hectares?

The rate at which alternative hectares are disappearing in some parts of the world materially increases the probability that a hectare preserved will meet these conditions, and thus its mean expected value for genetic conservation.

The contrary force is that of discounting: the perpetual stream of potential good which arises from genetic conservation is reduced to a finite, not very significant value. For criteria without a discount rate, the opposite problem arises. The loss of benefit through extinction of irreplaceable genes has indefinitely large value. Thus every species is of infinite worth, and every provenance, and variety, and possibly every individual.

Conservation for its own sake

From the human viewpoint, when a species becomes extinct there is an immediate sense of affront to the idea of natural justice. This may decline over time, though we remain offended, 300 years later, by that most famous extinction, of the dodo. Natural justice is, in principle, as much affronted by extinction of nameless invertebrates, but our feeling of loss is negligible.

Then there is the satisfaction we might have enjoyed, but no longer can, from existence of a species. We are unaware of past losses because we have no datum against which to measure them: that does not make the loss unreal. Nevertheless, there is only a certain amount of interest we can derive from the natural world, only a certain measure of regret at its depletions. Some of the loss is repaired by substitution: there are always other rarities to protect, other creatures whose behaviour can fascinate us instead. It is only the fact that the small net losses persist for ever that gives them much significance, under non-discounting criteria.

But added to this is the forgone life of the creature itself, whatever value that life might have had and no longer has because of the extinction. There is the countervailing value of the *realized* lives of other creatures, perhaps common ones, who take over the vacant ecological niche. Economists are inclined to be dismissive of such considerations, arguing that value means 'value to humanity'. CBA need not adopt that philosophy, however.

Even conservationists are inclined to inexactness in their thinking, arguing that the case against extinction derives from the right to live. Yet in natural justice the right to live applies to individuals as much as to species, to common species as much as to rarities. And if every elephant has a right to life, just because it is a living thing, then so has every leech. Each equally. And if we shift to arguing that there is satisfaction in the life of the animal (the larger the animal, the greater the satisfaction), it is satisfaction derived as an individual, not as a rarity, not as a member of a species.

These are metaphysical, but not irrelevant matters. They are not matters on which economists are well-qualified to pronounce. They provide the limiting case in valuation of externalities. We are dealing with the most awesome of responsibilities, the responsibility for life: we should at least refrain from trivializing discussion of its value.

27　The Value of Traded Goods

The next chapters consider the effect of a forestry project on a particular resource, and why the shadow price of that resource should differ from its market price. Methods of deriving economic and social prices are presented, drawing on the techniques described by Little and Mirrlees (1974), Squire and van der Tak (1975) and Hansen (1978), together with applications to forestry. Although these matters are normally discussed in the context of economic development, divergence between shadow and market prices occurs in all economies: developing and developed; tropical and temperate; capitalist and Marxist; inspired by whatever faith or none.

Foreign exchange effects of forestry

Most countries trade forest products, generally valuable raw materials (like veneer logs) or highly processed products (like writing papers). Whether such products are exports, or substitutes for imports, their production saves foreign exchange. Further timber processing adds to the foreign exchange effect (hence the restriction by some countries of roundwood exports).

But the foreign exchange effects of forestry and processing industries are more complex. Project inputs may include machinery and oil (imported or potentially exportable). Workers have foreign exchange opportunity costs if they are withdrawn from jobs with a tradable product. Where purchase and use of foreign exchange is unrestricted, higher wages prompt extra spending by project employees on tradable goods (the proportion of extra income spent on imports in Britain lies between 20% and 30%). Even change in environmental quality could influence foreign exchange earnings from tourism.

When a country contributes or absorbs a small proportion of world trade in a commodity, it can be treated as an individual seller or buyer in a competitive market – it cannot significantly affect price. Foreign exchange earnings from exports are then the f.o.b. (free on board) price, that is, the world price for the product loaded on ship at the port of export or on a lorry at the national frontier. The foreign exchange cost of imports is the c.i.f. (cost, insurance, freight) price. Because this includes a price for transport to the frontier and insurance in transit, this is higher than the f.o.b. price for a given commodity. Both f.o.b. and c.i.f. prices are called *border prices*.

Border price is not the same as price of inputs delivered to, or products despatched from, the project. Internal transport costs and marketing margins must be added to and deducted from c.i.f and f.o.b. prices respectively. Some internal costs (e.g. fuel) themselves have a foreign exchange component.

Marginal export revenue and marginal import cost

Sometimes a country is the only, or the dominant supplier of a product. For example Sudan supplies approximately 70% of world trade in gum arabic, the exudate of *Acacia senegal*. As a result, the world price for gum varies significantly with variation in quantities exported by Sudan. The US price elasticity of demand for Sudanese gum is estimated at -1.13 (Mahmoud, 1983). Thus for every 1% increase in quantity supplied there is a $1\%/1.13 = 0.88\%$ decrease in price. Sudan's total export earnings therefore increase by only $0.12 for every dollarsworth of extra gum sold. The case for planting *Acacia senegal* lies with its role in soil improvement and arresting desertification rather than in extra foreign exchange earnings (Sharawi, 1987).

The general formula for *marginal export revenue* from additional exports is

$$\text{MER} = \text{f.o.b.} \times \left(1 - \frac{1}{\eta}\right) \qquad (27.1)$$

where η is the price elasticity of demand for the *country's own* supply of the product, without its minus sign.

A parallel concept is *marginal import cost*. If a country imports a large proportion of world production of a commodity, significant price change is induced by increasing imports. The impact on foreign exchange is given by

$$\text{MIC} = \text{c.i.f.} \times \left(1 + \frac{1}{\varepsilon}\right) \qquad (27.2)$$

where ε is the price elasticity of supply for the *country's own* import demand for the product.

This conversion applies to both cost of project inputs, and the value of project output when the product is an import substitute. Few countries import a large enough share of world production to make a significant effect. (It is only upon the *imported portion* that the mark-up is due.) Any one country, for example, imports only a small fraction of the world supply of tractors; the world's major timber importer (Japan) only imports about 3% of total world production.

Bulk cellulose is grown in virtually every country; major contributions to world supplies come from several countries, so no country greatly reduces the price of exports by expanding their volume. Thus, with the exception of such special and barely substitutable products as gum arabic and balsa wood, elasticity effects do not seem very significant for forestry.

However, certain categories of product are grown largely in a particular *group* of countries – high-density tropical hardwoods, for example. While the demand for the product of *a particular country* is quite price-elastic, demand for the production *of the countries as a group* may be quite inelastic. Thus it is possible for aggregate foreign exchange earnings of the countries taken together to decline, while a greater volume of timber is sold.

Even where this effect is not directly relevant to forestry, it may be important to products competing with forestry for land. Two examples are coffee and cocoa, whose price elasticity of demand is around –0.2. When this value is substituted in equation (27.1), the marginal export revenue is a loss equivalent to four times the world price!

There is a widespread illusion among economists that, if the project is small, the price effect is insignificant. In fact, scale of project does not affect the proportionality between nominal foreign exchange earnings and detrimental price effects. Selling an extra million dollarsworth of cocoa reduces foreign exchange earnings of all cocoa producers by about $4 million: selling an extra dollarsworth of cocoa reduces these earnings by about $4.

If world income distribution were optimal, this price effect would have no importance. Loss of foreign exchange to exporters means saving in foreign exchange to importers. However, income is no more equally distributed between nations than between individuals. Projects which increase supplies to rich nations of a price-inelastic product of poor nations redistributes income from the poor to the rich.

This effect cannot be properly mitigated by quotas. Quotas and prices, under constant pressure from producers, are susceptible to modifications that mimic the market mechanism. Even if quotas hold firm, the best that can result from increased production is an unchanged earning of foreign currency.

Evidently social CBA should account for these trade effects. The forms of

CBA purveyed by economists from developed countries do not usually do so, because

(a) development aid is specifically designed to encourage the flow of cheap raw commodities to countries giving the aid, or
(b) the remit of cost–benefit analysts is to evaluate benefits and costs in the country where the project is implemented.

The sad feature of this latter case is that individual countries can do little about it. This is yet another version of the prisoner's dilemma. A country which refuses to implement an export-oriented project helps to maintain the export price for other developing countries, whilst itself suffering the price decrease caused by other countries' increasing exports. Although aggregate foreign exchange earnings decrease with increased output, it is in each country's interest to assure for itself the maximum share of those declining earnings.

But it is reprehensible that development agencies, whose nominal concern is the well-being of all developing countries, should apply such narrow analysis, and on that basis continue to fund these self-immolatory projects.

The official value of foreign exchange

It is commonly accepted that foreign exchange is scarce in developing countries. It is scarce in the general sense that its availability constrains investment and consumption. In a more particular sense, 'scarce' means that the official domestic currency price of foreign exchange understates its true value. Judging by the traumas experienced in balancing exports and imports, foreign exchange is also 'scarce' in many developed countries too.

In the idealized free market economy, nothing stays 'scarce' in this sense. If it is scarce, its price rises until the number of willing purchasers at that price just matches availability; individual purchasers can have as much as they wish at the prevailing price. Trade is self-regulating through the market in foreign exchange. Demand is high for the currencies of countries whose products are cheaper than comparable products of their competitors; that currency price rises till world-wide commodity prices are equalized. Low demand for the currency of an expensive producer causes the currency to fall until its world prices become competitive. Countries with comparative efficiency in a particular product find that product competitive on world markets; they export it and use foreign exchange to buy products in which they lack comparative advantage. Currency prices adjust so each nation is in trade balance. Under the sensitive adjustment of the market, each nation maximizes its wealth by making products where profits are high, and trading for the remainder.

Reality is very different. For several reasons governments may fix the official exchange rate at a level which exaggerates the value of domestic currency.

(a) The value of domestic currency against hard currencies supposedly measures the country's prestige; when the currency 'falls against the dollar' it is an indictment of the country's economic achievements.

(b) A high official value of the domestic currency increases foreign exchange earnings when nationals of other countries 'buy into the economy' by acquiring land or other domestic assets.

(c) When domestic inflation is faster than that of major international currencies, last year's market price for the domestic currency represents less purchasing power on international markets, so the price of that currency is overstated.

The economic wisdom of these arguments may be doubted. However, it is not the role of CBA to change government policy, but to evaluate projects under the policy expected to prevail over the project's life.

The shadow exchange rate

One method of finding the free market value of foreign exchange is to enter the free market, carrying foreign exchange. Where hard currencies are under strict government control, 'informal' markets for them flourish near airports and on back-streets of the national capital. Invariably more domestic currency is given than the official exchange rate indicates.

While the exchange rate so determined may be more realistic, it has deficiencies.

(a) Its origins cannot be disclosed in official documents.

(b) The illegality of the transaction means that the domestic currency offered is marked down to allow for risk of detection.

(c) The scarcity value in such transactions may be related to the scarcity of luxury consumption items on which domestic taxes are high and for which the affluent cannot obtain foreign exchange through regular channels. This scarcity need not match the scarcity of foreign exchange for the country's wider development aims.

A more acceptable shadow price is the ratio between summed internal prices and summed world prices of all traded goods, thus:

$$\text{SER} = \frac{D_i + D_e + D_t}{FE_i + FE_e} = \frac{[\text{internal willingness to pay for traded goods}]}{[\text{foreign exchange cost of traded goods}]} \quad (27.3)$$

where SER is the shadow exchange rate
D_i, D_e, and D_t are domestic currency values of imports and exports, and of import tariffs plus internal taxes that would have applied to exports, had they been consumed internally
FE_i, FE_e are foreign exchange values (c.i.f. and f.o.b. respectively) of imports and exports

The shadow exchange rate is thus the domestic willingness to pay for traded goods *per unit of foreign exchange*. The numeraire of this shadow price is consumption measured in domestic currency units. All the figures needed in the calculation are normally recorded in national accounts.

But there are complications. Table 27.1 shows the skeletal annual trade between Micronia, a small mountain state reliant on natural resources, and a more developed neighbour Magnesia, its only trading partner. Values are in millions of Magnesian dollars and (post-tax) microns. The official exchange rate is 4.5 microns to a dollar.

Table 27.1 Micronian trade figures

Item	Micronian	Magnesian	Comment
Luxury cars	2.2	0.4	A quota imported and auctioned by the government
Nylon rainwear	9.0	2.0	Imported and marketed freely by the Ministry of Rain
Timber	10.9	1.1	Import tariff of 120% to encourage local plantations
Coal	13.5	1.5	An export subject to a tax on consumption of 100%
Water		2.0	Subject to supply contract between Magnesian Water Board and Micronian Ministry of Rain
Total trade	35.6	7.0	

On the basis of these figures the shadow exchange rate is M5.09, representing the *average* value of a Magnesian dollar in total trade. But luxury cars and water are exchanged in fixed quantities: an additional dollar cannot affect these trade items. Using only the variable items rainwear, coal and timber, the shadow exchange rate becomes $1 = M7.26. Even this is valid only if these items vary in proportion to past expenditure – requiring very precise conditions on government policy and income elasticity of demand. For example, once everyone has a set of rainwear, no additional foreign exchange would be devoted to further purchases, and the shadow exchange rate would become $1 = M9.38. Unfortunately the necessary detail of elasticities is often unavailable: the crude (in this case badly wrong) equation (27.3) is used.

This evaluation also assumes an extra dollar leads to extra consumption of traded goods – marginal social benefit – rather than reduced production of these goods, with saved marginal social cost. The assumption would not matter, if internal markets were perfect and marginal social cost equalled marginal social benefit. If, however, the long-term cost of depleting coal is very high (see chapter 31), it is plainly better to reduce coal-mining than to increase consumption of coal. If an extra dollar allows coal to be conserved, its value is understated by a shadow exchange rate based only on changes of immediate consumption.

The final question concerns who is better off when an extra dollar becomes available. Conventionally, governments control trade, either directly or through supervision of foreign exchange deals. If the government uses an extra dollar to distribute extra rainwear, timber and coal free of charge to the citizens, then their consumers' surplus increases; the shadow exchange rate expresses the value of an extra government dollar in terms of the consumption numeraire. But if the government sells the goods, it receives their domestic currency value; the shadow exchange rate expresses the ratio between the value of the dollar and microns in government hands. A further conversion translates the value of microns in government hands into the consumption numeraire (see chapter 30).

These are matters of some sophistication which, for pragmatic reasons, most cost–benefit analyses avoid.

Conversion factors

Rather than converting foreign exchange into domestic currency, CBA methodologies using a foreign exchange numeraire convert domestic prices into world equivalents. This process inverts what has been done above, with two differences.

1 Conversion factors are calculated in terms of domestic prices, with and without taxes. The general conversion factor α is

$$\frac{D_i + D_e}{D_i + D_e + D_t} = \frac{[\text{world price at official exchange rate of traded goods}]}{[\text{internal willingness to pay for traded goods}]} \quad (27.4)$$

where D_i, D_e, and D_t are as in equation (27.3)

2 α may be refined into factors β_c for consumption goods and β_k for investment or capital goods. Since governments in developing countries generally wish to favour investment, import tariffs on capital goods are small or non-existent, and β_k may approach unity. Separate statistics for the two factors are not always available, however.

Premium for balance of trade equilibrium

A long-term balance of payments deficit incurs political and economic costs. It creates international indebtedness, with eventually crippling burdens of interest repayment. In the meantime countries or institutions to whom money is owed may exert pressure for unwanted change in internal matters (for example, on employment and distribution) or foreign policy (for example, alignment in UN).

Foreign exchange earnings or savings used to reduce indebtedness therefore yield a rather elusive benefit in increased political freedom and commuted interest payments, rather than an immediate benefit of additional consumption. On the other hand, if earnings are used for immediate benefit, the balance of trade position does not improve. You cannot have your premium for foreign exchange both ways.

28 The Shadow Wage Rate

Opportunity cost of labour has already entered discussion of forest decision-making in the context of revenue forgone *within the management unit*. CBA is concerned with the national economy, and with sacrifices of production incurred in other sectors when workers are recruited into forestry. While the difference between in-forest opportunity cost and wage usually reflects fluctuation in labour requirements, the difference in the economy has longer-term causes.

Unemployment and underemployment

A market economy does not employ a labour force just because it is available. Structural unemployment exists because workers lack the skills needed by the economy. Regional unemployment exists because surplus workers are unprepared to move in search of work. Cyclical unemployment arises periodically when economic activity slows down. Chronic unemployment occurs because not enough goods are demanded to give everyone a job.

Classical economics assumed that unemployment would solve itself through the price mechanism: unemployed workers would offer to work at lower wages, rather than starve, and it would eventually become profitable to employ them even in jobs yielding little revenue. Keynes (1936) argued that this mechanism might fail, since lower wages reduce ability to buy goods; with falling demand, prices and profits would fall too and industrial production would be further cut.

There are also institutional limits on how far wages can fall. Legislation may define a minimum legal wage. Dignity and justice demand that work is paid for, even if work is preferred to leisure. The collective strength of workers requires that no worker should undercut the agreed wage for a job. The total income of a given worker group may be maximized by exerting monopoly power, such that not all have jobs, but the wage is higher for those who do. (Contrariwise, a monopsonistic employer may offer fewer jobs, at a lower wage than the extra revenue generated by one more worker, simply to keep wage levels down.) Offered wage must exceed government payments to the unemployed before there is economic advantage in working. Hence even where unemployment is pervasive, where labour has zero opportunity cost and where leisure is so abundant that it is worthless, wages do not reach zero.

Underemployment exists when workers have jobs, but their contribution to useful production is less than their wage. This failure of pricing is variously explained.

1 The political kudos of having no unemployment: centrally planned economies in particular can direct workers into unproductive jobs, simply to show that the system 'works better than capitalism'.

2 Considerations of efficiency and justice: if all citizens are paid reasonably, just for being citizens, they might as well have a job too, even if its value is small.

3 Nepotism: particularly in bureaucratic economies, jobs are created by highly placed persons for relatives and friends, the jobs not necessarily contributing to profit or the enterprise's objectives.

4 Existence of a subsistence economy: in a non-monetized agricultural economy, workers on the family or village land-holding may be remunerated by an equal share (average product) in production, rather than by the extra production (marginal product) contributed by their efforts (Bottomley, 1973).

In all cases, remuneration overstates the opportunity cost of labour.

Often there is inflexibility too, in that a job offers a fixed number of hours per week: thus individuals cannot work precisely to the point where the value of one hour's extra leisure equals the wage.

The economic wage rate

Economic CBA is concerned with the loss of goods and services caused by diverting a worker into forestry. The loss depends on the skills required, the location of the project and the time when labour is needed: the first step in deriving an economic wage rate is to categorize the work-force accordingly.

Skilled workers (technically trained, or graduates in useful disciplines) are normally assumed to be in short supply; they are bought in competitive markets, where wages reflect opportunity costs. Recent unemployment among science and technology graduates casts doubt on this convention, but it may be adequate in particular circumstances. If on the other hand their skills are in great demand and legislation prevents them being paid the full value of their contribution to production, such workers can generally sell themselves in the less restricted international market. If technical and managerial expatriates are paid in hard currency, they can be treated as traded goods.

Skilled workers tend to be mobile between regions, but markets for unskilled workers are often local. Since unemployment rates, opportunity costs and willingness to travel in search of work vary spatially, a nationwide economic wage rate for unskilled workers can be misleading. Prevailing incomes also differ between regions, and this difference affects the *social* wage rate.

The rural economy, particularly in developing countries, has seasonal employment opportunities. Although a large surplus of agricultural labourers may exist in most months, the peak of labour demand in a forestry project not infrequently coincides with the agricultural harvest, when opportunity cost may soar. It is therefore essential to estimate monthly requirements for casual labour, and to assess the implications of forestry employment for agricultural output on the basis of actual monthly rather than average yearly labour demand in agriculture.

Long-term trends are also relevant: is it, for example, envisaged that the rural–urban migration stream will accelerate, and that agriculture will modernize till productivity of the remaining rural workers becomes very high?

Where project workers would otherwise have achieved useful production, it should be asked, what changes when they withdraw their labour? Is their product lost, or, in the case of subsistence agriculture, is the work simply taken on by other members of the family or village group? When workers are withdrawn from wage-labour, would their places be taken by new recruits to the work-force, or by increased use of machinery, or would the jobs lapse? What changes in each case?

It is relevant, given the premium on foreign exchange, whether the forgone product would have been consumed by the worker, sold domestically, or made available for export or import replacement.

Economic CBA deals not only with marketable output, but with non-market benefits and disbenefits. It is therefore pertinent whether extra time spent working (by workers or their families) represents loss of valued leisure time, and whether the project job entails extra unpleasantness or danger. Forestry is physically demanding, often requiring somewhat dangerous work in harsh terrain and unkind weather. If the decision to accept the work was rational, then

$$[\text{forestry wage}] - [\text{extra disbenefit}] > [\text{former wage}]$$

$$\therefore [\text{forestry wage}] - [\text{former wage}] > [\text{extra disbenefit}] \ (> 0)$$

Plate VIII Demanding conditions of work in an African forestry scheme
(Photo: Edwin Shanks)

Whence guesstimated disbenefit might lie halfway between the increase in wage and zero, so

$$[\text{economic wage rate}] = [\text{opportunity cost}] + \frac{[\text{forestry wage} - \text{former wage}]}{2}$$

$$(28.1)$$

The social wage rate

In addition to disbenefits, social CBA is concerned with monetary transfers resulting from employment. The question is 'who is advantaged, who disadvantaged, and by how much?' when a forestry job is created.

Those affected may include

(a) the worker
(b) those who take on some of the worker's prior employment

(c) the worker's former employer (if any)
(d) the worker's new employer
(e) the government, even if not involved as an employer.

The changes are complicated by taxation of income, and by governmental provision of the means of survival to the unemployed. Weights must be attached to monetary values. Table 28.1 gives data on a permanent forestry work-force.

Table 28.1 Components of project work-force

Worker	Income	Original income	Weight	Origin
Graduate	9000	8000	0.5	Competitive market
One worker	1200	600	5	Agricultural subsistence
One worker	1200	600	5	Urban unemployment
Clerk	4500	4500	1	Aunt's government office

The following information is also pertinent. The manual work is comparable to subsistence agriculture, and is regarded as no worse than enforced leisure time by the previously unemployed worker. The family of the worker from subsistence agriculture is expected to do about 80% of the work he previously undertook. Such additional work is regarded as unpleasant. The clerk's only previous duties were unproductive paper-shuffling: the new job involves no loss of leisure and no extra disutility. The government taxes money income, including £600 unemployment pay but excluding subsistence income, at a flat 25% rate. Government funds have a weight of 2.
Table 28.2 shows the relevant changes. Points arising are:

1 The previous employer of the graduate saves £8000, but loses the graduate's services, which in a competitive market are worth £8000 in added revenue.

2 The absence of tax on subsistence income means the rural worker has less benefit from the change than the urban worker, despite having the same previous gross income.

3 The rural worker's family do 80% of his work, worth £480. The disbenefit of extra work is costed at half the change in income, £240 (equation (28.1)).

4 By comparison with increased outlay on pay, the government receives little extra tax revenue. This is because the major pay item is the

Table 28.2 Effects of employment on well-being

Agent	Net income/ outlay	Previous net income/outlay	Change	Weight	Weighted change
Graduate	6 750	6 000	+750	0.5	375
Rural worker	900	600	+300	5	1 500
Family of above			+240	5	1 200
Urban worker	900	450	+450	5	2 250
Clerk	3 375	3 375	0	1	0
Government pay	−15 900	−5 100	−10 800	2	−21 600
Government tax	3 975	3 275	+700	2	1 400
Total					−14 875

graduate, who previously contributed £2000 in tax although being paid from non-government sources. To avoid confusion in such calculations, they should be tabulated in 'before and after' or, preferably, 'without and with project' style.

5 For the agents with weighting 5, wages actually represent a net benefit, since the weighting of government funds is lower.

6 No specific mention has been made of opportunity cost. Social CBA need not do so. All changes of consumption are assessed from an income viewpoint. Opportunity cost in subsistence agriculture is translated into income. The graduate's opportunity cost is offset by cost savings. However, there are unanswered questions about whether the net *social* benefit of the graduate's transfer is zero. If, for example the graduate was previously employed in an export or import-saving industry, the product should be accorded a foreign exchange premium, probably accruing to the government.

7 It has been assumed that project demand for labour is insufficient to raise the wage rate in the project area. This assumption is demonstrably false where projects take a substantial proportion of the local labour force, and is probably never really valid (see chapter 32).

Weights for income change

Consider the relationship between income and marginal utility of income (figure 28.1). The weight appropriate to pre-project income of the urban worker is w_0. But the weight appropriate to post-project income is w_1. The change in income should be weighted by an intermediate value. Technically, it is the mean of weights for each infinitesimal increment of income. Practically, it can be judged by eye, or by dividing area ABCD by its base, DC, giving a weight of $\bar{w}$ for the whole income change.

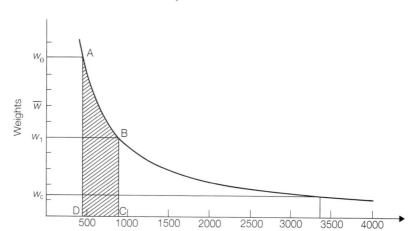

Figure 28.1 Graphical derivation of income weights

Area ABCD – this need not trouble readers unfamiliar with calculus – is obtained mathematically by integrating the marginal utility of income function, equation (24.1), between Y_0 and Y_1.

$$MU_Y = a \, Y^{-n} \qquad (24.1)$$

The relevant integrals, for $n = 1$ and $n \neq 1$, are

$$a \log_e Y \quad \text{and} \quad a \, Y^{(1-n)}/(1 - n) \qquad (28.2)$$

Taking $n = 1$ and substituting the values of Y_0 and Y_1 for the urban worker, $w_0 = 0.00222a$ and $w_1 = 0.00111a$. Area ABCD $= 0.693a$, and $\bar{w} = 0.00154a$.

The value of a need not be known, since only relative weights matter. The weight, w_c, applicable to the clerk is $0.00296a$, and the clerk, having the mean income for the nation, is assigned a weight of 1. The relative weight for the urban worker is

$$0.00154a/0.000296a = 5.20 \approx 5 \quad \text{(as used in the calculation)}$$

Those intimidated by calculus may see from figure 28.1 that these computed weights are reasonable. The weighting process may seem complex: it is, however, fundamental to social CBA, and to appropriate costing of workers in forestry projects.

29 The Social Discount Rate

One economic factor above all others emerges as a key influence on the economics of forestry: the discount rate. Since chapter 7 introduced the concept, barely a topic has passed without need to refer to it: it affects costing of machinery and roads, permeates every aspect of silviculture, influences the weight given to long-term non-market benefits. In many countries the discount rate used is what makes economic sense or nonsense of the whole process of growing trees. Even in economies which make no formal use of discounting, there is invariably some device, institutional or informal, which reflects a judgement that sooner is better, and now is best of all. Wherever this judgement is made, forestry is at risk.

For individual investors or land-owners, discounting is unquestionably a rational procedure to evaluate forestry investment. If an investment portfolio can generally earn 10% interest, and forestry has negative NPV at this rate, the implication is this: at any time when I make revenue from forestry, I could withdraw the same money from my portfolio, and at the end of the rotation I would have more money in that portfolio than would accumulate as timber value in the forest. Table 29.1 shows an example. Forestry's negative NPV (in this case −$480) indicates that the portfolio does better. If I prefer investment in forestry, it is because someone else is

Table 29.1 Comparison of forestry with portfolio investment

Portfolio	Compound interest	Cash out	Time	Forestry event
$1 000	$\times 1.1^{25}$		0	Planting
$10 835		−$1 500	25	First thinning
$9 335	$\times 1.1^{10}$			
$24 213		−$3 000	35	Second thinning
$21 213	$\times 1.1^{10}$			
$55 021		−$20 000	45	Clearfelling
$35 021				Excess money in portfolio

paying part of its costs, or because I derive non-market benefits from forestry, or because I am irrational. That should be accepted. The matter at issue – the matter which determines if a large part of the world's forestry investment is misguided – is whether the reasoning can legitimately be transposed into the national context.

Compound growth of national investment

The social rate of return on investment represents a miscellany of benefits in addition to revenues from marketable products: environmental and employment benefits, redistribution and increased consumers' surplus resulting from reduced prices. While all these have shadow prices, none generates reinvestible revenues. They are consumed in the moment and leave no impression on the investment stream. Whatever part of the social rate of return is attributable to them cannot be reinvested at compound interest.

There are also obstacles to reinvesting cash revenues.

1 *Questionable economic desirability*

If profits from an enterprise earning 10% are reinvested in more enterprises of the same kind, output rises at 10% compound. In no country in the world is population growing so fast, so consumption per head of the enterprise's product necessarily increases. Marginal utility and price of the good fall rapidly, eroding the value of such reinvestment.

Investment creates real machines, buildings and infrastructure, requiring real people to control and repair them. Again outstripping the growth of any population, such capital growth must either become more self-supporting or employ the entire population, 168 hours per week, within two decades.

Capital growth entails more throughput of raw materials, both for capital formation itself and for consequent increase of production. Rapid compound growth of pollution and resource depletion are likely concomitants of reinvestment.

These arguments do assume quantitative expansion of capital rather than qualitative development, but no mechanism ensures that qualitative development will match the rate of reinvestment.

2 *Questionable political feasibility*

Time preference means people want jam today: they cannot even be bought off with promises of jam at compound interest tomorrow. To reinvest all the profits of an economy, allowing no increase in immediate consumption, is unpopular, buying no votes in a democracy, inviting revolution under totalitarianism. It can be implemented only under the most repressive control, or the most unified sense of national purpose. Not all profits are spent on jam today, but if any of the 10% return is diverted into extra consumption, the rate of compound increase in investment falls below 10%.

3 Questionable physical reality

Investment is not just dollars moving from one box to another. It is real resources being converted into continuously productive form. This real process is observed in manufacture of lorries and construction of offices. Total reinvestment goes a stage further: any addition to the stock of lorries and offices is itself devoted only to creating capital goods. 'Reinvestment of oil revenues' is a phrase bandied around the financial world, but in reality oil is mostly used for heating, lighting, travel to work or pleasure, making and distributing consumption goods. A fraction does become incorporated in productive capital, in bulldozers, bridges and buildings, but even these yield largely a stream of consumption, rather than of investment.

4 Observed practice

Given these obstacles, it is unsurprising that total reinvestment of national profits does not happen. The real alternative to forestry is a portfolio that generates some reinvestment, but not increasing compound-wise at the prevailing rate of return. A stream of consumption is also generated. At the end of a forest rotation, the value of consumption derived from an investment portfolio may be less than that of consumption derived from a forest crop which uses the same initial investment. The choice of investment then hinges on the relative values of consumption generated during the rotation. This in turn depends on the time preference rate.

When do we want it? – NOW!

Time preference rates are not quantified like rates of return, yet they are implicit in consumers' choices. The choice to consume 100 poundsworth of goods this year rather than investing at a real rate of return of 5% and consuming 105 poundsworth of goods next year implies a time preference rate of at least 5%. Choices of consumption can be placed more explicitly before consumers: proffered choices between enjoyment tonight and enjoyment next year usually show that forest managers as individuals have a time preference rate exceeding 500%. The fact of time preference cannot be denied: more controversial is its interpretation.

Economists set great importance on consumer sovereignty – the right of consumers to place relative values on timber and televisions and toffees via their willingness to pay the price for these commodities. Consumers do not always choose wisely, but occasional ill-judgement is a small price to pay for freedom of choice. If cost–benefit analysts accept preferences between commodities (indexed by willingness to pay) as a valid measure of relative value of those commodities, should they not also accept time preference (indexed by interest rates) as a valid measure of relative value at different times?

There are two specific arguments against accepting individual time preference in social discounting. The first relates to the element of time preference due to mortality. It is rational for individuals to prefer consumption now to the same consumption next year, because over the intervening year they may die. For society as a whole, however, the passage of time bears the prospect of birth as well as the risk of death: a commodity next year has value to an ever-changing body of citizens, yet represents essentially similar consumption.

The collective time preference of the present generation is therefore partly an expression of group selfishness, with no place in an appraisal which includes costs and benefits 'to whomsoever accruing'. Yet the probability of an average citizen dying in any one year is rather low: between 1 and 2% for countries with reasonable health care. A substantial preference for present consumption remains after mortality risk is deducted, apparently on the pure grounds of its earliness in time.

The second argument concerns whether pure individual time preference does imply discounting. Given a quota of total consumption, individuals choose to consume now rather than next year, which agrees with the hypothesis that earliness is preferred. However, many consumers later regret their choices: in retrospect they wish they had forgone past consumption, in favour of consumption now. This is inconsistent with the hypothesis, which predicts that consumers should delight in the improvidence of their past!

An alternative hypothesis is that consumers prefer to consume *now* rather than at any other point in time. This is consistent both with choice of present rather than future consumption, and with retrospective (though ineffectual) preference that there should have been less consumption in the past and more in the present. All points in history have been *now* once and once only, and of all points in the future it can be predicted that they too will in due course be *now* only once. This gives no premium to any point in time on grounds of its earliness.

Some extra benefit does arise from early consumption within an individual's life, to the extent that it feeds happy memories: however, extra benefit also arises from consumption late within an individual's life, to the extent that it excites happy anticipation.

Retrospective preference also affects the inter-generational issue. Present generations prefer their own consumption to that of future generations.

Future generations will assuredly prefer their own consumption to that of the present, as present generations prefer their own consumption to that of the past. Inter-generationally, even happy memories do not favour early consumption, for the happy memories of future generations are as important as those of present generations.

Governments too, reflecting the will of the people and striving to maintain popularity, have a short perspective. Like individuals, they are constrained by circumstance from following the optimal path of investment. It is therefore vapid to derive social rates of discount from rates of return on accepted government investments (Harou, 1985; Price, 1988a).

Predicted utility and discounting

Instead of asking why we should *not* discount at a mean individual time preference rate, we ought to ask why we discount at all. Since mere lateness in time does not justify a discount, what features, if any, of consumption make it less valuable, the further into the future it occurs?

Six factors might influence the utility of consumption over time.

1 *The prospect of consumer elimination*

Technologies of war and environmental pollution have made collective destruction a real possibility for humankind. Timber is grown for the next generation, but if the next generation is never born, what utility will the timber have? Even the wildlife may not be there to 'enjoy' it.

Understandably, people do not want to accept this possibility, but possibility it is. The most potent argument against its inclusion is its tendency to self-fulfilling prophecy: if we believe the future will not exist, we will be so careless about it (using up resources and pouring out persistent pollutants) that its existence is imperilled.

2 *Fashion*

Passing popularity gives some goods a premium price. Fashion clothes and popular music recordings illustrate the point dramatically, fading as they usually do into unspeakable obscurity in a few months. Forestry examples are harder to find, but they exist in the vogue for a particular decorative timber in furniture. Wood-burning stoves too became a fashionable symbol of ecological awareness in Europe in the 1970s, only to be converted for fossil fuels as the novelty of wood-chopping declined among the middle classes!

Fashion, however, is not all. Some clothing designs become classic, some pop songs become 'golden oldies'. Oak, teak and mahogany continue to be preferred in high-quality furniture, and the calorific value of fuelwood is unimpaired by the passing of a trendy image. For some wood products a fashion discount is appropriate, but only a few, and not for the whole of their value.

3 *Technological advance*

When an iron-clad warship sank two wooden opponents at the Battle of Hampton Roads in 1862, the premium placed on specially shaped oak branches in thousands of hectares of British forests was wiped out. This is always possible for timber grown to precise specifications.

But technological advance has more general implications for the marginal utility of consumption. As nations become richer, their citizens consume more per head of most products. Accordingly, the marginal utility of those products diminishes over time. Past rising affluence has increased consumption per head of products like paper. For products like fuelwood, technological advance brought substitution by coal, oil, gas and electricity. Aggregate consumption per head of energy from all sources has increased in developed countries, so the marginal utility of fuelwood has declined even where it remains in use.

4 *The resources/population balance*

An influence contrary to technological advance has been increasing world population and declining base of concentrated mineral resources. These factors jointly tend to diminish consumption per head, and increase marginal utility over time. In developed economies, technological advance has so far kept ahead: the future may not follow this pattern.

5 *Uncertainty*

Many economists hold that uncertainty justifies discounting: the further into the future that a product is created, the more likely it is that unknown factors will reduce its value. But if there is genuine uncertainty (rather than a faintly perceived downward trend) it is equally true that the further into the future that a product is created, the more likely it is that unknown factors will *increase* its value. Indeed the extent of possible increase usually exceeds the extent of possible decrease, so a premium may exist on future consumption. This is appreciated by prudent individuals, who 'put something aside' in good times to provide for future uncertainties.

6 *Choice*

Having a resource now gives the choice of consuming now or saving for later. Having the resource later precludes the option of present consumption. But then, if the option of present consumption is taken, the option of later consumption is precluded, and future choice is diminished. This is not a sensible argument for discounting.

One discount rate or many?

The discount rate of social CBA is the 'rate of decline in value of the numeraire over time'. Our numeraire relates to consumption by a consumer of mean income. Conventional project appraisal, which emphasizes technological advance, assumes increasing mean consumption. In terms of the marginal utility of income/income relationship (see figure 28.1 and equation (24.1)), the discount rate measures the annual rate of decline of $\bar{w}$. If g is the rate of growth of mean income and n the absolute value of elasticity of marginal utility of income, the discount rate (often called the consumption rate of interest) is

$$n \times g + p \qquad (29.1)$$

p is the rate of pure time preference (preference for early rather than late consumption); as shown above, the grounds for including it are dubious. The ranges of values for n and g in economies round the world, nonetheless, give social discount rates between 0% and 30%.

Yet the factors 1–6 listed above clearly apply quite differently to different products. Nothing better characterizes the power of technological advance than the electronic calculator. In the 1960s, even in advanced university forestry departments, NPV calculations were performed using logarithms and tables of discount factors. Machines capable of raising 1.05 to the power 50 cost thousands of pounds, and were vital in advancing forest economics. Nowadays such capabilities are part of £10 calculators, which are given to children to keep them amused. In two decades the price of calculating power has slumped, as has its marginal utility. A heavy discount on calculators would have been entirely justified in financial, economic and social appraisal of calculator development in the 1960s.

By contrast, timber consumption per head has hardly increased in some countries (though that of some substitutes has done) and its real price has been rather stable. No dramatic rise in future consumption or fall in marginal utility can be expected. Chapter 35 examines the expected future of timber consumption, and also addresses the question of what the appropriate discount rate for it might be.

Consumption per head of undisturbed natural landscape may well have decreased over the years, and it is doubtful whether there is any case at all for discounting the future value of this or other constituents of high environmental quality (Price, 1978b). While recreation visits are increasing, and *additional* units have diminishing marginal utility, no discount should be applied to the number of visits *currently* made.

Nor will factors of production necessarily become scarcer or more abundant at the same rate as their products, so the same discount rate need not apply to revenues and costs, nor to profits or consumers' surplus.

In that discounting reflects the weight given to future income, appropriate discount rates clearly also vary between income groups. Using mean growth rates in determining a nation-wide consumption rate of interest fails to account for this variation. Table 29.2 shows the effect of discounting, separately and at an average rate, the benefits of a forestry project which at year 50 provides an equal amount of a product to a rich and a poor group. The parameter n is 1.5.

Table 29.2 Effect of differential and 'average' discounting of income

	Rich	Poor	Both
Willingness to pay for product (P)	20 000	20 000	40 000
Present income per head (Y_0)	10 000	1 000	5 500[a]
Income weight $(w \propto 1/Y_0^{1.5})$	0.1	3.162	
Income growth rate (g)	0.05	0.01	0.0483[b]
Income at year 50 $(Y_{50} = Y_0 \times (1 + g)^{50})$	114 674	1 645	58 160[a]
Discount rate $(r = n \times g)$	0.075	0.015	0.0724[c]
Weighted benefit $(B = P \times w)$	2 000	63 240	65 240
Discounted value $(B/(1 + r)^{50})$	54	30 039	1 980
Total discounted value for rich + poor	54	+ 30 039	= 30 093

Notes: [a] Mean for rich and poor. [b] Calculated from mean income at 50. [c] Calculated from mean income growth rate.

The contrast between the last two figures in the right-hand column is spectacular, yet it arises simply from averaging. The important benefit is that derived by the poor, yet the average discount rate is dominated by income growth of the rich. While this distortion has some significance in all project appraisal, its degree is extreme with the long waiting period of forestry, and becomes the more so where great disparities exist in income and income growth rate: these are precisely the circumstances in which social CBA has most to contribute to evaluation. This is further discussed by Hoekstra (1985) and Price and Nair (1985).

The appropriate discount rate also differs between predicted futures. In a future of increasingly scarce resources and inadequate technological advance, the discount rate would be zero or even negative. The problems caused for CBA are among the subjects discussed in the next two chapters.

Finally the appropriate discount rate might vary over time. It is, admittedly, difficult to predict how and when the rate might change: that, however, is a feeble excuse for committing the future to the charge of an indefinite and uniform negative exponential function, which is what conventional discounting really means.

Proponents of the conventional view sometimes suggest that these variations can and should be taken into account by adjusting shadow prices over time; discounting should simply reflect the changing value of the numeraire in which the prices are measured. This alternative approach to changing values over time should in theory give the same results as varying the discount rate. However, the difficulties of predicting trends for shadow prices serve in practice as an excuse for ignoring the problem: discounting is, after all, also a means of sweeping the problems of the future under the carpet.

30 The Shadow Value of Funds

Until now, scarce investment funds were priced by the interest rate. Discounting not only weighted costs and benefits according to when they accrued, but also ensured that funds were devoted to investments offering the best rate of return. This dual function cannot work when the social discount rate differs from the social rate of return on investment.

If the social rate of return exceeds the discount rate, the stream of discounted benefits flowing from investment of £1000 exceeds £1000. Like foreign exchange, investment funds are more valuable than their nominal price: they are scarce in that more potential investments have positive NPV at the prevailing discount rate than can be financed from available funds.

Scarcity of investment funds in this sense constrains economic development, probably in all countries. To reflect this scarcity, the capital-rationing function of high discount rates must be replaced by a shadow price which reflects the value of investment funds relative to consumption.

The shadow price of investment funds

Estimating the shadow price of investment funds requires CBA of alternative recipients of those funds. Either aggregate figures for investment in the economy generally, or data for a representative sample of potential projects must be obtained.

When funds are earmarked for forestry, evaluation is easier, as only the performance of competing forestry projects need be determined.

Suppose that investment of Rs10 000 has, on average, the following effects:

1 Permanent jobs are created, with post-tax wages of Rs4000, for workers whose contribution to agricultural output was valued at Rs3000 per year. (This output is not made up by family or anyone else.) A mean weight of 1.5 applies to workers' income.

2 Annual revenue of Rs5500 arises from marketable benefits, and Rs1000 is spent on repair, maintenance and management of the investment, using skilled labour from a competitive market.

3 Of financial profits, 20% are reinvested in similar investments, and 80% spent on free services for consumers at the mean level of income.

4 Non-market benefits are valued at 500 rupeesworth annually.

GNP per head is growing at 4% per year; n is 1.5. Table 30.1 shows the flow of benefits for the first two years. Financial flows and consumption flows are kept separate in table 30.1. Financial flows are instrumental only, as the means of creating the investment from which consumption flows arise.

Table 30.1 Flows of cash and benefit following investment

Investment	Govt cash	Other cash	Weight	Benefit	Item
10 000					start investment
↓ →→→→→→→→→→→→→→→→→→→→→→→→→				500	non-marketables
↓ →→→→→→→5500 →→→→→↓					revenues
Y ↓	−4000	4000			less wages
E ↓	−1000			0	less repair etc
A ↓	↓	−3000			lost subsistence
R ↓	↓				
↓	↓	=1000	×1.5	=1500	change in income
O ↓	↓				
N ↓	500 →→→→ 400		×1	=400	free services
E ↓	↓				
↓	↓			2400	TOTAL BENEFIT
↓←←←←←←←←−100					reinvestment
↓					
10 100					investment after one year
↓					
↓ →→→→→→→→→→→→→→→→→→→→→→→→				505	non-marketables
↓ →→→→→→→ 5555 →→→→→↓					revenues
Y ↓		↓			
E ↓	−4040	4040			less wages
A ↓	−1010			0	less repair etc
R ↓	↓	−3030			lost subsistence
↓	↓				
T ↓	↓	=1010	×1.5	=1515	change in income
W ↓	↓				
O ↓	505 →→→→ 404		×1	=404	free services
↓	↓				
↓	↓			2424	TOTAL BENEFIT
↓←←←←←←←←−101					reinvestment
10 201					investment after two years

The two important figures are total first-year benefit (2400 rupeesworth) and the rate of increase between year one and year two. Reinvestment of Rs100 after the first year increases total investment by 1%; since new investment has the same general character, each cash and benefit item also increases by 1%.

The NPV of this Rs10 000 investment is given by discounting the total benefit stream at $n \times g = 1.5 \times 4\% = 6\%$. If annual flow of benefit was constant, its value given by equation (7.3a) would be

$$2400 \text{ rupeesworth}/0.06 = 40\ 000 \text{ rupeesworth}$$

However, undiscounted benefits increase by a factor of 1.01 every year. This partly offsets the effect of discounting, which reduces value by a factor of 1.06 every year. The net effect is reduction by a factor of 1.05 every year, equivalent to using a 5% discount rate:

$$2400 \text{ rupeesworth}/(0.06 - 0.01) = 48\ 000 \text{ rupeesworth}$$

Thus each rupee invested earns 4.80 rupeesworth of benefit. This is the shadow price of a rupee invested.

Strictly, if benefits flow immediately and steadily, the continuous discounting formula (7.3b) should be used, giving a weight of 4.97. In practice, delays in distributing benefits may make 4.80 equally realistic.

For simplicity, services financed out of investment revenues were taken to benefit consumers at the mean income level for the nation (weighting = 1). But if these services are distributed equally among the population, the mean weight exceeds unity. Suppose that a third of the population have double the mean income per head and two-thirds have half the mean income per head. From equation (24.1), respective weights are $2^{-1.5} = 0.354$ and $0.5^{-1.5} = 2.828$; weighted mean weight is

$$0.354 \times 0.3333 + 2.828 \times 0.6667 = 2$$

Even if extra benefits are distributed in proportion to existing income, the mean weight is 1.179. Free services and cash handouts should be weighted by whichever mean weight reflects real distribution of these benefits. A weight of 2 on distributed benefits raises the shadow price of investment funds to

$$(500 + 1500 + 400 \times 2)/(0.06 - 0.01) = 5.6, \text{ that is}$$

$$\frac{([\text{non-marketables}] + [\text{weighted wage gain}] + [\text{distributed benefits}])}{[\text{annual reduction factor}]}$$

Variants on the theme

The compilation of shadow price of investment funds (SPIF) outlined above corresponds generally to that suggested in project appraisal handbooks:

$$\frac{(1 - s)q}{(r - sq)} \tag{30.1}$$

where s is *marginal propensity to save* (the proportion of revenues which is reinvested)

q is the financial rate of return on investment.

Our example is more sophisticated, since it includes non-market and employment benefits as well as financial ones, and benefits have been weighted according to their recipients. If 20% (the non-market rate of return) is added to the top line, equation (30.1) becomes

$$\frac{(1 - 0.20) \times 0.05 + 0.20}{(0.06 - 0.20 \times 0.05)} = 4.80 \qquad \text{(as before)}$$

It is sometimes proposed that, although investment funds are *presently* scarce, equilibrium will be achieved in the foreseeable future. (As q becomes more nearly equal to r, SPIF approaches 1.) However, there is little sign that such an event is imminent in developing countries; indeed, there is no reason why equality of q and r should ever be achieved under the market mechanism. Hence this 'refinement' (which requires complex formulas) actually entails less realistic assumptions.

If on the other hand $r = sq$, SPIF is infinite. If $r < sq$, SPIF is, algebraically, negative, but in fact is indefinitely large. These inconvenient results have prompted a search for other ways to define SPIF. Three suggestions are:

1 The investment lasts a year and pays back Rs10 000 $\times (1 + q)$ in a single lump: Rs10 000 $\times (1 + q) \times s$ are reinvested. The investment stream normally diminishes over time. This, however, is totally unrepresentative of social investments, whose life is typically measured in decades.

2 After several years, a proportion s of the value to which the investment has grown at compound interest is placed in fresh investments.

3 Each investment decision is taken independently of revenues from other investments, so reinvestment is not a consequence of revenue.

Other methods have been suggested by Marglin (1963).

These modifications reduce the probability of indefinitely large values arising. Yet there is nothing illogical about investment funds having indefinitely large value in the indefinite term: that is the valuation foresters intuitively give to forest land which is perpetually productive. Project evaluation is not actually difficult when investment funds have indefinite value: financial costs and revenues are appraised at the face value of their investible component, and consumption (which has indefinitely small relative weight) is ignored.

The formulation used should of course reflect how reinvestment occurs in reality. But, as no-one seems sure about this, the correct formulation is in doubt.

Figures to insert in the formula are not easily found. Financial rates of return can be estimated by various econometric methods (Trivedi, 1988), but judging the *social* return requires widespread yet profound familiarity with current projects. Parameter s can be estimated by relating fluctuations of gross capital formation to those of gross national product (derived from national economic statistics), although the figure is probably not very reliable.

The value of running costs and revenues

Amid this refined speculation, one rather extraordinary assumption has remained unchallenged in mainstream social CBA. The value of government funds is normally treated as though all surplus cash was assigned to investment (or to equally valuable purposes). Thus monetary costs of forestry projects have a weighting of (say) 4.8, as do revenues. Since all cash flows have the same high weighting, social and environmental benefits lose relative importance.

If, however, revenues from a forestry project are totally reinvested, *why are revenues from the alternative 'general' investment assumed to be split, say 20% to investment and 80% to immediate consumption?* This seems an inconsistency. And, since investment is more valuable than immediate consumption, the inconsistency favours forestry.

If on the other hand forestry revenues are split 20 : 80 between investment and consumption, Rs10 000 of revenue gives Rs8000 of consumption, and Rs2000 of investment, the latter having weight 4.8. The weight per rupee is therefore:

$$\frac{\text{Rs8000} + \text{Rs}(2000 \times 4.8)}{\text{Rs10 000}} = 1.76$$

This is a big difference: it is obviously crucial, not just what revenues and costs are, and when they occur, but under what heading they are placed.

Since the alternative 'general' investment remains productive (or is fully replaced) in perpetuity, forestry investment should be too. The cost of replanting should be deducted from clearfelling revenues, and the *remaining* funds split 20% : 80% between reinvestment and consumption.

Of course, government procedures may be inconsistent – forest replanting always needing a vote of new funds, while alternative investments receive funding in perpetuity. If so, CBA should reflect that real inconsistency.

It is certainly not irrelevant how replanting is treated. Consider the evaluation of two biomass rotations versus one unthinned sawlog rotation, when s = 25%, q = 6% and r = 3%. Using equation (30.1), SPIF = 3, while cash flows which are divided 25% to investment, 75% to consumption have weighting 1.5 (table 30.2).

In version I of the biomass rotation, replanting is considered part of the project. The net revenue, £3000, is divided 75 : 25 between immediate consumption and reinvestment. In version II, the £1000 for replanting is itself considered to constitute the 25% reinvestment and the profit is wholly consumed (weight 1). In version I, NPV of the biomass rotation is not only positive, but greater than the NPV of the 50–year rotation. However, in version II NPV is negative: the 50–year rotation is preferred, or, failing that, no planting at all.

Table 30.2 Alternative treatments of reinvestment

Year	Cash flow	Weight	PV (version I)	PV (version II)
Biomass				
0	−1000	3	−3000	−3000
25	4000 − 1000	1.5	2149	—
		or 1	—	1433
50	4000	1.5	1369	1369
Net present value			518	−198
Sawlog				
0	−1000	3	−3000	
50	10000	1.5	3422	
Net present value			422	

The shadow value of private income

Saving and investment are also undertaken by private individuals. Indeed, it is often argued that income to the rich should be treated favourably, because the rich have a high marginal propensity to save, whereas the poor spend their income on short-term survival. Social value of private income may be quantified by the techniques outlined for government funds, with the complication that private investment yields a stream of government tax revenues.

With any reasonable value of n, the weight assigned to consumption by the rich is small. The important social components of their income are therefore those attributable to tax and the invested portion.

The shadow cost of loans

All the above discussion assumes that governments finance projects from uncommitted domestic funds. Often, however, an international loan is available either for a specific project, or not at all. The cost of such loans is the discounted shadow price of the expected loan repayments. Since these repayments are specified in money terms, their real cost is reduced by the expected inflation (relative to domestic purchasing power) of the currency in which repayments are to be made. In what proportion repayments draw on investment and consumption funds depends on government policy.

International project agencies should calculate a SPIF for their own funds by the method demonstrated for domestic funds, but applied on a global scale.

31 Social Opportunity Cost of Natural Resources

Given the acute shortage of foreign exchange, investment and technology in developing countries, it is not surprising that the social cost of land receives little attention in texts on social CBA. Forests have been more often viewed as *sources* of foreign exchange and land for agriculture, than as *users* of land. Rural investment projects, such as irrigation schemes, tend to be capital- rather than land-intensive. Land-hunger is, however, an increasing feature of developing countries – in particular, shortage of good-quality land.

Land was central to the classical economics of Malthus and Ricardo. But its position was weakened by the concentration of twentieth-century economics on capital and labour theory and on national income accounting. In the early 1970s ecological concerns projected natural resources to the forefront of economics. Since then, however, preoccupation with international indebtedness and world economic recession has pushed these concerns into the background again. In the meantime, substitution of chemicals and machinery for land and labour, together with North American and European food surpluses, has given the impression that land is not a scarce factor of production. Yet land remains the best thing to grow trees on! Foresters must think of its cost even if economists do not. This chapter looks descriptively at some of the important cost factors in using land directly in urban and rural settings, and in the exploitation of natural resources derived from outside the forest.

Shadow price and alternative rural land uses

There is often no need to shadow price land for forestry. CBA should simply assess the net social benefit of alternative land uses, the preferred use being that which produces the highest net value. The exception arises when the alternatives under consideration are different locations for forests intended for a specific purpose like supplying pulpwood to a particular mill: shadow price is then the net benefit forgone by displacing the existing land use at each location.

Whether other uses of land are included as alternative courses of action, or are explicitly shadow priced, the same evaluative procedures should be applied to these other uses as to forestry. Non-market costs and benefits are appraised by the same techniques; an appropriate (though possibly different) discount rate is chosen; labour inputs and investment funds are shadow priced; taxes and subsidies, gained and forgone, are treated as transfers, weighted according to who pays and who receives.

In practice this procedure is rarely adopted. Land controlled by forestry agencies is usually considered, and often legally is, inalienably committed to forestry, unlike labour or investment funds. Even when there is no legal restriction, lack of expertise, reluctance to make concessions to another agency, or simply a separation of agency objectives from social ones frequently leads to alternative land uses being ignored (Price and Nair, 1984). Legal impediments cannot be overcome by individual land managers, and where they operate there is no opportunity cost other than that of alternative forestry uses. But institutional narrow-mindedness is inexcusable. A CBA which considers only one course of action (the intuitively preferred scheme) is at best a waste of time and at worst an obstacle to social well-being: arguably, it is not CBA at all.

Where change of land use entails purchase, social CBA also evaluates monetary transactions. Current land use may have low value, yet there may be strong competition to purchase the land for a different, more profitable use. Thus owners of large but presently unproductive tracts may become millionaires by advantageous sales. The weight for an extra £ consumed by a millionaire is small, whereas government or private investment funds have substantial weight: the transfer causes a net decline in utility. Double-counting land cost as both an opportunity cost and a transfer cost is best avoided by asking how much better off the seller is. A small but perpetual net income from farming may be given up. The utility of the purchase price depends on whether it is spent quickly (very low weight) or invested to generate a long-term income (moderate weight – see chapter 30). The cost to a state purchaser is price multiplied by the SPIF.

Large changes in value between one land use and another are characteristic where government restricts land use changes. Where the land market operates freely, the price of land should reflect its current use value; the seller would not be much advantaged by sale, and the shadow price of the land would be its sale price multiplied by the weight given to the purchaser's funds.

The cost of urban greenspace

Forestry providing a 'green lung' for central cities has become a popular concept recently. The opportunity cost of urban land is less often referred to. High land prices in city centres reflect willingness to pay for central locations, which in turn reflects the profits (for producers) or satisfactions or cost-savings (for consumers) derived from locating there.

For producers, the value of big cities comes from factors analogous to scale economies (Richardson, 1971). Concentrated industries can share research and educational facilities; they have good access to financial, legal and technical services; they can tap a large labour market for specialist skills. Similarly, cities offer consumers a wide range of health, welfare, leisure and educational services, entertainment opportunities, shopping facilities and jobs.

Large cities do have negative social and spatial externalities, but, taking a whole spectrum of city sizes together, these are incorporated in the locational choices of firms and households (Price, 1978a). High land prices on the whole reflect the high *net* benefit perceived from urban location.

The city centre is usually the zone most accessible to the whole population, and it is here that economic activities with the strongest urban character – high-level retailing, specialist services and office complexes – concentrate. Dramatic differences in land price over distances of only a kilometre reflect the relative advantage of locating in a compact central block rather than a dispersed pattern. Land price measures the extent to which urban parks and woodland disrupt the advantages of compactness.

Similarly, the moderately high prices of land in the inner ring of the main residential areas reflects accessibility to the centre (Evans, 1973). Greenspace intruding in this zone makes access more difficult for citizens beyond the zone. Indeed, if citizens of the inner city also occasionally travel to the countryside beyond the city bounds, land price understates the full extent of externalities imposed on within-city travel by urban greenspace (Price, 1982).

This is not, however, to deny the case for urban forestry. Urban parks confer a premium price on apartments overlooking them. Their recreational benefits accrue to poor inner city dwellers with no available subsitutes, at the cost only of walking time, and with high measurable benefit (Tucker, 1983).

Natural resources as inputs

Land as growing-space is not the only natural resource used in forestry. Irrigation water, fertilizer, roadstone and oil are just some of the inputs transported to site in the service of silviculture and harvesting.

Four classes of resource are distinguished by McInerney (1976): flow resources and regenerating resources (both renewable), recyclable resources and depletable resources (both non-renewable).

Flow resources are generated in a continuing stream through time, being impossible or expensive to store, and therefore being lost if not used immediately. Sunlight and rainfall are the two major flows to which land occupation gives foresters entitlement. Irrigation water is a flow 'bought in' to supplement intrinsic productivity of the site.

If an irrigation system provides water to one piece of land only, in a given profile over time, opportunity costs of land and of irrigation water are inseparable. If, however, water can be distributed flexibly, its opportunity cost depends on its potential contribution to productivity elsewhere. Irrigation water may resemble rural labour – there is surplus through much of the year, then everyone wants it at the same time. Ideally, under this constraint water should be allocated to land where it contributes the largest incremental net social benefit per litre. If storage is available, allocation over time should follow the same rule. Unfortunately for foresters, the quick return from allocating water to agriculture often overrides long-term benefits to tree growth, and, as with land, they are allocated what is left when farmers have taken what they want (when the opportunity cost is nil).

In CBA of a plantation which can have an assured supply, irrigation water should be shadow priced as the loss of production incurred when that water is withdrawn from other potential users. Given seasonal fluctuations of demand, a uniform price for water does not always reflect opportunity cost. Thus some economic entities are better or worse off when water is diverted to forestry. This distributional effect ought to be included in social CBA.

Regenerating resources can be built up, stored, depleted (and sometimes irreversibly destroyed) over time, usually by biological processes. Trees are a perfect example. Regenerating resources are not normally brought into the forest (being produced on site), though carbon dioxide belongs in this category. As carbon dioxide is not privately owned, it has no marketable value. There is still uncertainty about whether it is a limiting factor on photosynthesis (Kauppi, 1987) and so whether it might have an opportunity cost.

Organic fertilizers are also renewable. They are generally by-products of other processes, for example sewage sludge (McNab and Berry, 1985). Their supply is rather inelastic, so their shadow price is either an opportunity cost, or the excess cost of transporting them to site rather than using alternative means of disposal.

Recyclable resources are non-renewable in that (like gold) they exist in a limited stock. They do not deteriorate irrecoverably in use. Their cost is thus either a 'hire' value (an opportunity cost) for each year they are dedicated to forestry, or the (discounted) cost of restoring them to their original condition after the period of use. The only memorable forestry example is reusable roadstone.

Marginal social benefit and cost of depletable resources

Depletable resources are lost irrevocably by use. Oil burned by machinery, and fertilizers leached into watercourses are important forestry examples.

Depletion being irreversible, there are inevitably consequences for future generations, who will suffer reduced availability of depletable resources. Consequently opportunity costs cannot be determined only from the willingness to pay of present competitors for these resources.

Depletable resources cannot be properly treated, either, through the simplistic notion of a given homogeneous quantity which either does or does not exist. These resources show a spectrum of concentration or accessibility, such that current depletion is from high-grade, low-cost sources. By eliminating these, present use obliges later generations to turn to ever-lower-grade and ever-higher-cost sources.

As available stocks of a resource become more costly to extract, its price rises, reducing future marginal consumption. Reduced consumption progressively compensates for initial depletion, but never does so completely. Loss of consumption, with continuously increasing marginal utility, is incurred indefinitely. A simulation model (Price, 1984a) of the process shows that forgone marginal social benefit through using the resource, summed in perpetuity, is:

$$\frac{C \times |\varepsilon|}{(|\varepsilon| - 1)} \quad \text{which} \to \infty \text{ as } \varepsilon \to -1 \qquad (31.1)$$

where C is the present equilibrium price
 $|\varepsilon|$ is the absolute value of price elasticity of demand for the resource.

Strangely, no other economic characteristic of the resource's supply or demand enters the formula. There is no reason why the price elasticity of demand should not be -1, giving an indefinitely large shadow price. For resources with inelastic demand, the formula gives meaningless negative values: in fact the shadow price is again indefinitely large. It is sometimes alleged that low or zero discount rates lead to more investment and resource depletion (Scott, 1955): this is a naïve view, ignoring the effect of discount rates on the *cost* of depletion.

Ultimately the cost of extracting virgin resources may reach the point where it is economic to turn to renewable substitutes (for example in energy and fertilizers), or to recycle certain metals which are currently junked. In this case the summed social cost of depletion is intermediate between present cost and ultimate recycling costs (Price, 1983b).

Does technology change everything?

Economists do not usually quantify the long-term implications of resource depletion. But when they do, discounting is frequently invoked to show that long-term costs are barely significant. Discounting, when not based on time preference or market rates of return, is itself generally justified by referring to technological advance, which is assumed to increase consumption per head and so reduce marginal utility of consumption through time.

However, in this context the technological advance proposition contains a degree of circularity. By throwing emphasis onto technology as the major factor limiting abundance of goods, the argument implicitly assumes that natural resources are an unimportant limitation. Indefinite technological advance then implies indefinitely increasing consumption. This perpetually diminishes the marginal utility of the future consumption which is forgone because of present depletion. Hence depletion has little consequence for utility, and the thesis is justified that technology, rather than natural resources, is limiting.

But the converse starting assumption, that natural resources rather than technology are the ultimate limit on consumption, can be justified by a similar circular argument. The relative merits of these opposite arguments must be judged on some external criterion.

History provides no deterministic evidence about the future efficacy of technology. In a purely statistical sense, history is a biased sample of the population of all possible courses of events. This population of events may be represented as the various outcomes in a game of chance, where humanity progresses according to the number shown by a tossed die. A throw of six represents circumstances in which resource constraints not susceptible to technological alleviation lead to annihilation. Among the possible sequences of throws are many that are not terminated by a throw of six; the history that humanity has survived must be drawn from this sub-population of non-terminal sequences. But examining the sequence which has actually constituted history gives a biased estimate of the frequency of sixes in all possible throws: it gives no basis to predict the outcome of the next throw. History does not say how probable terminal events are, or indeed whether they could exist or not.

Neither is history just a tale of resource constraints falling inexorably before technological advance. The past increasing abundance of products derived from declining resources resulted as much from increased energy input as from improved technology. Without increased exploitation of the biological stock of forest energy, and later fossil fuels, the enormous growth of economic activity with a declining resource base could not have been achieved. As the accessibility of fossil fuel resources also declines, a double penalty in energy consumption is incurred. More energy is needed to extract a given product from declining ores, and more energy and other resources are expended in exploration for and exploitation of declining energy resources.

Furthermore, the present relationship of humankind to natural resources is quite different from what prevailed through most of history, when concentrated resources were exploited only locally. Depletion of resources to the limits of existing technology did occur (Seymour and Girardet, 1986), and individual civilizations collapsed as a result. But there were always other civilizations and new resource bases to perpetuate the species and allow continued development of technology. Today, resource decisions are interdependent. Worldwide resort to low-grade ores and fertilizer-based agricultures brings dependence of all civilizations on a common pool of depletable energy resources and of insufficiently tested technologies for their replacement. Despite the proliferation of research, humanity's technological and resource portfolio is in practice less diversified and more risk-prone than ever before. The rapidity of resource use and interdependence of the world economy has caused a large majority of eggs to be put in the few baskets with a potential pay-off adequate for the desired growth of the world economy. The risks facing all civilizations are linked risks, and now, unlike in historical times, humanity may stand or fall together.

Probabilistic Technological Change

Looking to the future, technological optimists (e.g. Beckerman, 1974) often do not trouble to predict specific paths for technological development, contenting themselves with generalities about the potential of technology to 'produce substitutes for raw materials that have become scarce', 'improve the utilization of a given resource base', or 'create new sources of cheap, abundant and safe energy'. *Potential* is the key word. These are achievements that *might* happen: because of the complexity of factors affecting their realization, it is impossible to show that they *will* happen.

This does not of course validate the assumption of technological pessimists (Ecologist, 1972; Ehrlich et al., 1977) – that technology cannot overcome natural resource limitations. Even in a future for which no specific technological salvation can be predicted, a technological breakthrough, for example in safe nuclear fusion energy, is the *deus ex machina* that could avert resource limitations. Yet *deus ex machina* has its aptness as a description of technological feats whose exact form cannot be defined. The unpredictability of the future can equally generate unforeseen problems for what presently appear as safe technological predictions. We face not so much risks, quantifiable from past experience, as uncertainties of awesome magnitude. Such formal decision-rules as there are (see chapter 12) suggest that it is prudent to act on pessimistic expectations.

The pessimistic view of technology changes fundamentally not just decisions on *exploitation* of non-renewable resources, but decisions on their *use* also. Forestry is energy-efficient, producing about 20 times the calorific value in wood output as it requires in fossil fuel input (Barrow et al., 1986): biomass forestry would gain importance in a fossil-fuel-constrained future. Nonetheless, there are implications for the type of forestry practised, particularly choice of technique (labour-intensive or energy-intensive) and balance between using biological and technological processes to maintain and enhance site productivity.

There are also implications for all shadow prices (Price, 1984b). Is SPIF negative – even indefinitely so – if investment leads to exponential expansion of the economy's capacity to deplete resources? What is the value of a competing, energy-inefficient agricultural use? Is the opportunity cost of labour negative, if it is withdrawn from resource-depleting industries?

Assumptions about the efficacy of technology are clearly so crucial, that it seems criminally irresponsible to pick the assumption that suits one's purpose and to base all CBA on that. Yet that is the conventional position. Even if one were to include only a low probability that the upward path of consumption will be curtailed, the resulting mean expected cost of many non-renewable resources would still be indefinitely large: the whole system of shadow prices is thrown into chaos.

This is a personal view, but many others share its premises. Its full implications for forestry are, perhaps, too disruptive for any decision-maker to carry them through. But marginal adjustment in the indicated directions – towards a more biologically sustainable forestry – is a start.

32 Cost–Benefit Analysis: A Review

Since CBA has had so much space in this book, an attempt to collate its diverse elements is proper, and to review criticisms levelled against it.

Setting up the analysis

Take an hypothetical forest exploitation project in Uruzela. The Comissione Florestale has the normal assortment of objectives to do with sound silviculture and development of forest resources to benefit the people. The government has its own portfolio of objectives, especially earning foreign exchange.

The government has many relevant options: establishing import-saving manufacturing industry; joining a multi-national project to develop tourism; exporting more canned beef, etc. These options are not specifically assessed in appraising the forestry project: they are included in a general way in the SPIF.

The Comissione Florestale has many projects, but, to keep the analysis manageable, attention is confined to the alternatives of conserving a forest area, with benefit to the forest-living population and to international wildlife interest, or creating employment and foreign exchange by a five-year programme of exporting furniture-quality logs, whereafter the land will be sold for ranching. The data set below is much reduced compared with what would normally appear in a CBA. Domestic cash flows are in domestas (Ds) and foreign exchange in dollars.

Exploitation project

Initial investment: Ds600 000 plus $100 000
Log export: $500 000 per year
Imported inputs: $250 000 per year
Domestic transport and marketing costs: Ds250 000 per year.

Plate IX Forest exploitation in south-east Asia: short-term foreign exchange earning – long-term opportunity costs?
(Photo: International Centre for Conservation Education)

The standard conversion factor for transport, marketing and catering services (0.8) is applied to this figure to give its shadow price.

Sale of land at year 6: Ds500 000.

Large profits to ranch owner; no net employment benefit.

During logging, the forest-living population (with a present subsistence income equivalent to Ds300 per head) will obtain minor forest products and use residual timber for firewood: thereafter 50 individuals will lose this free consumption valued at Ds150 per person per year.

Employment to 100 workers withdrawn from subsistence.

Wage is Ds500 per year. Their previous production, valued at Ds200 per year per worker, is *not* taken over by their families, or anyone else.

Employment to 10 managers transferring voluntarily from the private sector.

The market salary, Ds5000 per year, is paid.

Conservation project (doing-nothing)

Firewood and minor forest products flow in perpetuity for the forest living population.

The international conservation interest of the forest is such that net foreign exchange earning of $10 000 per year (accruing to government) can be attributed to it, at an internal financial cost (transport and catering) of Ds12 000.

General information on the economy

Income tax is at a flat rate of 33% on income above Ds1000 per year.

Initial investment funds compete with investments which:

yield a net financial rate of return of 12% in real (domestic) terms;

create one job per Ds5000 of investment, for workers paid Ds500 and withdrawn from similar subsistence employment to that of the forestry workers;

yield no net non-market benefit.

Net revenue from all government investments is divided 10% to reinvestment, 90% to additional consumption to citizens earning the national average of Ds600 per year.

Annual growth rate of income per head is 3%.

The elasticity of marginal utility of income is -2.

The current balance of payments account is in equilibrium (exports equal imports), and a 70% tariff is charged on all the $100 000 000 of imports. The official exchange rate is $1 = Ds4.

A pure time preference rate of 2% is applied.

Evaluation

First the shadow exchange rate, appropriate weightings and the SPIF must be worked out. As the processes have been described previously, only an outline is presented.

The shadow exchange rate is approximated by dividing summed internal prices of traded goods by summed world prices, as in equation (27.3)

$$\frac{Ds4 \times (100\ 000\ 000 + (100\ 000\ 000 \times 170\%))}{\$(100\ 000\ 000 + 100\ 000\ 000)} = Ds5.4 \text{ per } \$$$

Relative weights are derived as in chapter 28. As figure 32.1 shows, marginal utility of income falls steeply: the reasonableness of weights can be checked against the curve, but those below were derived algebraically.

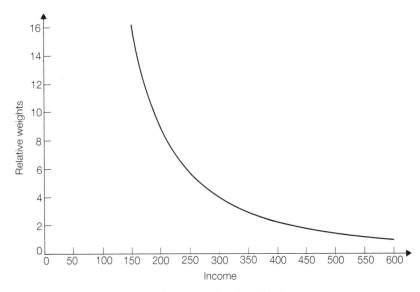

Figure 32.1 Relative income weights for project beneficiaries

Fall in income (Ds300 to Ds150) for forest-living population: 8.0
Rise in income (Ds200 to Ds500) for employed workers: 3.6
Marginal increase of consumption to population generally: 1.0

The SPIF is given by the process illustrated in table 30.1. Employment created by general investment yields increased weighted consumption of Ds300 × 3.6 per Ds5000 invested – a social rate of return of 21.6%, to add to the 0.9 × 12% = 10.8% financial return after reinvestment. The discount rate is 2 × 3% + 2% = 8% (equation (29.1)), and the rate of reinvestment is 0.1 × 12% = 1.2%. The SPIF is thus

$$\frac{(21.6\% + 10.8\%)}{(8\% - 1.2\%)} = 4.765$$

If running costs and revenues are divided 90 : 10 between consumption and investment, their weight is 0.9 + 0.1 × 4.765 = 1.377.

Table 32.1 shows costs and benefits for both alternatives.

These evaluations follow the practice of modern CBA. The boundary of the analysis is the national frontier. No allowance is made for consumers' surplus within the international community attributable to wildlife conservation. The price effect of increased exports is ignored. If price

Table 32.1 Costs and benefits for the two projects

Item	Foreign exchange	Domestic	Weight	Weighted value
Exploitation				
Investment	−100 000	−540 000	4.765	−2 573 100
Investment		−600 000	4.765	−2 859 000
Initial investment total				−5 432 100
Log exports	500 000	2 700 000	1.377	3 717 900
Input costs	−250 000	−1 350 000	1.377	−1 858 950
Transport and marketing		− 250 000	0.8	−200 000
Subsistence		50 × 150	8	60 000
Workers' extra income		100 × 300	3.6	108 000
Managers		No change		
Wages and salaries		−100 000	1.377	−137 700
Annual net benefit				1 689 250
Land sale		500 000	1.377	688 500
Ranching profits		large	0	0
Doing-nothing				
Subsistence		50 × 150	8	60 000
Conservation	10 000	54 000	1.377	74 358
Conservation costs		−12 000	0.8	−9 600
Annual net benefit				124 758

elasticity of demand for the type of timber exported is −2, then according to equation (27.1) the marginal export revenue of all exporting countries is half the direct export earning, or $250 000. As this equals the foreign exchange cost of exploitation, there is no net gain of foreign exchange to the exporters as a group. If greater weight is given to exporters than to importers, the international benefits of doing-nothing are understated, and those of exploitation overstated by the figures tabulated.

Discounting

Table 32.2 shows flows of weighted benefit, their time of occurrence and their value discounted at 8%. On this basis, exploitation seems marginally better than doing-nothing.

The table is, however, based on debatable assumptions about discounting. Including a pure time preference rate is normal, but ethically questionable. Without it, three things change.

Table 32.2 Project NPV, discounting costs and benefits at 8%

Item	Time	Benefit	Discount factor	Present value
Exploitation				
Investment cost	0	−5 432 100	1	−5 432 100
Net benefit	1	1 689 250	0.92593	1 564 120
Net benefit	2	1 689 250	0.85734	1 448 260
Net benefit	3	1 689 250	0.79383	1 340 981
Net benefit	4	1 689 250	0.73503	1 241 649
Net benefit	5	1 689 250	0.68058	1 149 675
Sale of land	6	688 500	0.63017	433 872
Total				1 746 457
Doing nothing				
Net benefit	1 − ∞	124 758	12.5	1 559 475

(a) The SPIF rises to 6.75; the weight on running costs and revenues is now 1.575. The standard conversion factor for transport, marketing and catering also changes to, say, 0.95 (the data given do not allow computation of the new value).

(b) Annual discount factors for all benefits of both alternatives come closer to one.

(c) If the discount rate for benefits to subsistence population is set arbitrarily low at 0.5%, the value of doing-nothing improves further.

The balance in table 32.3 decisively favours doing-nothing. Even if subsistence benefits are discounted at 6%, its NPV is still Ds2 227 500. The NPV of exploitation actually drops under a lower discount rate, because of increased SPIF. This emphasizes the importance of treating alternative investments the same way as forestry.

To persuade financial agencies that exploitation merits investment, incremental IRR and incremental *social* IRR might be calculated. The calculation is based on table 32.4, in which forgone cash/benefit flows of doing-nothing have been deducted from those of the exploitation alternative. In calculating social IRR a weight of one is used for government funds: in IRR calculations the discount rate equals the rate of return, so there is no premium on investment funds.

The IRR and SIRR on general government investment are respectively 12% and 33.6% (including employment benefit). These are the required rates of return which an acceptable investment should exceed: multiple IRRs make it ambiguous whether exploitation is acceptable.

Table 32.3 Project NPV, discounting costs and benefits at lower rates

Item	Time	Benefit	Discount factor	Present value
Exploitation				
Investment cost	0	−7 695 000	1	−7 695 000
Net benefit	1	1 839 250	0.94340	1 735 142
Net benefit	2	1 839 250	0.89000	1 636 926
Net benefit	3	1 839 250	0.83962	1 544 270
Net benefit	4	1 839 250	0.79209	1 456 858
Net benefit	5	1 839 250	0.74726	1 374 395
Sale of land	6	787 500	0.70496	555 156
Total				607 747
Doing nothing				
Subsistence	1 − ∞	60 000	200	12 000 000
Conservation	1 − ∞	73 650	16.667	1 227 500
Total				13 227 500

Table 32.4 Incremental IRRs of intensified investment

Item	Time	Incremental cash flow (Ds)	Incremental benefit (Domestasworth)
Investment cost	0	−1 140 000	−1 140 000
Profit	1 − 5	1 000 000	1 000 000
Employment benefit	1 − 5		108 000
Sale of land	6	500 000	500 000
Lost conservation	1 − ∞	−42 000	−42 000
Lost subsistence	6 − ∞		−60 000
IRR = 1.0% & 80.5%		Social IRR = 2.1% & 90.2%	

Presentation and after

NPVs and IRRs represent economists' final synthesis of value. If just one of these criteria has been adopted, decision-makers are presented with (say) an NPV of Ds607 747 for exploitation and Ds2 227 500 for doing-nothing. This seems to leave little to be decided! If these figures match decision-makers' intuitions or political interests, the adoption of doing-nothing will be declared to have been based 'on the most meticulous objective economic analysis'. If decision-makers prefer exploitation, the analysis may be declared 'faulty, biased or superficial', or be taken as 'one of many relevant factors' in deciding to adopt exploitation.

This is very discouraging for economists, who may well have a better grasp of relevant factors than decision-makers do, and may rightly wonder what else they could have done to make the CBA more acceptable. To pre-empt this depressing outcome, sensitivity analysis is often advocated.

Sensitivity analysis seeks a sensible balance between presenting masses of apparently unrelated raw economic data, and characterizing each alternative by a single figure. It shows the effect of adjusting contentious figures in the appraisal, such as future timber or oil prices, weighting factors, or discount rate. Decision-makers can thus see how robust the results are, and judge the appropriate figures themselves.

Sensitivity analysis also shows whether uncertainty really affects the choice of project, and allows economists to identify critical variables, which can thus receive more attention in future. It also has the political function of involving decision-makers in the analysis, and providing feedback to economists about decision-makers' values.

Tables 32.2 and 32.3 show the effect of different discount rates. The value of n in the marginal utility of income function may also be crucial, changing both weights and discount rate. A third element might be to vary assumptions made in calculating the SPIF: for example, if net revenues of exploitation are entirely invested, its NPV would exceed that of doing-nothing. Different assumptions might also be made about the distribution of benefits from investment.

Another possibility is using economic CBA, with unweighted values for products, labour priced at its opportunity cost, Ds200, and investment funds costed by discounting at an opportunity cost rate of return. Exploitation would be preferred at both 12% (the financial opportunity cost of capital) and 18% (the economic opportunity cost of capital, given the low opportunity cost of labour in alternative employment).

Despite its scope to enlighten, sensitivity analysis has dangers and drawbacks.

1 With several values inserted for each doubtful variable, the multiplicity of possible NPVs may become as bewildering as the original unprocessed data.

2 Decision-makers get maximum scope to justify a preferred project by selecting the set of shadow prices which gives it the highest NPV.

3 The shadow prices selected may be inconsistent between one decision and the next, leaving economists with no clear estimate of decision-makers' values after all. If a political decision on these values is required, it is better to elicit it before rather than after the analysis.

4 Economists are arguably better placed than decision-makers to judge matters like the discount rate and timber prices.

On whatever basis the decision is made, economists have one further job. *Ex post* evaluation reviews what actually happens to the adopted project, what volume growth eventuates, what usage of facilities is achieved, what unpredicted factors overturn expectations, by what factor costs are under-estimated and benefits overstated (or *vice versa*). Through this useful but often humbling experience, the team of assessors may be able to do better next time.

CBA in developed countries

Cost–benefit analyses for forestry projects in developed countries place more emphasis on environmental effects. Income weights might not be used (because the incomes of project beneficiaries are all close to the national mean). Investment might be considered optimal, and a free market in foreign exchange assumed, so no premium would be given to investment funds or foreign exchange. Heavy unemployment and subsidized agriculture might exist in remote rural areas, justifying opportunity costing of labour and land resources. However, if heavy unemployment also existed in urban areas, the net social return on all investments, and hence SPIF, would rise.

Chapter 31 makes the case for raising the customary shadow price of the non-renewable resources on which developed economies depend heavily.

Other systems of CBA

CBA is not a unified and agreed methodology, but a general philosophy of evaluation, within which differences of opinion flourish amongst theoreticians and practitioners alike. The version described in chapters 24–31 represents my preferred combination of techniques and assumptions. Many experts would regard it as idiosyncratic, if not misguided, particularly its view of discounting and natural resource costing. It sympathizes with social cost–benefit analysts in its concentration on income and the weights assigned to it. These choices of viewpoint have, it is hoped, been explained, and enough said to indicate how other forms of analysis differ.

The perspective on development CBA resembles that promulgated by UNIDO (Hansen, 1978) in its choice of domestic consumption as numeraire, and its adoption of existing rather than ideal government policy as the context in which the project matures. By contrast, the Little/Mirrlees system (Little and Mirrlees, 1974; Squire and van der Tak, 1975) uses a foreign exchange numeraire and assumes that economists can influence politicians in such matters as trade policy. The differences between systems are not crucial. In particular, the different numeraire gives different numerical results, but never produces different rankings among a given set of projects.

More radical is the system devised by Nair (1981). This takes at face value the stated commitment of many governments to fulfilling basic needs. Rather than applying a spectrum of weights, it gives weights of one to income up to Rs4800 per year (basic needs income), and zero to income above that. Willingness to pay for basic needs goods (those essential for a life of reasonable comfort) is weighted one, that for luxury goods, zero. Opportunity costs are those of forgone basic needs goods; the values of foreign exchange and of investment funds are the proportions representing basic needs goods; the discount rate for basic needs is zero. The 'income account' and the 'goods account' are aggregated at the end of the analysis, a heavier weight being given to income if changes in trade are easily accomplished. In its mixed emphasis on goods and income, it lies between economic and social CBA, but its weighting procedure is firmly in the social tradition. Its sharp distinction between what is and is not basic can be criticized, but that too is its strength: it bluntly confronts decision-makers with the real consequences of their policy pronouncements.

The viewpoint of economic CBA is argued by Gregersen and Contreras (1979) and Mishan (1988). It omits items which represent weighted transfers. The alternative with highest NPV is preferred, unless decision-makers reject it on grounds of undesirable redistribution (as might be done in the Uruzela example to favour doing-nothing). Objections to economic CBA are discussed in chapter 24.

The ideal CBA values only consumption of goods, according to imputed marginal utility; the role of income is to distribute available goods among consumers (Price, 1987a). The information base, however, rarely suffices to achieve this ideal.

Economic critique of CBA

CBA is ambitious in its objectives, so is judged by stringent standards. Some criticism is internal, from its own theoreticians: some comes from opponents of the whole concept, levelled particularly against its political implications.

Environmentalists present strong external criticism, on the grounds that CBA is in essence a thinly disguised version of profit-maximization, a tool of development rather than conservation. Environmental impact assessment is advocated instead. While this technique may give *greater* weight to the environment, that need not imply that it gives it *appropriate* weight. As chapters 25 and 26 showed, CBA has its own approach to environmental evaluation. Environmental impact assessment is perhaps best regarded as a complementary technique, whose role is to *identify* effects which CBA may at least attempt to evaluate.

Nonetheless, previous chapters have offered some criticism of prevalent conventions of CBA. Particularly, the assumption has been questioned that perpetual technological advance and economic growth justify both discounting and current-cost pricing of non-renewable natural resources. While *lower* social discount rates and *higher* shadow prices for non-renewable resources are often discussed by cost–benefit analysts, anyone proposing a *zero* discount rate and an *indefinite* shadow price for non-renewables is considered a cranky extremist. Consciously or unconsciously, everyone must take a position on this issue, but remembering that future generations (if any) may regard present profligacy as extremism of another, more selfish kind. *There is nothing moderate about the single-minded pursuit of maximum short-term profit.*

The narrow spatial concerns of CBA have also been criticized, especially the customary neglect of price changes which affect other nations' foreign exchange earnings. This is an example of the general habit of ignoring *ripple effects* of projects. When a project is implemented, it withdraws factors of production from its economic context, and supplies goods into it. In so doing it triggers price changes both locally and internationally, and stimulates adjustment in sectors which act in the same markets. These adjustments in turn provoke other price changes and further adjustments, the ripples spreading outward without obvious limit.

Ignoring these effects could be justified if CBA was less explicitly concerned with *costs and benefits to whomsoever accruing*, or if the economic context approximated an ideal market system without distortion or maldistribution. However, CBA declares its wide concern, and exists precisely because the economic context is not ideal.

Here is a profound practical problem, because ripple effects become harder to measure the more widely they spread out. But simulation models can be made of how interactions might occur. The main conclusions from one such model (Price, 1988c) are:

(a) The importance of ripple effects in relation to direct effects is independent of project scale – small projects cause significant ripples.

(b) CBA significantly undervalues goods for consumption by the poor, but overvalues goods for consumption by the rich.

(c) Distortion between price of goods and the marginal cost of producing them leads to unpredictable ripples.

(d) Increased consumption funded by project profits has a greater distributional effect than its direct value suggests.

(e) Employment of low-paid workers raises their market price, causing unmeasured redistribution to other low-paid workers. Conversely, employment of highly paid staff has unfavourable indirect effects.

Mis-estimation increases with the degree of distortion and mal-distribution. Thus the more CBA is needed to correct these defects, the less effectively it fulfils its role. It may accept projects which decrease net benefit, reject others which increase it, and rank projects incorrectly.

The relevance of these results to forestry projects should be clear. But the difficulty of obtaining reliable data allows only very general indications of how NPV is likely to be affected.

Less complex but no better understood are the reinvestment effects of running costs and revenues of projects. Analysts must attempt to establish the most realistic assumptions for particular circumstances. Every forest service has norms about whether revenues are remitted to central funds or retained for reinvestment, and the same applies to investments more generally.

Political critique of CBA

The above are not really criticisms of CBA itself, but of how it is applied. Other critics reject CBA altogether (Self, 1976).

One criticism is that it intrinsically cannot achieve what it attempts; that it is impossible to deduce value from willingness to pay, particularly for non-marketable goods (Pant, 1975). Critics contend that distribution, among contemporaries or between generations, is a matter of judgement, not susceptible to quantification. Dubious issues and points of difference among analysts are concealed behind a united, uncontroversial front, as in 'cookbook' approaches to project evaluation.

Secondly, there is a deadly tendency for selection of a 'pet' project to be supported by deliberately putting up unsound alternatives or no alternatives at all, or by evaluating alternatives under less favourable procedures than apply to the 'pet' project (Price and Nair, 1984).

The third criticism concerns the way in which CBA is used: single-NPV results pre-empt the role of politicians (Wildavsky, 1966), removing decisions from the people's representatives and delivering them to faceless and unaccountable technical experts. This criticism gains power because the terminology of economics makes its evaluations difficult for politicians and public to understand and challenge.

These charges have some justice: people do, by a slender margin, trust politicians, whom they can see, more than experts, whom they cannot; and there is benefit in the very process of involving the widest constituency in public decision-making. Against this must be weighed the probability that cost–benefit analysts evaluate any given effect more impartially than politicians do, and that the obscure-sounding terminology, like that of legal documents, overlies a precision which confutes ambiguity and exposes real issues. While some economists do try to extend the powers of CBA in order to gain greater control over decision-making, others do so to *improve* decision-making.

The two main criticisms of CBA, then, are

(a) that it has not yet gone far enough (in its economic capabilities)
(b) that it has already gone too far (in its political influence).

The viewpoint adopted is usually determined by political ideology rather than by informed deliberation.

The arguments have been presented so that readers may form their own judgements. Even if they conclude that CBA is not in the public interest, it is still important to know how it is done. CBA of some kind is frequent in forestry appraisals. Forest managers need to distinguish the honest analysis from the bogus or politically motivated one, the analysis which takes serious account of the real issues from the one which is superficial.

It must always be remembered that the complexities of CBA, daunting though they are, reflect complexities of the real world, and that in the real world decisions must be based on *some* form of evaluation. Evaluation by CBA has imperfections: but those imperfections should be compared with the imperfections of other forms of evaluation.

Part IV   The Wider Issues

33 Regional Income and Employment

This book focuses on decision-making at forest level, whether in determining harvesting method, thinning regime, or acceptability of projects. CBA may view broadly the costs and benefits to be evaluated, but it does so at a level which may involve only a few hectares.

There are, however, wider issues in forestry economics which touch on both political economy and forestry policy. Not many foresters reach positions of such authority as to exert visible influence upon such issues. Yet each informed individual can contribute to the debate, and, by shifting the climate of public and institutional opinion, affect the wider context of forestry.

Part IV examines some of these issues: the effect of forests on the well-being of localities; the reasons for state involvement in forestry; prediction of world price for forest products. Chapter 36 returns to the implications of the wider context for decision-making at forest level.

Rural depopulation

Rural–urban migration is a feature of most countries. It has existed ever since the specialized functions of cities – as opposed to large settlements – began to be defined thousands of years ago. The stream gathers momentum as countries industrialize, and becomes a flood that is sometimes a major national problem.

Rural depopulation is a demographic phenomenon with economic causes. It occurs when rural people perceive that cities offer a better deal (jobs, income and services available) than their current settlement. Its roots lie in 'rural push' and 'urban pull'.

'Push' relates to low incomes and declining job opportunities. Low income elasticity of demand for food and displacement of agricultural labour by machines mean that the rural share of GNP declines as industrial development proceeds, while the surplus of rural labour gives low wage bargaining power and sometimes declining real wages. Forestry-based communities, often relegated to the least productive and tractable land, are additionally handicapped by a harsh and inhospitable environment for human habitation.

As workers leave, demand for services in rural communities shrinks. Specialized services (retail, education, health, religious, cultural, welfare) which need a substantial population before they can be efficiently provided are at risk. The number of establishments offering other services declines, restricting choice. Owners and employees of these services depart too, accelerating the downward trend of population and spending power.

With the disappearance of local services, public transport to larger centres becomes necessary. But with declining population the quality and frequency of transport is reduced. Where possible, the more affluent acquire private transport, further reducing demand for and quality of rural public tranport.

At the same time the city offers the antithesis of the rural area, with the 'bright lights' factor and, in some cultures, a broader prospective marital choice added to economic pull factors listed in chapter 31. Apart from rural areas with special functions ancillary to cities – dormitory areas for commuters, or areas with environment favourable for retirement or tourism – a vicious downward spiral is initiated.

Nor is depopulation simply quantitative. Out-migrants tend to be young, fit, active, enterprising; the educated professionals; the relatively affluent; those best fitted to bring money into the economy, stimulate improvement of local environment and facilities, and lead campaigns to attract the attention of government and private enterprise. Left behind are elderly, infirm, lacklustre, impoverished; those least able to pull themselves up by their bootstraps and fight for their remaining rights.

Why stop depopulation?

The more hopeless a cause, the more the human spirit yearns to fight for it. It is thus almost axiomatic that a process so inexorably downward, so replete with positive feedbacks, should be resisted with every fibre of a nation's being. It is impolitic to suggest that depopulation is people voting with their feet for better conditions, or that migration is the market place in which people express willingness to make sacrifices for a better style of life.

Many reasons are given for resisting depopulation.

1 Social justice: migration hurts those left behind, often those least equipped to sustain hardship.
2 Political stability: areas whose problems are seen to be neglected by governments become cradles of unrest; great urban concentrations supply the focus of revolutions.

3 Cultural continuity: long-established communities are repositories of the folk-traditions on which the nation's identity and integrity depend.

4 Strategic safety: for countries not self-sufficient in agricultural and forestry products, there is insurance value in maintaining rural skills and local knowledge in case they are needed in times of war or other national crisis; formerly military security was served by containing population within an efficiently large city wall, but the nuclear era favours dispersion of economic activity.

5 Economic rationality: the more directly economic reasons fall under several headings.

   (a) Use of a labour force with low opportunity cost (due to high unemployment or underemployment), with beneficial effect on GNP.

   (b) Maintaining rural infrastructure and services throughout the year, so that it is available in the tourist season (if any).

   (c) Saving the social cost of building urban infrastructure for migrants.

   (d) Negative externalities of urban over-expansion (high rates of crime, disease and mental ill-health).

   (e) Countering false information on prospects of jobs, income and facilities in cities, which leads to over-estimation of benefits of migration.

   (f) Avoiding further unemployment in cities, where often many excess workers chase a limited pool of jobs: an extra migrant obtains a job only at the expense of already-resident workers.

These reasons appeal to benefits of remaining in a rural location, or costs of migrating to an urban one, which are not perceived as such by the migrant.

There are economic arguments for allowing or even encouraging migration, however. Subsidized or free government services are costly to provide to dispersed rural communities. Migration from settlements with undesirable economic characteristics allows reconstruction of the settlement pattern in a more economical and efficient form. Obstructing the migration flow simply preserves an inefficient and undesirable pattern, and defers solution of the population redistribution problem.

Relative efficacy of forestry in halting depopulation

Employment is the crux of rural depopulation. If sufficient quantity and variety of jobs can be provided in rural areas, it is believed, the population will stay, income will pass to rural services, and the economic fabric of the area will be sustained.

Although employment within a whole country can be created by a combination of policies on taxation and money supply, employment in rural areas depends on more specific measures: provision of free services, infrastructure, subsidies or tax advantages, imposition of restrictions or directives, or simply locating government activities in target areas.

Debates about rural depopulation and forestry employment tend to be emotional and illogical. It is often argued that forestry has achieved major triumphs both in creating rural employment and in improving labour productivity (its success in one measures its failure in the other). It is asserted both that mechanization is needed to cope with the enormous work-load in forestry and that forestry is needed to supply jobs to an enormous unemployed population. Means and ends become indistinct in the argument that forestry is needed to prevent depopulation so that there are people to do the work in forestry.

Forestry nevertheless has specific claims as a suitable means of providing employment. It is often under direct state control. It has a necessarily rural location, unlike light industry, which frequently locates in rural areas when incentives are high, but which equally frequently reverts to cities when incentives are withdrawn, or in economic recessions.

Forestry also supplies long-term employment. By contrast, mining or construction projects offer high employment per hectare, but only in the short term. When such projects start in rural areas, surplus local labour may not meet the project's whole need. High wages attract workers away from established local employers, who may be forced out of business. Workers arrive from outside the region; when construction finishes or reserves are worked out, these workers reinforce the unemployment problem.

Creating rural jobs is not just a matter of employing people directly. Some production processes require inputs from other firms, creating *backward linkages*. Others make products used as inputs by yet other firms (*forward linkages*). In the regional context, what matters is not only how strong these linkages are, but where the employment is located.

Forestry has strong linkages – backward ones such as repair and servicing of machinery; forward ones such as haulage and processing of timber. Forest products and ancillary services are expensive to transport long distances, so economic pressures encourage rural locations. Sawmilling has a low conversion percentage into final product, so total tonne-kilometres of haulage is reduced by locating close to the resource rather than close to mar-ket. Input–output analysis is a well-developed economic technique which relates additional requirements and availability in other sectors to changes in forestry activity (e.g. Schallau and Maki, 1983). But industries competing for land and funding also have backward and forward linkages, which should be included when comparing their employment-generating ability with that of forestry.

Plate X Forest village: an effort to stem rural depopulation
(Photo: Forestry Commission)

Nor can the rural location of economically linked industries be assumed. Urban locations have general economic advantages for processing industries. Haulage economies of rural locations are eroded if sawing residues are used in further processes, such as particle-board manufacture, or if other inputs like chemicals or plastic laminates are required in bulk. The need of chemical pulpmills for a large supply of pollutable water is an overriding determinant of location. As for backward linkages, the increasing sophistication of forest machinery may carry repair and servicing beyond the competence of local garages.

On a world scale, log export, and its banning, arise from the same conflicting forces.

Of income accruing to local factors of production, some is spent on purchases from outside the locality (*leakage*), some is spent on locally produced goods and services, giving additional local income. Respending of this money creates further jobs. This is the *multiplier* effect.

Numerically, the multiplier equals $1/(1-MPSL)$, where MPSL is the marginal propensity to spend locally – the proportion of additional gross income spent on local components of goods and services. The greater the range of goods and services supplied locally, the greater the MPSL and the multiplier. Thus expenditure on job creation is more cost-effective where services have not yet deteriorated badly. This, together with the greater efficiency of servicing larger communities, favours a policy of concentrating assistance for rural development on such communities, and allowing continued decline of very small ones. With given funding, more can be achieved to sustain the rural economy by spending it where a small injection has significant results. Forestry is more suited to this pattern of settlement than is farming (especially stock farming), which needs workers to live on or near the job. Where forestry requires gangs to move round widely dispersed sites over a cycle of several years, the best location for the gangs is in a settlement central to the whole forest, rather than dispersed evenly about it.

The multiplier effect depends on local wages, so the labour-intensity of an industry is crucial. Because of low mechanization in silviculture, forestry has traditionally been regarded as labour-intensive. Most work, however, arises in harvesting. This has been mechanized rapidly over recent decades, chainsaws completely replacing axes and felling saws in many countries, while tractors have ousted draught animals. Where older technologies persist, they may nevertheless be displaced during the next rotation.

The hiatus in employment between establishing a new crop and subsequent harvesting, together with further advance of mechanization, undermines forestry's claim to provide 'sustained yield' employment (Johnson and Price, 1987). Even where forestry would, with current technology, supply more jobs per hectare over a rotation than agriculture, increases in worker productivity may in practice give fewer worker-years during that period, with perhaps a tiny fraction of the originally estimated work-force required by the end of the rotation. Between the peaks of labour-demand in establishing and harvesting a forest, workers may drift away, and full mechanization or utilization of migrant labour may be the only way to undertake harvesting. Only when forestry takes over otherwise unused land is increased rural employment guaranteed.

Mechanization should not, of course, be automatically resisted: change which increases worker comfort, safety and job satisfaction is to be welcomed. Neither should employment linkages in producing forest machinery be neglected, when unemployment is a problem in urban as well as rural areas. But mechanization need not be an inexorable trend. If energy conservation and care of site productivity become more important in a natural-resource-constrained future, more labour-intensive working methods may be revived, where high worker productivity now seems the dominant criterion.

There are signs too, in mature industrial economies, that the migration stream is reversible. A semi-rural lifestyle, living in the country and working in the city, is becoming popular. But in the remotest areas, where forests are often concentrated, decline continues.

Tourist income generation

For obvious historical and economic reasons, forests are often abundant in economically undeveloped countries or regions. In a world where prices of rural raw materials are often static or falling at present, tourism based on the natural beauty of forests and their setting offers valuable and increasing income, for many countries in the form of precious foreign exchange.

Tourism is essentially labour-intensive. Personal service, in accommodation, catering, sports instruction and guiding, is part of the leisure experience: technological substitutes are unacceptable. A relatively small proportion of tourist expenditure leaks immediately from the local economy, especially if local foodstuffs are used in catering and locally produced craftwork is sold as souvenirs (Brownrigg and Greig, 1975). Moreover, tourism has a high income elasticity of demand, expenditure often increasing more than in proportion to rising income.

Regional support and managerial decisions

In so far as the arguments for stemming depopulation are valid, they should be reflected in managerial decisions about silviculture as well as choice of technique in harvesting. The shadow wage rate offers a mechanism for doing so. If retention of a rural population is an imperative, then shadow wage calculations should assume that an individual is restricted to living and working in the locality. In a generally fully employed economy, where migration in search of jobs would be normal, this substantially reduces the shadow wage.

However, the benefits of providing employment go beyond individual workers, into the community which their wages help to sustain. There are two classes of further effect to evaluate.

1 A ripple effect occurs because the shadow cost of providing local services or running linked local industries may be less than the market cost. The difference constitutes an additional net benefit.
2 The social, political, cultural and environmental benefits of retaining a rural population are externalities. To the extent that they depend on a forestry project, these can be included as project benefits.

Given the complexity of making these appraisals, it is unsurprising, though discouraging, that rural depopulation continues to be evaluated largely by political judgement.

It is also open to managers to vary the use of factors of production within the project. If rural depopulation is undesirable, and if forestry prevents it, then labour-intensive silviculture is particularly desirable and should be evaluated in a way that fully reflects its social as well as its silvicultural benefits (Price, 1978c). It is unethical to use rural depopulation as a political device to secure investment in a forestry project, then to ignore the argument in determining how forestry should be practised.

34 The Economics of State Involvement in Forestry

It is a notable feature of capitalist economies that, while state land ownership in agriculture is confined to a few experimental farms, there is usually a substantial state forestry enterprise. The reasons lie partly in history: the state may have been nominal owner of the virgin forest; as the need for cultivation grew, farm land was disposed of to individuals while the wooded residue remained in state ownership; the sporting interests of the head of state also dictated their retention.

There are, however, strictly economic reasons for continuing, and often increasing, state ownership of forest land, and for control by the state of private forestry activity. Some are general arguments, based on the defects of profit-maximization, and applicable to most economic activities: others however, have special force in forestry. At times when the flood and ebb of politics threaten to leave forestry aground on the mud-flats of ideology, it is important that foresters should distinguish clearly the good and the bad arguments for state intervention, the general arguments, and those particular to forestry.

The case against intervention . . .

One political viewpoint sees state intervention in economic matters as an intrinsic evil: either to be avoided at all costs, or to be tolerated only in special circumstances. Cogent reasons are advanced.

1 The individual's freedom is restricted by any state activity. To the extent that the state owns land, absorbs resources, produces goods and services, enacts legislation, it impinges on individual citizens; to the extent that its objectives differ from individuals' own, its impact is likely to be adverse. Exceptions must be recognized, for example, enforcement of reasonable laws to protect citizens from over-zealous

pursuit of freedom by fellow-citizens. The presumption, however, is in favour of leaving citizens alone.

2 Even benevolent intervention may be the thin end of the wedge. Governments start with benign intentions, but the exercise of power becomes attractive in itself. Small bureaucracies set up to administer the minimal set of state functions grow so as to protect their own interests against those of other bureaucracies, politicians and the public; they devise functions for themselves to generate a sense of importance; they make the obvious obscure and the direct tortuous to ensure that their own services become indispensable in using the system they have created.

3 State economic bodies, funded by taxation, avoid the pressures of making a profit and being accountable to shareholders. They are hence less cost-conscious, and tend not to seek innovative profit-making opportunities. Inefficiency in production combines with superfluous bureaucracy and tardiness in decision-making, the whole being reflected in excessive overheads and large scope for corruption. Any challenge on grounds of inefficiency or unprofitability is evaded by referring to vague multiple objectives whose achievement cannot be satisfactorily demonstrated.

4 Unlike the market mechanism, which responds swiftly and sensitively to needs which people themselves feel, state intervention imposes a value system which, even when it does respond to consumers, does so slowly.

. . . and against free enterprise

The above arguments have counterparts for the private sector, usually levelled against large (often multinational) companies.

1 Private enterprise itself restricts freedom, when large companies exert political pressure, for example over job creation. Freedom in a free market system is always limited by ability to pay, and the system does not distribute this equitably.

2 The advantages claimed for private enterprise tend to be dissipated by large businesses, which themselves have large internal bureaucracies with their own objectives and interest in maintaining an aura of indispensability. Shareholders are misinformed and misguided by skilled professionals at the behest of top management.

3 If monopoly power is achieved, giving control over the market, the pressures of profit-maximization are relaxed. Private corruption and

other illegal activities flourish under the umbrella of economic and political domination.

4 Consumer demand in the market reflects not so much consumers' real needs, but desires implanted by unscrupulous manipulative advertising.

There is truth in all these arguments, but protagonists tend to highlight one set or the other. They quote selected examples of the iniquities of either government or big business, and compare these with the theoretical perfection of the alternative system working well.

On the other hand, all are argued against large organizations, without considering scale economies. Some economic activities are 'natural monopolies': the larger the organization, the lower its unit costs and the greater its competitiveness. The communications and power industries are examples.

Foresters, as foresters, have no particular role in this debate (what they believe as citizens is another matter). The arguments are naturally deployed when further nationalization or privatization of the forest industry is discussed, but foresters may have more influence (depending on the ideological intransigence of the government) by presenting the special nature of forestry as an economic enterprise.

Forestry is not a natural monopoly. Enterprises of all sizes survive, and sometimes flourish. It is not particularly prone to the failings of bureaucracy or the excesses of misinformation. But it does have a distinctive character as a land use, in relation to identifiable failures of the market mechanism.

Land use and externality

Environmental externalities relate to the location of land: smoke and noise become nuisances because sufferers occupy land adjoining pulp and sawmills. Householders benefit as neighbours of amenity woodland. Forestry, being an extensive land use, has not only *many* but *widespread* externalities.

Externalities exist because of problems in creating a market. With negative effects, either the law does not entitle sufferers to compensation, or the effect is difficult to assess. For example, forestry may reduce volume and pH of streamflow, but it is unclear whether the prior right is for supply of unpolluted water downstream or for unstinted use of land on which rain falls, nor is it easy to establish who is affected and to what extent. The implication of international pollution in acidification of runoff makes market resolution quite intractable.

On the other hand many beneficial environmental effects either cannot be or are not worth being sold. Landscape is experienced by legal right, either on established rights of way through forests, or from viewpoints outside them. Wildlife conservation impinges on those not at site. Forest recreation can only be completely prevented by expensive exclusion measures, while the cost of charging for use of small car parks may not be covered by fees received. Even where charges can profitably be made, refusal to pay the charge on grounds of poverty or principle lead to under-utilization of site potential.

Since market solutions are ineffective, intervention is desirable to curb negative externalities and encourage positive ones.

Economies of co-ordinated planning

A feature distinguishing land from other resources is the uniqueness of each piece, in location if nothing else. In this sense every land-owner is a monopolist: there is no perfect substitute for that one piece of land. Thus the state may maintain the right to acquire a given area if that piece and no other serves the public purpose. Where precise location is crucial, as with the line of a road, this power is reasonable. It is less reasonable to exert it for forest acquisition, where it can be argued that land on the open market serves the public purpose just as well.

But land markets operate in a piecemeal way. Land holdings are sometimes sold when the existing use is no longer profitable, but sometimes through personal circumstances having nothing to do with economic use. Other holdings remain in the use which matches the traditions and skills of the present owner, although it is not the most lucrative or desirable one.

Evolution of land use pattern therefore occurs disjointedly, land being bought, not because it is ideal for a purpose, but because it is the best holding on the market. The existing pattern of land use could often be rearranged so as to increase production of every commodity and service, at less than current cost and to no-one's detriment. Yet the inertia and perhaps the mutual distrust of present users prevent the rearrangement being made.

Co-ordination of locational decisions therefore makes some sense. The mutual location of forests and processing industries are an instance. Even with perfect market information and mobility, the advantages of concentration are not totally captured by individual production units. Increasing the concentration of forests within the catchment of a major processing complex increases scale economies and gives a greater possibility of offering growers a high price, but most advantage from the action of one grower accrues to others. The opposite case of economies of dispersion occurs when several small processing firms each concentrate at the centre of a large forest to gain access to the widest supplies. Transport costs can be saved by dispersing firms throughout the forest, yet any one firm decentralizing reduces its share of timber supplies.

The common ownership problem

Where the state is a recent institution, the legacy of history is often cultivated farmland owned individually and forest and grazing land owned commonly. Common ownership by many individuals of the right to benefit from a land area is not the same thing as ownership by a single body representing the common interest, nor does it have the same effect. The following adverse effects can be identified.

1 Typically, a biological resource is most productive at moderate stocking. Natural forest and denuded wasteland both have zero net productivity, while managed forest from which timber removals are controlled is highly productive. As exploitation of natural forest begins, net productivity rises to replace removals, up to the point of maximum sustained yield. Discounting apart, this appears to be the optimal level of use. Once the stock is depleted below this level, yield declines. Yet, under common ownership, exploitation may continue to intensify. Each individual perceives only the benefit obtained from individual exploitation: the opportunity cost – loss of long-term productivity – is communal, falling largely on other individuals. Even conscientious individuals, acting to conserve the resource at its highest productivity, cannot improve matters: their 'share' of exploitation will probably be annexed by less conscientious individuals.

2 A less concentrated resource is more costly to exploit, in terms of time to gather a given amount of dead wood for fires, or nuts or fruits, or to track and kill forest animals. Communal costs imposed by reducing the resource concentration are not recognized by commoners acting in their individual interests. In an industrial economy, increased costs of search lead to substitution of other resources and products, but in a subsistence economy scarcity increases marginal utility of products, with ever-greater efforts yielding an ever-smaller harvest. Also some products – typically animal horn or bird feathers – are prized for their very rarity, so that, as the resource diminishes, the pressure on it mounts.

3 The end of this process may be irreversible loss of a species or a whole ecosystem. No individual can prevent this: it is in each individual's interest to secure a maximum share of the resource while it remains – the threat of extinction may even be an incentive to faster depletion.

4 There is a qualitative dimension too. Where choice exists, the best trees are taken, leaving badly formed stems, less workable species, the un-healthiest specimens, without regard for the genetic quality of the forest. Over time undesirable species and genotypes gain dominance. Similarly in unregulated sport-trophy hunting, the poorest specimens are left to form the future population.

5 Obversely, it is in no individual's interest to invest in improving the resource, by planting superior trees, fencing overgrazed areas etc., because the investor receives only a small share in the total benefits of improvement.

Even when forest concessions grant the exclusive right of exploitation to one company, that company has no guarantee of gaining the concession for the second-growth crop. Why leave good seed trees, why take care of soil conservation, why follow replanting conditions over-meticulously, when the beneficiaries will probably be another company? Why bother about the effect of exploitation on species which are not currently commercial? Far better to cut and clear out, moving on to another concession, in another country!

The commons problem has been widely considered a major threat to rational use of the world's resources (Hardin, 1968), though some question whether it is so pervasive and insoluble (Livingstone, 1986). One solution is to replace commons by individual tenure, the land being portioned among present title-holders. But this may be resisted where no tradition of such ownership exists, where there are no clear means of marking boundaries, or where experience has shown that land is divided inequitably. Replacement of communal cultures by imported individualistic ethics does not guarantee an improved outcome. Commoners may rationally prefer the devil they know!

The alternatives are communal regulation (with quotas fixed or taxes imposed on the quantity of product taken, or exploitation restricted to certain periods of the year) or formal state ownership and management of the resource in exchange for cash or concessions. Whether these concessions exist or not, continued but illicit use of the forest by former common-holders is not unknown.

Whatever solution is attempted, collaborative action is needed. Common lands are no-one's to sell, so the market cannot solve the problem, even by creating individual ownership.

The time period problem

The time period of production is the heart of forest economics. Chapter 29 made the case against accepting either market rates of return or individual time preference rates as a social discount rate. Yet it also pointed out that the *individual's* welfare is not maximized by accepting forestry if it earns less than the market rate of return, and the fact is that individuals *do* discount at individual time preference rates. Consequently pursuit of profit and perceived private well-being leads to under-investment. All investments are affected, but forestry's exceptional time period makes it particularly vulnerable.

Despite this, the NPV mentality has yet to overtake many land-owners with a long forestry tradition. Their economic reasoning may be outdated, but if it achieves a socially desirable forestry governments should leave them alone! The problem, for countries which have depleted their forest resource below an acceptable level, is that tradition does not create new forests.

In such circumstances, the 'infant industry' argument is often raised. This asserts that industries take some time to establish themselves, and initially require state protection or subsidy to survive against established producers in other countries. But the production period is a continuing problem in countries with a normal age-class structure. Chapter 11 argued that as an investment replanting is not different from initial planting. Law or tradition may oblige replanting of felled forests, but economic self-interest is often against it. Without legislation or state ownership, forest area does tend to decline.

Discounting affects also the type of forest and its location. Regulation may be needed if desiderata are to be achieved here.

State intervention is of course only beneficial if the state view of the future is longer-term than that of private investors. Unlike externalities, which affect the interests of present population, a low social discount rate favours voters and political supporters not yet born, and runs against the perceived interest of those alive today. Day-to-day political pressures encourage a short-term view.

Surprisingly, however, many governments *have* undertaken major afforestation, even against recommendations from their economic advisers, and in so doing have given direction to a broader national effort. The overt logic of the policy (like contestable claims about the environmental benefits of exotic plantations) may be suspect, but again its effect is like that of low social discount rates.

Research and the public goods problem

Forest research combines the time period problem and the commons problem: it takes a long time to achieve; once achieved, everyone else benefits. By contrast with industrial processes, forest and farm methods are on public display. Publicly available knowledge has no sale value. It can only be provided free, and therefore is only provided by public or charitable bodies. It is no accident that agricultural research, unlike production, also usually has a major public component.

Private and public risk

The direction and magnitude of change in world timber prices is uncertain. This affects private and public perception of forestry investment quite differently.

Private investors see forestry in the producers' role. The possibility of a high price is welcome, but, as argued in chapter 12, the utility gain of unexpectedly high prices for timber has less impact, per unit of currency, than the utility losses of unexpectedly low ones. This is especially so if a substantial part of the investment portfolio is in forestry. Risk aversion makes forestry less attractive.

The position of the state is very different. The state usually has only a small part of its investments in forestry, so treats possible reductions in revenue at parity with the same monetary increase. The state acts also as and on behalf of consumers. For a nation importing a large proportion of its timber, high prices cause major additional drain on foreign exchange and seriously reduced consumption. Risk aversion makes forestry more attractive.

That argument can be raised for any product in which the nation is not self-sufficient. However, for most products action to alleviate shortages can be taken within a few years. Again, the production cycle of forestry makes it exceptional.

The case against state forestry

It can be argued that the widespread and long-term nature of forestry make it particularly susceptible to certain malign aspects of state bureaucracy. Its remoteness (geographical and practical) from the seat of government opens a chasm between policy-makers and practitioners. Attacks on its economic inefficiency may be softened by pervasive but nebulous non-market effects, plus a financial buffer of 'free' forest capital (or a time-frame which makes comparisons difficult). The dispersed nature of the enterprise shelters corruption. Yet the proneness of state organizations to monoculture of ideas becomes more-than-usually exposed in monocultures of species and uniform silvicultural systems.

These are all potential failings: the success of a state forest service might well be measured by its ability to overcome them.

Styles of economic intervention

Intervention requires not only a justification, but a mechanism. The spectrum of potential measures passes from the left-wing extreme of nationalization without compensation, through the liberal preference of persuasion and encouragement, to the land-owners' idyll of generous subsidy.

The instruments of intervention themselves are not neutral to the social purpose. Subsidy or tax relief to forest owners is not a costless bounty, showered down on them as a mark of divine favour, but represents a remission of valuable government funds, often to the relatively wealthy; any social evaluation of the merit of financial support should include that factor.

Given the longevity of forestry and the transience of politics, measures commanding broad support are the most effective. Retention of state lands, state purchase in the open market, a mixture of subsidies and legal controls over the private sector, and a state-run research and advisory service, seems a moderate recipe for the best of both worlds.

For nations self-sufficient in timber and with a long tradition of responsible private forestry, the state can play a more passive role. But desperate diseases require desperate remedies: where forest destruction is far advanced and fast advancing, responsible public ownership and management is the mildest measure with much chance of success.

35 World Timber Price

World timber price is at once the most embracing summary of the economic position of forestry, and the most intimate concern of the field forester. It expresses the global forces on one of humanity's most valuable resources, yet has its bearing on every detail of choice among silvicultural regimes. The course of its future change is the one thing no serious forest economist would be foolish enough to predict, and none would be stupid enough to ignore.

The determinants of timber price are among the first factors that students encounter in economics texts: supply, demand and the elasticities thereof. In a textbook world it seems straightforward. In the real world this is the toughest nut to crack.

Supply

Supply has different meanings to economists and laypeople. To one group it is a relationship between market price and quantities offered for sale: to the other it is just 'how much there is' of something. In this case, the lay view provides a better starting point.

How much timber there is in the world is not known with great precision. Recent estimates by Food and Agriculture Organization and United Nations Environmental Programme suggest there are somewhat over 4000 million ha of forest, 1400 million of which is open woodland with low density of trees. No reliable estimate of total volume is available.

For the economist, however, the physically existing quantity is less relevant than the amount that can be harvested at given cost. About half the forest area is considered to be 'operable', that is, neither too inaccessible, nor too low-quality, nor restrained from commercial production for environmental reasons. 'Operability' must plainly relate to offered price. The higher the price, the more can be profitably harvested. Chapter 6 showed on the micro-economic scale that higher prices enabled extension of haulage and extraction limits, and exploitation of smaller tree sizes. On a world scale, such increases become the upward-sloping supply curve.

But supply curve on what time scale? In the short term not all the timber that could profitably be harvested at a given price is actually available (even if owners were willing to sell) because the infrastructure is not there to make it accessible, and because machinery and staff take time respectively to manufacture and train. In the long term the available timber does not represent supply either, because it is a stock, rather than a capability for continuous supply. Supply, like demand, has a time dimension which often does not feature in introductory texts. Long-term supply focuses on volume yield *per year* that can be made available at a range of prices. This relates to increment, not standing volume.

For semi-natural forests in the developed world, mean growth rate is 2–3 m^3/ha/year, decreasing towards the poles. Tropical forests show little net increment, since they are in a state of equilibrium, decay balancing growth. Productive potential is much higher than this: plantations in northern latitudes are capable of growing at 10 m^3/ha/year, and in the tropics growth rates up to 50 m^3/ha/year are obtainable. The distribution of these productivities can be reasonably guessed at, and comparative assessments of profitability made (Sedjo, 1983). If the potential was fully developed, it would be capable of supplying around 20 times the current rate of timber harvest.

If foresters were in charge of the world (which palpably they are not), such figures, together with estimates of growing and harvesting cost, would allow compilation of a supply curve. Since the world would change only very slowly under their rule, the market could evolve gradually to equilibrium, where the required sustained yield would be drawn from forests at minimum cost (provided some forest economists were in the ruling junta too).

But the world is ruled by other forces, and change occurs at a faster tempo. The time dimension is problematic yet again, causing timber supplies to adjust in perpetual arrears of current needs. Today's prices are based on the supply laid down between five (for the fastest-grown tropical planta-tions) and several hundred (for boreal forests) years ago. Present foresters must anticipate markets five to several hundred years ahead. But this anticipated market condition itself depends on decisions taken by other foresters, who are responding to a mixture of *present* price signals, anticipated *future* price signals, and to no price signals at all.

The theory of market dynamics includes reference to perverse cycles, in which the scarcity of one year induces high prices in that year and hence over-production and low prices in the following year. This is not a likely result in world forestry, even over decades, since the production cycle varies so much from zone to zone. Yet there is evidence of such cycles in the production of Christmas trees, and the predicted shortage of world pulping capacity for the mid-1970s seemed to lead to over-installation of such capacity, with consequent closures at the end of that decade.

We are thus involved in a global strategic game, where each decision to plant should be taken with some conception of how the foresters of other nations are responding to prices, how they view future prices, and how they will modify their programmes to meet the price trend emerging over a rotation.

For tropical and sub-tropical nations with rapid tree growth, the problem is not too acute. World supplies will not have changed much when first rotations are harvested. But in the temperate zones prediction of supplies involves guessing how the tropical and sub-tropical nations will act, bearing in mind that some could grow sawlogs in the time period between the last thinning and the final felling of a conventional European regime. Response can, indeed, be even faster than that, because a nation with many fast-growing plantations can begin cutting its forest capital without prejudicing long-term sustained yield. Increased yield can also be found with a short lead-time, simply by increasing the intensity of management of semi-natural forest.

With a given land-base, it becomes possible to evolve very sophisticated models of changing prices, changing harvest and trade, processing into different products, planting in response to prices and evolving supply in successive time periods (Kallio et al., 1987). But this pre-supposes that foresters are free to implement such programmes. In reality, land use competition may obstruct the desired development of forest area. Thus, although global deforestation is currently running at only about 0.25% of total area, we must look urgently in some critical areas (and in the long term everywhere) at the expected needs of agriculture, the evolution of *its* cost and price structure, the political influence *it* will exert when foresters claim more land.

Given these sources of uncertainty, it may be that in the medium term the economist's conception of a greater quantity coming forward when the offered price is higher is actually less relevant (once again) than the lay conception of a sustainable flow of timber which cannot, perhaps, increase much on the land area available to it.

Comparative advantage and self-sufficiency

The forester has not been born who cannot argue that his or her own country has comparative advantage in wood production; whether it is Scandinavians or Canadians with scale economies, New Zealanders with their good soils, tropical countries with fast growth and low labour costs, or Britons proclaiming that 'we have the best climate for growing trees in Europe'. The implication is that in the long term it is right for those who can grow trees efficiently (us!) to do so, and that in due course the world will come to its senses.

Economists have different criteria of judgement, which often leads them to assert that it would be better (for most countries) to import timber (but from which countries?) using foreign exchange gained by growing the crops or manufacturing the goods or providing the services in which the country really does have comparative advantage. Other countries may have no more comparative advantage than we do, but if they are so foolish as to continue growing timber and exporting it to us at less than the cost (including interest) of growing it, so be it: it is not our job to put other countries' foresters in order. Efficiency, like charity, begins at home.

The argument of economists, no less than that of the foresters, depends on a certain style of thought prevailing in the rest of the world: foresters assume that all the world will behave like economists, while economists all too often assume that the rest of the world will behave like foresters. These are risky premises when all other countries may be receiving the same message and playing the same game.

In relation to timber supply, the fewer the assumptions the better. The objective is not to score points for timber productivity or economic slickness, but to judge the most likely course for world timber prices. Comparative advantage plays only a secondary role in this.

Demand

The factors affecting demand – population, income, taste and technology of substitution – were alluded to in chapter 2. They are less susceptible to complex feedbacks than supply. Nonetheless, they are not easy to predict. Projected world populations and gross world income in relation to forestry time-scales are shown in table 35.1.

It is reasonable to suppose that demand will rise in proportion to population, and income elasticity studies indicate that it will also rise strongly with income per head of population. But all this assumes that the required quantities can be supplied at present prices.

Table 35.1   Population, income and forest production period

Date	Population (1000 million)	Income 1990 = 100%	Stage of plantation formed in 1990
1990	5.5	100	Planting
1995	6.0	122	Pulp harvest, Brazil
2015	7.9	250	Sawlog harvest, New Zealand
2060	13.8	1 241	Teak harvest, India
2170	55.5	64 290	Veneer oak harvest, France

Price elasticity and substitution

The difficulties of predicting the factors shifting world demand pale to insignificance, compared with those attending estimation of the elasticity of that demand. Most serious studies examine price elasticity of demand for final products. A wide range of values is reported in the literature, from -3.5 for sawnwood (McKillop, 1967) to -0.01 for paper (Buongiorno, 1978). Even the values presented within one volume (Kallio, *et al.*, 1987) show no evident consensus, and the differences are not trivial. With a price elasticity of demand of -3.5, a shortfall of supply by 10% would give a price rise of 3%: with an elasticity of -0.01, the price rise would be 3 764 762%!

For foresters, there is the further problem of translating price/quantity relationships in wood products markets into an elasticity for timber in the forest.

Two principal determinants of elasticity, time-period and product specification, also cause trouble. Both act on the effectiveness of substitution for timber. If the market is under-supplied, in the short term the options are to pay the higher price or go short. In the longer term, however, new technologies can be devised, either to improve the utilization percent of a resource (increasing the effective supply of services from a given resource quantity) or to replace the resource by another. Thus in the long term demand is more price elastic: a given shortfall of supply can be sustained with a smaller price increase.

The overall profitability of forestry depends on long-term response of prices to shortage, rather than on short-term fluctuations. Unfortunately long-term elasticity effects are hard to measure, tending to be swamped by many other long-term trends.

The possibilities of substitution are eliminated progressively as a product is defined in broader terms. Thus demand for sawlogs from a particular forest is very price elastic. Sawlogs from adjacent forests are near-perfect substitutes, and any price rise is readily compensated by consumers buying from another source. Demand for all sawlogs is much less price elastic, but, given time, composite products made from lower-grade wood can replace many uses of sawlogs. Quantity demanded of all wood products, similarly, shows even smaller price elasticity, but in some uses plastics or steel may be substituted. Finally for structural materials taken together, demand is very price inelastic, as there is little possibility of substitution.

Two concepts are relevant for forest managers. High elasticity at forest level places each manager at the mercy of world price, and is immediately relevant. However, in predicting world timber price over a long period the important factor is the effect of *total* timber supplies on expected price: this demand is much less price elastic. Furthermore all structural materials are derived from and by use of natural resources, which are subject to supply constraints and increases of demand like timber itself. The traditional view sees substitutes as available in more-or-less unlimited supply at a particular price. Taking all resources together, however, substitution possibilities are very restricted, and demand becomes even more price inelastic. It is perhaps as likely that timber will be required as a substitute for other resources, as that other resources will be available to replace timber.

It is worth considering also the implications of substitution for depletion of non-renewable natural resources (McKillop et al., 1981); the shadow cost of such depletion arguably lies far above the conventionally attributed value. An analysis which aims to maximize human welfare cannot legitimately ignore this.

It is all too easy to include the possibility of substitution more than once, and thus to overestimate its power. Substitution can be included once by diverting demand to other resources; twice by broadening the scope of defined supply to include timber and its substitutes; a third and fourth time by using price elasticities of supply and demand which implicitly incorporate these effects. Substitution cannot be omitted; it will mitigate the effects of *specific* shortages: but its benefits ought not to be overstated; its ability to alleviate *general* shortages is much more restricted.

Forest economists thus find themselves adrift in a wider context than they either expect or wish. Setting out in search of a price applicable to the product of one small forest, they are dragged inexorably into considering the balance between all resources and populations of the world.

It is disquieting, after reading the evidence of scientific study, to be left saying 'but on the whole I think ...'. Nevertheless, the wide spread of scientific results and the number of important factors which they either omit or do not resolve leave little real alternative. For price elasticity of demand, the self-questionnaire approach (see chapter 24) is perhaps a more reliable (though less impressive) guide to reality than thorough scientific studies. Ask: 'if I were obliged to manage with half the supply of wood products that I now enjoy, how would my willingness to pay for them change?' or 'if the price of final products were to increase by a factor of four, by how much would I curtail my consumption?' My own answer is that the two situations match each other reasonably well, the implication being that long-term price elasticity of demand is around -0.5.

Next should come considered estimations of how (say) a sustained four-fold price increase would affect the technology of wood processing: to what extent capital and labour could replace raw materials, to what extent recycling and re-use would become economically attractive. On this basis a price elasticity of demand for the raw resource can be derived, remembering that harvesting and processing costs may also be affected by shortages.

It could be argued that this approach aggregates too much, since the kinds of timber and the markets they serve show marked differences. However, at the margin – and particularly given time for adaptation – substitution between different kinds of material (for example tropical and temperate saw-timber) is possible. A chain of potential substitutions links all wood supplies, though the chain's distant ends are utterly distinct.

This is all very unscientific, likely to draw either uncontrollable mirth or incoherent anger from professional economists, but at least we can see what we are doing, which is more than can be said of many econometric studies.

Price, discounting and value

It is clear enough, for anyone whose dignity is not tied to Getting the Right Answer, that future world prices of timber are very uncertain, and that a deterministic approach evinces inexcusable arrogance. Yet decisions must be based on something. Our sense of values and a range of reasonable guesses seem more likely to produce a useful answer than a single, scientific, precisely wrong calculation. This is not to say that economics has no role to play, and that we should act on hunch: it does mean that it is worth exploring a road along which economics and common sense are equal partners.

Universally, economists attempt to impute a relative value of some future timber product from its predicted price, rather than predicting its price from some notion of relative future value. Price is perceived as the fundamental variable, from which value arises as a secondary event. But this is not the only, nor the most sustainable view of fundamentals. Goods and services have a price only because consumers value them.

Value at present may be inferred from the price people are willing to pay. But there is no record of future willingness to pay. The prices which in due course are paid will be inflated monetary prices. In time series analyses these prices will be deflated to a 'real' price in a reference year; yet there is *nothing* real about such prices. As prices they never did exist, nor ever will exist, and it is a strange aberration that anyone should wish to predict them. Nor are they measures of 'real' value, for the constant purchasing power which they are intended to represent itself has diminishing or increasing marginal utility, according to whether consumption per head of that product and its substitutes is increasing or decreasing.

That is why the issues of discounting and price prediction cannot be separated, once the passage of time itself and the rate of return on investment are rejected as the basis for discounting. Positive discounting is a prediction of diminishing marginal utility, which is valid provided the future is an era of greater consumption per head. In such an era we may predict what the implications for price of that diminishing marginal utility may be, but the price change is a *reflection*, not a *determinant* of that marginal utility.

If on the other hand we predict increasing scarcity and reduced timber consumption per head at some future date, then that itself is the guide towards how we should weight timber consumption now against timber consumption then, without recourse to price estimation, and without applying any kind of discounting procedure to allow for the passage of time. Time in this context is irrelevant, except as it ushers in shortages or new supplies. Prices are estimated from shortages, in order that in the very long term we may make predictions about those new supplies.

Changes in terms of trade and exchange rates

If the purpose of timber production is to save (or earn) foreign exchange, evaluations must be cast in terms of what that saving will be worth to the nation when the forest investment reaches maturity. What goods will be bought with it, by whom and to what effect? It can be argued (Sedjo, 1983) that terms of international trade have a bearing on this value; the constant shifts in these terms, and in official and shadow exchange rates, seem therefore to create a major problem for evaluation.

However, as figure 35.1 shows, the problem of international adjustments is more apparent than real. Rapid movements in exchange rates reflect differential rates of domestic inflation. And, as with domestic inflation itself, the most realistic treatment is to ignore them. (This is not to assume that they will go away.) Deteriorating terms of trade result from increasing abundance of exports or increasing scarcity of imports. Hence the smaller volume of imports which is equivalent in value to a tree is balanced by the increasing marginal utility of consuming them; the larger equivalent volume of domestic products is balanced by the diminishing marginal utility of consuming them. Terms of trade affect the value of a tree only when extra foreign exchange is gained (as is often done in the Third World) by devoting more resources to import saving and export creation, rather than by forgoing consumption. Potential world timber shortage, with increased price, is the most general factor affecting the value of growing an extra tree.

In the broadest perspective of CBA, the benefit of forest investment lies in the value of timber produced, rather than in foreign exchange saving. The approaches may be roughly equivalent, for if timber is scarce in the world it will both have a higher value itself, and command a greater foreign exchange price. There are, nonetheless, price ripple effects like those described in chapter 32: shortages of a particular timber are good news for the producing country, and if the producing country is poor it is good news for international redistribution.

Probabilistic best-guessing

Meanwhile, forest managers want to make profit-maximizing decisions, and need a figure for future timber prices. The following set of probabilistic estimates is intended to illustrate an approach, not to give a result.

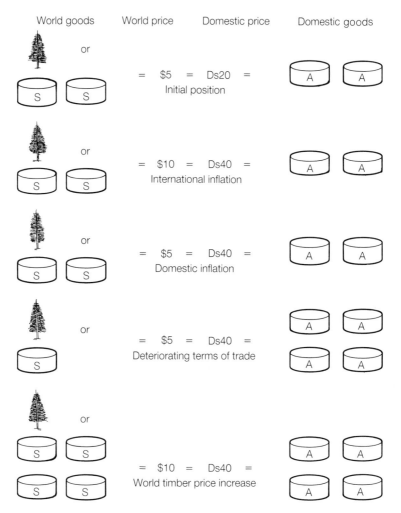

Figure 35.1   Influence of international changes on tree value
Items across one row have equivalent value
The imported 'world goods' are trees and tins of salmon: the domestic
goods are tins of exportable asparagus.

Suppose that a plantation is established in 1990 for felling in 35 years.
Consider three scenarios. The first has the world economy performing well
on all fronts. GNP per head is predicted to grow at 2% per year in real terms.
The value of n is 2, so the discount rate is 4%. Rising GNP implies rising
timber consumption, but any tendency to world shortages is counteracted by
vigorous programmes of investment in roads into forests and creation of

plantations, and the real price of timber stays constant. In these circumstances, to which a 30% probability is assigned, the PV to year 1990 of 400 m³ of timber, of a grade presently priced at £15/m³, is £1520; the contribution to mean expected value is £456.

The second scenario, assigned a 60% probability, foresees growth in timber demand associated with growth of GNP, which is not matched by increasing supply. Thus prices are expected to rise. World consumption of timber in 2025 *at present prices* is estimated at 7700 million m³, and the availability of wood (without infringing sustained yield constraints) is 6200 million m³. Unless supply is increased, prices must rise. With a price elasticity of demand for wood products of −0.5 (guessed, but reasonable) equilibrium is achieved with a 54% increase in product price. If growers presently receive on average only 15% of the consumers' price of timber products, a 54% rise in that price without increase in harvesting and processing costs implies a 360% increase of residual value. However, such an increase in raw material price is likely to prompt more efficient utilization, more re-use and recycling, which may make up, say, half the shortfall of supply. Under these assumptions growers' price rises by 152%. Timber is still available on world markets, however, and continuing growth of GNP means that the sacrificed foreign exchange has diminishing marginal opportunity cost. The discount rate remains at 4%, the PV is £3830/ha and the contribution to mean expected value is £2298.

Thirdly, consider a scenario with 10% probability, in which natural resource constraints stop growth of the national economy, and timber on the world market becomes prohibitively expensive. The nation, currently aiming at 40% self-sufficiency in timber by 2025, is obliged to become completely self-sufficient. Assuming no improvement in timber use, the result is an astounding 36-fold increase in price to growers. Even with amelioration of utilization, the price rise would be 8-fold. Under the natural resource constraint, however, the oil cost of harvesting might increase substantially: let the increase in stumpage therefore only be 7-fold. It is now the scarcity of timber itself, rather than the opportunity cost of foreign exchange, that sets the value of extra production. Direct estimation of this scarcity value supplants discounting, in the context of social evaluation. The PV of the plantation is now £42 000 and its contribution to mean expected value is £4200. The summed mean expected value is £6216. The point to note most particularly is that it is the least likely scenario that has contributed most to mean expected value.

Under the optimistic, neutral and pessimistic scenarios, the opportunity cost of both land and investment funds would be different. Table 35.2 outlines the complex (and unconventional) appraisal required. A sensitivity analysis, with several elasticity assumptions, is also in order, if the matters discussed in this chapter are taken seriously.

Table 35.2 Shadow pricing one rotation under different price scenarios

	Optimistic	Neutral	Pessimistic
s	0.1	0.1	0[a]
q	0.08	0.08	0.08
r	0.04	0.04	—
SPIF†	2.25	2.25	2.8[b]
SPRF*	1.125	1.125	1[a]
Planting cost in 1990 × SPIF	−1000 × 2.25 = −2250	−1000 × 2.25 = −2250	−1000 × 2.8 = −2800
Receipts in 2025	6000	15120	42000
split between investment funds in lieu of replanting[c] × SPIF, discounted to 1990	$1000 \times 2.25 \div 1.04^{35} = 570$	$1000 \times 2.25 \div 1.04^{35} = 570$	1000[d]
and running funds × SPRF, discounted to 1990	$5000 \times 1.125 \div 1.04^{35} = 1425$	$14120 \times 1.125 \div 1.04^{35} = 4026$	$41000 \times 1 \div 1.00^{35} = 41000$
Forgone annual agricultural profit 1990–2025 × SPRF × discount factor‡	$-60 \times 1.125 \times 18.66 = -1260$	$-60 \times 1.125 \times 28.02^{e} = -1891$	$-60 \times 1 \times 110.95^{f} = -6657$
Total	−1515	455	31543
× probability	×0.3	×0.6	×0.1
MEV contribution	−455	273	3154

Notes: [a] Under natural resource constraints, expansive reinvestment is not encouraged. [b] Forgone accumulated simple interest at 8% on general investment during the 35 years of the plantation's life. [c] £1000 is abstracted from the investment stream during the rotation. As the forestry investment is not maintained, this £1000 is switched back into 'general' investment at the end of the rotation. [d] Allocation to restore forgone general investment from 2025 onward: consumption resulting from this general investment is unchanged thereafter. [e] Food prices rise at the same rate as timber prices, partly offsetting discounting. [f] Food prices rise at the same rate as timber prices. † equation (30.1); * see chapter. 30 for these derivations; ‡ equation (7.4a).

There are major implications not only for land use policy, but for the detail of silviculture (see chapter 36). It is tempting to shy away from these problems, with the excuse that 'these things cannot be predicted'. But an implicit single prediction that 'things will stay much the same' underlies the normal approach to forest investment appraisal. Those who believe in this sentiment should at least declare their faith firmly.

36 The Wider Economic Purpose at Forest Level: Taxes, Subsidies, Shadow Prices and Silviculture

Forest policy is an important subject, decided by important people. But it is what happens at forest level, not what is written in statute books, that makes forest policy effective or ineffective. Part of that policy, therefore, must concern how policy is transmitted to forest level. On the one hand there are directives, passed down through the hierarchies of organizations, public and private, and usually made more explicit at each level, until the forest worker is told to plant 2000 eucalypts on a particular hectare. Such organizational directives are worked out within the constraints of the law relating to forestry, land use, employment and civil behaviour. Norms and standards are also filtered down through representative bodies and professional associations.

Top down or bottom up?

There are also more subtle and flexible economic interpretations of the public interest. Within a state organization, these can be and are increasingly entered into CBA. Such computations have traditionally been executed at national or regional level. Yet their financial counterpart, NPV calculations, are regularly applied by field-level managers for individual stands. This is the bread and butter of forest economics – the reason the subject is routinely studied during professional training. Nothing but custom prevents calculations based on shadow prices – those broader reflections of desirable resource use – being performed by the same people at the same level.

The private equivalents of shadow prices are taxes and subsidies. These cash sums often represent deliberate intervention to introduce the public interest into private decision-making. They may be conceived simply as a general incentive to more (or less) forestry, or may aim to promote (or suppress) a specific kind of forestry. Chapter 4 suggested that taxes and subsidies should be treated as modifications of costs or revenues. If this view is adopted by private sector decision-makers, resource allocation is affected and – whatever the intentions of politicians – one form or other of forestry is favoured.

The potential of fiscal policy to cause replication of the results of CBA should now be apparent. Environmental economics asserts that optimal pollution is achieved by a tax equal to the marginal social disbenefit of the pollutant, and that the right level of amenities is promoted by a subsidy equal to marginal social benefit. The same principle can be adapted to forestry by making the subsidy (or tax) equal to the difference between market and shadow prices: in the case of externalities, subsidies and taxes are consequently equal to shadow prices.

The effect of decision-making in response to non-market prices should be to reflect the highest level of national economic purpose (foreign exchange saving, optimal investment strategy, etc.) at the lowest decision-making level. Because decisions refer to local conditions, they better express *appropriate* response to the national purpose than any policy delivered down from the seat of government, the board-room or forest service headquarters. If freedom is granted for such decisions to be made locally, forestry policy in effect becomes the bottom-up aggregation of actions made in direct response to *national* economic policy.

Some economic functions for headquarters still remain:

(a) strategic planning and co-ordination of the kind mentioned in chapter 34;
(b) providing formulas and protocols for calculations by decision-makers at lower levels;
(c) calculating shadow prices which do not vary at forest level, like shadow exchange rate, SPIF, or world timber price;
(d) giving specific assistance with evaluation problems that are proving intractable.

Effects on silviculture

Although under such a dispensation managerial economics becomes very different, the implications for silviculture have already been indicated in chapters 13–20, where the effect of varying costs, revenues and discount rate was frequently alluded to. Alterations made by shadow pricing, and by taxes and subsidies which mimic shadow pricing, are:

1 *Reduced shadow price of labour*

Labour-intensive husbandry (treatment of individual sites and trees) becomes more socially 'profitable'. Pruning and selective thinning are especially likely to increase. A subsidy for each hectare planted has no such effect; a subsidy or tax relief proportional to expenditure promotes more intensive silviculture generally; an explicit subsidy of labour (or labour-intensive operations) is needed to substitute labour for machinery, if this result is desired.

2   *Increased shadow price of fossil fuel, and other non-renewable resources*

This encourages less capital-intensive techniques. For any given mechanized or non-renewable-resource-based operation, such as fertilizing, lower intensity and lesser extent is indicated, all else being equal. However, a scenario which foresees high shadow prices for these resources probably also places a high price on wood. The overall balance might then favour *greater* intensity of operations. There is no difficulty in reflecting such shadow prices financially: fuel tax already does so.

3   *Reduction of discount rate*

Among all possible changes, this affects silviculture most. Lower discount rate extends rotations, increases intensity of inputs (including tree numbers per hectare), but decreases intensity of removals in thinning. Thinning regimes are silviculturally traditional ones, full site utilization and long-term quality improvement being dominant arguments.

But a lower discount rate means a higher weighting for investible funds. If all costs and revenues are given the SPIF weight, the unit of currency is simply revalued: weighting has no relative effect, except to diminish the importance of non-market costs and benefits.

A higher weighting of investment funds as opposed to running costs and revenues does, however, moderate the desirability of increased silvicultural investment. Indeed, short-term investment while the crop is still absorbing expenditure may become less attractive under a low discount rate and high SPIF. The importance of successor rotations depends somewhat on whether replanting costs are accounted part of the ongoing investment, part of running net revenue or as fresh investment (see chapter 30). The lower discount rate always increases the importance of maintaining site productivity.

Reflecting a long-term view in the fiscal system is not easy, except by giving incentives for long-term activities. This cannot promote detail such as extended rotations – planting grants, for example, shorten financially optimal rotations. Conversely, a 'negative wealth tax' (a proportional sum paid on the value of the growing stock) or an annual grant increasing with age would stimulate longer rotations.

4 *Rising timber price*

The effect is like that of lowering the discount rate (more intensive silviculture, longer rotations) without corresponding adjustment in SPIF. Possible future rises in timber price might be considered less favourably by private individuals than by the state. Apart from this, there is no need for a subsidy: private perception of likely price rises itself is an incentive to invest (and to invest more intensively) in forestry.

Rising prices combined with low discount rates may generate a negative effective discount rate. Routine insertion of negative values of r in discounting formulas yields sensible results for one-off investments like pruning. All permanent site amelioration becomes worthwhile. Optimal rotations, surprisingly, are the same as given by the maximum forest rent criterion (Price, unpubl.).

Non-market benefits and costs

While some cost–benefit analyses have used regional average figures for environmental values (Treasury, 1972), these effects vary enormously with location and form of forestry: every scheme should be assessed locally.

Hydrological effects vary not only with climatic and physical conditions, but according to whether there is any requirement for water (volume or quality) downstream. Silvicultural variables like species choice, thinning regime and rotation length have hydrological consequences and may thus be modified (generally towards less intensive intervention) by inserting hydrological shadow prices. Water quality requirements normally prohibit absolutely the use of certain chemicals on the catchment. However, economic evaluation is possible, for example via the effects of fertilizing on water eutrophication with consequent clogging of filter beds. This raises incremental shadow cost of application, and optimal level of application drops.

Species mixture, plantation layout and rotation length are all important in determining landscape, recreation, wildlife and sporting values. In chapter 26 the difficulty of obtaining purely objective valuations for small differences in regime was discussed. Nonetheless, some evaluation, conscious or unconscious, enters choice made on these matters. Sometimes the choice is relatively obvious: it is widely agreed that environmental value of plantations tends to increase with age, favouring longer rotations. (But see Johansson and Löfgren (1988).) *How much longer* depends on subjective response. But subjective response need not be purely qualitative or non-monetary: chapters 24–26 suggest techniques for monetizing it.

The extreme variability of environmental benefits (costs) makes them a very inappropriate target for general subsidy (tax) to induce private sector conformity with the social good. A less economically elegant, but more operationally useful practice is to offer compensation for loss of profit when a land-owner adopts a particular scheme in pursuit of social advantage. This does not obviate the need for CBA, since the decision still must be taken as to whether the social advantage gained justifies both production lost and compensation paid.

Applications of shadow prices to decision-making

Three brief examples are offered of shadow pricing applied to forest decision-making. Many others can be added by adjusting the costs, benefits or discount rates used in the examples in Parts I and II.

1 *Landscape value and regeneration pattern*

A 4-ha mixed deciduous woodland 100 years old has three regeneration alternatives: immediate clearfelling and replanting; natural regeneration; taking two sets of equal-sized and carefully designed coupes, one immediately, one in fifty years.

Silvicultural costs per hectare per year do not vary between options, but harvesting costs over 100 years will be increased by £600/ha for two-period felling, and £3000/ha by natural regeneration. This latter cost, together with delay of establishment and lack of control over ensuing species mixture (mostly ash and sycamore) suffices to exclude natural regeneration from further consideration.

Under either of the remaining options, the timber produced will be worth £35/m^3 on average. By clearfelling now, mean annual increment of 6 m^3/ha and annual revenue of £35 × 6 × 4 = £840 is expected. Two-period felling entails growing 2 ha to age 150, during which time increment is expected to be only 4 m^3/ha. After replanting, 6 m^3/ha will once again be attained. Mean increment for this sub-area over 100 years is therefore 5 m^3/ha. The value of increment for the whole crop is £35 × (6 × 2 + 5 × 2) = £770. The extraction cost penalty is (£600 × 4/100) = £24 per year. Discounting is intentionally avoided.

Over a longer time, the two-period scheme incurs no further forgone revenue, as all fellings are made at age 100 years: the £24 per year harvesting penalty is the only continuing cost.

Both regeneration schemes would reduce the present landscape value. However, two-period felling has clear landscape advantage, maintaining the general impression of tree cover throughout the next 100 years. On a cardinal rating scale (see chapter 26), the aesthetic contribution of the schemes to the overall landscape, at different ages, is assessed in table 36.1. Averaged over a rotation, clearfelling has a rating of 0.64, and two-period

Table 36.1 Cardinal weights for aesthetic value over time

Scheme	0	30	49	50	99
Current crop	1				
Two-period felling	0.75	0.9	1	0.75	1
Clearfelling	0	0.5		0.75	1

Table 36.2 Summary of costs and revenues for alternative regeneration patterns

Scheme	Revenue	Harvesting penalty	Scenic loss	Total
Two-period	770	−24	−180	566
Clearfelling	840	0	−540	300

felling 0.88. If the woodland is further supposed to contribute 25% of present scenic value, clearfelling reduces value on average by 9%, and two-period felling by 3%.

A survey of expenditure by visitors shows that the gross value of holidays in this scenic area is at least 75p per waking hour. An estimated 4000 visitors per year each spend 2 hours on the riverbank looking at the woodland area, giving a total value of £6000. Clearfelling reduces this value by £540 per year, two-period felling by £180. The full comparison is given in table 36.2.

The evaluation on which this example was based took two days' work. The study lacked finesse, but contained enough information, as a pilot study, to aid a decision on whether correct treatment of the woodland was in enough doubt to merit deeper analysis, including increasing visit rates and prices of timber.

2 Shadow costing and choice of technique

Consider the effect of shadow costing on comparison between forwarders and cable systems shown in table 36.3. The shadow cost of labour is 40% of financial cost (the figure used in one CBA of forestry (Treasury, 1972)). Oncost is essentially a payment to labour and has been similarly adjusted. Fuel cost is increased by a factor of five on the basis of the argument advanced in chapter 31. Machine cost is split into 60% labour cost (shadow costed at 40%) and 40% forgone future consumption of materials (shadow costed at 500%). This increases machine cost by a factor of 2.24.

Table 36.3 Choice of technique under financial and shadow pricing

	FORWARDER		CABLE SYSTEM	
Item	Financial	Shadow	Financial	Shadow
Machine cost	22.22	49.77	6.25	14.00
Operator/oncost	7.00	2.80	14.00	5.60
Fuel	2.50	12.50	0.50	2.50
Total cost	31.72	65.07	20.75	22.10
Output	12	12	5	5
Unit cost	2.64	5.42	4.15	4.42

Shadow costing reverses the financial cost advantage of the forwarder. This is because the cable system is cheaper per cubic metre in machine and fuel costs, which financial costing understates, but is heavily penalized for its labour cost, which financial costing overstates. The shadow costs of fuel and capital are speculative; nonetheless, they show the sensitivity of decisions to plausible changes in shadow price. As the cable crane is in any case cheaper in machine and fuel costs ($£1.35/m^3$) than the forwarder ($£2.06$), a low shadow wage rate ($\leqslant 32\%$ of market wage) would itself justify the cable system.

3 Illicit felling, distribution and rotation length

Unauthorized incursion into plantations, both for grazing and removal of firewood, is a widespread forestry problem. Illicit felling may make plantations unprofitable; it also affects optimal rotation, since the longer the crop is left, the greater the loss of timber. In a study of eucalypt plantations in India, Trivedi (1988) has applied financial, economic and social CBA to the problem. Only a few results are summarized here.

In one model, illicit felling is scattered through the crop. Total crop increment is reduced, but illicit felling acts as a thinning, so that individual increment of remaining trees increases (see chapters 14 and 15). The removals accrue to the lower half of all income groups. NPV_∞ in rupees for different rotations are given in table 36.4.

Economic NPV_∞ uses a higher discount rate (14.5% – representing marginal productivity of capital) than financial NPV_∞ (10% – representing adjusted bank lending rate). It would hence be expected that NPV_∞ would be lower and rotation shorter under economic criteria. This is not so because economic analysis includes illicit fellings as benefits, treated at parity with similar legitimate fellings.

Table 36.4 Optimal rotations under financial, economic and social prices
* indicates optimum

Rotation	Financial NPV_∞	Economic NPV_∞	Social NPV_∞ (rupeesworth)
6	21 971	20 548	503 847
7	*23 283	22 117	635 284
8	23 150	22 809	725 294
9	22 125	22 941	785 808
10	21 996	23 557	867 369
11	21 357	23 871	932 958
12	20 201	*23 878	980 229
13	18 721	23 678	1 012 858
14	17 057	23 349	1 033 837
15	15 312	22 943	*1 045 588

The much larger social NPVs are due to:

(a) a social discount rate less than 2% (based on slow growth of income per head) which enhances the value of first and (particularly) successor crops;
(b) the weights given to costs and benefits – 11.894 for investment funds, 3.878 for government revenues and 2.705 for illicit revenues.

Under certain circumstances, overall social NPV_∞ from plantations may increase by illicit felling. This is partly because of the 'thinning' effect on diameter growth, but partly due to weighting. For example, in less productive crops illicit felling is beneficial if government revenues are only partly reinvested (weight 3.878), but detrimental if government revenues are wholly reinvested (weight 11.894), or if illicit removals accrue to consumers across the whole income range (weight 1.618) rather than across its lower half (weight 2.705). A high weight to government revenues also tends to shorten rotations, since the relative value of illicit removals is thereby diminished.

This example shows not only that shadow pricing may influence optimal silviculture, but that the particular assumptions adopted may do so too.

Small decisions and large concepts

To some foresters, forestry just represents a job, a means of obtaining a salary. For such, economics implies adopting whatever objectives – like profit-maximization – and performance standards – like keeping within the budget – the employing organization may set. The simpler the requirements, the better life is. As economics becomes more sophisticated, however, the more complex and wide-ranging are these requirements likely to become.

Given the variability of shadow prices, decision-making based on them can often only be done realistically at local level. Just-for-the-money foresters might feel that economics is enough trouble as it is; thus the suggestion that mini-CBA is needed for every silvicultural decision is likely to meet implacable lack of enthusiasm. However, many shadow prices needed for such analyses may already have been calculated for national decision-making purposes, or for the decision on whether to adopt that particular plantation scheme or not. Managers need only replace market prices with shadow prices in evaluating silvicultural options.

On the other hand, many foresters believe in the merit of what they are doing. Before economists became influential, such people acted intuitively 'for the common good'. Nowadays these are often the managers who complain that 'economists at headquarters' do not understand local conditions, or are too narrow in their perception of value. Shadow pricing presents an opportunity for them to combine a wide national perspective with local knowledge in an analysis which is both realistic (in its view of physical conditions) and idealistic (in the breadth of costs and benefits of forestry to which it refers).

However, the case for local CBA is stronger than that. No matter how abstruse the concepts described in Part III may have seemed, they represent an attempt to grasp the real impact of forestry on social benefit, not only to the nation, but to humanity. In this sense they relate to ultimate realities. Given that forestry is often justified by sweeping reference to its social benefits, foresters cannot logically avoid the task, onerous though it may be, of incorporating the best estimate available of those social benefits in fundamental silvicultural and harvesting decisions at forest level.

The result will not invariably favour traditional 'sound forestry', or even forestry at all, because the analysis reaches beyond the objectives of forestry towards the purpose of existence. Foresters' instincts may shy at some conclusions; but it is a great gift to recognize that one's instinct may refute an argued conclusion because one's instinct is wrong.

Economists are not always right either, but their failures lie in inadequate definition of objectives or lapses of logic, rather than in their habits of quantitative thought. Quantification in large and unfamiliar spheres is precisely what is needed to assist resolution of the many and conflicting desiderata in natural resource use. Forestry economics becomes useful when it can relate what is done in the forest to ultimate objectives: to what the individual believes are right and proper ends.

Glossary

Note: Foresters use a rich variety of local and regional terms to describe operations: in this book I have used what I perceive as the most general English-language terms. Economics has a more modern, but not less abstruse, terminology. My attempt has been to confine myself to a minimum set of terms. Many terms not defined here are defined on the pages indicated in bold in the index.

agroforestry	a term used with a wide range of precise meanings, but generally referring to land use systems in which forestry and agriculture interact beneficially
blanking	additional planting done to fill in blanks due to scattered failure of a regenerated crop
browsers	animals which eat foliage, twigs, etc. – and hence are a threat to a young crop
cabling	extracting a log by a system of winches and cables
chokering	attaching a log by wire, chain or rope to the tractor, winch cable or animal used to extract it
cleaning	removal of 'weed' species of trees and shrubs from a young stand
clearfelling	felling the entire standing crop in an area at one time
coppice	a woodland stand which has been regenerated from shoots formed at the stumps of the previous crop trees, and normally grown on a short rotation for small material
coppice-with-standards	a woodland stand consisting of coppice among which a number of trees are retained on a long rotation to provide large material
cost-effective	achieving a certain target at low or minimum cost; achieving a good or maximum performance at certain cost
coupe	a felling made at one time; the forest area so felled
demand	a schedule of the quantities of a good or service

willingly purchased at a range of prices, by a given population in a given time period

double-counting   including a cost or benefit twice in an evaluation, usually by measuring it in two different forms and adding the two results

elasticity   responsiveness of one economic variable to another

equilibrium economy   one in which supply and demand of every good and service are in balance, so that marginal cost is equal to marginal revenue in each market

extraction   the phase of harvesting in which felled trees are moved to a permanent transport network, for example a road or canal

factor of production   a resource used in production of goods or services

forwarding   extracting a log completely supported on a wheeled device or sled towed behind (or integral with) a tractor or animal

harvesting   = logging

haulage   the phase of harvesting involving movement along a permanent transport network, for example by lorry along a road

income elasticity of demand   the percentage change in quantity purchased at a given price with a 1% increase in income

inflation   general increase in the price of goods and services, with consequent fall in the quantity of goods and services which may be purchased with a given sum of money

light-demanding   of a tree, requiring high light intensities in order to achieve satisfactory growth

logging   the process of felling timber and removing it from a forest

miombo   open woodland in which trees are scattered in a savanna-like setting

monopoly   a condition in which a product or service is supplied exclusively by one economic entity

monopsony   a condition in which one economic entity is the sole purchaser of a product or service

normal forest   one in which an equal area of every age class up to the most mature is present

normative   pertaining to what ought to be done: of economics, the study of how resources should be allocated, according to some particular objective

oligopoly   a condition in which the supply of a product or service is dominated by a small number of major suppliers

price elasticity of demand	the percentage change in quantity purchased after a 1% change in price: demand is said to be price elastic if quantity increases by more than 1% after a 1% decrease in price, and price inelastic if quantity increases by less than 1%
probabilistic	pertaining to a situation where results are treated as having a known probability of coming about
provenance	strictly, the place from where seed was collected; loosely, the variety of tree grown from seed collected there
pruning	removal of side-branches flush with the tree's stem
ring-porous	of timber or trees, having particularly large pores in the wood formed at the beginning of the growing season
rotation	the complete life-cycle of a crop, from initiation, through to final felling
shade-bearing	of trees, able to survive and grow in the shade of other trees
skidding	extracting a log by dragging it along the ground behind a tractor or an animal
supply	a schedule of the quantities of a product willingly made available, over a range of prices, in a given time period
sustained yield	a management regime under which equal volumes of timber are cut in each time period
thinning	removal of some of the trees in a crop before the end of the rotation

References

Adams, S. N. 1986: Sheep performance and tree growth on a grazed Sitka spruce plantation. *Scottish Forestry*, 40, 259–63.

Barnett, H. J. and Morse, C. 1963: *Scarcity and Growth: the Economics of Natural Resource Availability*. Johns Hopkins University Press.

Barrow, P., Hinsley, A. P. and Price, C. 1986: The effect of afforestation on hydro-electricity generation: a quantitative assessment. *Land Use Policy*, 3, 141–51.

Beckerman, W. 1974: *In Defence of Economic Growth*. Jonathan Cape.

Beesley, M. E. 1965: The value of time spent in travelling. *Economica*, 32, 174–185.

Blandon, P. 1985: Agroforestry and portfolio theory. *Agroforestry systems*, 3, 239–49.

Borough, C. J. 1979: Agroforestry in New Zealand – the current situation. *Australian Forestry*, 42, 23–9.

Bottomley, J. A. 1973. The paradox of factor-pricing in under-developed rural areas. *Journal of Agricultural Economics*, 24, 493–520.

Bowes, M. D. and Loomis, J. B. 1980: A note on the use of travel cost models with unequal zonal populations. *Land Economics*, 56, 465–70.

Boyle, K. J., Bishop, R. C. and Welsh, M. P. 1985: Starting point bias in contingent valuation bidding games. *Land Economics*, 61, 188–94.

Brazier, J. D. 1977: The effect of forest practices on quality of the harvested crop. *Forestry*, 50, 49–66.

Brookshire, D. S., Ives, B. C. and Schulze, W. D. 1976: The valuation of aesthetic preferences. *Journal of Environmental Economics and Management*, 3, 325–46.

Brownrigg, M. and Greig, M. A. 1975: The economic impact of tourist spending on Skye. *Scottish Journal of Political Economy*, 22, 261–75.

Bunn, E. H. 1981: The nature of the resource, *New Zealand Journal of Forestry*, 26, 162–99.

Buongiorno, J. 1978: Income and price elasticities in the world demand for paper and paperboard. *Forest Science*, 24, 231–46.

Buongiorno, J. and Gilless, J. K. 1987: *Forest Management and Economics*. New York: Macmillan.

Busby, R. J. N. and Grayson, A. J. 1981: Investment appraisal in forestry. *Forestry Commission Booklet* 47.

Cannell, M. G. R. 1979: Biological opportunities for genetic improvement in forest productivity. In E. D. Ford, D. C. Malcolm and J. Atterson (eds.), *The Ecology of Even-Aged Forest Plantations*, Institute of Terrestrial Ecology.

Cannell, M. G. R. 1980: Productivity of closely-spaced young poplar on agricultural soils in Britain. *Forestry*, 53, 1–21.

Chambers, T. W. M. and Price, C. 1986: Recreational congestion: some hypotheses tested in the Forest of Dean. *Journal of Rural Studies*, 2, 41–52.

Chang, S. J., Foster, B. B. 1980: Discounting under risk [an interchange]. *Journal of Forestry*, 78, 634–6.

Chang, S. J. 1981: Determination of the optimal growing stock and cutting cycle for an uneven-aged stand. *Forest Science*, 27, 739–44.

Christensen, J. B. 1985: An economic approach to assessing the value of recreation with special reference to forest areas. Ph.D. thesis, Department of Forestry and Wood Science, UCNW, Bangor.

Christensen, J. B. and Price, C. 1982: Weighting observations in the derivation of recreation trip demand regressions – a comment on Bowes and Loomis. *Land Economics*, 58, 395–9.

Christensen, J. B., Humphreys, S. K. and Price, C. 1985: A revised Clawson method: one part-solution to multidimensional disaggregation problems in recreation evaluation. *Journal of Environmental Management*, 20, 333–346.

Clark, C. 1973: The marginal utility of income. *Oxford Economic Papers*, 25, 145–59.

Clawson, M. 1959: *Methods of Measuring the Demand for and Value of Outdoor Recreation*. Resources for the Future, Reprint 10.

Collett, M. E. W. 1970: External costs arising from the effects of forests upon streamflow in Britain. *Forestry*, 43, 87–93.

Common, M. S. 1973: A note on the uses of the Clawson method for the evaluation of recreation site benefits. *Regional Studies*, 7, 401–6.

Connolly, D. S. and Price, C. unpubl.: *The Clawson method and site substitution: hypothesis and model*. MS available from the author.

Cown, D. J. 1974: Comparison of the effects of two thinning regimes on some wood properties of radiata pine, *New Zealand Journal of Forestry Science*, 4, 540–51.

Cubbage, F. 1983: Economics of forest tract size: theory and literature. *United States Department of Agriculture Forest Service General Technical Report* SO-41.

Davies, E. J. M. 1980: Back to the drawing board. *Scottish Forestry*, 34, 43–7.

Dupuit, J. 1844: Sur l'utilité des travaux publics et sa mésure. Reprinted in translation in: D. Munby (ed.), *Transport*, Penguin, 1968.

Dykstra, D. P. 1984: *Mathematical Programming for Natural Resources Management*. McGraw-Hill.

Earl, D. E. 1973: Does forestry need a new ethos? *Commonwealth Forestry Review*, 52, 82–9.

Ecologist 1972: *Blueprint for Survival*. Penguin.

Edwards, P. N. and Grayson, A. J. 1979: Respacing of Sitka spruce. *Quarterly Journal of Forestry*, 73, 205–18.

Ehrlich, P. R., Ehrlich, A. H. and Holdren, J. P. 1977: *Ecoscience: Population, Resources, Environment*, 3rd ed. Freeman.

Evans, A. W. 1973: *The Economics of Residential Location*, London: Macmillan.

Fellner, W. 1967: Operational utility: the theoretical background and measurement. *Ten Economic Studies in the Tradition of Irving Fisher*. Wiley.

Fenton, R. T. and Dick, M. M. 1972: Economics of afforestation with *Pinus radiata* in New Zealand. *New Zealand Journal of Forestry Science*, 2, 289–388.

Fenton, R. T. and Sutton, W. R. J. 1968: Silvicultural proposals for radiata pine on high quality sites. *New Zealand Journal of Forestry*, 13, 220–8.

Forestry Commission 1974: *Fifty-third Annual Report and Accounts of the Forestry Commission*. HMSO.

Forestry Commission 1983: Tables of discounted revenue. *Forestry Commission Planning and Economics Paper* 4.

Foster, B. B. and Cote, J. B. 1970: Rates of return from Christmas tree plantations. *Journal of Forestry*, 68, 98–9.

Garfitt, J. E. 1986: The economic basis of forestry re-examined. *Quarterly Journal of Forestry*, 80, 33–35.

Gogate, M. G. 1983: An assessment of high density energy plantations (HDEP) in Gujarat on silvicultural, ecological, management and economic aspects. *The Indian Forester*, 109, 427–44.

Grah, R. F. 1960: The effect of initial stocking on the financial return from young growth Douglas fir. *Hilgardia*, 29, 613–79.

Gray, S. J., Price, C. unpubl.: Urgency index ratios: a simple tool for forest management. MS available from the author.

Grayson, A. J. 1987: Evaluation of forestry research. *Forestry Commission Occasional Paper* 15.

Gregersen, H. M. and Contreras, A. H. 1979: Economic analysis of forestry projects. *FAO Forestry Paper* 17.

Gregory, G. R. 1955: An economic approach to multiple use. *Forest Science*, 1, 6–13.

Groves, K. W., Pearn, G. J. and Cunningham, R. B. 1987: Predicting logging truck travel times and estimating costs of log haulage using models. *Australian Forestry*, 50, 54–61.

Haight, R. G. 1987: Evaluating the efficiency of even-aged and uneven-aged stand management, *Forest Science*, 33, 116–34.

Hammack, J. and Brown G. M. Jnr. 1974: *Waterfowl and Wetland: towards Bioeconomic Analysis*. Johns Hopkins University Press.

Hansen, J. R. 1978: *Guide to Practical Project Appraisal*. United Nations.

Hardin, G. 1968: The tragedy of the commons. *Science*, 162, 1243–8.

Harou, P. A. 1985: On a social discount rate for forestry. *Canadian Journal of Forest Research*, 15, 927–34.

Hart, C. E. 1986: *Taxation of Woodlands*. Hart, Chenies, Coleford, Glos.

Heberlein, T. A. and Shelby, B. 1977: Carrying capacity, values, and the satisfaction model: a reply to Greist. *Journal of Leisure Research*, 9, 142–8.

Hill, M. 1968: A goals-achievement matrix in evaluating alternative plans. *Journal of the American Institute of Planners*, 34, 19–29.

Hoekstra, D. A. 1985: Choosing the discount rate for analyzing agroforestry systems/ technologies from a private economic viewpoint, *Forest Ecology and Management*, 10, 177–83.

Hoekstra, D. A. 1987: Economics of agroforestry. *Agroforestry Systems*, 5, 293–300.

Johansson, P-O. and Löfgren, K-G. 1985: *The Economics of Forestry and Natural Resources*. Basil Blackwell.

Johansson, P-O. and Löfgren, K-G. (1988): Where's the beef? a reply to Price. *Journal of Environmental Management*, 27, 337–9.

Johnson, J. A. and Price, C. 1987: Afforestation, employment and depopulation in the Snowdonia National Park. *Journal of Rural Studies*, 3, 195–205.

Johnson, K. N. and Scheurman, H. L. 1977: Techniques for prescribing optimal timber harvest and investment under different objectives – discussion and synthesis. *Forest Science Monograph* 18.

Kallio, M., Dykstra, D.P. and Binkley, C. S. (eds.) 1987: *The Global Forestry Sector*. Wiley.

Kao, C. and Brodie, J.D. 1980: Simultaneous optimization of thinnings and rotation with continuous stocking and entry levels. *Forest Science*, 26, 338–46.

Kauppi, P. 1987: Forests and the changing chemical composition of the atmosphere. In M. Kallio, D. P. Dykstra and C. S. Binkley (eds.), 1987.

Keynes, J. M. 1936: *The General Theory of Employment, Interest and Money*. London: Macmillan.

Kula, E. 1981: Future generations and discounting rules in public sector investment appraisal. *Environment and Planning A*, 13, 899–910.

Kula, E. 1986: The developing framework for the economic evaluation of forestry in the United Kingdom. *Journal of Agricultural Economics*, 37, 365–76.

Little, I. M. D. and Mirrlees, J. A. 1974: *Project Appraisal and Planning for Developing Countries*. Heinemann.

Livingstone, I. 1986. The common property problem and pastoralist behaviour. *Journal of Development Studies*, 23, 5–19.

MacGregor, J. J. 1972: Forestry concessions in the British Commonwealth countries. *Commonwealth Forestry Review*, 50, 43–57.

MacGregor, J. J. and Balman, F. E. 1973: Problems in the measurement of direct and overhead costs in forestry. *Quarterly Journal of Forestry*, 67, 104–10.

Mahmoud, A. E. 1983: Viscosity modification of gum arabic as a means of enhancing marketability. M.Sc. thesis, Polytechnic Institute, Virginia, USA.

Marglin, S. A. 1963: The opportunity costs of public investment. *Quarterly Journal of Economics*, 77, 274–89.

McInerney, J. 1976: The simple analytics of natural resource economics. *Journal of Agricultural Economics*, 27, 31–52.

McKillop, W. 1967: Supply and demand for forest products, an econometric study. *Hilgardia*, 38 (1), 1–132.

McKillop, W., Adams, D. M. and Haynes, R. W. 1981. National impacts of softwood product price increases. *Journal of Forestry*, 79, 807–10.

McNab, W. H. and Berry, C. R. 1985: Distribution of aboveground biomass in three pine species planted on a devastated site amended with sewage sludge or inorganic fertilizer. *Forest Science*, 31, 373–82.

Medema, E. L. and Lyon, G. W. 1985: The determination of financial rotation ages for coppicing tree species. *Forest Science*, 31, 398–404.

Mills, W. L. Jnr. 1988: Forestland: investment attributes and diversification potential. *Journal of Forestry*, 86 (1), 19–24.

Mills, W. L., Jnr and Tufts, R. A. 1985: Equipment replacement: a comparison of two methods, *Forest Science*, 31, 661–70.

Mishan, E. J. 1988: *Cost–Benefit Analysis*, 4th ed. Allen and Unwin.

Misomali, E. D. 1987: Economic cost–benefit analysis in relation to fuelwood plantations in Malawi. B.Sc. dissertation, Department of Forestry and Wood Science, Bangor.

Mitlin, D. C. 1987: Price–size curves for conifers. *Forestry Commission Bulletin* 68.

Moore, D. G. and Wilson, B. 1970: Sitka for ourselves: the 25 year rotation. *Quarterly Journal of Forestry*, 64, 104–12.

Murchison, H. G. and Nautiyal, J. C. 1971: When to replace a vehicle. *The Forestry Chronicle*, 47, 205–9.

Mutch, W. E. S. and Hutchison, A. R. 1980: *The Interaction of Farming and Forestry.* East of Scotland College of Agriculture.

Nair, C. T. S. 1981: Basic needs fulfilment and the evaluation of land use alternatives with special reference to forestry in Kerala State, India. Ph.D. thesis, Department of Forestry and Wood Science, UCNW, Bangor.

Newcombe, K. 1984: An economic justification for rural afforestation: the case of Ethiopia. *Energy Department Paper* 16, World Bank.

Nwonwu, F. O. C. 1987: Cost minimization through the use of taungya system in pulpwood plantation establishment. *Agroforestry Systems*, 5, 455–62.

Openshaw, K. 1980: *Cost and Financial Accounting in Forestry.* Pergamon.

Palo, M. 1987: Deforestation perspectives for the tropics: a provisional theory with pilot applications. In M. Kallio, D. P. Dykstra and C. S. Binkley (eds.), 1987.

Pant, M. M. 1975: Benefit–cost analysis – a possibly overemphasized criteria in forestation evaluation. *The Indian Forester*, 101, 367–84.

Pingle, G. 1978: The early development of cost–benefit analysis. *Journal of Agricultural Economics*, 29, 63–71.

Price, C. 1976: Subjectivity and objectivity in landscape evaluation. *Environment and Planning A*, 8, 829–38.

Price, C. 1978a: Individual preference and optimal city size. *Urban Studies*, 15, 75–81.

Price, C. 1978b: *Landscape Economics.* London: Macmillan.

Price, C. 1978c: Mechanization or husbandry? an economist's speculation. In R. B. Tranter, (ed.), *The Future of Upland Britain.* Centre for Agricultural Strategy.

Price, C. 1979: Public preference and the management of recreational congestion. *Regional Studies*, 13, 125–39.

Price, C. 1981a: Charging versus exclusion: choice between recreation management tools. *Environmental Management*, 5, 161–75.

Price, C. 1981b: Are extra recreation facilities unproductive? *Journal of Environmental Management*, 12, 1–5.

Price, C. 1981c: When does windthrow risk happen and does it matter? *Y Coedwigwr*, 33, 14–25.

Price, C. 1982: Residential density and spatial externalities. *Urban Studies*, 19, 293–302.

Price, C. 1983a: Evaluation of congestion and other social costs: implications for systems of recreation parks. *Sistemi Urbani*, 5, 119–39.

Price, C. 1983b: The strange case of the missing time period $n + 1$. *Environment and Planning A*, 15, 357–64.

Price, C. 1984a: Project appraisal and planning for over-developed countries: (I) The costing of nonrenewable resources. *Environmental Management*, 8, 221–232.

Price, C. 1984b: Project appraisal and planning for over-developed countries: (II) Shadow pricing under uncertainty. *Environmental Management*, 8, 233–242.

Price, C. 1984c: The sum of discounted consumption flows method: equity with efficiency? *Environment and Planning A*, 16, 829–33.

Price, C. 1986: Differential depreciation and the cost of forest operations. *Scottish Forestry*, 40, 264–75.

Price, C. 1987a: *Does Shadow Pricing Go On For Ever?* Department of Forestry and Wood Science, UCNW, Bangor.

Price, C. 1987b: Further reflections on the economic theory of thinning. *Quarterly Journal of Forestry*, 81, 85–102.

Price, C. 1987c: The developing framework for the economic evaluation of forestry in the United Kingdom: a comment. *Journal of Agricultural Economics*, 38, 497–500.

Price, C. 1988a: Investment, reinvestment and the social discount rate for forestry. *Forest Ecology and Management*, 24, 293–310.

Price, C. 1988b: One more reflection on the economic theory of thinning. *Quarterly Journal of Forestry*, 82, 37–44.

Price, C. 1988c: Does social cost–benefit analysis measure overall utility change? *Economics Letters*, 26, 357–61.

Price, C. unpubl.: *Optimal rotations with negative discount rates: not just an abstraction.* MS available from the author.

Price, C. and Dale, I. D. 1982: Price predictions and economically afforestable area. *Journal of Agricultural Economics*, 33, 13–23.

Price, C. and Nair, C. T. S. 1984: Cost–benefit analysis and the consideration of forestry alternatives. *Journal of World Forest Resource Management*, 1, 81–104.

Price, C. and Nair, C. T. S. 1985: Social discounting and the distribution of project benefits. *Journal of Development Studies*, 21: (4), 25–32.

Price, C. and Wan Sabri, W. M. unpubl.: *Transformation and weighting in recreation demand functions.* MS available from the author.

Rahman, Afzalur. 1981: Price–size relationship and rate of return from teak plantations in Bangladesh. *Bano Biggyan Patrika*, 10, 44–8.

Raymond, O. H. 1985: Unmarked pine thinning – a commercial option. *Australian Forestry*, 48, 193–8.

Richardson, H. W. 1971: *Urban Economics.* Penguin.

Riitters, K., Brodie, J. D. and Hann, D. W. 1982: Dynamic programming for optimization of timber production and grazing in ponderosa pine. *Forest Science*, 28, 517–26.

Routledge, R. D. 1987: The impact of soil degradation on the expected present net worth of future timber harvests. *Forest Science*, 33, 823–34.

Rowan, A. A. 1976: Forest road planning. *Forestry Commission Booklet* 43.

Sar, L. and Crane, W. 1984: Economic returns from fertilization of *Pinus radiata* stands. *Australian Forestry*, 47, 225–9.

Savage, L. J. 1951: The theory of statistical decisions. *American Statistical Association Journal*, 46, 55–67.

Schallau, C. H., and Maki, W. R. 1983: Interindustry model for analyzing the regional impacts of forest resource and related constraints. *Forest Science*, 29, 384–94.

Schallau, C. H. and Wirth, M. E. 1980: Reinvestment rate and the analysis of forestry enterprises. *Journal of Forestry*, 78, 740–2.

Schuster, E. G. and Zuuring, H. R. 1986: Quantifying the unquantifiable. *Journal of Forestry*, 84 (4), 25–30.

Schweitzer, D. L., Sassaman, R. W. and Schallau, C. H. 1972: The allowable cut effect. *Journal of Forestry*, 70, 415–18.

Scott, A. 1955: *Natural Resources: the Economics of Conservation.* University of Toronto Press.

Sedjo, R. A. 1983: *The Comparative Economics of Plantation Forestry.* Resources for the Future.

Sedjo, R. A. 1984: An economic assessment of industrial forest plantations. *Forest Ecology and Management*, 9, 245–57.

Self, P. 1976: *Econocrats and the Policy Process. The Politics and Philosophy of CBA.* London: Macmillan.

Sessions, J. and Paredes, G. 1987: A solution procedure for the sort yard location problem in forest operations. *Forest Science*, 33, 750–62.

Seymour, J. and Girardet, H. 1986: *Far from Paradise.* BBC Publications.

Shahwahid, Mohd. 1985: Determining an economic cutting regime for the tropical rainforest. *The Malaysian Forester*, 48, 57–74.

Sharawi, H. A. 1987: *Acacia senegal* in the gum belt of Western Sudan: a cost–benefit analysis. M.Sc. thesis, Department of Forestry and Wood Science, UCNW, Bangor.

Shechter, M. and Lucas, R. C. 1978: *Simulation of Recreational Use for Park and Wilderness Management.* Johns Hopkins University Press.

Sheikh, M. I. and Raza-ul-Haq 1982: Effect of spacing on the growth of *Dalbergia sissoo* (shisham). *The Pakistan Journal of Forestry*, 32, 73–4.

Sinden, J. A. and Worrell, A. C. 1979: *Unpriced Values.* Wiley.

Sobik, I. 1982: Economic effectiveness of drainage (translated from the Russian in *Forestry Abstracts*, 46, no. 3199).

Speechly, H. T. and Helms, J. A. 1985: Growth and economic returns after pre-commercial thinning non-uniform white fir stands in California. *Forest Ecology and Management*, 11, 111–30.

Squire, L. and van der Tak, H. 1975: *Economic Analysis of Projects.* Johns Hopkins University Press.

Sunda, H. J. and Lowry, G. L. 1975: Regeneration costs in loblolly pine management. *Journal of Forestry*, 73, 406–9.

Sutton, W. R. J. 1969: Overhead costs in relation to forest size. *New Zealand Journal of Forestry*, 14, 87–9.

Sutton, W. R. J. 1973: The importance of size and scale in forestry and the forest industries. *New Zealand Journal of Forestry*, 18, 63–80.

Talbert, J. T., Weir, R. J. and Arnold, R. D. 1985: Costs and benefits of a mature first generation loblolly pine tree improvement programme. *Journal of Forestry*, 83, 162–6.

Teeguarden, D. E. 1973: The allowable cut effect. *Journal of Forestry*, 71, 224–6.

Treasury 1972: *Forestry in Great Britain: an Interdepartmental Cost/Benefit Study.* HMSO.

Trivedi, S. N. 1988: Utility–based social shadow pricing and its comparison with other evaluation techniques: a cost–benefit study of fuelwood plantations in Bihar, India. Ph.D. thesis, Department of Forestry and Wood Science, UCNW, Bangor.

Tucker, J. C. 1983: An estimation of the use and social benefit from urban parks. M.Sc. thesis, Department of Forestry and Wood Science, UCNW, Bangor.

von Thünen, J. H. 1875: *Der Isolierte Staat in Beziehung auf Landwirtschaft und Nationalökonomie.* Schmaucher Zarchlin.

Wald, A. 1950: *Statistical Decision Functions.* Wiley.

Wardle, P. A. 1967: Spacing in plantations – a management investigation. *Forestry*, 40, 47–69.

Weisbrod, B. A. 1972: Income redistribution effects and cost–benefit analysis. In R. Layard (ed.) *Cost–Benefit Analysis*. Penguin.

Westgate, R. A. 1986: The economics of containerized forest tree seedling research in the United States. *Canadian Journal of Forest Research*, 16, 1007–12.

Westoby, J. C. 1987: *The Purpose of Forests*. Basil Blackwell.

Weston, J. F. and Brigham, E. F. 1979: *Managerial Finance*. Holt Rinehart and Winston.

Wildavsky, A. 1966: The political economy of efficiency: cost–benefit analysis, system analysis and program budgeting. *Public Administration Review*, 26 (4), 292–310.

Winch, D. M. 1972: *Analytical Welfare Economics*. Penguin.

Zivnuska, J. A. 1961: The multiple problems of multiple use. *Journal of Forestry*, 59, 555–60.

Index